# China and Asia

It is difficult to overstate the growing importance of China and Asia in the global economy. Despite the sharp downturn experienced in the 1997 financial crisis, China and Asia have bounced back strongly in the new millennium and delivered solid economic growth. In this book, Yin-Wong Cheung and Kar-Yiu Wong have gathered together 35 renowned researchers from four continents to examine contemporary issues on economic and financial interactions with a focus on China and Asia.

Four broad areas are discussed. The first part deals with China and her interactions with other economies, the second with economic interactions within the region, the third with foreign exchange rate issues facing Asian economies and the fourth with financial market development in the region.

Within these chapters, some interesting results are explained, many of which differ from what is commonly believed. For example it is explained how exports from China and other Asian economies follow the 'flying geese' pattern and that these economies can grow in harmony; that appreciating the Asian exchange rates would not have much impact on their current account surpluses; and that financial liberalization in Thailand did not create the short-term debt problem, which is believed to be a major cause of the 1997 financial crisis. It is also described how developments in the US have very strong influences on Asian economies and that mainland China was a less important source of external shocks than is commonly held.

This book will be of considerable interest to students and researchers engaged in Asian studies and international macroeconomics, as well as those specifically interested in the Asian economy.

**Yin-Wong Cheung** is a Professor in the Economics Department at the University of California, Santa Cruz, California, USA. He is also a Professor in the School of Economics and Finance, University of Hong Kong and a guest Professor of the School of Economics, Shandong University, China.

**Kar-Yiu Wong** is a Professor of Economics at the University of Washington, Seattle, USA.

# Routledge studies in the modern world economy

# China and Asia

Economic and financial interactions

**Edited by**
**Yin-Wong Cheung and**
**Kar-Yiu Wong**

LONDON AND NEW YORK

First published 2009
by Routledge
2 Park Square, Milton Park, Abingdon, Oxon, OX14 4RN

Simultaneously published in the USA and Canada
by Routledge
711 Third Avenue, New York, NY 10017

*Routledge is an imprint of the Taylor & Francis Group,
an informa business*

Typeset in Times New Roman by Keyword Group Ltd.

First issued in paperback in 2013

*British Library Cataloguing in Publication Data*
A catalogue record for this book is available from the British Library

*Library of Congress Cataloguing in Publication Data*
A catalogue record has been requested for this book


ISBN13: 978-0-415-74836-0 (pbk)
ISBN13: 978-0-415-77609-7 (hbk)
ISBN13: 978-0-203-88639-7 (ebk)

# Contents

# Figures

# Tables

# Contributors

**Alan G. Ahearne**  National University of Ireland, Ireland

**Nedim M. Alemdar**  Bilkent University, Turkey

**Tony Cavoli**  University of South Australia, Australia

**Xikang Chen**  Chinese Academy of Social Sciences, China

**Leonard K. Cheng**  Hong Kong University of Science and Technology, Hong Kong

**John G. Fernald**  Federal Reserve Bank of San Francisco, USA

**K.C. Fung**  University of California, USA

**San Sau Fung**  Bank for International Settlements

**Hans Genberg**  Hong Kong Monetary Authority, Hong Kong and Graduate Institute of International Studies, Switzerland

**Federico Guerrero**  University of Nevada, USA

**Jakob de Haan**  University of Groningen, The Netherlands

**Juann H. Hung**  Congressional Budget Office, USA

**Richard Jong-a-Pin**  University of Groningen, The Netherlands

**Marc Klau**  Bank for International Settlements

**Lawrence J. Lau**  Chinese University of Hong Kong, Hong Kong and Stanford University, USA

**Jaewoo Lee**  International Monetary Fund

**Jie Li**  The Central University of Finance and Economics, China

**Guijun Lin**  University of International Business and Economics, China

**Jose A. Lopez**  Federal Reserve Bank of San Francisco, USA

**Prakash Loungani**  International Monetary Fund

**Guonan Ma**  Bank for International Settlements

**Robert McCauley**  Bank for International Settlements

**Mark Mink**  University of Groningen, The Netherlands

**Eiji Ogawa**  Hitotsubashi University and RIETI, Japan

**Elliott Parker**  University of Nevada, USA

**Ramkishen S. Rajan**  George Mason University, USA

**John W. Schindler**  Board of Governors of the Federal Reserve System, USA

**Gunther Schnabl**  Leipzig University, Germany

**Ronald M. Schramm**  Columbia University, USA

**Junko Shimizu**  Meikai University, Japan

**Sibel Sirakaya**  University of Washington, USA

**Mark M. Spiegel**  Federal Reserve Bank of San Francisco, USA

**Ozan Sula**  Western Washington University, USA

**Stephen J. Turnovsky**  University of Washington, USA

**Thomas D. Willett**  The Claremont Colleges, USA

# Introduction

*Yin-Wong Cheung and Kar-yiu Wong*

It is difficult to overstate the growing importance of Asia in the global economy. Despite the sharp downturn experienced in the 1997 financial crisis, the region has bounced back strongly in the new millennium and delivered solid economic growth. The crisis experience, however, revealed a shortcoming in the region of being only a stronghold of trade and the need of a well functioning financial section. Since the 1997 event, the region has made considerable efforts to improve the governance and efficiency of its financial section. While the region's financial markets are still in the development phase, the region is exerting its financial prowess to the rest of the world via outward direct investment and sovereign wealth fund activity.

Undeniably, China plays a significant role in the recent success of Asian economic performance. Indeed, China's huge trade surplus and international reserve holding are often described in terms laden with hyperbole. The strong re-emergence of China changes not only the economic landscape of East Asia but also the world. For instance, in the last two decades, China has evolved into a major production hub in the region. The relocation of manufacturing process has altered trade patterns within the region and between Asia and the rest of the world.

This book examines some contemporary issues on the economic and financial interactions with a focus on China and Asia. To this end, we bring together 35 renowned researchers from esteemed universities, government research units, and international organizations across four continents. These researchers investigate and analyze critically various important issues, which are grouped into four different parts. The first part deals with China and her interactions with other economies, the second with economic interactions within the region, the third with foreign exchange rate issues facing Asian economies, and the fourth with financial market development in the region.[1]

The trade relationship between China and other Asian economies is a contentious issue. The main concern is whether China's exports drive out the exports of other Asian economies or if these economies' exports can growth together. In the first paper, Ahearne, Fernald, Loungani, and Schindler examined the trade data and found that exports from China and other Asian economies follow the 'flying geese' pattern – in which China moves up in technological developments and gets into the product space vacated by the other Asian economies. At the same time, other

Asian economies' exports benefit from the integration of trade in the production process and China's income growth. Overall, the evidence shows that exports of all economies can grow in harmony.

The interplay of savings and investment drives China's growth. Nonetheless, there are not many studies on capital deployment. Lin and Schramm in the second paper assessed China's flow of funds at both national and sectoral levels. It is found that the large volume of direct investment inflow allows China's own savings to be invested overseas. In contrast with collective enterprises that incur losses, the state-owned enterprises are on average found to be profitable. The private corporate sector also has positive savings. One interesting finding is that about one third of domestic savings are turned into investment via informal intermediation. In the third paper, Hung offers an overview of China's policy on international capital flow, which is conceived to be cornerstone of its economic success.

The phenomenon of China's economic growth in the last 20 plus years is usually accredited to its impressive export sector performance. A natural question to ask is: What are the implications of an increase in exports on China's output and employment? Chen, Cheng, Fung and Lau undertook a painstaking job and estimated the increases in output and employment in response to increases in exports in the aggregate as well as disaggregated by commodity and by destination. As expected, compared with processing exports, non-processing exports yield stronger output and employment effects. Both effects vary across industries and final destinations of exports. Their calculations show that an amount of US$1,000 Chinese exports to the world has a direct effect of US$240 and a total effect of US$545 on national output and direct and total employment (person/year) effects of, respectively 0.130 and 0.375.

Economic interactions are the theme of the second part of the book. Hans, in the fifth paper, examined the inflation experience of seven small economies in East Asia: Hong Kong, Malaysia, Korea, Philippines, Singapore, Taiwan, and Thailand. It is found that developments in the US have a very strong influence on these countries. Observed differences in the degree of dependence on the US can indeed be ascribed to differences in exchange rate/monetary policy responses to external shocks. Indeed, the findings show that, during the sample period, mainland China was a less important source of external shocks than is commonly believed.

Since the 1997 financial crisis, a number of Asian countries have turned their current account deficits into surpluses. The sharp change in current account balances raises the concern of whether persistent exchange rate undervaluation is behind these surpluses. In the sixth paper, Lee analyzed the interactions of current account balances and real exchange rates in five Asian economies; namely China, India, Indonesia, Korea, and Thailand. The semi-structural approach reveals that, after the financial crisis, a large part of observed current account surpluses are of permanent nature and unrelated to exchange rate undervaluation. An implication is that appreciating these Asian exchange rates would not have much impact on these countries' current account surpluses.

The last paper in the second part of the book examines business cycle of 17 Pacific Rim countries. Using the correlation between detrended GDP series from

1960 to 2004 to measure the degree of business cycle comovement, the authors de Haan, Jong-A-Pin and Mink found no clear trend towards increased business cycle synchronization among the Pacific Rim countries. Further, trade intensity is found to be related to business cycle comovement, but financial integration is not.

The paper by Cavoli and Rajan and that by Schnabl evaluated the exchange rate arrangement pursued by selected Asian economies after the 1997 financial. In the eighth paper, Cavoli and Rajan used different criteria and found some evidence that Korea, Thailand and Indonesia have migrated from soft US dollar pegs to a more flexible exchange regime setting after the crisis.

Schnabl, on the other hand, found that the exchange rates of Indonesia, Korea, Philippines, Singapore, Taiwan, and Thailand are more responsive to yen movement after the crisis. Economies including China, Hong Kong, and Malaysia appear to have the US dollar as their dominant anchor currency. The role of the euro as a reserve currency in East Asia remains uncertain.

The tenth paper by Fung, Klau, Ma and McCauley considered refined measures of effective exchange rates of China and other Asian countries. The refined measure is motivated by the trade data distortion induced by the Hong Kong and Singapore entrepôt trade. For instance, Hong Kong is a main entrepôt of Chinese trade. Without adjusting for entrepôt trade activity, the calculation of the Chinese Renminbi effective exchange rate would overstate the influence of the US dollar because Hong Kong maintains a US dollar currency board. By the same token, the effective exchange rates of other Asian countries understate the weight of Renminbi relative to Hong Kong dollar.

The fourth part of the book contains five papers on issues related to financial markets. Lopez and Spiegel examined foreign intermediation activity in Japan during the so-called 'lost decade' of the 1990s in the eleventh paper. They found that, during the 1990s, foreign bank lending in Japan fell, both in overall numbers and as a share of total lending. However, there was marked growth in foreign underwriting activity in the international yen-denominated bond sector. Lopez and Spiegel identified a key factor in the disparity between these activities is their different clienteles: While foreign banks in Japan lent primarily to domestic borrowers, international yen-denominated bond issuers were primarily foreign entities with yen funding needs or opportunities for profitable swaps.

The Asian Bond Markets Initiative (ABMI) is an amplification of regional efforts to develop efficient and liquid bond markets in Asia. In the twelfth paper, Ogawa and Shimizu proposed to issue Asian bonds denominated in core-Asian Monetary Unit, which is a synthesis currency unit comprising the Japanese yen, the Hong Kong dollar, the South Korean won, the Singapore dollar, the Thai baht, and the Indonesian rupiah. The authors argued that the proposed Asian bond offers a low risk liquid instrument and presents an alternative for countries in the region to diversify internationally.

Li, Sula and Willett investigated the topical issue of reserve accumulation in the thirteenth paper. These authors observed that capital flow variability observed in normal times can be drastically different from the variability exhibited in crisis periods. Thus a wise international reserve policy should involve forward looking active management. A new theoretical framework was derived to illustrate that there may be an 'inaction zone' over which reserve levels deviate from their optimal values without these deviations being sufficiently costly to prompt adjustment actions.

What are the major causes of the Asian financial crisis? Excessive short-term debts that were brought about by financial liberalization are a commonly perceived culprit. Guerrero and Parker took the issue to the data and examined the maturity of corporate debt in Thailand – a country first hit by the crisis. In the fourteenth paper, Guerrero and Parker found that during the period 1993–7 financial liberalization may be associated with an increase in maturity of corporate debts instead of a decrease in maturity. The finding casts some doubts on the generality of the idea that financial liberalization created the short-term debt problem.

In the fifteenth paper, Alemdar, Sirakaya and Turnovsky developed a model of a two-sector small open economy to study a self-enforcing lending scheme in which a debtor's repayment resources never fall below the default alternative at any point in time. Simulations of the model by genetic algorithms under a wide range of parameter values demonstrate the extent of inefficiencies due to limited enforcement. An irreversible export-led growth strategy, though mitigating the commitment problem inherent in sovereign lending, cannot support full enforcement openness.

The economic and financial interactions within Asia and between Asia and the rest of the world are complex and dynamic issues. We are under no illusion that these issues and, more importantly, their policy implications be understood and analyzed precisely. However, we believe that the papers in this book add significantly to our knowledge about China and Asia and will be a valuable reference for future research.

# Part I
# China

# 1 Flying geese or sitting ducks

## China's impact on the trading fortunes of other Asian economies

*Alan G. Ahearne, John G. Fernald,*
*Prakash Loungani and John W. Schindler*

## Introduction

Discussions of trade linkages among the emerging markets of Asia often include polarised views. Under one view, China and other Asian economies can grow in harmony, as exemplified in the 'flying geese' paradigm (Akamatsu 1961, 1962).[1] Okita (1985) noted that the great diversity among the Asian nations in their stages of development and resource endowments 'works to facilitate the flying geese pattern of shared development as each is able to take advantage of its distinctiveness to develop with a supportive division of labour'. Some recent analyses (e.g. Kwan 2002) also take the view that economies in Asia share mutual benefits from the potential of greater integration of product lines across the region and the increased incomes of Chinese consumers, both of which are reflected in expanding intra-regional trade in Asia (see also Zebregs 2004).

The other view sees China and other Asian economies largely as competitors: They specialize in the production of export goods that are relatively close substitutes and compete for market share in major export markets. A 2001 *White Paper on International Trade* by Japan's Ministry of Economy, Trade and Industry captures this view well. It suggests that:

> … owing to the emergence of China in East Asia, there has been some disruption in the conventional orderly catch-up process of the flying-geese pattern led by Japan, followed by the newly-industrialized economies (NIEs), ASEAN members, and China. It argues that, through receiving direct foreign investment, China has been gaining competitiveness not only in labour-intensive products, but also IT and other technology-intensive products. As a result, the complementary international division of labour according to the level of economic development has given way to stiffer competition, including in high-tech industries. In the long-term, such increased competition could bring overall benefits to the regional economy by improving productivity. In the short-term, however, increasing competition between China and ASEAN members could have negative repercussions on the latter, as illustrated by the 1997–98 Asian financial crisis.
>
> Quoted in Kwan (2002)

In one provocative but popular rendition of this view, Asian economies are 'sitting ducks' being picked off by a China armed with a huge pool of cheap labour and an allegedly undervalued exchange rate (Bhalla 1998). Calls for an appreciation of the renminbi are a staple in policy circles (see Bergsten 2006 and Williamson 2003 for example).

The evidence in this paper suggests that the polar views do not do justice to the rapidly evolving trade relationships among Asian economies.[2] In Section 2, we present evidence that at the aggregate level, Chinese export growth and that of other Asian economies move in tandem, suggesting that both depend on common shocks. We verify this evidence on the relative importance of foreign income and exchange rates in the determination of Asian export growth using a three-variable vector autoregression (VAR) model. An important finding is that, while exchange rates do matter for export performance, the income growth of trading partners matters even more. In this sense, China and emerging Asia are on the same side, with the export performance of both still heavily dependent on income growth in common major trading partners, namely, the United States, the European Union and Japan.

Turning from the aggregate to sectoral data, we find, nevertheless, that there is clearly considerable shifting of trade patterns taking place. In Section 3, we present evidence from industry-level data on the extent of export competition between China and other Asian economies in the US market, where competition is likely to have been most intense. We find that China has gained market share in the US as a whole and in almost every industry, while the share of other Asian economies has declined. However, many other Asian economies, particularly the ASEAN-4 economies (Indonesia, Malaysia, the Philippines, Thailand), have also experienced gains in market shares in a number of industries at the expense of the Asian NIEs. In many industries, therefore, the results are suggestive of a 'flying geese' pattern in which China and the ASEAN-4 move into the product space vacated by the NIEs. In addition, as China continues its rapid development, other economies in the region have an incentive to try and move up the value chain as their comparative advantage shifts to higher-value added, less labour intensive industries. We also summarize the evidence on the beneficial effects of China's growth on the rest of Asia through the channel of rising Chinese imports from the rest of Asia.

That said, the other view is also right in claiming that China's increased integration into the global economy has meant that sectoral transitions in other Asian economies are likely to be occurring at a faster pace than would otherwise have been the case. Asian economies therefore need to take steps to ease the transition of their labour force into other sectors, including through the provision of social safety nets to lower the costs of adjustment.

## Aggregate evidence on trade linkages between China and other Asian economies

Figure 1.1 shows the striking co-movement between China's export growth and that of other Asian economies. The figure shows export growth (measured in dollar

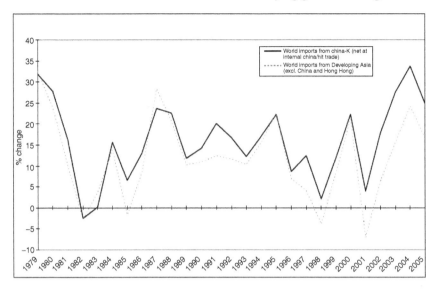

*Figure 1.1* Exports of China and emerging Asia (per cent change).
Source: IFS.

Note: Figure shows annual growth in nominal value of exports of China and Hong Kong (excluding trade between China and Hong Kong), and exports of other developing Asian economies. As noted in the text, we use trading-partner data on imports from these regions.

values) to the world from China (including Hong Kong SAR)[3] and from the 'rest of Asia',[4] using trading partner statistics.

The co-movement in export growth between China and other Asian economies suggests that common factors – such as growth in advanced economies, movements in the world prices of key exports such as semiconductors, and movements in the yen-dollar rate – were probably more important determinants of Asian exports than was competition with China.

In addition, the vertical integration of many product markets in Asia would likely add to this similarity in growth rates. As an example of how vertical integration might make export growth rates similar, take the example of a small electronic device like a DVD player. The manufacturing of some components – e.g. motherboards and memory, etc. – might be handled in one or several of the ASEAN economies or the NIEs. Those components are then exported to, say, China, where they are assembled into the DVD player. The DVD player is then shipped out to its final destination. Several economies in the region might thus provide value-added to a single device. Hence, as demand for DVD players fluctuates, one would expect export growth to be positively correlated across economies.

Discussions of China's export performance tend to emphasize factors peculiar to China, such as economic reform initiatives, rapid investment, tax incentives, or its World Trade Organization (WTO) accession.[5] Some observers focus almost solely on the perceived undervaluation of the renminbi exchange rate to explain China's export performance. There have been, of course, times when China-specific factors have had a large impact on China's exports (e.g. China's WTO accession almost certainly had a larger effect on China than on its trading partners/competitors). However, these discussions tend to miss the prevalence of common shocks, which Figure 1.1 suggest are of equal or greater importance.

Tables 1.1 and 1.2 provide some further evidence of the co-movement by controlling for the obvious common factors: Growth in industrial country GDP and real exchange rates. (For example, for much of the period emerging Asia pegged implicitly or explicitly to the dollar, so that changes in the yen/dollar rate would be a common shock for these economies.) In particular, we show results from fixed-effects panel regressions of the real volume of non-China Asian export growth on Chinese real export growth as well as control variables. For these purposes, we include Hong Kong in the NIEs, rather than with China.

The first three columns of Table 1.1 do not include controls other than fixed effects and an (insignificant) lagged dependent variable. These columns show the main implication of Figure 1.1 that when China's exports rise, exports of other economies also tend to rise.

The next three columns include controls. We measure foreign GDP as a weighted average of export-partner GDP, where the weights are country-specific export weights. The real effective exchange rate for each economy uses trade weights with major trading partners and corresponds to the methodology used by staff at the Board of Governors of the Federal Reserve System in calculating their published US real exchange rate indices (see Loretan 2005 for details).

Note that in the case of China's exchange rate, we do not use the 'official' exchange rate between 1987 and 1994. For that period, China had a dual exchange rate system with an official rate and a parallel floating rate (the so-called swap market rate). Following Fernald *et al.* (1999), we use a trade-weighted average of the official and swap rates for this period. This correction substantially changes China's real exchange rate around the 1994 unification of the two rates, but does not qualitatively change the results that follow.

Even with the foreign-GDP and real-exchange-rate controls, the conditional correlation remains positive: When China's exports rise, other economies' exports also tend to rise. This is true even when we allow lags of the explanatory variables in the last three columns.

Table 1.2 allows the coefficient on China's exports to change in 2001, when China entered WTO. The coefficient on China's exports tends to be higher and more significant for the pre-2001 period. But even after 2001, the conditional correlation remains positive (though insignificant).

As noted in the introduction, in recent years commentary has often focused on real exchange rates as a channel for competition among Asian economies. At the onset of the Asian financial crisis in 1997, for example, many observers suggested that China had undergone a large depreciation at the beginning of 1994, which ultimately brought pressure to bear on other Asian economies to devalue their own currencies. This view was challenged in IMF (1997, 1998) and Fernald *et al.* (1999) on two grounds. First, there was little effective nominal depreciation of the

*Table 1.1* Conditional correlations between China's real export growth and real export growth in other Asian economies

| Independent Variable | NIEs | ASEAN-4 | All countries | NIEs | ASEAN-4 | All countries | NIEs | ASEAN-4 | All countries |
|---|---|---|---|---|---|---|---|---|---|
| | (1) | (2) | (3) | (4) | (5) | (6) | (7) | (8) | (9) |
| **China's Real Exports** | 0.29 (0.09) | 0.36 (0.12) | 0.32 (0.07) | 0.10 (0.08) | 0.19 (0.11) | 0.14 (0.07) | 0.13 (0.09) | 0.20 (0.12) | 0.20 (0.08) |
| Lag 1 | · | · | · | · | · | · | -0.00 (0.09) | -0.01 (0.12) | -0.00 (0.08) |
| Lag 2 | · | · | · | · | · | · | -0.05 (0.09) | -0.03 (0.13) | -0.05 (0.08) |
| Foreign Demand | · | · | · | 2.75 (0.51) | 3.24 (0.61) | 3.06 (0.40) | 3.44 (0.66) | 4.14 (0.79) | 3.78 (0.55) |
| Lag 1 | · | · | · | · | · | · | -1.57 (0.58) | -0.02 (0.75) | -0.90 (0.50) |
| Lag 2 | · | · | · | · | · | · | 1.11 (0.52) | 0.85 (0.66) | 0.76 (0.44) |
| Real Exchange Rate | · | · | · | -0.34 (0.10) | -0.34 (0.07) | -0.33 (0.05) | -0.31 (0.10) | -0.32 (0.07) | -0.37 (0.06) |
| Lag 1 | · | · | · | · | · | · | -0.30 (0.10) | 0.29 (0.07) | 0.17 (0.06) |
| Lag 2 | · | · | · | · | · | · | -0.00 (0.10) | 0.06 (0.08) | -0.03 (0.06) |
| Lagged Dependent Variable | 0.12 (0.10) | -0.06 (0.10) | 0.00 (0.07) | 0.10 (0.09) | -0.07 (0.08) | -0.01 (0.06) | 0.20 (0.11) | 0.01 (0.11) | 0.11 (0.08) |
| Adjusted $R^2$ | 0.09 | 0.12 | 0.13 | 0.35 | 0.42 | 0.40 | 0.48 | 0.50 | 0.43 |

Notes: Standard errors are in parenthesis. Dependent variable is growth in exports in local-currency units. Regressions estimated as a panel from 1981-2005. NIEs comprise of Korea, Singapore, Taiwan, and Hong Kong. ASEAN-4 comprise Indonesia, Malaysia, Philippines, and Thailand. All regressions include country fixed effects (not shown).

*Table 1.2* Regressions with break in coefficient on China's exports

|  | NIEs | ASEAN-4 | All countries |
|---|---|---|---|
|  | (1) | (2) | (3) |
| China's real exports (Pre-2001) | 0.13 | 0.27 | 0.19 |
|  | (0.10) | (0.13) | (0.08) |
| China's real exports (Beginning in 2001) | 0.10 | 0.16 | 0.12 |
|  | (0.09) | (0.11) | (0.07) |
| Foreign demand | 2.68 | 2.96 | 2.89 |
|  | (0.54) | (0.66) | (0.42) |
| Real exchange rate | −0.35 | −0.33 | −0.33 |
|  | (0.10) | (0.07) | (0.05) |
| Lagged dependent variable | 0.10 | −0.07 | −0.01 |
|  | (0.09) | (0.08) | (0.06) |
| Adjusted $R^2$ | 0.34 | 0.42 | 0.40 |

Notes: Standard errors are in parenthesis. Dependent variable is growth in exports in local-currency units. Regressions estimated as a panel from 1981–2005. NIEs comprise of Korea, Singapore, Taiwan, and Hong Kong. ASEAN-4 comprise of Indonesia, Malaysia, Philippines, and Thailand. All regressions include country fixed effects (not shown).

renminbi at the time, because the apparent devaluation of the official rate simply unified it with the unofficial rate at which most trade transactions already took place. Second, the moderate real depreciation was rapidly reversed by China's quite high inflation in 1994 and 1995. As a result, China's real exchange rate appreciated rather than depreciated over the 1993–7 period. Nevertheless, many Asian economies did have sharp real depreciations whereas China did not.

If China and emerging Asia were important competitors, such exchange rate movements should lead to corresponding changes in real export growth. Hence, a particular focus of the results in this section is whether movements in real exchange rates explain a large share of the variance in exports across Asian economies. In order to quantify the importance of various shocks on Asian exports, we estimate a simple model for Asian export growth. The data used in the estimation are annual, and extend from 1981 to 2005. To obtain sufficient degrees of freedom, we pool the data for eight Asian economies, China, the Asian NIEs (Korea, Singapore, Taiwan) and the 'ASEAN-4' (Indonesia, Malaysia, Philippines, Thailand).

We then run a panel vector autoregression (VAR) with three variables: (1) real income growth among major trading partners, (2) real exchange rate growth, and (3) real export growth. In estimating the VAR, we order the variables as listed; other orderings of the variables have little effect on results. We include two lags of each variable in the estimation, along with country fixed effects.

Figure 1.2 presents the estimated impulse responses from the VAR showing the response of export growth to standard-sized (i.e. one standard deviation) increases in each of the three sources of shocks. Focusing on the last column, it is evident that the contemporaneous responses of exports to foreign income and real exchange rate movements have the expected signs and are statistically significant.

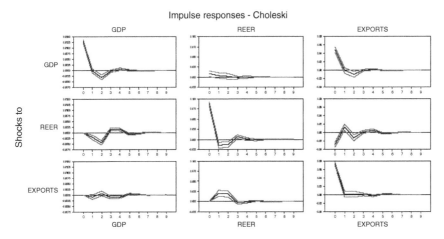

*Figure 1.2* Impulse responses from trivariate VAR system.

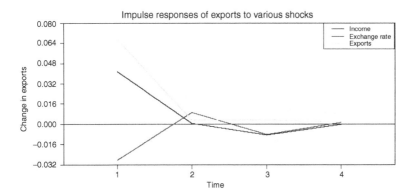

*Figure 1.3* Impulse responses of exports to various shocks.

The most interesting impulse responses are reproduced in Figure 1.3, which shows only the point estimates going out four years after the shock. An increase in income growth among trading partners leads to an increase in a 'representative' Asian economy's export growth: there is a strong – and statistically significant – contemporaneous impact. Over the next few years, the impact dissipates and is not statistically significantly different from zero. Depreciation in the currencies of major trading partners has the predicted adverse impact on export growth in the representative economy. Here, too, it is only the contemporaneous impact that is significantly different from zero.

Table 1.3 presents the variance decomposition of real export growth. As shown, income effects account for a much larger percentage of the variance than relative price effects. For instance, at the one-year horizon, income growth accounts for 25 per cent of the variance, compared with 8 per cent for real exchange rate changes.

*Table 1.3* Variance decompositions

*Decomposition of variance for export growth (EXPORTS)*

| Step | GDP | REER | EXPORTS |
|------|------|------|---------|
| 1 | 25.4 | 8.3 | 66.4 |
| 2 | 24.7 | 10.5 | 64.7 |
| 3 | 25.2 | 11.1 | 63.8 |
| 4 | 25.1 | 11.1 | 63.8 |

Notes: GDP = GDP growth of major trading partners and REER = growth in real effective exchange rate.

Not surprisingly, shocks to exports themselves show the largest dynamic response (as shown in Figure 1.2) and also account for the largest share of the variance.

These results suggest that, over the last 25 years, changes in real exchange rates have not been the primarily determinant of export growth for the major Asian exporters. A more important determinant has been income growth in the major trading partners (which, over the bulk of our sample period, reflects growth in the industrialized economies, particularly the United States). Industrial country demand and the effects of structural changes are likely to have outweighed exchange rate fluctuations as determinants of China's export growth.

These findings can explain why, for instance, China's export growth remained strong during the Asian crisis in 1997–8. Overall demand remained high (with strength in the United States and Europe countering weakness among Asian trading partners). As a result, export growth remained quite robust despite the drag from the depreciations of many Asian currencies. Prasad and Rumbaugh (2003) make a similar point about the more recent period. While acknowledging that 'the recent depreciation of the U.S. dollar, to which the renminbi is linked, has no doubt added temporarily to China's competitiveness', they suggest that it is unlikely that exchange rates are the primary determinant of China export growth because 'China's exports continued to grow rapidly virtually across the board even when the U.S. dollar was appreciating against other major currencies'.

## Sectoral evidence on export competition among Asian economies in the US market

This section describes how the market shares of exports of the various Asian economies have changed over time. We focus on exports to the United States, which is likely to have been the market where competition has been most intense. In addition to looking at changes in the overall market share (i.e. exports across all industries combined), we present evidence on changes in two high-profile industries that were identified in our previous work as being ones that displayed large changes in trade shares and accounted for a sizable fraction of total US imports from these Asian economies.

By focusing on relative export performance in a single geographic region and for specific industries, we hope to obtain product-level evidence on 'export competition'. For these purposes, we define export competition as 'shifts in market share' across four groups of Asian economies, China, the Asian NIEs, ASEAN-4 and a South Asia bloc (Bangladesh, India, Pakistan). In particular, we want to see if China's market share has increased markedly within a particular industry.

Note that by focusing on shares in particular markets we are strongly stacking the deck in favour of the export-competition view. After all, since shares sum to 100 per cent, it is arithmetically impossible for all shares to move in the same direction. So a country may have its share in a particular market decline without necessarily experiencing a decline in the level of its exports to that market. It may be losing market share in one market but gaining it in another. Moreover, some changes in shares may be deliberate, as in the case of industries that have shifted to a more vertically integrated approach to manufacturing.

Nevertheless, the changing shares give some sense of how trade patterns are evolving in the various economies. Also, from the perspective of a producer within a narrow industry, these figures give some sense of who they are competing against. Thus, the changing trade patterns discussed here provide indirect evidence of whether China and emerging Asia better fit the 'flying geese' or 'sitting ducks' paradigm.

Trade shares were computed for the period 1989 to 2005, thus providing a long-term perspective on changes. The data are at the three-digit industry level (on an end-use basis) and are published by the US Department of Commerce's Bureau of Economic Analysis (BEA). Tables 1.4 and 1.5 present data for 1989 and 2005 for the four country groups and for each of the 47 industries that make up the aggregate.[6] The tables contain a huge amount of data but some salient features emerge.

First, looking at Table 1.4, there is no doubt that China has emerged as a significant exporter across virtually the entire spectrum of industries: its share has increased in 41 industries. In contrast, there are only four industries in which the NIE share is higher in 2005 than in 1989 and these are all in the industrial supplies and materials category (1-digit code '1', i.e. 3-digit codes that begin with a '1'). In addition, there is one industry, 300 (new and used passenger cars), in which the NIEs have nearly maintained a 100 per cent share of US imports from emerging Asia since 1989, although with foreign direct investment in China's auto sector growing rapidly it may not be too long before that dominance is challenged as well.

Second, increases in the shares of ASEAN-4 are also quite prevalent, increasing in 17 of the 47 industries. This means that cases in which the shares of both China and ASEAN-4 have increased are almost as likely as cases in which their shares have moved in the opposite direction.

Third, an interesting finding is that South Asia shows an increase in 30 of the 47 industries. Though this region's overall share of the US market still remains small, the increases at the sectoral level suggest that that the region may start to be a contender in future.

Table 1.4 Shares of US imports from Asia by sub-region

| End Use Code | Industry description | 1989 | | | | 2005 | | | |
|---|---|---|---|---|---|---|---|---|---|
| | | China | NIEs | ASEAN | S. Asia | China | NIEs | ASEAN | S. Asia |
| 000 | Green coffee, cocoa beans, and cane sugar | 0 | 3 | 89 | 8 | 0 | 2 | 97 | 1 |
| 001 | Other agricultural foods | 19 | 15 | 55 | 11 | 35 | 10 | 41 | 14 |
| 002 | Feedstuff and foodgrains | 2 | 4 | 82 | 13 | 27 | 2 | 54 | 17 |
| 010 | Nonagricultural products | 20 | 27 | 45 | 8 | 31 | 5 | 53 | 11 |
| 100 | Petroleum and products, excluding gas | 18 | 8 | 62 | 12 | 15 | 51 | 20 | 15 |
| 101 | Fuels, n.e.s.-coal and gas | 71 | 1 | 29 | 0 | 75 | 0 | 23 | 2 |
| 103 | Nuclear Fuel Materials and Fuels | 100 | 0 | 0 | 0 | 100 | 0 | 0 | 0 |
| 110 | Paper base stocks | 15 | 41 | 43 | 0 | 12 | 0 | 85 | 3 |
| 111 | Newsprint and other paper products | 19 | 76 | 5 | 0 | 43 | 45 | 11 | 1 |
| 120 | Agricultural products | 12 | 5 | 77 | 6 | 19 | 3 | 66 | 13 |
| 121 | Textile supplies and related materials | 25 | 47 | 13 | 15 | 37 | 35 | 10 | 18 |
| 123 | Other materials, except chemicals | 16 | 37 | 45 | 2 | 16 | 74 | 9 | 1 |
| 125 | Chemicals, excluding medicines and food additives | 19 | 62 | 8 | 11 | 45 | 31 | 13 | 11 |
| 130 | Lumber and other unfinished building materials | 2 | 27 | 68 | 3 | 59 | 9 | 21 | 11 |
| 131 | Building materials, finished | 8 | 75 | 17 | 0 | 73 | 10 | 17 | 1 |
| 140 | Steelmaking and ferroalloying materials-unmanufact. | 60 | 5 | 24 | 11 | 92 | 6 | 2 | 0 |
| 141 | Iron and steel mill products-semifinished | 1 | 90 | 3 | 6 | 26 | 51 | 9 | 14 |
| 142 | Major nonferrous metals-crude and semifinished | 52 | 14 | 33 | 1 | 67 | 12 | 15 | 6 |
| 150 | Iron and steel products, except advanced manufact. | 9 | 76 | 10 | 5 | 49 | 33 | 9 | 9 |
| 151 | Iron and steel manufactures-advanced | 12 | 84 | 3 | 2 | 46 | 48 | 2 | 9 |
| 152 | Other finished metal shapes and advanced manufact. | 16 | 72 | 4 | 8 | 63 | 23 | 6 | 3 |
| 160 | Unfinished | 51 | 16 | 14 | 19 | 54 | 31 | 7 | 7 |
| 161 | Finished | 23 | 66 | 10 | 1 | 52 | 37 | 8 | 9 |
| 200 | Electric and electric generating equipment | 22 | 70 | 8 | 0 | 62 | 23 | 12 | 3 |

| Code | | c1 | c2 | c3 | c4 | c5 | c6 | c7 | c8 |
|---|---|---|---|---|---|---|---|---|---|
| 210 | Oil drilling, mining and construction machinery | 4 | 74 | 21 | 1 | 38 | 51 | 5 | 6 |
| 211 | Industrial and service machinery, n.e.c. | 15 | 81 | 2 | 2 | 57 | 33 | 6 | 4 |
| 212 | Agricultural machinery and equipment | 10 | 83 | 3 | 4 | 45 | 30 | 1 | 24 |
| 213 | Computers, peripherals and semiconductors | 7 | 72 | 21 | 0 | 48 | 25 | 27 | 0 |
| 214 | Telecommunications equipment | 21 | 66 | 13 | 0 | 38 | 13 | 49 | 0 |
| 215 | Other business machinery and equipment | 28 | 66 | 6 | 0 | 86 | 9 | 5 | 0 |
| 216 | Scientific, hospital and medical machinery | 22 | 61 | 6 | 12 | 42 | 26 | 27 | 4 |
| 220 | Civilian aircraft, engines and parts | 12 | 83 | 4 | 0 | 24 | 68 | 6 | 1 |
| 221 | Railway transportation equipment | 16 | 81 | 2 | 1 | 71 | 12 | 2 | 15 |
| 222 | Vessels, except military and pleasure craft | 11 | 83 | 6 | 0 | 59 | 37 | 3 | 1 |
| 223 | Spacecraft, engines and parts, except military | 0 | 100 | 0 | 0 | 0 | 30 | 67 | 3 |
| 300 | Passenger cars, new and used | 0 | 100 | 0 | 0 | 1 | 99 | 0 | 0 |
| 301 | Trucks, buses, and special-purpose vehicles | 0 | 99 | 0 | 1 | 98 | 2 | 0 | 0 |
| 302 | Parts, engines, bodies, and chassis | 11 | 74 | 13 | 2 | 44 | 38 | 14 | 4 |
| 400 | Apparel, footwear, and household goods | 34 | 49 | 12 | 5 | 68 | 5 | 13 | 14 |
| 401 | Other consumer nondurables | 45 | 46 | 8 | 1 | 64 | 25 | 4 | 7 |
| 410 | Household goods | 23 | 64 | 10 | 3 | 72 | 17 | 9 | 2 |
| 411 | Recreational equipment and materials | 38 | 57 | 5 | 0 | 88 | 9 | 3 | 0 |
| 412 | Home entertainment equipment | 19 | 63 | 18 | 0 | 67 | 15 | 18 | 0 |
| 413 | Coins, gems, jewelry, and collectibles | 46 | 22 | 28 | 4 | 50 | 2 | 21 | 27 |
| 420 | Nondurables-unmanufactured | 14 | 34 | 38 | 14 | 29 | 33 | 21 | 17 |
| 421 | Durables-unmanufactured | 12 | 13 | 10 | 65 | 28 | 2 | 6 | 64 |
| 500 | Imports, N.E.S. | 28 | 55 | 15 | 2 | 44 | 38 | 15 | 3 |

Notes: All figures are per cent, and sum to 100 for a given year.

Table 1.5 Dollar value and import share from Asia, by product

| End Use Code | Description | Total imports from Asia 1989 (US $ billions) | Total imports from Asia 2005 (US $ billions) | Asia's share of US imports 1989 (per cent) | Asia's share of US imports 2005 (per cent) |
|---|---|---|---|---|---|
| 000 | Green coffee, cocoa beans, and cane sugar | 0.3 | 0.4 | 9 | 11 |
| 001 | Other agricultural foods | 1.4 | 3.9 | 11 | 9 |
| 002 | Feedstuff and foodgrains | 0.1 | 0.4 | 14 | 21 |
| 010 | Nonagricultural products | 1.6 | 4.9 | 23 | 30 |
| 100 | Petroleum and products, excluding gas | 2.5 | 4.0 | 5 | 2 |
| 101 | Fuels, n.e.s.-coal and gas | 0.0 | 0.5 | 0 | 1 |
| 103 | Nuclear Fuel Materials and Fuels | 0.0 | 0.1 | 0 | 2 |
| 110 | Paper base stocks | 0.0 | 0.0 | 0 | 1 |
| 111 | Newsprint and other paper products | 0.1 | 0.9 | 1 | 9 |
| 120 | Agricultural products | 1.2 | 2.6 | 30 | 37 |
| 121 | Textile supplies and related materials | 1.6 | 4.8 | 30 | 37 |
| 123 | Other materials, except chemicals | 0.0 | 0.1 | 2 | 9 |
| 125 | Chemicals, excluding medicinals and food additives | 0.7 | 7.1 | 5 | 13 |
| 130 | Lumber and other unfinished building materials | 0.5 | 3.0 | 11 | 17 |
| 131 | Building materials, finished | 0.5 | 2.8 | 19 | 17 |
| 140 | Steelmaking and ferroalloying materials-unmanufactured | 0.1 | 0.4 | 5 | 7 |
| 141 | Iron and steel mill products-semifinished | 0.4 | 2.6 | 5 | 16 |
| 142 | Major nonferrous metals-crude and semifinished | 0.3 | 1.2 | 2 | 4 |
| 150 | Iron and steel products, except advanced manufactures | 0.6 | 2.2 | 20 | 30 |
| 151 | Iron and steel manufactures-advanced | 0.8 | 3.5 | 33 | 50 |
| 152 | Other finished metal shapes and advanced manufactures | 0.4 | 3.4 | 16 | 27 |
| 160 | Unfinished | 0.1 | 0.6 | 8 | 14 |

| Code | Category | | | | |
|------|----------|------|------|----|----|
| 161 | Finished | 1.1 | 8.1 | 21 | 33 |
| 200 | Electric and electric generating equipment | 2.4 | 12.9 | 19 | 30 |
| 210 | Oil drilling, mining and construction machinery | 0.3 | 3.0 | 6 | 19 |
| 211 | Industrial and service machinery, n.e.c. | 2.7 | 17.5 | 9 | 18 |
| 212 | Agricultural machinery and equipment | 0.1 | 0.8 | 3 | 12 |
| 213 | Computers, peripherals and semiconductors | 14.8 | 88.7 | 44 | 75 |
| 214 | Telecommunications equipment | 2.6 | 19.6 | 28 | 53 |
| 215 | Other business machinery and equipment | 0.8 | 4.1 | 18 | 48 |
| 216 | Scientific, hospital and medical machinery | 0.3 | 4.2 | 8 | 17 |
| 220 | Civilian aircraft, engines and parts | 0.1 | 0.8 | 2 | 3 |
| 221 | Railway transportation equipment | 0.0 | 0.2 | 2 | 14 |
| 222 | Vessels, except military and pleasure craft | 0.0 | 0.1 | 13 | 11 |
| 223 | Spacecraft, engines and parts, except military | 0.0 | 0.0 | 0 | 0 |
| 300 | Passenger cars, new and used | 1.6 | 9.2 | 3 | 7 |
| 301 | Trucks, buses, and special-purpose vehicles | 0.0 | 0.3 | 0 | 1 |
| 302 | Parts, engines, bodies, and chassis | 1.9 | 12.2 | 7 | 13 |
| 400 | Apparel, footwear, and household goods | 24.6 | 65.6 | 69 | 61 |
| 401 | Other consumer nondurables | 2.0 | 9.7 | 19 | 13 |
| 410 | Household goods | 9.4 | 64.2 | 51 | 66 |
| 411 | Recreational equipment and materials | 6.0 | 24.9 | 48 | 67 |
| 412 | Home entertainment equipment | 5.1 | 27.5 | 43 | 59 |
| 413 | Coins, gems, jewelry, and collectibles | 1.6 | 6.9 | 23 | 36 |
| 420 | Nondurables-unmanufactured | 0.0 | 0.1 | 3 | 4 |
| 421 | Durables-unmanufactured | 1.8 | 5.1 | 32 | 27 |
| 500 | Imports, N.E.S. | 1.4 | 8.3 | 10 | 15 |

*Table 1.6* Shares of US imports from Asia from selected sub-regions

A. All industries

|  | 1989 | 1993 | 1997 | 2001 | 2005 |
|---|---|---|---|---|---|
| China | 23 | 31 | 35 | 42 | 57 |
| NIEs | 56 | 42 | 36 | 31 | 21 |
| ASEAN-4 | 17 | 22 | 24 | 22 | 17 |
| South Asia | 5 | 5 | 5 | 5 | 6 |

B. Industry 213: Computers, peripherals and semiconductors

|  | 1989 | 1993 | 1997 | 2001 | 2005 |
|---|---|---|---|---|---|
| China | 7 | 7 | 10 | 19 | 48 |
| NIEs | 72 | 68 | 61 | 47 | 25 |
| ASEAN-4 | 21 | 25 | 29 | 34 | 27 |
| South Asia | 0 | 0 | 0 | 0 | 0 |

C. Industry 400: Apparel, footwear, and household goods

|  | 1989 | 1993 | 1997 | 2001 | 2005 |
|---|---|---|---|---|---|
| China | 34 | 51 | 55 | 56 | 68 |
| NIEs | 49 | 23 | 13 | 11 | 5 |
| ASEAN-4 | 12 | 18 | 21 | 20 | 13 |
| South Asia | 5 | 8 | 11 | 14 | 14 |

Notes: All figures are per cent and all shares sum to 100 for a given year.

Overall, the message from Table 1.4 is that China and ASEAN-4 appear to have been moving into the product space vacated by the NIEs. The evidence is only reinforced if one takes into account the amount of imports from Asia in each industry, which is shown in Table 1.5. In five of the seven largest industries, the shares of China and ASEAN-4 have moved in the same direction (these are industries 213, 400, 412, 214 and 211); in the other two (industries 410 and 411) the shares have moved in opposite directions but the declines in the ASEAN-4 share are small.

We now turn to a closer look at the changes over time in trade shares. Table 1.6.A. shows export shares for the four groups for the US market as a whole. As shown, in 1989 China and Hong Kong together accounted for about a quarter of total exports to the United States from the four groups. By 1993, China's share had increased to a third. Mainland China alone nearly doubled its share of the US market, helped perhaps by the real depreciation of the renminbi over this period. The ASEAN-4 group also increased its market share, but by a smaller magnitude than the increase in mainland China's share. Correspondingly, the share of the NIEs fell from 56 per cent to 42 per cent. There is, therefore, some evidence of 'competition' – shifts in market share – among these three groups over the period 1989 to 1993. South Asia's share did not change over this period.

By contrast to the 1989–93 period, the period between 1993 and 1997 is far more tranquil. The shares of China and ASEAN-4 inch up over this period at the

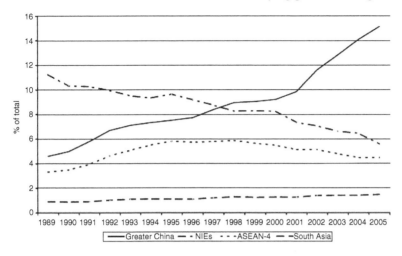

*Figure 1.4* Shares of world exports to the United States.

expense of the NIEs. The Asian crisis and the associated sharp real depreciations in the currencies of many Asian economies, did not lead to any dramatic changes in market shares: The relative stability that characterized the period 1993 to 1997 continued through 2001. During the most recent period, however, China's share jumped dramatically from 42 per cent to 57 per cent, at the expense of both the NIEs and the ASEAN-4. Thus, the period 2001 to 2005 again shows strong signs of competition.

The story is much the same when we examine the country groups' shares of world exports to the United States. As shown in Figure 1.4, China's share of world exports to the United States has risen steadily since 1989, with a sharp increase since 2000. The share of the ASEAN-4 also rose through much of the 1990s, but has fallen a little over the most recent period. The NIEs have experienced a steady decline in their share. The share of the South Asia bloc has trended up but remains small.

A similar perspective is offered in Figure 1.5, where we plot the dollar value of the country groups' exports to the United States. Again, we only see strong signs of competition in the most recent period, from 2001 onwards, during which China's exports to the United States have soared, while exports of the NIEs and the ASEAN-4 have stagnated. During the 1990s, the dollar value of each groups' exports actually rose, providing evidence that – as we noted above – that focusing on shares can overstate the extent of competition.

We now turn to a more detailed analysis of the two largest industries based on US imports from Asia in 2005, namely, industry 213 (computers, peripherals and semi-conductors) and industry 400 (apparel, footwear and household products). First consider the changes in industry 213 (Table 1.6.B). China's market share rose from 7 per cent in 1989 to 19 per cent in 2001, while the share of ASEAN-4 rose from 21 per cent to 34 per cent. There is a corresponding fall in the share

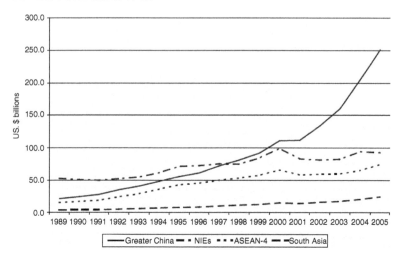

*Figure 1.5*  $ Value of Asian exports to the United States.

of the NIEs. In the period since 2001, China's gains in this industry have been dramatic and have come at the expense of both the NIEs and ASEAN-4.

The story in the case of industry 400 is a bit different (Table 1.6.C). Here too, China does experience a big increase in market share between 1989 and 2001, from 34 per cent to 56 per cent, but the bulk of this increase occurs between 1989 and 1993. The share of the ASEAN-4 also increased over the 1989 to 2001 period, with the change again being more substantial in the earlier part of the period. Since 2001, ASEAN-4 has lost market share to China, while South Asia has held its own over this period.

In sum, contrary to some popular perceptions, China's gains in market share have not come about primarily at the expense of the labour-intensive ASEAN-4 or South Asian economies. Instead, China displaced the NIEs in industries that these more advanced economies were relinquishing. This is a healthy development. It mimics an earlier period, when the NIEs moved into the industries relinquished by a more advanced Japan. In the most recent period, however, from 2001 to 2005, we do see that China's share has risen considerably, still primarily at the expense of the NIEs, but also at the expense of the ASEAN-4.[7]

## The destination of Asian NIE exports

An interesting fact that emerges from the data is that the NIEs are losing import shares in the US market in almost all categories of goods at the same time that their overall exports are growing. This raises an obvious question: Where are exports from the NIEs going? In Table 1.7, we attempt to answer this using data from the IMF's Direction of Trade Statistics (DOTS).[8] The table shows the average annual growth rate of exports from China, the NIEs, the ASEAN-4 and South Asia (as we have defined them in this paper) to the world, the G-3 (United States, Japan,

*Table 1.7* Average annual growth of exports from emerging Asia by destination

|           |            | World | G-3  | Greater China | NIEs | ASEAN-4 | South Asia |
|-----------|------------|-------|------|---------------|------|---------|------------|
| 1989–1993 | China/HK   | 15.8  | 18.4 | 12.7          | 17.6 | 13.2    | 13.0       |
|           | NIEs       | 9.3   | 2.5  | 27.7          | 15.6 | 16.9    | 14.3       |
|           | ASEAN-4    | 15.3  | 12.9 | 19.8          | 20.7 | 17.3    | 8.1        |
|           | South Asia | 8.3   | 3.4  | 7.9           | 12.5 | 18.4    | 18.3       |
| 1993–2001 | China/HK   | 9.1   | 9.9  | 7.4           | 10.2 | 12.2    | 12.8       |
|           | NIEs       | 6.2   | 5.0  | 8.8           | 8.7  | 7.0     | 6.1        |
|           | ASEAN-4    | 7.8   | 6.8  | 11.4          | 7.0  | 14.8    | 15.1       |
|           | South Asia | 9.1   | 8.2  | 11.2          | 7.0  | 10.1    | 11.0       |
| 2001–2005 | China/HK   | 23.2  | 21.7 | 21.6          | 25.6 | 25.4    | 36.3       |
|           | NIEs       | 14.5  | 7.3  | 26.8          | 14.8 | 13.1    | 18.9       |
|           | ASEAN-4    | 14.6  | 9.1  | 34.0          | 10.7 | 20.5    | 24.2       |
|           | South Asia | 19.5  | 15.5 | 34.0          | 18.1 | 19.4    | 17.0       |

Notes: IMF Direction of Trade Statistics, CEIC, and National Sources.

and European Union, which we use as a proxy for industrial economies), China, the NIEs, the ASEAN-4 and South Asia.[9] The growth rates are broken down into the time periods we identified earlier: the first period of China's increasing shares from 1989–93, the relatively stable shares period from 1993–2001, and the recent period in which China's shares have risen rapidly from 2001–2005.

In the early period, it is obvious that China's share of the G-3 import market was growing at the expense of the NIEs. The average growth in Chinese exports to the G-3 was almost 20 per cent during that period, while NIE export growth to the G-3 was just 2 per cent. However, NIE exports to China were growing at an almost 30 per cent annual rate at that time. In the stable share period from 1993–2001, the export growth rates of all three groups were fairly similar. The NIEs experienced a more rapid period of export growth to the G-3, perhaps due to the US high-tech boom and the NIEs exports to China continued to rise, albeit at a slower rate.

In the period 2001 to 2005, however, the differences are striking. In this period, both the NIEs and ASEAN-4 have experienced export growth to China at a rate that far outstrips their export growth to other regions.[10] We offer two explanations for the rise in NIE exports to China and the relative weakness of exports to the G-3. First, demand in China remained strong throughout the period we examined, despite several episodes of global weakness. Most noticeably, during the 2000–2002 period, the US high-tech bubble burst, global demand fell, and yet China continued to grow at a robust pace. Thus, it is not surprising that exports to China rose significantly in that period. Second, the shifting of production facilities to China from the NIEs likely has boosted NIE exports of intermediate products to China for processing and export of the finished product.[11] The data presented here do not shed light on the relative importance of these two explanations, but it is likely that both are partly responsible.

## Conclusions

We have examined trade linkages among China and other economies in emerging Asia at both the aggregate and sectoral levels. At an aggregate level their relationship appears complementary, with export growth driven by common factors such as global growth. Moreover, China's rapid growth itself represents a significant opportunity for emerging Asia – China's imports have grown in lock step with its exports, and China is thus an important source of demand for goods from emerging Asia. For example, Korean exports of steel products to China have surged, reflecting robust spending on infrastructure and other construction projects in China.

When one looks at the sectoral data on US imports from Asia, there is no doubt that China is displacing other Asian economies across a wide spectrum of markets. Not all of this displacement is symptomatic of competition. First, a significant portion of the final assembly of Asian-made products takes place in China. In that sense, as McKinnon and Schnabl (2006) state, 'China is merely the face of a worldwide export surge into American consumer markets'. Second, to some extent the changes in trade shares reflect a longer-term trend of China moving into the product space vacated by the Asian NIEs as they move to higher value-added products.

Nevertheless, it seems likely that the shifts in trade shares require actual shifts in resource allocations, which can often be painful for those who lose out. The appropriate policy response would be to take steps to smooth the flow of resources across sectors.

## Acknowledgement

The views in this paper are solely the responsibility of the authors and should not be interpreted as reflecting the views of the Board of Governors of the Federal Reserve System or of any other person associated with the Federal Reserve System or of the International Monetary Fund. We thank Jason Tjosvold and David Thipphavong for research assistance.

## References

Abeysinghe, Tilak and Ding, Lu (2003) 'China as an Economic Powerhouse: Implications on its Neighbors', *China Economic Review*, 14(2): 164–85.

Ahearne, Alan, John Fernald, Prakash Loungani and John Schindler (2003) 'China and Emerging Asia: Comrades or Competitors?', *Seoul Journal of Economics*, 16(2): 183–213.

Akamatsu, Kaname (1961) 'A Theory of Unbalanced Growth in the World Economy', *Weltwirtschaftliches Archiv*, 86: 196–217.

———— (1962) 'A Historical Pattern of Economic Growth in Developing Countries', *The Developing Economies*, 1(1): 3–25.

Bergsten, C. Fred (2006) 'The US Trade Deficit and China', Testimony before the Hearing on US-China Committee on Finance, United States Senate, March 29.

Bhalla, Surjit (1998) 'Chinese Mercantilism: Currency Wars and How the East was Lost', ICRIER Paper, No. 45, July, New Delhi: Indian Council for Research on International Economic Relations.

Carolan, Terrie, Nirvikar Singh and Cyrus Talati (1998) 'The Composition of U.S.–East Asia Trade and Changing Comparative Advantage', *Journal of Development Economics*, 57(2): 361–89.

Cerra, Valerie and Anuradha Dayal-Gulati (1999) 'China's Trade Flows—Changing Price Sensitivities and the Reform Process', IMF Working Paper, No. 99/1.

Diwan, Ishac and Bernard Hoekman (1999) 'Competition, Complementarity and Contagion in East Asia', in *The Asian Financial Crisis: Causes, Contagion and Consequences*, Pierre-Richard Agénor, Marcus Miller, David Vines, and Axel Weber (ed.), New York: Cambridge University Press. pp. 312–56.

Fernald, John G., Hali Edison, and Prakash Loungani (1999) 'Was China the First Domino? Assessing Links Between China and the Rest of Emerging Asia', *Journal of International Money and Finance*, 18(4): 515–35.

Gochoco-Bautista, Maria Socorro (1995) 'ASEAN-China Economic Relations into the 21st Century', *Philippine Review of Economics and Business*, vol. XXXII, No. 2, December.

IMF (1997) World Economic Outlook, December.

——— (1998) 'The Asian Crisis: Causes and Cures', *Finance and Development*, June, 35: 2.

Kojima, Kiyoshi (2000) 'The "flying geese" model of Asian economic development: origin, theoretical extensions, and regional policy implications', *Journal of Asian Economics*, 11(4): 375–401.

Kwan, C.H. (2002) 'The Rise of China and Asia's Flying-Geese Pattern of Economic Development: An Empirical Analysis Based on US Import Statistics', The Research Institute of Economy, Trade and Industry (RIETI) Discussion Paper Series 02-E-009, July.

Loretan, Michael (2005) 'Indexes of the Foreign Exchange Value of the Dollar', *Federal Reserve Bulletin*, Winter 2005: 1–8.

Loungani, Prakash (2000) 'Comrades or Competitors?: Trade Links Between China and Other East Asian Economies', *Finance and Development*, June, 37: 2.

McKinnon, Ronald Ian and Gunther Schnabl (2006) 'China's Exchange Rate and International Adjustment in Wages, Prices, and Interest Rates: Japan Déjà Vu?' CESifo Working Paper, No. 1720.

Prasad, Eswar and Thomas Rumbaugh (2004) 'Beyond the Great Wall', *Finance and Development*, 40(4): 46–9.

Okita, Saburo (1985) 'Special presentation: prospect of Pacific economies', Korea Development Institute. *Pacific cooperation: issues and opportunities*: 18–29. Report of the Fourth Pacific Economic Cooperation Conference, Seoul, Korea, April 29–May 1: 21.

Tambunan, Tulus (2006) 'Is ASEAN still relevant in the era of the ASEAN-China FTA?' Paper prepared for the 2006 APEA conference, Seattle, USA, July 29–30, 2006.

Voon, Jan P. (1998) 'Export Competitiveness of China and ASEAN in the U.S. Market', *ASEAN Economic Bulletin*, 14(3): 273–91.

Williamson, John (2003) 'The Renminbi Exchange Rate and the Global Monetary System', Lecture at the Central University of Finance and Economics, Beijing, October 29.

Zebregs, Harm (2004) 'Intraregional Trade in Emerging Asia', *IMF Policy Discussion Paper*, No. 04 (1).

# 2 A decade of flow of funds in China (1995–2006)

*Guijun Lin and Ronald M. Schramm*

## Introduction

In this paper we examine the balance between savings and investment (the flow of funds) for the People's Republic of China (China) at both a macroeconomic level and at disaggregated sectoral levels. Specifically, we look at the flow of funds at the national level and then at the sectoral level as divided into the government sector, the production sector and the individual (small entrepreneurs/households) sector.[1] Finally, we subdivide the production sector into three component sectors: the state-owned enterprise sector (SOE), the collective sector (COE) and the corporate sector.

We take a top-down approach starting at the macroeconomic flow level and then moving down to individual sectors. Earlier research in this area has been rather limited. Kujis (2005), relying on the National Bureaus of Statistics (NBS) flow of funds tables presents a breakdown identical to the sectoral breakdown used here, but does not independently link that breakdown upward at the macro level nor to the lower sub-sector level. We also make explicit assumptions regarding the share of government in the flow of funds accounts and allow for different estimates of household savings. These alternative scenarios allow for a range of possible flow of funds and balances. Other approaches have taken as a starting point the sources of finance (e.g. loans, grants and self-raised funds etc.) to individual sectors consistent with the NBS presentation. Some studies have focused on the profitability of a single sector such as the SOE sector (Carsten, 2002). Zhang (2001) has written a number of insightful articles on the evolving structure of enterprise finance. It is hoped that our more integrated approach provides both a different angle in analyzing China's flow of funds and a broader range of estimates. In the process, we learn more about data availability, consistency and shortcomings.

A number of results emerge from this paper. Some are new and some confirm the work of earlier authors but with a different approach. We summarize our findings and observations.

---

1 Foreign Direct Investment (FDI) in part has freed Chinese national savings to take the form of capital outflows (to date most of which has been used in the accumulation of foreign exchange reserves).

2    Though the individual sector in absolute terms has lower savings than does the production sector, it is the largest source of funds to both the government sector and the production sector.

3    Related to (2), our estimates of profitability in the production sector are much higher than Kujis (2005) estimates, but the flow balance has been shrinking over the past decade and may have become negative around 2000–2001.

4    The SOE sector in the aggregate has been profitable over the past decade. Nevertheless, its savings/investment balance has been either very low or negative in that period. The balance may have turned positive around 2004; COEs have had a deteriorating balance with investment remaining stable, but savings (profitability) declined over most of the decade.

5    The corporate sector has had a positive balance throughout the decade which has allowed it to lend to the SOE and collective sectors.

6    A substantial share of national savings is not financially intermediated either via bank deposits, insurance premiums, debt or equity instruments or increased cash holdings. This suggests a substantial informal intermediation market within and between companies and individuals. This, in part, quantifies the often cited 'triangle of debt'.

Section 2 of the paper presents the accounting framework for our analysis. Section 3 identifies sources of data and the methodological approach. Sections 4–6 provide results for flow of funds at the macroeconomic, sectoral and production sub-sector levels. Section 7 briefly analyzes the flow of financial intermediation instruments and Section 8 summarizes and hints at some policy implications.

## China: Flow of funds analysis

Our approach in examining China's flow of funds is to combine the well known macroeconomic methodology with the more disaggregated data presentation of China's NBS. We start by segregating Chinese output $(Y)$ into its uses: Consumption $(C)$, investment $(I)$, government $(G)$ and net exports + net factor payments $(X - M + NFP)$ and obtain the familiar identity

$$Y_{GNP} \equiv C + I + G + (X - M + NFP) \qquad (2.1)$$

After some adjustments using the definition of the budget deficit and the breakdown of personal income into consumption $(C)$, savings $(S)$, and taxes $(T)$, we have:

$$S' - I = (X - M + NFP) + (G + Tr - Taxes) \qquad (2.2)$$

Here we have the traditional breakdown of the economy into three sectors (from left to right in (2.2)) we have the domestic savings/investment balance, the external sector and the government sector. Equation (2.2) states that the difference between savings $(S')$ and investment $(I)$ on the part of individuals and productive entities will equal the current account on the balance of payments plus the budget deficit (where $G + Tr$ – taxes is a positive number when there is a budget deficit). Importantly, we note that $G$ in (2.2) represents government consumption; Government investment is included in $I$ along with individual and productive sector investment. Savings includes savings of just the private and productive sectors and excludes government savings. We also note that $I$ includes 'stock-building' or inventory accumulation – both planned and unplanned.

We would now like to rearrange and specify (2.2) in a way more suitable to China's statistical presentation. First we collapse the budget deficit into $S'$ and redefine $S'$ as $S$ or domestic savings. We next decompose $S$ into its variant sectors:

1   the government sector, representing all levels of government;
2   the production sector, representing production by state-owned enterprises (SOEs), collective entities (COEs) and corporate entities; and
3   the private or individual sector representing non-production and non-government domestic entities and individuals.

We classify sub-sectors of investment, $I$, in exactly the same way. We summarize these relationships in (2.3) and (2.4):

$$S = I + (X - M + NFP) \tag{2.3}$$

$$S^G + S^{Prod} + S^{Priv} = I^G + I^{Prod} + I^{Priv} + (X - M + NFP) \tag{2.4}$$

Equations (2.3) and (2.4) have sources of funds on the left-hand side of each equation and uses of funds (savings) on the right-hand side. To be complete, we identify $S^{Prod}$ and $I^{Prod}$ and its components:

$$S^{Prod} \equiv S^{SOE} + S^{Collective} + S^{Corporate} \text{ and}$$

$$I^{Prod} \equiv I^{SOE} + I^{Collective} + I^{Corporate} \tag{2.5}$$

We refer to $S$ and $I$ in the form of equation (2.3) as domestic savings and domestic investment. Finally, it is useful to define national savings and national investment. Subtracting out foreign direct investment (*FDI*) from each side of (2.3) and rearranging, we have:

$$S - (X - M + NFP) - FDI = I - FDI \tag{2.6}$$

On the right-hand side of (2.6) national investment represents investment undertaken by domestic (not foreign) entities within China. The left-hand side represents national savings by Chinese entities which are directed toward investment (physical) within China. The expression $(X - M + NFP) - FDI$ represents gross capital outflows (mainly financial and mainly channelled into reserve holdings) by Chinese entities and individuals beyond China's borders.[2] Equation (2.6) is important in that it allows us to isolate Chinese flow of funds which are directed toward national investment activities. In addition, we will present results regarding those flows which are channelled abroad.

Our general approach is to apply the definition of domestic savings and national investment at a sectoral level and then compare savings and investment and the resulting balance between the two at the sectoral level (see, for example, Teplin (2001)). Formally, we examine:

$$S^i - I^i = Balance^i \qquad (2.7)$$

where superscript *i* represents either a sector such as the production sector or a sub-sector of a sector such as the collective sector of the production sector.

Our general strategy is to use data for sectors where the 'level of comfort' with that data is high. We then use our accounting framework above to identify data for the residual sector. Specifically, the Production sector is the residual sector or 'plug sector' for both savings and investment. The residual sub-sector of the production sector is the corporate sector on the savings side while on the investment side, there was sufficient data to make a residual sector unnecessary.

## Sources of data and definitions

Data on the distribution of investment across sub-sectors, profitability of various sub-sectors and private savings comes from various issues of the *China Statistical Yearbook* (CSY).[3] While this provided the bulk of information on the relative sizes of various sub-sectors, this information was supplemented by data from *International Financial Statistics* and estimates from the *Economist Intelligence Unit*. Updates to all these sources can be found in *China Monthly Statistics*. The *China Financial Stability Report* (2005) provides a useful historical summary of financial data on bank deposits, equity and bond issuance and loan amounts. Regarding assumptions on 'fiscal reach' in investment we used both International Monetary Fund and World Bank estimates.

We use the same definitions for state-owned and state-controlled enterprises, state-owned units, collective enterprises, private enterprises and self-employed enterprises as found in the China Statistical Yearbook. Specifically, the appendices for Chapters 6 and 14 of the 2005 CSY provide detailed definitions of these different types of entities. Any entity which is not included in any of the above definitions, we define as a 'corporate entity'. As such, this latter definition includes shareholding units, joint ownership units, foreign funded units and units funded from Hong Kong, Macao and Taiwan. Again, these latter types of entities are defined in the above-mentioned appendices.

## Flow of funds at the macro level

The results of this section are well-known, but provide the basis for two more disaggregated sections on flows that follow. We therefore, discuss in some detail the methodology and assumptions employed in deriving the results found in Table 2.1 and Figures 2.1–2.3. Figures 2.1 and 2.2 provide the sources and uses of

Table 2.1 Flow of funds at the macro level

| | National Savings or sources of funds | | | | | | | | | | | |
|---|---|---|---|---|---|---|---|---|---|---|---|---|
| | US$ Millions | | | | | | | | | | | |
| | 1995 | 1996 | 1997 | 1998 | 1999 | 2000 | 2001 | 2002 | 2003 | 2004 | 2005 | 2006 |
| Savings (imputed) private + prod + gov | 298681 | 343853 | 398467 | 409709 | 419162 | 441401 | 497882 | 585877 | 721944 | 904258 | 1145030 | 1430139 |
| Domestic savings as a per cent of GDP | 41% | 40% | 40% | 39% | 38% | 37% | 38% | 40% | 44% | 47% | 50% | 52% |
| National uses of funds | | | | | | | | | | | | |
| Total investment as a per cent of GDP | 41% | 39% | 37% | 36% | 36% | 35% | 36% | 38% | 41% | 43% | 43% | 43% |
| Current account balance | 0% | 1% | 4% | 3% | 2% | 2% | 1% | 2% | 3% | 4% | 7% | 9% |
| Total investment breakdown | | | | | | | | | | | | |
| FDI as a share of total investment | 13% | 13% | 13% | 12% | 10% | 10% | 7% | 9% | 8% | 7% | 6% | 4% |
| FDI (gross) | 33849 | 38066 | 41674 | 41117 | 36978 | 36567 | 30473 | 44272 | 47381 | 51327 | 56515 | 42435 |
| National Investment Pri + pro + gov | 263213 | 298544 | 319830 | 337120 | 361069 | 384316 | 450008 | 506183 | 628688 | 784272 | 927697 | 1137838 |
| National savings vs. domestic savings | | | | | | | | | | | | |
| Domestic savings as a per cent of GDP | 41% | 40% | 40% | 39% | 38% | 37% | 38% | 40% | 44% | 47% | 50% | 52% |
| National savings as a per cent of GDP | 36% | 35% | 32% | 32% | 33% | 32% | 34% | 35% | 38% | 41% | 40% | 41% |
| National investment vs. domestic investment | | | | | | | | | | | | |
| Domestic investment as a per cent of GDP | 41% | 39% | 37% | 36% | 36% | 35% | 36% | 38% | 41% | 43% | 43% | 43% |
| National investment as a per cent of GDP | 36% | 35% | 32% | 32% | 33% | 32% | 34% | 35% | 38% | 41% | 40% | 41% |

Sources: China Statistical Yearbook (various issues); Economist Intelligence Unit; International Financial Statistics; China Monetary Policy Report (various issues).

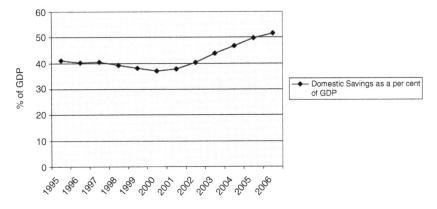

*Figure 2.1* Domestic sources of funds or savings as a per cent of GDP.

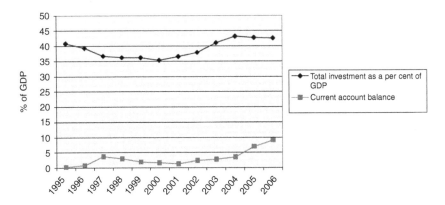

*Figure 2.2* Domestic uses of funds or savings as a per cent of GDP.

China's domestic savings. Inclusion of budget surpluses makes China's prodigious domestic savings rate even higher (52 per cent of GDP) by 2006.[4] As is the case with virtually all countries, most of these savings are channelled into investment (43 per cent of GDP). The remainder is channelled in foreign savings (lending abroad) as represented by the current account surplus (9 per cent of GDP in 2006). We note that both domestic savings and investment have accelerated as a share of GDP since 2000 consistent with an economic growth expansion that began in 1999.

Domestic savings is a residual estimate along the lines of equation (2.2) after taking into account budget deficit/surplus, current account and domestic investment data. The budget deficit/surplus data is based on International Monetary Fund IFS data (2006) and various Article IV estimates. These estimates exclude government investment since we are including that investment as a use under national investment. It is for this reason that our budget series is in

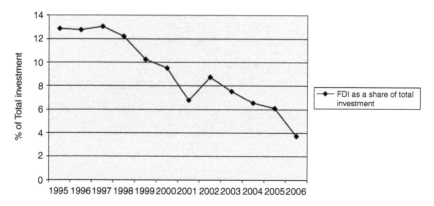

*Figure 2.3* FDI as a share of total investment.

surplus – it only includes government consumption and various government transfers as expenditure items. Domestic investment includes both investments in plant, property and equipment as well as inventory accumulation. Current account balance is based on International Monetary Fund (IMF) estimates. Since the current account and capital account must sum to zero (if we broadly define the capital account to include changes in reserve holdings), we interpret current account surpluses as net lending abroad.[5]

Referring to Figures 2.4–2.5 and with reference to equation (2.6), we see that the gap between domestic and national savings has remained relatively stable while that between domestic and national investment has narrowed somewhat. In part the stable gap for the former pair reflects the narrowing share of FDI as a share of domestic savings (as seen in Figure 2.3) being offset by the widening current account surplus. In the sectoral analysis below we use the national investment and domestic savings measures because these measures tell us about the financing and investing decisions of the various economic entities within China as opposed to the investment and savings decisions of the rest of the world as they affect China at an accounting level.[6]

An immediate observation using the national vs. domestic distinction is that FDI over the years has allowed some of China's substantial savings to be used elsewhere – that is as gross lending – either in the form of reserve accumulation or other outward financial flows. In fact the cumulated sum of the difference between domestic savings and national savings for the 1995–2006 period is approximately US$ 1.2 trillion.[7] This is remarkably close to recent measures of China's gross foreign exchange reserve holdings.

## Flow of funds at the sector level

In this section we attempt to divide the flow of domestic savings and national investment identified in the last section into three sectors: Government, production and individual. Government refers to all levels of government – central, provincial

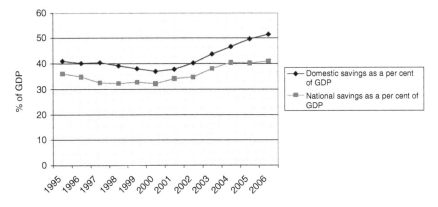

*Figure 2.4* National vs. domestic savings.

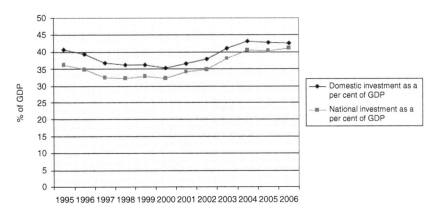

*Figure 2.5* National vs. domestic investment.

and township but as we will discuss below our definition attempts to exclude output of a non-public good nature.[8] Production refers to productive activities by enterprises, including output by SOEs, COEs and corporate entities for use by the non-government sector. The individual sector includes both households in their role as workers and as entrepreneurs – here we use the NBS definitions of 'self-employed units' and 'private enterprises' found in Chapters 6 and 14 of the CSY (2007) and data on consumption and savings for individuals found in Chapter 10.

Separating what constitutes government savings and investment hinges on our ability to determine what share of production by SOEs can be attributed to the production of public goods and what share to private goods – not an easy task. We examine two possible benchmarks to delineate government investment from SOE non-government investment. The first relies on estimates found in Article IV (IMF) reports for various years which range from 2.1 per cent (1996) to 3.5 per cent (1999) of GDP and average 2.9 per cent as government's investment share of

GDP for the entire period 1995–2006. We refer to this as the 'LowG Investment Scenario'. For the 'HighG Investment Scenario' we use an average share of GDP of 6.5 per cent for government investment. This number assumes an intermediate role of the government in investment (World Bank 1995) and is consistent with the share of the national budget allocated to investment in 1992.[9]

Individual sector investment is based on the estimates found in the CSY (Chapter 6) but is pro-rated based on the larger EIU aggregate figure. Production sector investment is also based on CSY pro-rated data and has been adjusted by removing government investment as suggested in the previous paragraph, individual investment and FDI (since we are working with a national investment measure).

Government savings is based on IFS and Article IV (IMF) data and is taken as the difference between government revenues and government consumption and transfers. This measure is indifferent to either the high or low investment scenario assumption for the government. An 'intermediate scenario' is estimated as the simple average of the high and low scenarios.

Individual savings (for both urban and rural residents) is estimated in two ways. The first, the LowHS scenario is based on the difference between disposable income and consumption CSY data based on the 'People's Livelihood' CSY Chapter 10. Between 1995 and 2006 it is estimated that individual savings as a share of individual disposable personal averaged about 20 per cent and as a share of GDP averaged only 11 per cent. A second scenario for savings, where individual savings is higher in absolute terms, is based on CSY national income accounts of overall consumption expenditure (CSY, Chapter 3, Section 14). This figure is used to impute a higher household disposable income than found in LowHS (certainly an overestimate since it includes government consumption as well). We then estimate absolute individual savings from this higher base. This yields our high estimate for household savings, HighHS scenario. HighHS is 4 percentage points as a share of GDP higher than LowHS. Significantly, since total domestic savings acts as a constraint throughout, any assumption about higher individual savings implies a lower level of savings for the production sector. Production sector savings is estimated as the residual of domestic savings minus the sum of government savings and individual savings. An 'intermediate scenario' is estimated as the simple average of the HighHS and LowHS scenarios.

### Results

With respect to the government sector flow of funds balance, we see in Tables 2.2 and Figures 2.6–2.10 that under either a high or low scenario, the government's primary surplus (savings) is insufficient to cover its investment needs throughout the decade and therefore the government needs to borrow outside of its sector in order to meet its financing needs. As is obvious from the discussion related to IMF vs. World Bank assumptions the difference in borrowing needs for the government between high and low scenarios averages about 3.6 per cent of GDP for the decade. HighHS and LowHS do not impact the government balances using our framework.

Table 2.2 Sectoral savings analysis intermediate assumption

| | Flow of funds at the sectoral level Per cent of GDP: % | | | | | | | | | | | |
| | 1995 | 1996 | 1997 | 1998 | 1999 | 2000 | 2001 | 2002 | 2003 | 2004 | 2005 | 2006 |
|---|---|---|---|---|---|---|---|---|---|---|---|---|
| *Government* | | | | | | | | | | | | |
| Savings government | 1 | 1 | 1 | 0 | 0 | 0 | 1 | 1 | 1 | 2 | 2% | 2% |
| Investment government | 4 | 4 | 4 | 5 | 5 | 5 | 5 | 5 | 5 | 5 | 5% | 5% |
| Balance | −4 | −4 | −4 | −4 | −5 | −5 | −4 | −4 | −4 | −3 | −3% | −3% |
| *Productive S(prod)−(I(prod)−FDI)* | | | | | | | | | | | | |
| Savings productive | 32 | 30 | 30 | 28 | 24 | 23 | 21 | 19 | 19 | 22 | 35% | 36% |
| Investment productive $ dom | 27 | 25 | 23 | 23 | 23 | 22 | 24 | 24 | 27 | 29 | 29% | 30% |
| Balance | 5 | 5 | 7 | 5 | 1 | 1 | −3 | −5 | −8 | −7 | 6% | 6% |
| *Privates (priv) − I(prov)* | | | | | | | | | | | | |
| Savings private | 9 | 10 | 10 | 11 | 14 | 14 | 17 | 21 | 23 | 22 | 12% | 13% |
| Investment individual | 5 | 6 | 5 | 5 | 5 | 5 | 5 | 6 | 6 | 6 | 6% | 6% |
| Balance | 3 | 4 | 5 | 6 | 9 | 9 | 11 | 15 | 17 | 16 | 6% | 7% |

Sources: China Statistical Yearbook (various issues); Economist Intelligence Unit; International Financial Statistics; China Monetary Policy Report (various issues).
Note Balances do not sum to the difference between domestic savings and domestic investment but sum to the difference between domestic savings and national investment.

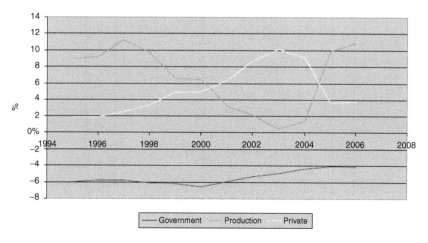

*Figure 2.6* Sectoral flows High G Low HS scenario.

The High vs. Low and HighHS and LowHS assumption do make a qualitative difference for the production sector flow of funds. Under all scenarios, the savings/investment balance declines through the decade and then improves in 2005–06. In the HighG LowHS scenario the balance is positive for the entire decade. In the LowG HighHS scenario it is positive, then negative mid-decade and then positive around 2005–06. Under the intermediate scenario, the balance is always low but becomes negative in 2001 in tandem with a higher level of investment. That is to say, the production sector becomes a net user of savings of the only surplus sector (the private sector) between 2001 and 2004. In the next section, we will look at the production sector at a more disaggregated level for further insight into these results. We note that our estimates for production sector savings is considerably higher than that of Kujis (2005) suggesting an even higher rate of profitability of this sector over the past decade. This, in part, reflects our forced linkage of sectoral savings to macro-level savings.

The private sector flow of funds is not affected by our HighG or LowG assumption but is affected by HighHS vs. LowHS. Results are presented in Figures 2.6–2.10 and Table 2.2. Under all scenarios, private sector balances are high, positive and increasing over the decade but fall in 2005–06. The balance as a share of GDP reached its highest levels in 2003 at 13 per cent according to the intermediate scenario. The individual sector has a increasing surplus of funds to lend out to the other two sectors rising from 3 per cent in 1995 to 14 per cent in 2003. This surplus of funds is either lent out to the government or productive sector. Though the individual sector in fact has a lower savings ratio out of GDP than the production sector (16 per cent of GDP for individual as compared to 26 per cent for production in 2003), the production sector's investment uses is significantly higher than the individual sector's.[10] This creates either a much smaller production surplus (HighG LowHS scenario) or an actual deficit (LowG/HighHS scenario).

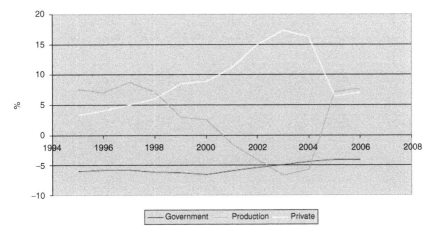

*Figure 2.7* Sectoral flows High G High HS scenario.

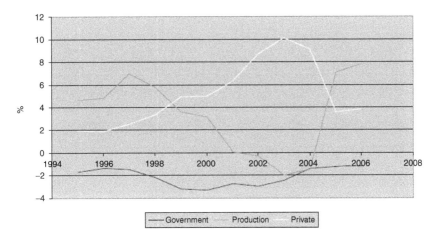

*Figure 2.8* Sectoral flows Low G Low HS scenario.

## Flow of funds at the production sub-sector level

We disaggregate the production sector into SOEs, COEs and corporate entities as discussed and defined earlier. This allows us to examine the declining flow balance of the production sector. We assume the 'intermediate scenario' from the sectoral level in order to keep the discussion tractable. Limited information is available on what is, in effect, an absolute level of net profitability across the three sectors – SOEs, COEs and corporate entities.[11] We therefore need to make assumptions regarding their distribution. Two measures of how profits might be distributed are available. One is based on the distribution of value-added across the three sub-sectors. The other is based on actual profitability of the three sub-sectors.

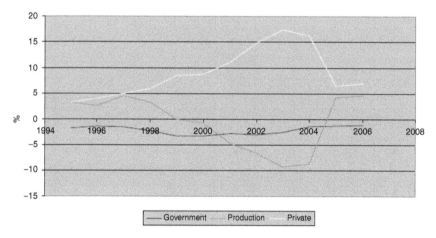

*Figure 2.9* Sectoral flows Low G High HS scenario.

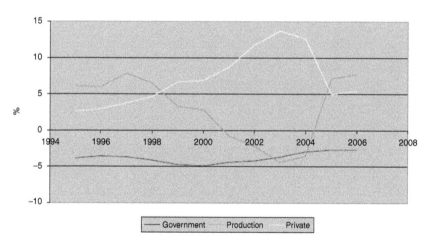

*Figure 2.10* Sectoral flows intermediate scenario.

Both measures can be found in CSY (2006) Chapter 14. These measures are for enterprises 'above a designated size' and may therefore not adequately represent the full sample of enterprises.[12] We rely on the value-added distribution as the basis for the distribution of profits or savings across the three sub-sectors. Qualitatively, the results in this paper do not change using the profitability distribution and the value-added data has a longer tradition in the accounting system and was therefore deemed more reliable.

### Results

Our results suggest that all three sub-sectors had positive savings (or profitability) over the entire decade under consideration. This is surprising in light of so much that has been written particularly with respect to the SOE sector (Carsten 2002). This result is also consistent with the findings of Kujis (2005). The HighG/LowG and HighHS/LowHS scenarios combined would create five possible combinations of outcomes if we include the intermediate scenario. Our results suggest that, qualitatively, results are similar across all scenarios, so we only present the intermediate sub-sector results. Tables 2.3 and Figure 2.11 provide the intermediate scenario results. The SOE flow balance has been either low or negative throughout the entire period but in 2005 became positive.[13] This recent improvement may reflect government efforts at moving SOEs to operate more in line with market forces – and improvements in management and financial practices.

On the other hand, COEs moved into a negative flow of funds balance beginning in 1998 and that situation appears to have deteriorated each year thereafter. The movement downward appears to be a result of continuing investment in the face of ever decreasing savings (profitability). Though the COEs represent a relatively small share of total GDP (about 3 per cent of value-added of all state-owned and controlled industrial enterprises), their net uses of funds are in absolute terms the highest among the three sub-sectors. The corporate sector is the only sector that consistently had a positive flow of funds balance throughout the decade reflecting in part an ever-rising level of profitability. We need to remember that this sector receives the lion's share of FDI and that is not reflected as a use under our national investment measure. Meanwhile, savings is domestic savings and the difference between the two contributes to the positive balance.

To summarize, it would appear that of the three sub-sectors, the corporate sector appears most likely to have a positive flow of funds balance and the collective sector most likely to have a negative balance. The state-owed sector has experienced somewhat of a turnaround in 2005. All three sub-sectors, however, have positive savings throughout the entire period – suggesting that in the aggregate at least all were profitable over the past decade.

## Savings/investment financial intermediation

Figure 2.12 presents the flow of various intermediating instruments, additions to cash holdings, net financial institutional deposits and insurance premiums paid over the past decade.[14] Apparently, increases in bank deposits make up the largest share of the flow of domestic savings (average 49 per cent) while other financial instruments represents only a small portion. An average of 33 per cent of domestic savings appears to be informally intermediated. That is, this share of domestic savings does not appear to pass through a financial instrument, a government issued instrument, an insurance company or a bank.[15] The highest share occurred in 1997 with informal intermediation accounting for 41.4 per cent of domestic savings. After 2001, the share of informal intermediation fluctuated and in 2003, it dropped to 16 per cent but by 2006 had risen again to 37 per cent. As shown in Figure 2.12, there seem to be a large negative correlation between the amount of informally intermediated funds and to the changes in financial institution deposits.

Table 2.3 Sub-sector (production) savings analysis intermediate assumption

Flow of funds at the sub-sectoral level

| | Per cent of GDP | | | | | | | | | | | |
| | 1995 | 1996 | 1997 | 1998 | 1999 | 2000 | 2001 | 2002 | 2003 | 2004 | 2005 | 2006 |
|---|---|---|---|---|---|---|---|---|---|---|---|---|
| SOE balance | | | | | | | | | | | | |
| Savings soe based on scene ratio | 0.174634 | 0.147645 | 0.140634 | 0.163686 | 0.134819 | 0.103155 | 0.085459 | 0.072202 | 0.070115 | 0.077879 | 0.114518 | 0.116228 |
| SOE investments of net of govt | 0.16125 | 0.149895 | 0.138683 | 0.140288 | 0.132915 | 0.121172 | 0.119038 | 0.105316 | 0.103645 | 0.09964 | 0.097737 | 0.099192 |
| Balance | 0.013384 | -0.00225 | 0.001951 | 0.023397 | 0.001905 | -0.01802 | -0.03358 | -0.03311 | -0.03353 | -0.02176 | 0.01678 | 0.017036 |
| Collective balance | | | | | | | | | | | | |
| Savings collective | 0.081276 | 0.102542 | 0.092513 | 0.051777 | 0.037109 | 0.024921 | 0.016838 | 0.012772 | 0.010764 | 0.011344 | 0.01788 | 0.014216 |
| Collective investment | 0.062829 | 0.067889 | 0.060109 | 0.052399 | 0.051908 | 0.052034 | 0.054537 | 0.054372 | 0.061985 | 0.066887 | 0.067359 | 0.069623 |
| Balance | 0.018447 | 0.029466 | 0.028162 | -0.00059 | -0.01405 | -0.02502 | -0.03416 | -0.03767 | -0.04519 | -0.04727 | -0.0416 | -0.046 |
| Corporate balance | | | | | | | | | | | | |
| Savings corporate | 0.064281 | 0.064279 | 0.076047 | 0.068382 | 0.071884 | 0.106152 | 0.107019 | 0.101711 | 0.11262 | 0.135332 | 0.219307 | 0.234194 |
| Corporate investment | 0.013324 | 0.014169 | 0.0146 | 0.016539 | 0.022789 | 0.033602 | 0.047142 | 0.059952 | 0.082955 | 0.10028 | 0.100209 | 0.104526 |
| FFE investment | 0.02849 | 0.028835 | 0.025201 | 0.02313 | 0.022205 | 0.020384 | 0.023961 | 0.023875 | 0.030693 | 0.037544 | 0.037514 | 0.039109 |
| Balance | 0.022467 | 0.021275 | 0.036246 | 0.028713 | 0.02689 | 0.052166 | 0.035915 | 0.017885 | -0.00103 | -0.00249 | 0.081585 | 0.090559 |

Sources: China Statistical Yearbook (various issues); Economist Intelligence Unit; International Financial Statistics; China Monetary Policy Report (various issues).

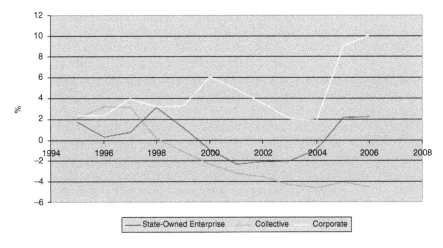

*Figure 2.11* Sub-sector (production) flows intermediate scenario.

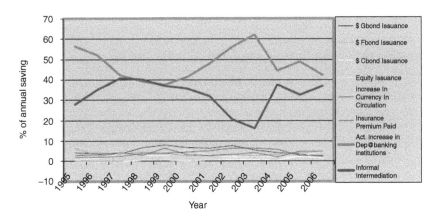

*Figure 2.12* Formal vs. informal financial intermediation.

Assuming that all external capital outflows were not intermediated, the estimate of non-intermediation would still be close to 30 per cent.[17]

By comparison, we note that even if we exclude financial institution deposits, the various vehicles for financial intermediation offered by corporations, government at all levels and foreign entities constitute 90 per cent of savings in the United States (Board of Governors of the Federal Reserve System, 2006). This suggests a much higher share of financial intermediation per unit of savings in the United States than in China.[17] Outside the formal financial system, there may exist a relatively large unregulated market in China. Also based on our estimates, while the production sector's savings was on average 82 per cent higher over the decade than the individual sector, the production sector's financial institution deposits were 60 per cent lower. The implication is that much of the informal intermediation may be occurring in the production sector. Even more significantly, the analysis suggests that Chinese financial markets have not as of yet provided a large (and broad) enough range of financial assets to absorb the tremendous creation of wealth that has been taking place. That absence has implications for those financial assets which do exist and their pricing and for the employment of China's vast pool of savings in their most productive uses.

The above estimates for non-intermediation assume that the financial instruments issued are all used to absorb new savings rather than to simply recycle current wealth through the creation of new liabilities and assets. This is particularly relevant to bank deposits which we know get recycled as loans and further deposits – a phenomenon known as the money multiplier. For China, the money multiplier on money plus quasi-money is between 5 and 6. If we were to take this phenomenon into account, the amount of formal intermediation for new savings by bank deposits (which is the largest source of formal intermediation) would be substantially lower and informal intermediation, of course, substantially higher than the figures mentioned above. The authors hope to provide a more comprehensive analysis related to the question of intermediation versus non-intermediation in a later paper.

## Summary, policy implications and direction for further research

China's massive savings and investment has helped fuel the tremendous growth that we have seen in that economy over the past several decades. Surprisingly, very little research exists attempting to analyze the decomposition of those flows. This is an early attempt. A better understanding of these flows can only lead to their improved utilization. At a macro level we have identified the role of FDI in freeing up some of China's vast savings to flow abroad (FDI inflows averaged about 56 per cent of gross external outflows over the past decade). Over time those outflows will need to be diversified across a broader spectrum of foreign assets in order to provide both higher returns along with reduced risk. Our assumptions regarding the size of the government sector in SOE investment highlights the need for greater transparency in this area – something that will inevitably occur over time. At the sub-sectoral level, the finding that SOEs have in the aggregate been profitable over the past decade, suggests a dramatic change in their financial structure – a reduction in the debt/equity ratio via the accumulation of retained earnings. In turn, the focus shifts from the creditor-company relationship to the shareholder-company relationship and an entailing host of corporate governance issues. Our results suggest that perhaps the spotlight may need to be turned to the collective sector which, albeit small, appears to have suffered a continuous decline in profitability over the decade yet a steady level of investment. Further research will be needed to verify these results. Finally, the finding that about one third of domestic savings is informally intermediated raises a host of research and policy questions. Specifically, how are these informal financing decisions being made and will reform of the financial sector ultimately move these funds into the formal financial system and will that in turn enhance the economic efficiency of their use?

## Acknowledgement

Special thanks to Yin-Wong Cheung and other participants at the WTO, China and the Asian Economies Conference at the *University of International Business and Economics in Beijing* (June, 2006). Also thanks to the Harvard Club of New York's *China Business and Economy Group* for their useful comments on an earlier draft of this paper.

## References

Board of Governors of the Federal Reserve System (2006) *Z1 Statistical Release*, 'Flow of Funds', http://www.federalreserve.gov/Releases/Z1/.

Carsten A. Holz (2002) 'Long live China's state-owned enterprises: deflating the myth of poor financial performance', *Journal of Asian Economics*, 13 (4), July–August: 493–529.

China Statistical Information & Consultant Center, SSB (CSICC) (2006) *China Monthly Statistics*, March 10.

Economist Intelligence Unit (2006) EIU Database, www.eiu.co.

Financial Stability Analysis Group of the People's Bank of China (2005) 'China Financial Stability Report', China Financial Publishing House, Beijing.

International Monetary Fund (2006) International Financial Statistics, International Monetary Fund, http://www.imf.org.

―――― (various years) 'People's Republic of China', Article IV Consultation.

Kujis, Louis (2005) 'Investment and Saving in China', World Bank Policy Research Working Paper 3633, The World Bank Office, Beijing, China, June.

National Bureau of Statistics of China (various years), *China Statistical Yearbook*, China Statistics Press, Beijing.

Teplin, Alan (2001) 'The U.S. Flow of Funds Accounts and Their Uses'. *Federal Reserve Bulletin*, Board of Governors of the Federal Reserve System, July: 431–441.

World Bank (1995) 'China Public Investment and Finance', Country Operations Division, China and Mongolia Department, East Asia Operations Division, Report Number 14540-CHA, October 18.

Zhang, Weiying (2001) 'Developments in Chinese Corporate Finance and its Implication for Ownership Reform', August 7, http://www.macrochina.com.cn/english/analysis/outlook/20010807001948.shtml

# 3 China's approach to capital flows since 1978

## A brief overview

*Juann H. Hung*

## Introduction

China began finding its way cautiously toward pro-market reforms and opening its economy in late 1978. Its management of capital flows has followed a learning-by-doing approach, guided by the goal of propelling and sustaining economic growth while minimizing risk to economic (and political) stability.

The government has frequently fine-tuned its restrictions of foot-loose portfolio flows, claiming that China's financial infrastructure is still not ready to deal with large swings of those flows. During periods when capital flight was a more serious threat, controls over those outflows tended to tighten while those over inflows became more relaxed. In contrast, when hot money inflows (betting on an appreciation of the yuan or prices of financial assets in China) became more problematic, controls of portfolio inflows tended to become more restrictive. In recent years, as China has grown more confident of its economic power, it has also resorted to lowering barriers on portfolio outflows as a way to help ease the pressure of the rapid rise in its balance of payments.

Promoting foreign direct investment (FDI) inflows has remained an important element of China's development strategy since the (post-1978) reform era began. In the early years of the reform era, China had little foreign exchange (FX) reserves and was far behind in the technology ladder. Against that backdrop, attracting FDI inflows was viewed as a way to jump-start China's economic growth. Nevertheless, initiatives to promote those inflows were timid and tentative at first and FDI were allowed only in special economic zones. Since 2004, China's policymakers – enabled by its large holdings of FX reserves – have also permitted outward FDI to rise rapidly. Both inward and outward FDI deals are aimed at accessing foreign technologies, management skills, and export markets. Outward FDI deals appear to have also given an added emphasis on securing raw materials which are critical to the sustainability of China's rapid growth.

There is some evidence that China's approach to capital flows has contributed significantly to the uninterrupted high growth rates of its economy since 1994. Some studies – though not all – have found that the rapid rise in FDI inflows has made an important contribution to China's growth.[1] Most analysts agree that the government's control over portfolio flows shielded its economy from the 1997–8

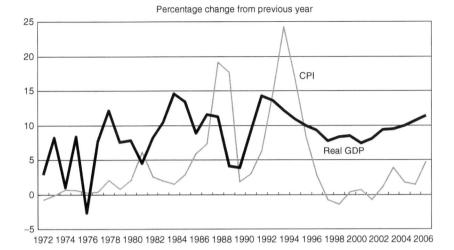

*Figure 3.1* China's real GDP and CPI.
Source: China National Bureau of Statistics.

Asian financial crisis, when many of its neighbouring economies were buffeted by the large swings of foreign capital flows. Some analysts also argue that China's ability to sustain its currency-peg regime since 1994, which was underpinned by its tight controls of portfolio flows, played an important role in maintaining China's price stability and uninterrupted economic growth.[2] Up until 1994 China was afflicted by cycles of boom and bust (Figure 3.1). After it consolidated the official exchange rate and the swap rate and fixed it at the lower swap rate in 1994, price inflation was quickly brought down to 3 per cent in 1997 (from over 20 per cent in 1994). So far, the devastating cycles of boom and bust have not yet resurfaced. From 1996 to 2007, China's annual real GDP growth rates averaged 9.2 per cent, while inflation averaged about 2.8 per cent.

Nevertheless, China's approach to capital flows appears to also have problematic legacies. Encouraging FDI only in selected industries and in limited geographical areas, combined with its restrictions on labour mobility, may have contributed to an unbalanced growth pattern that's partially responsible for the sharp rise in income inequality between the urban and rural populations. The sharp rise in China's net exports, much of which is net exports of foreign-invested enterprises, has also added to international community's perception and criticism of China's mercantilist policies.

China's tight controls over portfolio flows and an inflexible exchange rate system also face mounting challenges: the sharp rise in its trade surplus and large net FDI inflows have fuelled China's overheating economy in recent years, causing troubling asset-price inflation. Speculation in domestic stock markets has been rampant in part because domestic stocks available for public trading are limited while private portfolio outflows are restricted. Since 2005, the authority has rapidly relaxed controls over portfolio outflows as part of its efforts to cool down the overheating economy and to relieve the pressure on its exchange rate. However, in part because most investors are still betting that the yuan – which has been allowed to appreciate only tiny steps each day until lately – will continue to rise against the dollar, such partial liberalizations of capital controls have not yet succeeded in cooling the Chinese economy.[3] Moreover, as international pressure for a more flexible yuan grows, the downside of China's past tight controls of portfolio flows has also grown more obvious. Those tight controls helped to insulate China's financial markets from destabilizing swings of hot money, but they have also retarded the development of China's FX infrastructure (i.e. the development of sufficient numbers of market makers and instruments for hedging currency risks, such as forward contracts and derivatives) that needs to be in place for a smooth functioning of a flexible exchange rate system.

## Foreign direct investment

This section looks into the role of the Chinese government, among other factors, in propelling the rapid rise of FDI inflows, and the impact of those inflows on the Chinese economy. It also discusses the surge in China's FDI outflows since 2003.

### *The government's role in the rise of FDI inflows*

China opened up to inward FDI in a cautious and trial-and-error manner. In the earlier years of the reform era, changes were slow and laws and regulations remained rather restrictive. Pro-market reforms and open-up policies were first experimented with in four special economic zones (SEZs) in 1980. In 1984, those experiments were expanded to another 14 open coastal cities (OCCs); and generous tax incentives were set up in both SEZs and OCCs to attract FDI that would bring along advanced technology. For example, in the first two years that a foreign-invested enterprise (FIE) in those special economic zones or cities made a profit, it was exempt from corporate income tax. In subsequent years, the same FIEs would be subject to an average corporate income tax of 15 per cent, less than half the standard 33 per cent paid by Chinese companies. As a result, FDI inflows jumped 98 per cent in 1984 and continued to grow at double digit rates for several years (Figure 3.2). The government's brutal suppression of the Tiananmen Square protest in 1989, however, caused growth of FDI inflows to fall sharply. In response, the government began to take measures to reassure foreign investors. For example, a law was enacted in 1990 to prohibit the state from nationalizing joint ventures and simplify the procedures for new foreign investment. In 1991, the government eliminated a 10 per cent tax imposed on distributed profits remitted abroad by FIEs. In 1992, Deng Xiaoping's speech during his tour of the South further reaffirmed China's commitment to pro-market reforms, and FDI soared in 1992 and 1993 (Figures 3.2 and 3.3). When those inflows declined somewhat following the 1997–8 Asian crisis, the government extended preferential treatments to FDI in energy, transportation, and infrastructure industries.

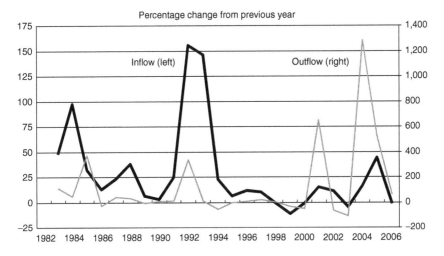

*Figure 3.2* China's FDI flows.
Source: State Administration of Foreign Exchange.

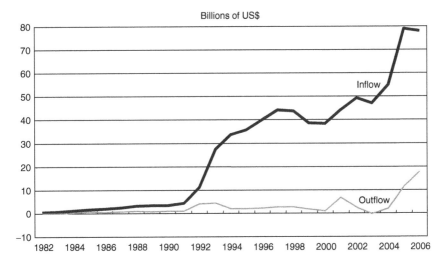

*Figure 3.3* China's FDI flows.
Source: State Administration of Foreign Exchange.

After China's accession to World Trade Organization (WTO) in 2001, FDI inflows began to surge again. Since then FDI flows from industrial countries have risen substantially and they have mainly gone to the financial service sector. After 2002, foreign banks were allowed to buy equity in domestic banks, although the share of ownership could not exceed 20 per cent for a single foreign investor or 25 per cent for total foreign ownership. In addition, foreign banks were allowed to provide yuan service to domestic firms in open cities since 2003. One aim of easing restrictions of foreign ownership of domestic banks was to improve the corporate governance and banking practices of domestic banks, thereby speeding up the development of the financial markets and institutions.

Clearly, the government's role in promoting FDI inflows has gone beyond improving the legal framework to make China a more friendly and credible environment for direct investment. As domestic enterprises have stepped up their complaints against unfair tax treatment, and perhaps also to reduce the distorting effects of those taxes laws, the government passed a new corporate income tax law (which took effect on January 1, 2008) that consolidated tax rates of both domestic enterprises and FIEs at 25 per cent. But significant preferential tax treatments remain.[4]

### *Other drivers of FDI in China*

Two factors – inexpensive labour and the potentially large market – are probably the most notable and most agreed-upon market forces driving FDI into China.

Low labour costs have been especially important for attracting vertical investment (investment intended to take advantage of low cost production for re-exporting of its products abroad). In early years of the reform era, FDI into China was mostly dominated by such export-oriented FDI. That export-oriented FDI in China mainly came from other Asian economies which had pursued export-led growth but whose domestic labour had become too costly to compete with Chinese labour. In particular Hong Kong and Taiwan, with their geographical proximity and cultural ties to China, became the prime source of such FDI inflows. In 1992, combined FDI from Hong Kong and Taiwan accounted for about 78 per cent of total inward FDI, with Hong Kong alone accounting for 68.2 per cent (Table 3.1).[5]

Since the mid-1990s, however, other countries with even lower labour costs – such as Thailand and Vietnam – also began to pursue an export-led growth path

*Table 3.1* Changing sources of FDI inflow to China

|  | 1990 | 1992 | 2001 | 2002 | 2003 | 2004 | 2005 | 2006 |
|---|---|---|---|---|---|---|---|---|
| Hong Kong | 53.9 | 68.2 | 35.7 | 33.9 | 33.1 | 31.3 | 24.8 | 29.1 |
| European Union | 4.2 | 2.2 | 8.9 | 7.0 | 7.4 | 7.0 | 7.2 | 9.8 |
| United States | 13.1 | 4.6 | 9.5 | 10.3 | 7.9 | 6.5 | 4.2 | 9.4 |
| Japan | 14.4 | 6.5 | 9.3 | 7.9 | 9.5 | 9.0 | 9.0 | 6.6 |
| Korea | – | – | – | 5.2 | 8.4 | 10.3 | 7.1 | 5.6 |
| Singapore | – | – | – | 4.4 | 3.9 | 3.3 | 3.0 | 3.4 |
| Taiwan | 6.4 | 9.5 | 6.4 | 7.5 | 7.4 | 5.1 | 3.0 | 3.1 |
| Other | 8.0 | 9.0 | 30.3 | 23.8 | 22.7 | 27.4 | 41.6 | 33.0 |
| Virgin Islands | – | – | – | 11.6 | 10.8 | 11.1 | 12.5 | 16.2 |

Sources: MOFCOM FDI Statistics.
Web address: http://www.fdi.gov.cn/pub/FDI_EN/Statistics/AnnualStatisticsData/default.jsp

Note: Per cent of total realized value for year.

that built on inward FDI. That and the fact that Chinese consumers have grown wealthier, the enormous market potential of China has become an increasingly more important factor, relative to inexpensive labour, in attracting FDI. Thus, direct investments from North America and Western Europe, which are heavily tilted to horizontal investments (i.e. investments whose products are intended to service the Chinese domestic market), have grown more sizable.[6] After 2001, as China allowed foreign entry into its financial sector and banking industries (to comply with conditions of its accession to the WTO), direct investments from the US and other OECD countries began to account for an increasingly large share of total FDI inflows to China, as those countries' financial firms elbowed each other to get a foothold in the untapped Chinese market. In 1992, FDI from the EU, the US and Japan accounted for about 13 per cent of total FDI in China; by 2006, that share rose to 26 per cent (Table 3.1).

### *Effects of inward FDI on China's economy*

China's economic growth in the reform era has been propelled mainly by rapid growth in net exports, productivity growth and investment.[7] FDI inflows have made important contribution to China's growth through its effect on net exports and productivity growth, even though they directly financed only about 6 per cent of fixed investment from 1981 to 2006. Given the existence of various obstacles restricting labour mobility in China, however, the policy of encouraging FDI only in designated areas and selected sectors also contributed to rapidly rising income inequality in China.

### *Contribution to net exports*

FIEs have become an increasingly important contributor to the rise in China's net exports since 2000 (Figure 3.4). From 2000 to 2005, FIEs' net exports share in China's total net exports surged from a mere 10 per cent to 53 per cent. (During that period, China's net exports rose from $24 billion to $102 billion). That contribution to net exports, however, appears to have peaked in 2005, perhaps reflecting the rising importance of horizontal FDI (whose products are intended for the Chinese market) as opposed to those of vertical FDI (whose products are intended for the export market).

The transformation of FIEs from net importers to net exporters in 1998 perhaps in part reflected the high cost of imported capital goods needed in the initial stages of establishing a new enterprise. In part, it also appears to have stemmed from their shift toward producing higher-value products, as suggested by the rise in the share of FDI in communication, computer and other electronic equipments in total FDI (especially 1997 to 2001) and the decline in the share of textile (Table 3.2).

FIEs may also have contributed to growth in net exports indirectly through technology spillover to local Chinese firms. This is suggested by the shift in the composition of overall China's exports toward higher-value products at a faster speed than the composition of FDI inflows has. In the early 1990s, exports still

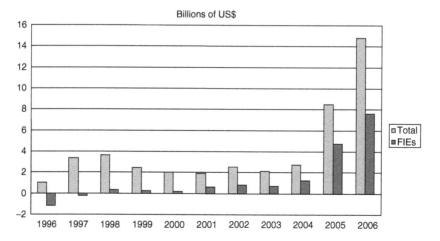

*Figure 3.4* China's trade balances: Total vs. FIEs.
Source: CEIC.

Note: FIE = Foreign invested enterprise.

*Table 3.2* Distribution of China's FDI inflows by sector, selected years

|  | 1997 | 2001 | 2004 | 2006 |
|---|---|---|---|---|
| Agricultural | 1.4 | 1.9 | 1.8 | 0.9 |
| Construction | 3.2 | 1.7 | 1.3 | 1.0 |
| Electricity, Gas, and Water Supply | 4.6 | 4.8 | 1.9 | 1.8 |
| Manufacturing | 62.1 | 65.9 | 71.0 | 57.7 |
|   Textile | 4.1 | 4.1 | 3.9 | 3.0 |
|   Chemical Material and Product | 3.2 | 4.7 | 4.4 | 3.8 |
|   Communication, Computer and Other Electronic Equip. | 5.9 | 15.1 | 11.6 | 11.8 |
|   Other Manufacturing | 49.0 | 42.0 | 51.0 | 39.1 |
| Mining | 2.1 | 1.7 | 0.9 | 0.7 |
| Transport, Storage and Postal Service | 3.7 | 1.9 | 2.1 | 2.9 |
| Real Estate | 11.4 | 11.0 | 9.8 | 11.8 |
| Banking and Insurance | – | 0.1 | 0.4 | 9.7 |
| Information Transmission, Computer Service and Software | – | – | 1.5 | 1.5 |
| Scientific Research | – | – | 0.5 | 0.7 |
| Leasing and Commercial Service | – | – | 4.7 | 6.1 |
| Other[a] | 11.6 | 10.9 | 4.2 | 5.2 |

Sources: CEIC.

Note: Per cent of total realized value for year. [a]Includes wholesale and retail trade, catering, water conservancy, residential and other service, social organization, education, health care and recreation.

mainly consisted of garments and other low-value manufactured goods. But since then, they are increasingly composed of higher-value items such as electronic goods. For example, from 1994 to 2006, the share of higher-end exports categorized as machinery and transport equipment surged from 18.1 per cent of total exports

*Table 3.3* Composition of China's exports, selected years

|  | 1994 | 2001 | 2004 | 2006 |
|---|---|---|---|---|
| Food | 8.3 | 4.8 | 3.2 | 2.7 |
| Crude Materials (Except Fuel) | 3.4 | 1.6 | 1.0 | 0.8 |
| Mineral Fuels | 3.2 | 3.2 | 2.4 | 1.8 |
| Chemical Products | 5.2 | 5.0 | 4.4 | 4.6 |
| Basic Manufactures[a] | 19.2 | 16.5 | 17.0 | 18.0 |
| Machinery and Transport Equipment | 18.1 | 35.7 | 45.2 | 47.1 |
| Office and ADP Machines | 2.2 | 8.8 | 14.7 | 13.9 |
| Electrical Machinery | 4.9 | 9.5 | 10.0 | 10.5 |
| Telecom and Sound Recording Equip. | 5.6 | 8.9 | 11.5 | 12.8 |
| Other Machinery and Transport Equip. | 5.4 | 8.4 | 9.0 | 10.0 |
| Misc. Manufactures | 41.3 | 32.7 | 26.4 | 24.6 |
| Apparel and Clothing Accessories | 19.6 | 13.8 | 10.4 | 9.8 |
| Footwear | 5.0 | 3.8 | 2.6 | 2.3 |
| Travel Goods and Handbags | 2.0 | 1.5 | 1.1 | 0.9 |
| Other Misc. Manufactures[b] | 14.7 | 13.7 | 12.3 | 11.6 |
| Other[c] | 1.4 | 0.6 | 0.4 | 0.4 |
| Total | 100.0 | 100.0 | 100.0 | 100.0 |

Sources: CEIC.

Note: Per cent of total. [a]Includes leather, rubber, wood, paper, yarn, fabric, iron, steel, non-metallic mineral manufactures and non-ferrous metals. [b]Includes furniture, photographic equipment, watches, prefabricated buildings, professional instruments and sanitary plumbing. [c]Includes beverages, tobacco, and animal and vegetable oils.

to 47.1 per cent, while the share of miscellaneous manufactures (mostly apparel and clothing accessories, and footwear) fell from 41.3 per cent to 24.6 per cent (Table 3.3).

### Contribution to productivity growth

Several studies have found that the rapid growth in total factor productivity (TFP) is a main pillar of China's real GDP growth in the reform era, second only to capital formation. For example, Kuijs and Wang (2006) found that capital accumulation contributed over 50 per cent, and TFP growth about 33 per cent, to China's output growth between 1978 and 2004, with employment growth contributing the modest remainder. Bosworth and Collins (2007) also have similar findings.

Some researchers argue that inward FDI has spurred TFP growth significantly in China. Whalley and Xin (2006) suggest that inward FDI may have contributed to real GDP growth by as much as 3.9 percentage points annually in 2003 and 2004, about 41 per cent of total GDP growth during that time. Their findings, though they may appear shockingly high, do not seem to be outside the realms of likelihood in light of the sharp rise in the share of FIEs' contributions to the rise in China's overall value-added. Even though the share of foreign investment in financing China's total fixed investment has stayed modest (around 6 per cent), FIEs' share of value-added in the industrial sector (i.e. the manufacturing and mining sector)

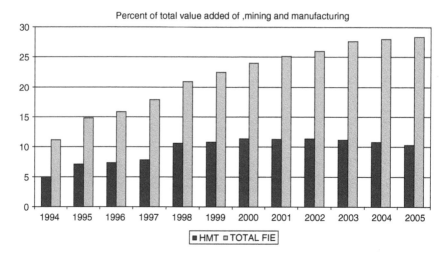

*Figure 3.5* Value added of mining and manufacturing in China: Total FIE vs. HMT.
Source: CEIC.

Note: FIE = Foreign invested enterprise; HMT = Hong Kong, Macau, and Taiwan; 2004 is interpolated.

soared to 28 per cent in 2004 from 11 per cent in 1994 (Figure 3.5).[8] Since the industrial sector accounted for about 47 per cent of China's GDP in 2004, the contribution of industrial FIEs to GDP in 2004 amounted to about 13 per cent (= 0.28 ∗ 0.47). But since FIEs in the industrial sector only accounted for 64 per cent of all FIEs in China, that 13 per cent is the lower bound of FIEs' total contribution to China's GDP in that year. If we assume that the contributions of FIEs to GDP are about the same across all industries to which an FIE belongs, then the contribution of all FIEs to GDP would have been higher at about 20 per cent (= 0.13/0.64) in 2004. This is a significant increase from FIEs' contribution to GDP in 1996, which was about 13 per cent based on similar imputations.[9]

### Contribution to unbalanced growth

The government's policy of promoting FDI inflows in high-tech industries and only in SEZs and selected cities, however, may have also contributed to an unbalanced growth that is now threatening the stability and sustainability of China's future growth. Given the existence of various obstacles restricting labour mobility and the faster growth of the FIE sub-economy than the non-FIE economy, the high concentration of FDI in urban areas has contributed to the high concentration of job creation in the urban area.[10] That uneven distribution of job creation in turn has contributed to the rapidly rising income inequality in China.

Income inequality in China has risen rapidly even as China rapidly climbs up the economic ladder. Based on official data, annual income per capita of urban dwellers rose by more than sixfold from 1985 ($250) to 2006 ($1600); in contrast, per capital income of rural dwellers during that period rose only threefold, from

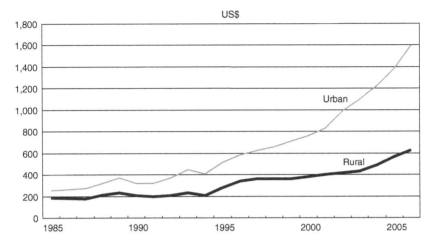

*Figure 3.6* Annual income per capita in China: Urban vs. rural.
Source: CEIC.

Note: 1986 rural income per capita is interpolated.

about $200 to $600 (Figure 3.6). Since a potentially large number of rural people may not be counted in the official data because of the one-child policy, that gap could be even larger than the official data indicate.

### Outward FDI

China's FDI outflows remained relatively insignificant for most the post-1978 reform era (Figure 3.3). However, as China's rapidly growing FX reserves began to put increasing upward pressure on the Chinese exchange rate and asset prices in 2004, China's policy on FDI outflows shifted toward a more liberal regime and those outflows began to surge. The shift was aimed at relieving the extent to which its currency needs to appreciate and the urgency of that appreciation. That shift was also well-timed: it occurred when ensuring a steady supply of raw materials to sustain its rapid economic catch-up had become more urgent than ever, and after China had acquired enough FX reserves to afford direct investment abroad.

China's approach to outward FDI, like its approach to inward FDI, is closely tied to its strategy of accelerating its economic development through accessing foreign technology and management skills, export markets, and raw materials. For now, however, ensuring a steady supply of raw materials to sustain its rapid economic catch-up appears to have topped other objectives. For example, from 2003 to 2006, the lion's share of China's outward FDI (36 per cent) went into the mining sector (Table 3.4). Two other major sectors that also received large shares of China's outward FDI were those that are important in facilitating sales of Chinese products in their overseas markets as well in transmitting marketing

*Table 3.4* Distribution of China's non-financial outward FDI, by sector

|  | 2003 | 2004 | 2005 | 2006 | *Average, 2003–2006* |
|---|---|---|---|---|---|
| Agricultural | 2.9 | 5.3 | 0.9 | 1.0 | 2.5 |
| Construction | 0.8 | 0.9 | 0.7 | 0.2 | 0.6 |
| Electricity, Gas, and Water Supply | 0.8 | 1.4 | 0.1 | 0.7 | 0.7 |
| Manufacturing | 21.9 | 13.7 | 18.6 | 5.1 | 14.8 |
| Mining | 48.3 | 32.7 | 13.7 | 48.4 | 35.8 |
| Transport, storage and postal service | 2.7 | 15.1 | 4.7 | 7.8 | 7.6 |
| Real estate | −0.5 | 0.2 | 0.9 | 2.2 | 0.7 |
| Information Transmission and Computer Service | 0.3 | 0.6 | 0.1 | 0.3 | 0.3 |
| Scientific Research | 0.2 | 0.3 | 1.1 | 1.6 | 0.8 |
| Leasing and Commercial Service | 9.8 | 13.6 | 40.3 | 25.6 | 22.3 |
| Other | 12.9 | 16.2 | 19.0 | 7.0 | 13.8 |
| Total | 100.0 | 100.0 | 100.0 | 100.0 | 100.0 |

Source: CEIC.

Note: Per cent of total.

and logistic skills to Chinese firms at home. For example, the transport, storage, and postal service sector received 7.6 per cent, while the leasing and commercial services sector 22.3 per cent, of total FDI outflows from China.

Nevertheless, the impression that one gets from the press that China's foreign direct investments have concentrated heavily in strategic sectors in Africa and in Latin America turns out to be unsupported by the data. Indeed, other Asian countries have persisted as the largest recipients of China's FDI outflows, followed by Latin America at a distance. Even though it appears Latin America has overtaken Asia as the largest recipient of those outflows after 2004, that pictures is misleading because the Cayman Islands – a popular tax haven – accounted for over 80 per cent of China's outward FDI received by the region (Table 3.5). Indeed, assuming for illustration purposes, that all China's FDI in the Cayman Islands eventually went somewhere other than either Asia or Latin America (i.e. North America, Europe, or Africa), then the share of China's FDI in Latin America excluding the Cayman Islands would have been only 4 per cent in 2006, considerably below the share in Asia which was 44 per cent that year.

Despite the flurry of headline news about China's overseas investment, China's FDI outflows are still dwarfed by its FDI inflows or portfolio outflows. Even after a couple of years of sharp growth, China's FDI outflows only reached a modest $18 billion by 2006, just a fraction of its FDI inflows ($78 billion) or portfolio outflows ($110 billion) in that year. The much larger portfolio outflows than FDI outflows seems to confirm a report by *The Economist* that Chinese firms are less keen in acquiring a majority stake in foreign companies than trying to gain experiences (in management skills, industry-specific technology and other know-how, etc.) by taking minority stakes in them.[11]

*Table 3.5* Destinations of China's non-financial outward FDI

|              | 2003 | 2004 | 2005 | 2006 |
|--------------|------|------|------|------|
| Asia         | 52.7 | 54.6 | 35.7 | 43.5 |
| Hong Kong    | 40.3 | 47.8 | 27.9 | 39.3 |
| Japan        | 0.3  | 0.3  | 0.1  | 0.2  |
| Korea        | 5.4  | 0.7  | 4.8  | 0.2  |
| Singapore    | −0.1 | 0.9  | 0.2  | 0.7  |
| Europe       | 5.1  | 2.9  | 3.2  | 3.4  |
| Russia       | 1.1  | 1.4  | 1.7  | 2.6  |
| North America| 2.0  | 2.3  | 2.6  | 1.5  |
| United States| 2.3  | 2.2  | 1.9  | 1.1  |
| Latin America| 36.4 | 32.1 | 52.7 | 48.0 |
| Cayman Islands| 28.3| 23.4 | 42.1 | 44.4 |
| Africa       | 2.6  | 5.8  | 3.2  | 2.9  |
| Other        | 1.2  | 2.4  | 2.5  | 0.7  |

Source: CEIC.

Note: Per cent of total non-financial outward direct investment.

## Portfolio Investment

The Chinese government's control over portfolio flows has been closely inter-twined with its exchange-rate policies, evolving roughly along a learning-by-doing approach.[12] Maintaining exchange rate stability has been one of several aims of China's capital-control measures. The government has declared it will not consider floating the yuan until the authorities feel they are ready for full capital-account liberalization. China has fine-tuned its policies toward portfolio flows to maintain the stability of its exchange rate and its economy since the beginning of the reform era, but that approach is now facing many challenges.

### *The evolution of China's control over portfolio flows*

The Chinese authority has been constantly adjusting its exchange rate and capital-control arrangements since the late 1970s, aiming to find a system that would facilitate the country's economic growth and development with minimum risk to economic and political stability. In the initial years, the yuan was substantially overvalued and China began running a current account deficit in 1985. The authority was forced to devalue the yuan several times for the first two decades of the reform era (Figure 3.7). The exchange rate system changed from a centrally-planned administrative mechanism to a dual exchange rate system, then to a managed float with a narrow band, followed by a *de facto* peg to the US dollar and finally returned to a managed float with slightly widened band. Along the way, the authority revised its capital-control measures several times, aiming to stem capital flight at some times and hot money inflows at other times, to support the stability of those exchange rate regimes.

Overall, the evolution of China's capital-controls can be roughly broken into seven phases.

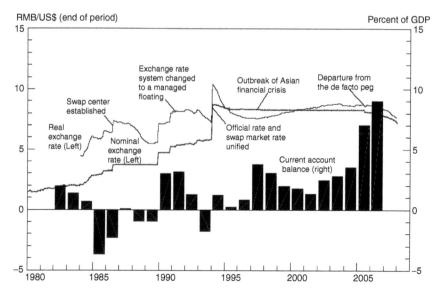

*Figure 3.7*  China's current account balance and the RMB official exchange rate.
Source: Min Zhao, External Liberalization and the Evolution of China's Exchange System: an
Empirical Approach (2006); China National Bureau of Statistics; China State Administration of Foreign
Exchange; OECD; Haver Analytics.

### *First phase 1978–1985: China cautiously opened up to capital inflows*

In December 1978, the Chinese government initiated economic reform and started
opening up to the rest of the world. The aim of the opening-up policies was
to jump start the economy by tapping foreign capital to fund investment and
attracting foreign technology to promote export growth and import substitution.
The exchange-rate system was supposed to facilitate those goals in an economic
system which keeps central-planning at the core while allowing market mechanism
to function at the margin.

Finding the 'equilibrium' exchange rate of the yuan without the help of a
well-functioning FX market turned out to be difficult. In 1981, China introduced
a dual exchange rate system: an internal settlement (2.8 yuan/dollar) rate for
authorized current account transactions, and an official rate for other transactions
(1.5 yuan/dollar). The dual exchange rate system was intended to boost foreign
exchange reserves, which stood at $2.3 billion in 1980. Domestic enterprises had
to surrender foreign exchange earnings to the state and received yuan at the official
exchange rate. Depending on the source of the exchange earnings, they could also
receive a share of the surrendered foreign exchange as 'retention quotas'.

The official rate also proved to be unsustainably high and was gradually
devalued. On January 1, 1985, the official rate was eventually unified with the
settlement rate at 2.8 yuan/dollar. However, China's current account balance
continued to fall (to −3.7 per cent of GDP in 1985). Subsequently, the official
rate fell to 3.72 yuan/dollar by the end of 1986.

*Phase 2 1986–1991: Capital controls were first eased but then retightened*

China reintroduced a dual-exchange-rate system in 1986. Foreign Exchange Adjustment Centers, the so-called swap centres, were established in some cities. Foreign-invested enterprises (FIEs) and Chinese enterprises with 'retention quotas' (of foreign exchange) were permitted to trade foreign exchange among themselves at a rate different from the official rate in those swap centres. All domestic banks were also allowed to conduct foreign exchange business.

By 1988, most cities had established foreign exchange swap centres. The swap rate was allowed to float, forming a platform for a market mechanism. The trading volume in swap centres steadily increased and more firms were allowed to trade in the swap market. As the swap rates continue to decline, the fixed official rate was under increasing downward pressure. The authorities managed to keep the official rate at 3.72 yuan/dollar for nearly three years, but finally gave in and began a sequence of devaluating the yuan in December 1989. In April 1991, the official exchange rate regime was changed from a periodical adjustment to a managed float, allowing the authorities to adjust the rate even more frequently.

The swap market rates generated market distortions and became problematic in the late 1980s and early 1990s. (China had one official foreign exchange rate and often many market exchange rates because of imperfect arbitrage between swap centers). Against this backdrop, rules and regulations were introduced to strengthen supervision of external transactions.

*Phase 3 1992–3: Capital controls on inflows were eased following the Tiananmen Square suppression*

After the growth of capital inflows ground to a halt following the harsh suppression of the Tiananmen Square protest, Deng Xiaoping called for an acceleration of reforms and opening-up during his famous 'tour through the south' in early 1992. His view was soon endorsed by the Congress of the Communist Party. The authorities officially accepted a market-based floating exchange regime and current account convertibility as the ultimate goals of the exchange reform. Besides FDI inflows, China started exploring more channels to use foreign capital. In 1992, the B-share market was launched in Shenzhen and Shanghai, allowing domestic corporations to issue foreign-currency denominated shares, which only non-residents were allowed to buy. In 1993, non-bank financial institutions were allowed to conduct business in foreign currency.

However, accelerated liberalization in the external and financial sectors appeared to have contributed to economic overheating in 1992 and 1993. Price inflation soared from about 5 per cent in 1992 to 24 per cent in 1994. The annual growth rate of real GDP surged to 14 per cent in 1992 and 1993 (Figure 3.2). The current account balance swung from a surplus of $13.3 billion (3.1 per cent of GDP) on in 1991 to a deficit 11.9 billion in 1993. The high inflation and a rapidly falling current account drove expectations of further yuan depreciation. The exchange rate in the swap market at one point fell to over 10 yuan/dollar in mid-1993, before intervention by the People's Bank of China lifted it to 8.7 yuan/dollar at the end of 1993. (Meanwhile, the official rate remained at a much higher 5.8 yuan/dollar). Against this backdrop, reforming the exchange rate regime became an urgent issue.

*Phase 4 1994–6: Controls on inflows were tightened, while controls on outflows eased, to support the new exchange rate regime and combat inflation*

On January 1, 1994, the official and swap market exchange rates were unified at the prevailing swap market exchange rate (8.7 yuan/dollar). The unified exchange rate regime was a managed floating rate with a narrow band $(+/-0.25$ per cent) in each trading day. The China Foreign Exchange Trade System (CFETS) became operational, creating an integrated system of foreign exchange trading centralized in Shanghai. The swap centres in the old regime became branches of the Shanghai market. A two-tier trading system was established. Firms traded foreign exchange with banks. Banks traded their net foreign exchange position in CFETS. As exchange rate flexibility increased, Foreign Exchange Designated Banks were allowed to offer yuan forward products for firms to hedge exchange risk.

Firms were no longer allowed to retain foreign exchange for current account transactions. They had to surrender their foreign exchange earnings from current account transactions at the official rate, and purchase foreign exchange when a payment in foreign currency was needed. Foreign exchange proceeds from capital account transactions could not be converted into RMB, unless approved by SAFE.

The tightened control on capital inflows and the exchange rate reform proved successful in cooling credit growth and overheating. The current account deficit turned into a surplus by 1994, and the yuan gradually appreciated to 8.45 by the end of 1994. However, the expectation of further yuan appreciation in turn induced large speculative capital inflows through loopholes and all sorts of schemes, partially offsetting the government efforts to contain the overheating.

In response, measures were taken to relax restrictions on capital outflows and to enhance controls over inflows. Except for FDI, all financial-account transactions were to be approved by SAFE case by case.

*Phase 5 1997–2000: Controls on outflows were tightened while restrictions on inflows eased in the aftermath of the Asian crisis*

Capital outflows became an increasing problem in late 1997 and early 1998, as the eruption of the Asian crisis in the summer of 1997 prompted concerns about the devaluation of the RMB. Foreign direct investment remained strong. But large portfolio outflows ensued as foreign banks sharply reduced their exposures, causing the financial account to turn from a surplus of $21 billion in 1997 to a deficit of $6 billion in 1998.

To minimize illegal capital outflows and maintain a stable exchange rate, the authorities tightened the screening of capital-account transactions and imposed severe penalties, such as imprisonment, for fraudulent behaviour. Meanwhile, controls of inflows were relaxed. Restrictions on extending external guarantees, issuing bonds in international market and FIEs' borrowing in yuan were relaxed.

The banking industry also began to open up to foreign investment. In 1997, 13 more cities were opened for foreign banks to conduct business in RMB, adding to the 5 open cities already in place. In 1999, the geographic restriction on foreign banks was repealed, though geographic restrictions on foreign banks' conducting business in the yuan remained. Moreover, foreign banks were allowed to invest in domestic banks, in hope that this would improve domestic banks' corporate governance and promote sound banking practices.

During the Asian financial crisis, the trading band of ±0.25 per cent was narrowed further. Even though the regime was still nominally a managed float, China had essentially operated it as a *de facto* peg to the dollar and the exchange rate was kept at 8.28 yuan/dollar until July 2005.

*Phase 6 2001–04: Portfolio inflows were eased following China's accession to the WTO*

China's accession to the WTO in December 2001 marked a new stage for China's external liberalization. In addition to tariff cuts, China has promised that a large number of key services – including important business services, courier services, wholesale trade, franchising, tourism services, rail and road transport, and freight forwarding services – would be fully or almost fully open to foreign entry by 2008. Substantial foreign entry would also be allowed in many other services – including in telecommunications, audiovisual services, construction, retail trade, insurance, banking, securities, and maritime transport.

Since then, China has made rapid progress toward opening up its financial sector to foreign investment. More cities were opened to foreign banks to conduct business in the RMB. In addition to the liberalization of direct investment by foreign banks, domestic investors were allowed to invest in B-shares with self-owned foreign exchange earnings since 2001. Starting from 2002, qualified foreign institutional investors (QFII) are allowed to invest in the domestic capital market (bond and stock markets). Thus, from 2001 to 2004, portfolio inflows dwarfed outflows, contributing to economic overheating and tremendous upward pressure on the yuan exchange rate.

*Phase 7 2005–present: Portfolio outflows are encouraged to ease the upward pressure on the yuan and cool the overheating economy*

The Chinese government has long maintained that the yuan is not ready to float until its FX and financial markets are ready to manage the potentially large swings of portfolio flows. Thus, instead of allowing the rapid rise in China's current account surplus and net capital inflows to freely drive up the yuan exchange rate,

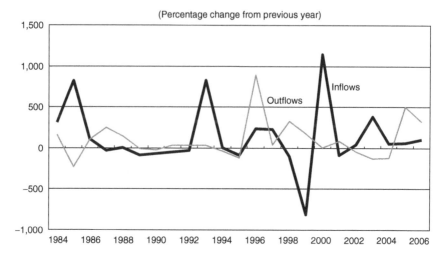

*Figure 3.8* Growth of China's portfolio inflows and outflows.
Source: State Administration of Foreign Exchange.

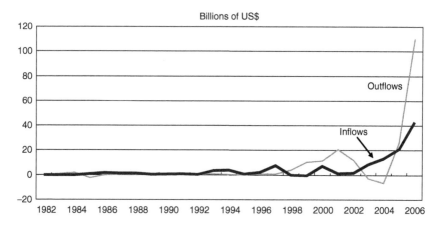

*Figure 3.9* China's portfolio flows.
Source: State Administration of Foreign Exchange.

the authorities began to lower barriers on capital outflows and tighten restrictions of portfolio inflows to help relieve that upward pressure on the yuan (besides widening the band of daily fluctuation to 0.3 per cent in July 2005 and then to 0.5 per cent in May 2007).[13] Consequently, portfolio outflows began to surge after 2004, outgrowing the rise in inflows (Figures 3.8 and 3.9).

### The challenges ahead

Even though China has begun liberalizing its financial-services industry at a rapid pace since its accession to the WTO, it still has a long way to go before its banks and capital markets can function efficiently as financial intermediaries. In view of China's past struggles with swings in capital flows, it is not surprising that China is reluctant to abolish capital controls before its financial market is ready. As long as its financial sector is still underdeveloped, portfolio inflows have a tendency to be used inefficiently, causing asset-price inflation (or even financial bubbles) rather than higher rate of output growth. The banking and corporate sectors may also tend to increase their exposure to currency risk faster than their ability to manage that risk, a problem that was central to the Asian crisis of 1997–8. At the same time, once capital is allowed to exit freely, large capital flight could occur if there is a sudden rise in perceived political uncertainty.

Most economists also agree that it is unwise for countries such as China, where FX trading is inhibited (either due to incomplete markets or government regulations, or both), to plunge into a floating exchange rate regime.[14] A sufficient number of market makers willing and able to take open positions is an important factor for a reasonably smooth market-based float.[15] Despite all the progress China has made so far, Chinese commercial banks are still constrained from taking large open positions in foreign exchange. Moreover, there is no liquid market in domestic bonds for banks to hedge their open positions in the domestic currency. With no natural market makers in the system, an immediate switch to free floating would very likely result in wildly erratic movements in the yuan exchange rate while the ability and options of traders (exporters and importers) to hedge currency risks would still be limited.

Some economists, such as Eichengreen (2006), argue that the progress already made toward partial liberalizations of capital controls actually make it even more urgent for China to allow the yuan greater flexibility (under a managed float). Currently, China's crawling-peg exchange rate regime only allows the yuan to move within a band of 0.5 per cent from the central parity announced the previous day, making it relatively easy for speculators to make one-way bets. Given that most investors consider the yuan to be still significantly undervalued, lowering restrictions on capital outflows could only encourage more speculative inflows, rendering the authorities less capable of insulating the economy from the effects of those inflows.

The authorities thus are facing a dilemma. The risk is high if China floats the yuan before its financial and FX markets are up to speed. The risk is also high if capital flows are liberalized while its financial market is still underdeveloped and its exchange rate is heavily managed. Continuing to restrict portfolio flows, however, will continue to inhibit the development of its financial and FX markets, delaying the time when the yuan is ready to float. Given the Chinese economy's sizeable weight in the global economy, especially in the Asian region, the stakes are high whether China can successfully manage the transition toward floating its exchange rate.

## Conclusion

China's achievements over the past two decades dazzling. Its annual GDP growth has averaged about 10 per cent, while inflation remained subdued. Growth of income per capital averaged about 9 per cent a year since 1990. In some aspects, its record is even better than that of the four Asian newly industrialized economies (Singapore, Hong Kong, South Korea, and Taiwan). This paper discusses the ways in which China's approach toward capital flows may have contributed to that record.

But China's approach to capital flows is not an unqualified success. It has likely contributed to a pattern of unbalanced growth and rising income inequality, which risks the sustainability of its rapid growth. China's fine-tuning and gradualist approach toward capital-account liberalization, necessary to sustain its currency-peg exchange rate policy, has retarded the development of an efficient domestic financial market and well-functioning foreign exchange market. The acceleration of liberalizing portfolio flows since 2001 has contributed to notable progress in the financial sector; however, given China's crawling-peg regime, it also further hampers the Chinese central bank's ability to rein in inflation and an overheating economy. Now that China has grown to be a major economy of the world, whether it can successfully manage the transition toward full capital-account convertibility and a free-floating exchange rate matters not only to China but also to the global economy.

## Acknowledgement

This paper is a shortened version of Congressional Budget Office Working Paper, No. 2008–02. The analysis and conclusions expressed in them are those of the authors and should not be interpreted as those of the Congressional Budget Office. The author thanks Adam Weber for his valuable research assistance, and Bob Dennis, John Peterson, and Kim Kowalewski, Bruce Arnold, Doug Hamilton, and Joseph Kile for their helpful comments.

## References

Bosworth, B. and Collins, S. (2007) 'Accounting for Growth: Comparing China and India', NBER Working paper, No. 12943.

Eichengreen, B. (2006) 'China's Exchange Rate Regime: The Long and Short of It', Manuscript, University of California Berkeley, CA.

Goldstein, M. (2004) 'Adjusting China's Exchange Rate Policies', Peterson Institute for International Economics Working Paper, No. 04-1, Washington DC.

——— (2007) 'A (Lack of) Progress Report on China's Exchange Rate Policies', Peterson Institute for International Economics Working Paper, No. 07 (5).

Goldstein, M. and Lardy, N. (2003) 'Two-Step Currency Reform for China', *Asian Wall Street Journal*, September 12.

Hung, J. (2008) 'China's Approach to Capital Flows since 1978', Congressional Budget Office Working Paper, No. 2008 (2), Washington, DC.

Kuijs, L. and Wang, T. (2006) 'China's Patten of Growth: Moving to Sustainability and Reducing Inequality', *China and World Economy*, No.1, 2006.

McKinnon, R. (2007) 'Why China Should Keep its Dollar Peg: A Historical Perspective from Japan', Stanford University Working Paper, No. 323, California.

Prasad, E. (2007) 'Is the Chinese Growth Miracle Built to Last?' Manuscript, Cornell University. New York.

Prasad, E. and Wei, S. J. (2005) 'The Chinese approach to capital inflows: patterns and possible explanations', NBER Working paper, No. 11306.

Tseng, W. and Zebregs, H. (2002) 'Foreign Direct Investment in China: Some Lessons for Other Countries', IMF Policy Discussion Paper, No. 02 (03), Washington DC.

Wei, S. J. (1993) 'The Open Door Policy and China's Rapid Growth: Evidence from City-level Data', NBER Working Paper, No. 4602.

Whalley J. and Xin, X. (2006) 'China's FDI and Non-FDI Economies and the Sustainability of Future High Chinese Growth', NBER Working Paper, No. 12249.

Whalley, J. and Zhang. S. (2004) 'Inequality Change in China and (Hukou) Labour Mobility Restrictions', NBER Working Paper, No. 10683.

Zhao, M. (2006) 'External Liberalization and the Evolution of China's Exchange System: an Empirical Approach', World Bank China Office Research Paper, No. 4.

# 4 The estimation of domestic value-added and employment induced by exports

An application to Chinese exports to the United States

*Xikang Chen, Leonard K. Cheng, K. C. Fung and Lawrence J. Lau*

## Introduction

The objective of this study is twofold: first, to develop a methodological framework for the estimation of the increases in domestic value-added (or equivalently, GDP) and employment in a country in response to increases in its exports, in the aggregate as well as disaggregated by commodity and by destination; and second, to apply this empirical methodology to the estimation of the increases in Chinese domestic value-added, and employment, as a consequence of increases of Chinese exports to the United States.

Our practical motivation is the large and rising trade imbalances between the People's Republic of China (PRC) and the United States. The PRC has, for the past few years, run large trade surpluses vis-à-vis the United States, although the exact magnitude of the trade surplus is in dispute.[1] For example, for 2005, official US estimates indicate a merchandise trade surplus of US\$ 201.6 billion in China's favour, whereas official Chinese estimates put the figure at only US\$ 114.2 billion. The best estimate by Fung *et al.* (2006) is US\$ 172.3 billion.

An important question of contention is the perceived relative distribution of benefits of the trade between China and the US. Traditionally, the focus of public interest, not shared by most professional economists, is on the bilateral trade balance. A country with a trade surplus vis-à-vis its trading partner country is presumed to have derived a greater benefit from the bilateral trade. China, however, takes the position that the domestic value-added of Chinese exports to the US is low, in particular its 'processing exports' (officially known as 'processing and assembly' exports). 'Processing exports' refers to exports produced by firms located in China (maybe owned and operated by firms from Hong Kong and Taiwan) using raw materials, components and parts (and sometimes machinery and equipment) as well as design supplied by foreign firms which as part of the contractual agreement will import the products into the foreign countries. The proportion of Chinese domestic value-added to gross value in Chinese processing exports has been roughly estimated to be 10 per cent in 1992, rising to 20 per cent in 1995 and 35 per cent in 1999 (See Lardy 1992 and Fung *et al.* 2004).

Our theoretical motivation is to derive the information necessary for a more objective assessment of the relative balance from trade between two trading partner countries. In this study, we propose to quantify the domestic economic impact resulting from increased exports in terms of value-added (GDP) and employment.[2] Thus, instead of, or in addition to, the bilateral trade balance, it is possible to compare the relative benefits between two trading partners in terms of the value-added and employment derived from their bilateral trade. Based on this theoretical framework, our principal empirical contributions are the first quantitative estimates of the economic benefits derived by China, both directly and indirectly, from its exports to the US and to the world, in terms of value-added and employment. To answer the question of measuring bilateral trade balances in terms of value-added more completely, it is necessary to apply the same methodological framework to the US economy, using an input-output table of the US. Studies along these lines include Lau *et al.* (2006a; b).

Our methodology is to extend Leontief *et al*'s (1953) input-output analysis in a number of directions to capture China's special production structure. These extensions include the following.

1    Since we are interested in estimating the extent of *domestic* value-added due to Chinese exports, and because domestically produced and imported intermediate inputs, even in the same sector classification, are imperfect substitutes for each other, the input-output table needs to distinguish between domestically produced and imported intermediate inputs. Technically, we need a table with 'non-competitive imports', not one with 'competitive imports' that lumps domestically produced inputs and imported inputs together.

2    To estimate value-added and employment, we need input-output coefficients for the primary inputs (capital, labour and natural resources (including land)) as well as the coefficients of intermediate inputs. That is, we need to expand the input-output table into an input-occupancy-output table.

3    Since we are interested in the effects of an increase of exports, as opposed to net exports,[3] we need to disaggregate the net exports final demand in the input-output table into separate exports and imports final demand.

4    Because more than half of Chinese exports are processing exports – in 1999 these exports accounted for 59.5 per cent of total Chinese exports, and they require different primary and intermediate inputs from ordinary exports, it is necessary to have two separate input-output tables, one for processing exports and another for ordinary exports.

In addition to the above extensions of the standard input-output analysis to fit our purpose and China's economic reality, we also need to pay special attention to the following issues about data processing.

1    We have to match the sectors contained in the input-output tables to the trade data that are reported under the HS (Harmonized Systems) of merchandise

trade classification, thus creating a concordance of 33 sectors for the Chinese economy. Furthermore, while the input-output tables measure the quantities of the commodities in terms of producers' prices on an 'ex-factory' basis, Chinese exports as contained in customs trade data are measured in FOB (free on board) prices and Chinese imports are measured in CIF (cost, insurance and freight) prices. It is therefore necessary to create conversion matrices that allow all commodities to be measured on the same basis.

2    Since the composition of the exports final demand vector varies across different trading partners, the exports final demand needs to be disaggregated by destination of the exports, even if it may be assumed that exports are perfect substitutes in production across destinations.

3    Because a significant proportion of Chinese exports are first shipped to Hong Kong, and then re-exported to other ultimate destinations, we need to include the re-exports through Hong Kong, disaggregated in accordance with the commodity classification of the input-output table, to arrive at the total exports to the destination countries.

In Section 2, we develop a general methodological framework for the assessment of the impact of increased exports on value-added and employment, on the basis of input-output analysis. In Section 3, we discuss in detail the assembly and construction of our basic data. In Section 4, we present our principal findings. Brief concluding remarks are made in Section 5.

## The methodological framework

The input-output analysis is a very useful tool to study the effects of a change in final demands on the national economy. As argued above, in order to study the effects of a change in exports it is necessary to have an input-output table of the non-competitive type, i.e. imported goods and domestically produced goods in the same sectors are treated as differentiated products. The characteristics of such an input-output table are given in Table 4.1.

The equations of supply and demand in the above table are as follows:

$$\sum_{j=1}^{n} X_{ij}^{D} + F_{i}^{D} = X_{i} \qquad (i = 1, 2, \ldots, n) \tag{4.1}$$

$$\sum_{i=1}^{n} X_{ij}^{M} + F_{i}^{M} = M_{i} \qquad (i = 1, 2, \ldots, n) \tag{4.2}$$

where superscript $D$ represents domestic products and $M$ denotes imported products; $X_{ij}$ represents inter-industry flow from sector $i$ to sector $j$; $F_{i}$ denotes final demands; $X_{i}$ denotes gross output value of sector $i$ and $M_{i}$ denotes value of imports of sector $i$.

*Table 4.1* An input-output table with non-competitive imports

| | Intermediate demands | Final demands | |
|---|---|---|---|
| | 1, 2, …, n total | Household consumption + government consumption + gross capital formation + exports | Gross domestic output ($X_i$) or imports ($M_i$) |
| Domestic intermediate inputs | | | |
| 1 | $X_{ij}^D$ | $F_i^D$ | $X_i$ |
| 2 | | | |
| ⋮ | | | |
| N | | | |
| Imported intermediate inputs | | | |
| 1 | $X_{ij}^M$ | $F_i^M$ | $M_i$ |
| 2 | | | |
| ⋮ | | | |
| n | | | |
| Total intermediate inputs | | | |
| Value-added | | | |
| Depreciation | | | |
| Compensation of labourers | | | |
| Net taxes on production | | | |
| Operating surplus | | | |
| Total | $V_j$ | | |
| Total inputs | $X_j$ | | |

$$A^D X + F^D = X \tag{4.3}$$

$$A^M X + F^M = M \tag{4.4}$$

where $A^D = [a_{ij}^D]$ is the matrix of direct input coefficients of domestic products and the direct input coefficient $a_{ij}^D = X_{ij}^D / X_j$; $A^M = [a_{ij}^M]$ is the matrix of direct input coefficient matrix of imported goods; $X$ = total output column vector; $F^D$ = column vector of final demands of domestic products; $F^M$ = column vector of final demands of imported goods; $M$ = column vector of imported goods.

Then we have

$$(I - A^D)X = F^D \tag{4.5a}$$

$$X = (I - A^D)^{-1} F^D \tag{4.5b}$$

$$M = A^M (I - A^D)^{-1} F^D + F^M \tag{4.5c}$$

where $(I - A)^{-1}$ is the well-known Leontief's inverse. Because $F^D$ includes household consumption, government consumption, gross capital formation (gross fixed capital formation and changes in inventories) and exports.

The increment of the gross output vector $(\Delta x)$ induced by the increment of exports $(\Delta E)$ is given by $\Delta X = (I - A^D)^{-1}\Delta E$, and consequently, the increment of the value added column vector induced by an increment in exports is given by

$$\Delta V = \hat{A}_V \Delta X = \hat{A}_V(I - A^D)^{-1}\Delta E \tag{4.6}$$

where $\hat{A}_V$ is a diagonal matrix whose $j$th element on the diagonal is given by $a_{Vj}$, sector $j$'s ratio of value added and gross output. Similarly, the effect of a change in employment induced by an increment in exports is given by,

$$\Delta L = \hat{A}_L \Delta X = \hat{A}_L(I - A^D)^{-1}\Delta E, \tag{4.7}$$

where $\hat{A}_L$ is a diagonal matrix whose $j$th element on the diagonal is given by $a_{Lj}$, sector $j$'s ratio of the amount of labour force and the gross output. The above formulae (4.6) and (4.7) will be used to estimate the effect of an increase in Chinese exports on Chinese domestic value-added and employment. Using such input-output tables, we can define the value added (VA) induced by exports in two different but equivalent ways. The first way of calculating total VA is to add up all of direct and indirect VA induced by exports.

$$\text{Total VA} = \text{Direct VA} + \text{Sum of all indirect VA} \tag{4.8}$$

Let us define $b_{Vj}$ as the coefficient of total value added induced by exports of sector $j$'s products. Then we have

$$b_{Vj} = a_{Vj} + \sum_{i=1}^{n} a_{Vi}a_{ij}^{D} + \sum_{i=1}^{n}\sum_{k=1}^{n} a_{Vk}a_{ki}^{D}a_{ij}^{D}$$

$$+ \sum_{i=1}^{n}\sum_{k=1}^{n}\sum_{s=1}^{n} a_{vs}a_{sk}^{D}a_{ki}^{D}a_{ij}^{D} + \ldots \quad (j = 1, 2, \ldots, n)$$

In order to export one dollar of textiles, one dollar of textiles has to be produced in China. As a result, a first round of domestic value-added is created directly. Let us call it the *direct* VA induced by exports of one dollar of textiles. In order to produce textiles, however, intermediate inputs such as agricultural products (cotton and hemp, etc.), and chemicals (chemical fibres, etc.) must be used, thus creating the first-round *indirect* value-added. In producing cotton and hemp, fertilizers are consumed, thus creating a second round of indirect domestic VA. And this process of creating indirect domestic VA goes on indefinitely as intermediate inputs are produced (see Figure 4.1). The total domestic value-added induced by one dollar of textiles exports is equal to the sum of direct domestic VA and all indirect domestic VA. Using the matrix notation, the column vector of $b_{Vj}$ is given by

$$B_V = A_V + A_V A^D + A_V A^D A^D + A_V A^D A^D A^D + \ldots$$

$$= A_V(I + A^D + A^{D^2} + A^{D^3} + \ldots)$$

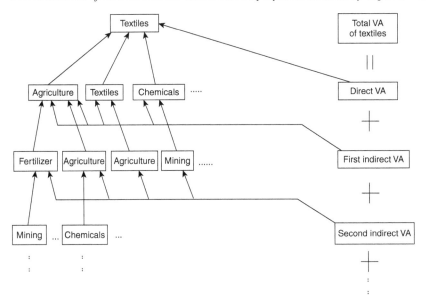

*Figure 4.1* The total value-added induced by exports of one-dollar textiles.

where $A_V$ is a row vector of direct value added coefficients and $B_V$ is a row vector of total value added coefficient.

Mathematically, matrix $A^D$ has two important properties: a) It is a non-negative matrix, i.e. $0 \leqslant a_{ij}^D \leqslant 1$, $(i, j = 1, 2, \ldots, n)$, and b) Its column sum is less than unity, i.e. $\sum_{i=1}^{n} a_{ij}^D < 1$, $(j = 1, 2, \ldots, n)$. Given these two properties, the power series of matrix $A^D$ is convergent and the inverse matrix $(I - A^D)^{-1}$ exists. Moreover, $(I - A^D)^{-1} = I + A^D + A^{D^2} + A^{D^3} + \ldots$ Thus, we get

$$B_V = A_V(I - A^D)^{-1} \tag{4.9}$$

This equation derives the total impact on value added induced by one dollar of exports.

Similarly, we can calculate the total impact on employment induced by exports as follows

$$B_L = A_L(I - A^D)^{-1} \tag{4.10}$$

where $A_L$ is a row vector of direct employment coefficients and $B_L$ is a row vector of total employment coefficient.

The second way of calculating total VA is to subtract imports from the gross outputs, i.e. we can obtain total value-added as follows:

Total Value Added = Gross Value of Output

− Total Imports Used in Producing the Output   (4.11)

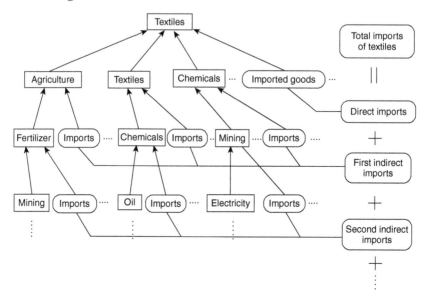

*Figure 4.2* Total imports induced by exports of one-dollar of textiles.

As illustrated in Figure 4.2, total imports are equal to the sum of direct imports and all indirect imports. In producing textiles, imported intermediate inputs are used. The imported inputs used directly in the production of textiles constitute the direct imports. To produce textiles, however, domestically produced inputs are also used, and to produce these domestic intermediate goods, some inputs have to be imported. These imported inputs constitute the first round of indirect imports. Analogous to the description under Figure 4.1, there are additional rounds of indirect imports. Total imports are given by the sum of direct imports and all rounds of indirect imports.

With the concept of total imports, we can derive total VA by using equation (4.11). Defining $b_j^M$ as the coefficient of total imports induced by one dollar of exports by the $j$th sector, we have

$$b_j^M = a_{0j}^M + \sum_{i=1}^{n} a_{oi}^M a_{ij}^D + \sum_{i=1}^{n}\sum_{k=1}^{n} a_{ok}^M a_{ki}^D a_{ij}^D$$

$$+ \sum_{i=1}^{n}\sum_{k=1}^{n}\sum_{s=1}^{n} a_{os}^M a_{sk}^D a_{ki}^D a_{ij}^D + \dots (j = 1, 2, \dots, n),$$

which can be expressed in matrix form as follows:

$$B^M = A_o^M + A_o^M A^D + A_o^M A^D A^D + A_o^M A^D A^D A^D + \dots$$

$$= A_o^M (I + A^D + A^{D^2} + A^{D^3} + \dots)$$

$$= A_o^M (I - A^D)^{-1}$$

where $A_o^M = (a_{o1}^M, a_{o2}^M, \ldots, a_{on}^M)$ denotes the sum of the direct import coefficients and $B^M = (b_1^M, b_2^M, \ldots, b_n^M)$ denotes the row vector of the total imports coefficients.

More precisely, $a_{oj}^M = \sum_{i=1}^{n} a_{ij}^M$.

Using the second definition of total value added as given by (4.11), we obtain the coefficient of total VA as $(1 - \text{coefficient of total imports})$, i.e.

$$b_{Vj} = 1 - b_j^M \qquad (j = 1, 2, \ldots, n),$$

or in matrix form,

$$B_V = i - B^M, \tag{4.12}$$

where $i = (1, 1, \ldots, 1)$ is a unity row vector.

It can be proven that total VA obtained from (4.9) is equivalent to that obtained from (4.12) (see Appendix 1 of Chen *et al.* 2004). To illustrate, using the first method (4.9), the direct domestic value-added contained in \$1 of textiles export is calculated as \$0.17766 but that for the production of textiles is \$0.1913. The first round indirect VA is \$0.174929, the second round indirect VA is \$0.119233, and the third round indirect VA is \$0.074092. As expected, the higher the round, the smaller the value of indirect VA. After adding up the direct and indirect VA, the total domestic value-added induced by one-dollar of textiles export is \$0.656993. Using the second method, in producing \$1 of textiles for exports, the value of direct imports is \$0.300461. The value of the first round of indirect imports is \$0.019695. The value of the second round of indirect imports is \$0.009117. The value of the third round of indirect imports is \$0.005367. After adding up the direct and indirect imports, the value of total imports is \$0.343007 dollar for every dollar of exports of textiles produced, implying a total domestic value-added of \$0.656993, exactly equal to that obtained using the first method.

Thus, theoretically we can use *either* approach to calculate the amount of total domestic value-added contained in Chinese exports to the world and to the US. However, since operationally it is easier to use the second approach, in the remainder of this paper we shall estimate the domestic value-added induced by exports as the difference between the gross value of exports and the value of imported intermediate goods.

## The data

The core of the data that we use is the 1995 input-output table of China, published in 1997.[4] It is an updated input-output table, compiled by the National Bureau of Statistics of China on the basis of the 1992 input-output table. In the 1995 table, there are 33 production sectors (see Appendix 2 of Chen *et al.* 2004). With the assistance of the MOFTEC, the Customs Bureau and the National Bureau of Statistics, we have constructed from unpublished raw data two separate sets of input-output tables – one for processing exports and the other for non-processing exports. Each table contains separate import and export columns for different countries of destinations.

In this study, several important tasks involving data construction and analysis are performed.

### *Separation of net exports into exports and imports columns*

This study is based on the input-output table of China for 1995, which had only a single 'net exports' final demands column. With the assistance of the National Bureau of Statistics, we disaggregated the net exports column into an export column and an import column with customs duties, and further disaggregate exports by the following destinations: the US, Hong Kong, Japan, Taiwan, Korea, Germany, and Rest of World. The data used for these purposes include the *Custom Statistical Yearbook of China, Balance of International Income and Expenditure of China*, and *Profits and Deficits of Exported and Imported Commodities of China*.

### *Construction of an input-output table with non-competitive imports*

Up until 2007, all national input-output tables of China were of the competitive type. The intermediate flows $X_{ij}$ of the table include (without distinction) intermediate inputs that are both domestically produced and imported. Since we need to subtract out from the gross value of exports the value of total imported inputs, we must separate out imported and domestically produced inputs. Using several data sets, including data of *China's Third National Industrial Survey* for 1995, and with the help of the National Bureau of Statistics, we separate out domestic and imported intermediate goods and constructed a non-competitive type input-output table. In the input-output table we use, there are 33 separate import rows, one for each sector.

### *Distinguishing between processing exports and ordinary exports*

An important feature of Chinese exports is the very high proportion of processing exports in the value of total exports. In 1995 the total value of Chinese exports was US$148.8 billion. Of this amount, the value of processing exports was US$73.7 billion, accounting for 49.55 per cent of the total value of exports in 1995 (Customs Bureau of PRC 1996, p. 12). In recent years, that proportion had actually been rising – from 54.7 per cent in 1997 to 59.5 per cent in 1999 and then decreased after 2004. The proportion in 2001 is 55.4 per cent, in 2004 is 55.3 per cent and in 2006 is 52.7 per cent.

The amount of domestic value-added generated by processing exports is generally believed to be much lower than that the other kinds of Chinese exports. In 1995 the value of Chinese processing exports was US$73.7 billion, while the value of imports related to these exports was US$58.4 billion. Thus, based on aggregate data, imported intermediate inputs accounted for as much as 79.2 per cent of the value of processing, implying that the direct value-added of such exports would be close to 20 per cent. Due to the importance of processing exports in Chinese trade and due to the significantly different value-added between ordinary exports and processing exports, we construct a 1995 processing exports input-output table (excluding final demands) and a non-processing exports input-output table. There are two direct input coefficient matrices, each with 33 import rows, one for processing exports production and the other for non-processing exports production. In constructing these two input-output tables, data from China's Third National Industrial Survey for 1995 were used and assistance from MOFTEC, the Customs Bureau and the National Bureau of Statistics was sought.

### Conversion tables between trade data and input-output data

Another important piece of work we do with the data is to integrate exports and imports data into the input-output table. We match the different commodity/sector classification by developing a concordance between the 33 sectors of China's input-output tables (see Appendix 2 of Chen *et al.* 2004) and the Harmonized System (HS) of international merchandise trade classification (see Appendix 3 of Chen *et al.* 2004). The concordance allows us to allocate customs exports and imports data to their respective input-output sectors.

There are also other differences in the measurement of quantities of inputs and outputs between the input-output tables and in the trade statistics. In the input-output tables, all commodities are measured in producers' prices (ex-factory prices) because the transportation and distribution margins are attributed to the transportation, commerce, finance and insurance sectors. As a result, the exports column in the final demands of the input-output table consists of two parts: the value of the exported commodities measured at producers' prices and the transportation and distribution margins incurred by these exports prior to their delivery to a port or airport for transportation to a foreign destination. Thus, to be consistent, exports and imports must be treated similarly. Since exports are measured on a FOB basis, we construct a conversion matrix that transforms exports as measured on the FOB basis in the customs statistics into exports as measured according to the convention of the input-output tables. Similarly, imports are measured in the customs statistics on the CIF basis, but in an input-output table, they are measured at the actual supply prices, which include not only cost, insurance and freight, but also customs duties and transportation and distribution margins. Again, to ensure that we are dealing with quantities measured in the same way, we construct a conversion matrix for imports that transforms imports as measured on the CIF basis in the customs statistics into imports as measured according to the convention of input-output tables.

As an illustration, suppose China exports US$1 of textiles, FOB, as recorded in the Chinese customs statistics. In the input-output table, the US$1 of Chinese exports of textiles is represented in the exports column as follows: US$0.8902 of exports of textiles; US$0.0256 of exports of freight transport and communication services; US$0.0120 of public utilities services; US$0.0110 of passenger transport services, and US$0.0096 of finance and insurance services. An example of such a conversion matrix is presented in Appendix 4 of Chen *et al.* (2004).

We encounter other problems in integrating exports and imports data from China Customs into the input-output tables. For example, the trade data obtained from the customs statistics do not include the exports and imports of services. In addition, imported goods that do not pass through customs are not included in the customs statistics. We understand these possible discrepancies but are not able to address them in this paper.

### Input-output tables that link employment to output

For our purpose of estimating the effects of exports on employment, it is necessary to construct input-occupancy-output tables (Chen 1990, 1999; Chen *et al.*1992) with rows for primary inputs such as labour force, natural resources, and capital (fixed assets and circulating assets). Based on the 1995 input-output table, we construct three additional rows: employment, fixed assets and circulating assets.

## Principal findings

### Effects of Chinese exports on Chinese domestic value-added by industry

In Tables 4.2 and 4.3, we present the Chinese domestic value-added of Chinese processing and non-processing exports. For each type of exports, two measures are reported: direct value-added, which includes only the first round use of domestic inputs; and the total domestic value-added, which includes the use of all the rounds of domestic intermediate goods. By definition, total domestic value-added is always larger than the corresponding direct value-added.

As expected, the estimates of domestic value-added of processing exports are uniformly lower than those of the non-processing exports. Generally, for processing exports, more than 90 per cent of the intermediate inputs come from abroad. The production of these exports uses primarily the following domestic inputs: electricity, coal, petroleum, gas, freight transport and communication, passenger transport, commerce, public utilities, and finance and insurance.

For processing exports, the lowest direct domestic value-added is 11.5 per cent (manufacture of machinery), while the highest is 45.7 per cent (finance and insurance). For total domestic value-added, the lowest is 13.8 per cent (manufacture of electronic and communication equipment), while the highest is 55.1 per cent (finance and insurance). For non-processing exports, finance and insurance has the highest direct domestic value-added (62.2 per cent), while coking, manufacture of gas and coal products has the lowest (14.4 per cent). For total domestic value added, the highest is in agriculture (96.4 per cent) and the lowest is in the sector manufacture of transport equipment (85.1 per cent).

When China joined the World Trade Organization (WTO), there was widespread concern in the US and other developed countries that there would be a flood of imports coming into the US market, particularly in the sensitive areas of textile (sector 7) and wearing apparel (sector 8). However, the trade benefits derived by China could be quite different from the gross values of its exports and the benefits

*Table 4.2* Chinese domestic value-added. Induced by US$1 of Chinese processing exports, 1995 (US$)

| Sector | Direct value-added | Total value-added |
|---|---|---|
| 01 Agriculture | 0.197 | 0.227 |
| 02 Coal mining | 0.242 | 0.296 |
| 03 Crude petroleum and natural gas production | 0.279 | 0.319 |
| 04 Metal ore mining | 0.156 | 0.198 |
| 05 Other mining | 0.228 | 0.278 |
| 06 Food manufacturing | 0.149 | 0.167 |
| 07 Manufacture of textiles | 0.147 | 0.165 |
| 08 Manufacture of wearing apparel, leather and products of leather and fur | 0.158 | 0.170 |
| 09 Sawmills and manufacture of furniture | 0.128 | 0.160 |
| 10 Manufacture of paper, cultural and educational articles | 0.138 | 0.166 |
| 11 Electricity, steam and hot water production and supply | 0.209 | 0.308 |
| 12 Petroleum refineries | 0.159 | 0.205 |
| 13 Coking, manufacture of gas and coal products | 0.163 | 0.279 |
| 14 Chemical industries | 0.139 | 0.167 |
| 15 Manufacture of building materials and non-metallic mineral products | 0.159 | 0.214 |
| 16 Primary metal manufacturing | 0.118 | 0.151 |
| 17 Manufacture of metal products | 0.129 | 0.155 |
| 18 Manufacture of machinery | 0.115 | 0.143 |
| 19 Manufacture of transport equipment | 0.133 | 0.160 |
| 20 Manufacture of electric machinery and instrument | 0.128 | 0.144 |
| 21 Manufacture of electronic and communication equipment | 0.128 | 0.138 |
| 22 Manufacture of instruments and meters, etc. | 0.135 | 0.159 |
| 23 Maintenance and repair of machinery and equipment | N.A. | N.A. |
| 24 Industries not elsewhere classified | 0.129 | 0.151 |
| 25 Construction | N.A. | N.A. |
| 26 Freight transport and communication | 0.372 | 0.416 |
| 27 Commerce | 0.174 | 0.259 |
| 28 Restaurants | 0.156 | 0.170 |
| 29 Passenger transport | 0.444 | 0.511 |
| 30 Public utilities and service to households | 0.268 | 0.334 |
| 31 Culture, education, health and scientific research | N.A. | N.A. |
| 32 Finance and insurance | 0.457 | 0.551 |
| 33 Public administration | N.A. | N.A. |
| Weighted average | 0.153 | 0.176 |

as perceived by policymakers. Let us first look at the processing exports of textile and wearing apparel. The estimates for their direct Chinese domestic value-added are 14.7 per cent and 15.8 per cent respectively, while the estimates for the total value-added are 16.5 per cent and 17.0 per cent, respectively. For non-processing exports of textile and wearing apparel, their direct value-added estimates are 19.5 per cent and 23.0 per cent, respectively, and the estimates of their total value-added are considerably higher, with 93.4 per cent for textile and 94.4 per cent for wearing apparel. Combining both processing and non-processing

*Table 4.3* Chinese domestic value-added. Induced by US$1 of Chinese non-processing exports, 1995 (US$)

| Sector | Direct value-added | Total value-added |
|---|---|---|
| 01 Agriculture | 0.598 | 0.964 |
| 02 Coal mining | 0.532 | 0.932 |
| 03 Crude petroleum and natural gas production | 0.606 | 0.923 |
| 04 Metal ore mining | 0.379 | 0.910 |
| 05 Other mining | 0.453 | 0.926 |
| 06 Food manufacturing | 0.345 | 0.956 |
| 07 Manufacture of textiles | 0.195 | 0.934 |
| 08 Manufacture of wearing apparel, leather and products of leather and fur | 0.229 | 0.944 |
| 09 Sawmills and manufacture of furniture | 0.286 | 0.907 |
| 10 Manufacture of paper, cultural and educational articles | 0.261 | 0.939 |
| 11 Electricity, steam and hot water production and supply | 0.485 | 0.927 |
| 12 Petroleum refineries | 0.280 | 0.892 |
| 13 Coking, manufacture of gas and coal products | 0.144 | 0.902 |
| 14 Chemical industries | 0.261 | 0.916 |
| 15 Manufacture of building materials and non-metallic mineral products | 0.332 | 0.926 |
| 16 Primary metal manufacturing | 0.273 | 0.900 |
| 17 Manufacture of metal products | 0.242 | 0.904 |
| 18 Manufacture of machinery | 0.289 | 0.862 |
| 19 Manufacture of transport equipment | 0.246 | 0.851 |
| 20 Manufacture of electric machinery and instrument | 0.261 | 0.894 |
| 21 Manufacture of electronic and communication equipment | 0.312 | 0.859 |
| 22 Manufacture of instruments and meters, etc. | 0.338 | 0.863 |
| 23 Maintenance and repair of machinery and equipment | 0.330 | 0.880 |
| 24 Industries not elsewhere classified | 0.250 | 0.914 |
| 25 Construction | 0.290 | 0.912 |
| 26 Freight transport and communication | 0.591 | 0.925 |
| 27 Commerce | 0.563 | 0.953 |
| 28 Restaurants | 0.401 | 0.957 |
| 29 Passenger transport | 0.595 | 0.924 |
| 30 Public utilities and service to households | 0.598 | 0.950 |
| 31 Culture, education, health and scientific research | 0.523 | 0.939 |
| 32 Finance and insurance | 0.622 | 0.958 |
| 33 Public administration | 0.478 | 0.928 |
| Weighted average | 0.329 | 0.925 |

exports of textile and wearing apparel, the estimates for direct Chinese value-added are 17.8 per cent and 18.3 per cent, respectively; the estimates for total Chinese domestic value-added are higher, with textile being 65.7 per cent and wearing apparel being 44.1 per cent.

The aggregate direct value-added and total value-added of all processing exports was 15.3 per cent and 17.6 per cent of the total value of processing exports. The aggregate direct value-added and total value-added of all non-processing exports was 32.9 per cent and 92.5 per cent of the total value of non-processing exports. The direct value-added and total value-added of aggregate Chinese exports is obtained by weighing the above figures by the shares of processing and non-processing exports in total exports. The estimates are 24 per cent and 54.5 per cent, respectively, of China's total exports.

### Effects of Chinese exports on domestic employment by industry

Examining the employment effects of Chinese exports is important with China being a member of the WTO. Being a member of the WTO will accelerate China's economic reforms, including the reform of the state-owned enterprises and one of the most feared impacts is massive unemployment. However, joining the WTO will also increase China's exports, which can generate employment and thus ease the unemployment situation.

In Tables 4.4 and 4.5, we present the employment effects of US$1000 of processing exports and non-processing exports, respectively. As can be seen in Table 4.4, in several sectors, there are no direct or total employment increases due to processing exports. The average direct and total employment effects are respectively 0.048 and 0.057 person-year. These average employment effects are substantially lower than those for non-processing exports (see Table 4.5), i.e. 0.214 and 0.703 person-year, respectively.

For processing exports, the largest direct and total employment effects occur in agriculture (0.171 and 0.181, respectively). Except industries with no employment effects at all, the electronic and telecommunication equipment industry has the lowest total employment effect (0.027). For processing textiles exports, the direct and total employment effects are 0.044 and 0.050, respectively. For wearing apparel, the direct and total employment effects are 0.048 and 0.052, respectively.

For non-processing exports, the highest employment effects occur in agriculture again, with the direct effect being 1.357 and the total effect being 1.8. For textiles, the direct employment effect is 0.107 and the total employment effect is 0.845. For wearing apparel, the direct and total employment effects are 0.108 and 0.745, respectively. The electronic and telecommunication equipment industry ends up as having the second lowest direct and total employment effects (0.064 and 0.329, respectively).

As in the case of value-added, the average direct employment and total employment effects of US$1000 of aggregate Chinese exports can be obtained by weighing the employing effects of processing exports and non-processing exports by their shares in total exports. The average direct domestic employment effect of US$1,000 of aggregate Chinese export is 0.130 person-year, while the average total effect on employment is 0.375 person-year. For either direct or total employment effect, the lowest occurs in the manufacture of electronic and communication equipment (0.029 and 0.07, respectively). For each US$1,000 of Chinese exports, the textile sector increases employment directly by 0.084 person-year and by 0.558 person-year in total. The figures for wearing apparel are 0.069 and 0.294, respectively.

*Table 4.4* Chinese domestic employment. Induced by US$1,000 of Chinese processing exports, 1995 (Person-Years)

| Sector | Direct employment | Total employment |
|---|---|---|
| 01 Agriculture | 0.171 | 0.181 |
| 02 Coal mining | 0.151 | 0.169 |
| 03 Crude petroleum and natural gas production | 0.054 | 0.066 |
| 04 Metal ore mining | 0.090 | 0.103 |
| 05 Other mining | 0.113 | 0.128 |
| 06 Food manufacturing | 0.048 | 0.054 |
| 07 Manufacture of textiles | 0.044 | 0.050 |
| 08 Manufacture of wearing apparel, leather and products of leather and fur | 0.048 | 0.052 |
| 09 Sawmills and manufacture of furniture | 0.062 | 0.075 |
| 10 Manufacture of paper, cultural and educational articles | 0.046 | 0.058 |
| 11 Electricity, steam and hot water production and supply | 0.030 | 0.069 |
| 12 Petroleum refineries | 0.017 | 0.039 |
| 13 Coking, manufacture of gas and coal products | 0.052 | 0.109 |
| 14 Chemical industries | 0.038 | 0.049 |
| 15 Manufacture of building materials and non-metallic mineral products | 0.065 | 0.085 |
| 16 Primary metal manufacturing | 0.035 | 0.048 |
| 17 Manufacture of metal products | 0.047 | 0.058 |
| 18 Manufacture of machinery | 0.041 | 0.052 |
| 19 Manufacture of transport equipment | 0.038 | 0.050 |
| 20 Manufacture of electric machinery and instrument | 0.035 | 0.041 |
| 21 Manufacture of electronic and communication equipment | 0.023 | 0.027 |
| 22 Manufacture of instruments and meters, etc. | 0.082 | 0.090 |
| 23 Maintenance and repair of machinery and equipment | 0.000 | 0.000 |
| 24 Industries not elsewhere classified | 0.054 | 0.061 |
| 25 Construction | 0.000 | 0.000 |
| 26 Freight transport and communication | 0.152 | 0.165 |
| 27 Commerce | 0.132 | 0.156 |
| 28 Restaurants | 0.100 | 0.104 |
| 29 Passenger transport | 0.135 | 0.153 |
| 30 Public utilities and service to households | 0.106 | 0.125 |
| 31 Culture, education, health and scientific research | 0.000 | 0.000 |
| 32 Finance and insurance | 0.103 | 0.133 |
| 33 Public administration | 0.000 | 0.000 |
| Weighted average | 0.048 | 0.057 |

## Aggregate effects of Chinese exports on Chinese domestic value-added and domestic employment

Tables 4.2–4.5 present the effects of Chinese exports by sector on China's domestic value-added and employment. By getting the weighted sums of the coefficients of the value-added estimates and employment effects of all sectors, we can obtain the average effects of China's exports to the US and to the world. These estimates are reported in Table 4.6, which shows that for every US$1000 of aggregate, Chinese

*Table 4.5* Chinese domestic employment. Induced by US$1,000 of Chinese non-processing exports, 1995 (Person-Year)

| Sector | Direct employment | Total employment |
|---|---|---|
| 01 Agriculture | 1.357 | 1.800 |
| 02 Coal mining | 0.485 | 0.709 |
| 03 Crude petroleum and natural gas production | 0.098 | 0.266 |
| 04 Metal ore mining | 0.257 | 0.567 |
| 05 Other mining | 0.278 | 0.580 |
| 06 Food manufacturing | 0.066 | 0.957 |
| 07 Manufacture of textiles | 0.107 | 0.845 |
| 08 Manufacture of wearing apparel, leather and products of leather and fur | 0.108 | 0.745 |
| 09 Sawmills and manufacture of furniture | 0.160 | 0.610 |
| 10 Manufacture of paper, cultural and educational articles | 0.121 | 0.696 |
| 11 Electricity, steam and hot water production and supply | 0.073 | 0.323 |
| 12 Petroleum refineries | 0.043 | 0.298 |
| 13 Coking, manufacture of gas and coal products | 0.130 | 0.591 |
| 14 Chemical industries | 0.078 | 0.522 |
| 15 Manufacture of building materials and non-metallic mineral products | 0.161 | 0.512 |
| 16 Primary metal manufacturing | 0.103 | 0.438 |
| 17 Manufacture of metal products | 0.120 | 0.485 |
| 18 Manufacture of machinery | 0.133 | 0.439 |
| 19 Manufacture of transport equipment | 0.095 | 0.414 |
| 20 Manufacture of electric machinery and instrument | 0.092 | 0.427 |
| 21 Manufacture of electronic and communication equipment | 0.064 | 0.329 |
| 22 Manufacture of instruments and meters, etc. | 0.259 | 0.542 |
| 23 Maintenance and repair of machinery and equipment | 0.201 | 0.496 |
| 24 Industries not elsewhere classified | 0.135 | 0.643 |
| 25 Construction | 0.207 | 0.558 |
| 26 Freight transport and communication | 0.383 | 0.548 |
| 27 Commerce | 0.325 | 0.571 |
| 28 Restaurants | 0.251 | 0.932 |
| 29 Passenger transport | 0.344 | 0.506 |
| 30 Public utilities and service to households | 0.262 | 0.479 |
| 31 Culture, education, health and scientific research | 0.577 | 0.839 |
| 32 Finance and insurance | 0.258 | 0.450 |
| 33 Public administration | 0.630 | 0.898 |
| Weighted average | 0.214 | 0.703 |

export to the world will directly increase China's GDP by US$240, while the total increase in GDP would be US$545.

By comparison, US$1000 of aggregate Chinese export to the US, China's GDP would be increased by US$190 directly but by US$481 if the repercussions on the rest of the economy are included, if Chinese exports to the US are based on adjusted US import quota; the direct value-added and total value-added figures become US$207 and US$458 if Chinese exports are instead based on adjusted Chinese export data.[5]

*Table 4.6* Chinese domestic value-added and employment. Induced by US$1,000 of aggregate Chinese exports to the United States and to the world, 1995

| | Chinese exports to the United States (based on adjusted US export data) | Chinese exports to the United States (based on adjusted Chinese export data) | Chinese exports to the world |
|---|---|---|---|
| Direct value-added (US$) | 190 | 207 | 240 |
| Total value-added (US$) | 481 | 458 | 545 |
| Direct employment (person-year) | 0.074 | 0.083 | 0.130 |
| Total employment (person-year) | 0.277 | 0.271 | 0.375 |

The table shows that the direct and total impact of Chinese exports to the world on employment are 0.13 and 0.375 person-year for every US$1,000 of exports, respectively. These effects are higher than those induced by Chinese exports to the US. Using adjusted Chinese export data, the estimated direct and total employment effects are 0.083 and 0.271 per US$1,000 respectively. If we use instead the adjusted U.S. import data, then the direct and total employment effects are 0.074 and 0.277 per US$1,000 of exports. Thus, regardless of which data set we use, the employment effects are quite similar.

## Concluding remarks

Professional economists measure the gains from trade by examining the increased utilities or increased consumption possibilities of representative consumers in each country. However, trade negotiators score trade gains and losses quite differently. While these scores may not always make economic sense, they have real and significant effects. In this paper we develop a methodology and empirically implement the methodology to obtain two key measures of these perceived benefits, namely domestic value-added and employment induced by Chinese exports to the United States.

There are several methodological, conceptual and data contributions by this paper to the literature of US–Chinese trade. We construct from raw data the imported intermediate goods by sector. We break down the Chinese exports into their destination markets, each with their imported inputs, and match them up with the 33 sectors as classified in the input-output table. Given that China's trade is characterized by a high proportion of processing exports, we construct from raw data two separate input-output tables: one for processing exports production and another for non-processing export production. To obtain the effects on employment, we extend the standard input-output tables to include labour as an input, again using raw data on industry-specific employment.

By providing the first quantitative estimates of the Chinese domestic value-added and Chinese domestic employment due to Chinese exports to the world and to the United States, we hope that our empirical measures can contribute to both the academic literature of China trade and to the policy discussion on the economic relationship between China and the US.

## Acknowledgement

The authors are, respectively, Professor, Academy of Mathematics and Systems Science, Chinese Academy of Sciences; Professor, Department of Economics, Hong Kong University of Science and Technology; Professor, Department of Economics, University of California at Santa Cruz; and Vice Chancellor, Chinese University of Hong Kong and Kwoh-Ting Li Professor of Economic Development, Department of Economics, Stanford University. The authors wish to express their heartfelt thanks to Guo Ju-e, Professor of Shaanxi Institute of Finance and Economics, Li Wenhua, Associate Professor of Zhengzhou Institute of Industry, and their students, for their time-consuming work in constructing the input-output table of China for processing exports and in augmenting the input-output table of China for 1995 with the non-competitive imports rows. Without their fundamental contribution, this study cannot possibly be completed. The authors also wish to thank Dr. Xu Yiping of the Institute of Systems Science, Chinese Academy of Sciences, for his efforts in processing the trade data from China's Customs Statistics and from the Hong Kong Special Administrative Region. In addition, they also wish to thank the Census and Statistics Department, Hong Kong Special Administrative Region, for its assistance in providing information on the re-export margins in accordance with the commodity classification of the input-output table of China for 1995. Finally, the authors wish to thank the Center for Economic Development at the Hong Kong University of Science and Technology for its generous financial support. The responsibility for any errors rests entirely with the authors.

## References

Batey, P. W. J. and Melvyn J. Weeks (1987) 'An Extended Input-Output Model Incorporating Employed, Unemployed, and In-migrant Households', Papers of the Regional Science Association, 62: 93–115.
——— (1989) 'The Effects of Household Disaggregation in Extended Input-Output Models', in Ronald E. Miller, Karen R. Polenske and Adam Z. Rose, (eds), *Frontiers of Input-Output Analysis*, New York: Oxford University Press. pp. 120–33.
Batey, P. W. J., M. Madden and Melvyn J. Weeks (1987) 'Household Income and Expenditure in Extended Input-Output Models: A Comparative Theoretical and Empirical Analysis', *Journal of Regional Science*, 27: 341–56.
Blackwell, J. (1978) 'Disaggregation of the Household Sector in Regional Input-Output Analysis: Some Models Specifying Previous Residence of Workers', *Regional Studies*, 12: 367–77.
Chen, Xikang (1990) 'Input-Occupancy-Output Analysis and Its Application in China', in Manas Chattezji and Robert E. Kuenne, (eds), *Dynamics and Conflict in Regional Structural Change,* London: Macmillan Press. pp. 267–78.

────── (1999) 'Input-Occupancy-Output Analysis and Its Application in the Chinese Economy', in Shri Bhagwan Dahiya, (ed.), *The Current State of Economic Science*, Rohtak: Spellbound Publications, Pvt. Ltd. pp. 501–14.

Chen, Xikang, *et al.* (1992) *Input-Occupancy-Output Analysis of Urban and Rural Economies of China*, Beijing: Science Press.

Chen, Xikang, Leonard K. Cheng, K. C. Fung, and Laurence J. Lau (2004) 'The Estimation of Domestic Value-Added and Employment Induced by Exports: An Application to Chinese Exports to the United States', Working Paper, Stanford University, September 2004.

Customs Bureau of P. R. of China (1996) *Customs Statistical Yearbook of China for 1995*, Customs Statistics Editorial Board.

Fung, K. C. and Lawrence J. Lau (1998) 'The China-United States Bilateral Balance: How Big is It Really?', *Pacific Economic Review*, 3(1) February: 33–47.

────── (2001) 'New Estimates of the United States-China Bilateral Trade Balances', *Journal of the Japanese and International Economies*, 15: 102–30.

Fung, K. C., Lawrence J. Lau and Joseph S. Lee (2004) *U.S. Direct Investment in China*, Washington, D.C.: American Enterprise Institute, Washington, D.C. Foreword by Former U.S. Secretary of State George P. Shultz.

Fung, K. C., Lawrence J. Lau and Yanyan Xiong (2006) 'Adjusted Estimates of United States-China Bilateral Trade Balances: An Update', *Pacific Economic Review*, 11(3), October: 299–314.

He, Shiqiang, and Karen R. Polenske (1998) 'Interregional Trade, The Heckscher-Ohlin-Vanek Theorem, and Leontief's Paradox', paper presented to the 12th International Conference on Input-Output Techniques, New York City, May 18–22.

Lardy, Nicholas (1992) 'Chinese Foreign Trade', *The China Quarterly*, 131, September: 691–720.

Lau, Lawrence J., Xikang Chen, Leonard K. Cheng, K. C. Fung, Jiansuo Pei, Yun-Wing Sung, Zhipeng Tang, Yanyan Xiong, Cuihong Yang and Kunfu Zhu (2006a) 'Estimates of U. S.-China Trade Balances in Terms of Domestic Value-Added', Working Paper, No. 295, Stanford Center for International Development.

────── (2006b) 'The Estimation of Domestic Value-Added and Employment Generated by U.S.-China Trade', Working Paper, No. 2, The Institute of Economics, Chinese University of Hong Kong.

Lee, Kuhn C. (1986) 'Input-Output Multipliers with Backward, Forward, and Total Linkages', paper presented to the 8th International Conference on Input-Output Techniques, Sapporo, Japan, July 28–August 2.

Leontief, Wassily W. *et al.* (1953) *Studies in the Structure of the American Economy*, New York: Oxford University Press.

National Bureau of Statistics of the People's Republic of China, Department of National Economic Accounting (1997) *Input-Output Table of China, 1995* (in Chinese), Beijing: China Statistical Publishing House.

Richardson, Harry W. (1985) 'Input-Output and Economic Base Multipliers: Looking Backward and Forward', *Journal of Regional Science*, 25, November: 601–61.

Round, Jeffery I. (1989) 'Decomposition of input-Output and Economy-Wide Multipliers in a Regional Setting', in Ronald E. Miller, Karen R. Polenske and Adam Z. Rose (eds), *Frontiers of Input-Output Analysis*, New York: Oxford University Press. pp. 103–18.

# Part II
# Economic interactions

# 5 External shocks, transmission mechanisms and inflation in Asia

*Hans Genberg*

## Introduction

The increasing importance of China in the world economy has given rise to explanations of inflation in the industrial and emerging markets that emphasize the role of price impulses in China for the low inflation in the first several years of the twenty-first century and for the build up more recently. In the case of East Asia, an additional explanation for the low inflation subsequent to the crisis in 1997–8 has centered on the role of the crisis itself as well as on the consequences of different monetary policy choices in the post-crises period. This paper is a contribution to the analysis of these questions. Section 1 sets the stage by recalling the main features of the inflation experiences in the region and presenting some preliminary evidence on the importance of external influences. Section 2 reviews some recent cross-country evidence from the literature, which suggests that the inflation process in the region can be understood in terms of an inflation equation driven by a relatively conventional open economy Phillips curve relationship combined with an aggregate demand relationship in which external demand has an important effect. Section 3 reports the results from an empirical analysis based on estimated vector auto regression models which attempts to isolate the role of world-wide shocks as opposed to shocks originating in China for the smaller countries in the region, and which discusses differences in the responses of individual countries to external events. Section 4 summarizes and concludes.

## The evolution of inflation in East Asian countries: an overview

Like in many other parts of the world inflation has been on a declining trend in East Asia since the early 1990s. Figure 5.1 presents the average CPI inflation rates for eight individual countries in the region together with that of the United States which is included as a reference representing the rest of the world.[1] The trend towards lower inflation is quite visible. In the first half of the 1990s the inflation rate was on average 6.4 per cent, it fell to 2.6 per cent in the second half of the decade and declined further to 0.8 per cent in the last three years of the sample.[2]

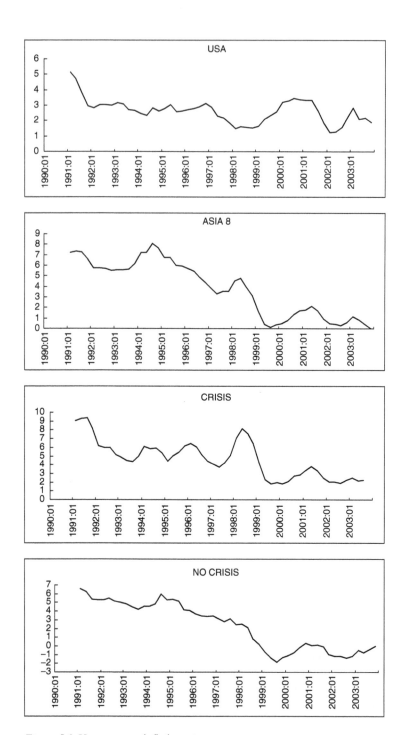

*Figure 5.1* Year-on-year inflation rates.

Two other groups are shown in the figure, a 'crisis' group consisting of countries that were most directly affected by the 1997–8 crisis, namely Korea, Malaysia, Philippines, and Thailand, and a 'no crisis' group consisting of Hong Kong, Singapore, and Taiwan.[3] The declining trend is present in both, although the inflation rates in the 'crisis' countries spiked up significantly in 1998 in response to the currency depreciations at the time, before falling in a similarly spectacular manner as the recessions took hold. In contrast, the 'no crisis' group experienced a more regular decrease in inflation during this period, consistent with their more stable exchange rates with respect to the US dollar and appreciating rates with respect to the 'crisis' countries.

The crisis episode is an example where country-specific factors had important impacts on the macroeconomic evolution in individual countries. Because of this and because it was so traumatic, it has figured importantly in explanations of the post-crisis deflation in the countries involved. But by focusing on this episode alone, one runs the risk of not seeing the woods for the trees.

This paper aims to provide a more unified explanation of the inflationary forces operating in the region and in order to do so it will attempt to isolate both common- and country-specific factors that have operated throughout the period. A working hypothesis is that the countries in our sample were influenced to a significant degree by external macroeconomic forces, because of their tendency to gear monetary policy towards stabilizing dollar exchange rates.

A first piece of evidence consistent with this hypothesis is that both prior and subsequent to the crisis, the cyclical patterns of inflation rates have been quite similar across the countries in the group. This is clearest in the 1999–2003 period which is characterized by a generalized slowdown in 1999, a recovery in 2000 and 2001, followed by another slowdown in 2002 and again a tentative turnaround in 2003. These common movements suggest that the cyclical pattern of inflation in the region may have a single underlying cause. Common reactions to the 1997–8 crisis have been mentioned in this context, as has been the evolution of inflation in China, which has followed a similar pattern as the smaller countries in the region. Although these explanations are plausible, they do not take into account the fact that the inflation rate in the US also followed a very similar pattern during the same time period. This could of course be a pure coincidence, but it could also be an indication that external factors have important impacts on the countries in the region.[4] Statistical evidence based on principal component analysis bring out quite clearly that there is a common element in the individual inflation rates even before the crisis. This analysis also shows that this element is related to the evolution of inflation in the US.

Table 5.1 contains the results obtained for two periods, one spanning the entire sample from 1991 to 2003 and the other covering the pre-crisis period until the end of 1997. In both cases the first principal component explains a substantial portion of the behaviour of inflation rates across countries. In the longer sample all countries load approximately equally on the first component, suggesting that this can be interpreted as the common element of inflation. The second principal

*Table 5.1* Principal component analysis of y-o-y inflation rates

| Sample period | 1991: –2003:2 | | 1991:1–1997:4 | |
|---|---|---|---|---|
| | $1^{st}$ principal component | $2^{nd}$ principal component | $1^{st}$ principal component | $2^{nd}$ principal component |
| Cumulative proportion of variance explained | 64% | 79% | 47% | 69% |
| | *Factor loadings* | | *Factor loadings* | |
| Mainland China | 0.28 | 0.60 | 0.00 | −0.57 |
| Hong Kong | 0.42 | 0.13 | 0.46 | −0.13 |
| Singapore | 0.32 | 0.41 | 0.38 | 0.00 |
| Taiwan | 0.38 | 0.22 | 0.33 | −0.38 |
| Korea | 0.38 | −0.27 | 0.45 | 0.23 |
| Malaysia | 0.35 | −0.34 | 0.37 | −0.13 |
| Philippines | 0.34 | −0.34 | 0.42 | 0.34 |
| Thailand | 0.34 | −0.31 | −0.02 | 0.56 |

component for the full sample appears to pick up the common response of the 'crisis' countries to the 1997–8 crisis.

The first principal component in the pre-crisis period appears to capture the common elements in all countries except mainland China and Thailand. The reason why the inflation process in mainland China is not captured is that the build-up of inflation until 1995 in this country is quite unique. The reason for Thailand's low loading on the first principal component is less obvious, but it may be a sign that the macroeconomic evolution in general in this country was out of step with the rest of the group leading up to the currency crisis in the summer of 1997.

The evidence in Table 5.1 suggests the presence of an important common factor in the inflation rates of the countries in our sample, but it does not give any hint as to what the driving forces behind this common factor might be. Table 5.2 contains preliminary results indicating that external forces, as proxied by the US inflation rate, are important. The table reports results from fitting a regression of the first principal component computed from the full sample on the US inflation rate. Whether one looks at the entire period from 1991 to 2003 or the pre-crisis period or the post-crisis period, the conclusion from these regressions is the same; the inflation rate in the US is strongly related to the common element in the inflation rates in the East Asian countries.

Finding a strong common element in the inflation rates among the countries in our sample and suggesting that this common element is related to the inflation rate in the US, does not mean that all countries react in the same way to external forces and that country-specific shocks are unimportant. Investigating further the mechanism whereby external shocks are translated into domestic inflation and identifying important domestic sources of inflation is therefore important, if we want to have a fuller understanding of the inflation process in each country. A review of recent comparative studies provides useful clues.

*Table 5.2* Determinants of the common factor in inflation rates

| Sample period | 1991:1–2003:2 | 1991:1–1997:4 | 1999:1–2003:2 |
|---|---|---|---|
| US Inflation | 0.71 | 1.31 | 1.88 |
|  | (0.26) | (0.28) | (0.38) |
|  | [0.008] | [0.0001] | [0.0003] |
| Post crisis dummy | −2.93 |  |  |
|  | (0.66) |  |  |
|  | [0.0001] |  |  |
| Constant | −0.87 | −2.30 | −4.88 |
|  | (1.13) | (0.66) | (0.62) |
|  | [0.26] | [0.002] | [0.0000] |
| Adjusted $R^2$ | 0.94 | 0.91 | 0.92 |

Note: Dependent variable: The first principal component as defined in Table 5.1, col. 2. Standard errors are reported in parentheses and p-values in square brackets. The equations are estimated taking into account the third order moving average structure of the data inherent in the use of overlapping y-o-y inflation rates. Standard errors are estimated with White's method to correct for heteroscedasticity.

## Empirical evidence from recent comparative studies

Several comparative studies of inflation in East Asia have been carried out in the last year. The most extensive is Gerlach *et al.* (2003) which reports results from a panel-structure regression analysis of inflation and output movements in ten countries in the region.[5] Disyatat (2003) studies the same set of countries using more informal empirical techniques and Kumar *et al.* (2003) investigate the particular role of mainland China in the price formation process of neighbouring countries. What follows is a summary of the major conclusions and open questions left by these studies.

Gerlach *et al.* adopt a framework based on a relatively conventional open economy Phillips curve for inflation and an IS-type relationship for the output gap.

Domestic inflation is a function of the domestic output gap, foreign inflation, the change in the effective exchange rate, and the deviation of the real exchange rate from its equilibrium level. The output gap depends on foreign demand and the real interest rate.

The results of the estimation show that foreign factors measured by inflation in trading partners and import demand from the US are important sources of inflation and output dynamics for all countries in the sample. Interest rate and exchange rate effects are also significant, indicating that domestic monetary policy could potentially have an impact. Of course, in some of the countries, the interest rate will also be heavily influenced by developments in international financial markets, so it can not be viewed as a purely domestic factor.[6]

As already noted, Gerlach *et al.* estimate their model in a panel set-up which means that slope coefficients are assumed to be equal across countries. Although this assumption can not be rejected for many of the variables, the authors report evidence showing that the responses to changes in nominal effective exchange rate vary across countries. This implies that responses to external shocks may be different across countries as suggested by the discussion in the previous section.

Although the study by Disyatat, op. cit., is a mainly descriptive, it raises a number of issues dealing with the transmission mechanism of deflationary impulses. Like Gerlach *et al.* the author argues that output gaps have been important explanations of inflation rates in the region and argues that these have been principally of domestic origin until the latest slowdown in 2000–2001.[7] Exchange rate developments are also emphasized and it is suggested that the countries which have pursued a fixed US dollar exchange rate regime were particularly affected by the strength of the dollar during the late 1990s and early 2000. More generally the author argues that it is important to recognize differences in monetary policy in order to fully understand the differences in inflation performance across countries.

Kumar *et al.* consider the particular role of China in the deflation process in the neighbouring countries. They point to a sharp increase in inter-regional trade as a possible conduit of stronger inflation links between the countries, and report results from estimates of a vector autoregressive model showing that prices in Taiwan and Hong Kong are particularly sensitive to inflation developments in the Mainland. Singapore is influenced as well but to a smaller extent, whereas Malaysia and Thailand do not seem to be affected at all.

All three papers suggest that asset price developments combined with balance sheet effects and credit crunches has had an important role to play in the inflation process in the region immediately following the 1997–8 crisis. While this seems a priori reasonable, the empirical evidence of these effects is limited. To be sure, asset prices did decline in many of the economies in the region during the crisis, and credit contracted. These factors may therefore have played a certain role in the transmission of shocks. To what extent they constituted independent shocks themselves or were endogenous to the deflation process is more controversial however.

The evidence in these studies point to several elements that must be considered in an analytic framework used to describe the price formation process in the countries in the region. Fluctuation in demand as measured by output gap or unemployment is an important element of the transmission. External sources of demand shifts are significant in addition to competitiveness effects transmitted through real exchange rate movements. Exchange rate changes and foreign price movements also appear to have an impact on inflation over and above the effects that impinge on demand. A possible channel may be changes in the cost of imported intermediate goods.[8] Finally it is important to keep in mind that the chosen monetary policy strategy may play an important role in insulating some countries from external deflationary impulses, while it strengthens the effects of these impulses in other countries. In the next section I will use an empirical framework that enables me to measure the importance of external relative to internal shocks for the dynamics of inflation and output in our group of countries.

## Some evidence on the nature, importance, and consequences of external shocks

### *The methodology*

The empirical methodology is motivated by the models reviewed in the previous section. The structure of these models is illustrated schematically in Figure 5.2. Inflation and output movements in any of the smaller countries in the region are influenced by three sets of factors. First there is what might be called 'world' factors, i.e. demand, price, and interest rate developments in world markets generally. These have a direct influence on output and inflation though trade and price transmission channels. They also have indirect influences through their impact on domestic interest rates, the exchange rate, asset prices etc. as well as on macroeconomic developments in mainland China which in turn exerts significant influence on the smaller economies (cf. the evidence in Kumar *et al.* 2003).

Economic development in mainland China can be a second source of macroeconomic shocks for the smaller economies in the region.[9] As already noted, this economy is influenced by, but is assumed not to influence, the rest of the world.

Finally there are domestic factors that influence and are influenced by inflation and output developments. These variables are also determined in part by external developments, both in mainland China and in the rest of the world, but because of the small size of the economies we are modelling, they are unlikely to have any impact in return.

To investigate the importance of differences in structure and economic policy one should ideally estimate structural models for each of the economies and simulate them jointly in the spirit of the work in, for example, Bryant *et al.* (1993). This is beyond the scope of the present undertaking.

The approach followed here is instead to conduct the analysis in a vector autoregression (VAR) framework which explicitly takes into account the recursive nature of the interactions illustrated in Figure 5.2. The reduced form nature of VAR models will of course limit the questions to which the analysis can provide answers, but it is hoped that the results will nevertheless provide novel and useful insights.

Consider each of the following seven small economies separately: Hong Kong, Korea, Malaysia, Philippines, Singapore, Taiwan, and Thailand. Fluctuations in inflation and growth in each country are assumed to be determined by external shocks coming from China and the rest of the world in addition to domestic shocks of various kinds. Fluctuations in the Chinese economy are assumed to depend on developments in the rest of the world but not significantly on those in the small neighbours. Finally, macroeconomic fluctuations in the rest of the world are determined independently of both the Chinese and the small economies we are interested in. The recursive nature of the interactions in the model permits drawing certain structural inferences from the estimated VAR. To be specific, let $y^i$, $y^C$, and $y^U$, represent relevant macroeconomic variables in country i, China, and the US (representing the rest of the world) respectively. Interactions among them can

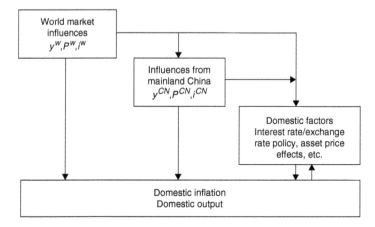

*Figure 5.2* Schematic illustration of the structure of macroeconomic influences on small East-Asian economies.

be described by the following general structural model.

$$\begin{pmatrix} A_0^{ii} & A_0^{iC} & A_0^{iU} \\ 0 & A_0^{CC} & A_0^{CU} \\ 0 & 0 & A_0^{UU} \end{pmatrix} \begin{pmatrix} y_t^i \\ y_t^C \\ y_t^U \end{pmatrix} = \begin{pmatrix} A^{ii}(L) & A^{iC}(L) & A^{iU}(L) \\ 0 & A^{CC}(L) & A^{CU}(L) \\ 0 & 0 & A^{UU}(L) \end{pmatrix} \begin{pmatrix} y_{t-1}^i \\ y_{t-1}^C \\ y_{t-1}^U \end{pmatrix} + \begin{pmatrix} u_t^i \\ u_t^C \\ u_t^U \end{pmatrix}$$

$$(5.1)$$

$A_0$ and $A(L)$ represent structural coefficients and the error vector contains structural shocks to the equations in each of the regions. The triangular form of the matrices that pre-multiply the vectors of endogenous variables reflects the assumed recursive nature of the interactions between them. This also ensures that the VAR representation of the system is triangular as in (5.2). Furthermore, the VAR residuals will be such that the elements of $\varepsilon^U$ will be linear combinations of the elements of $u^U$ only, that $\varepsilon^C$ will be linear combinations of $u^U$ and $u^C$, but not of $u^i$ and that $\varepsilon^i$ will be linear combination of all structural shocks.[10]

$$\begin{pmatrix} y_t^i \\ y_t^C \\ y_t^U \end{pmatrix} = \begin{pmatrix} D^{ii}(L) & D^{iC}(L) & D^{iU}(L) \\ 0 & D^{CC}(L) & D^{CU}(L) \\ 0 & 0 & D^{UU}(L) \end{pmatrix} \begin{pmatrix} y_{t-1}^i \\ y_{t-1}^C \\ y_{t-1}^U \end{pmatrix} + \begin{pmatrix} \varepsilon_t^i \\ \varepsilon_t^C \\ \varepsilon_t^U \end{pmatrix}$$

$$(5.2)$$

In the principal empirical implementation $y^i$ contains two elements, CPI inflation and growth of real GDP, $y^C$ consists only of the rate of CPI inflation in China, and $y^U$ contains three variables, the US Federal Funds rate, the CPI inflation rate in the US, and the growth of real GDP in the US.[11] I will make no attempt to identify separately the structural shocks that correspond to each of these variables.

The results I report below only rely on identifying the US shocks as a group, the Chinese shock, and the shocks to the country being analyzed as a group.[12] To achieve this identification I can rely on the standard Cholesky factorization of the covariance matrix of the VAR residuals.

Before we proceed, two types of complications have to be dealt with: the implications of expectations variables in the structural equations, and the effects of leaving out (in the empirical implementation) some relevant variables.[13] It turns out that neither of these will change the basic structure of the VAR representation at least as far as our use of it is concerned. If expectations of future values of the elements in $(y_t^i, y_t^C, y_t^U)'$ belong in the structural model, then we can eliminate them by invoking an expectations generating mechanism where the expectations of future values are replaced by projections of current and past information. This means that expectations of future $y_t^i$ will be functions of current and past values of $y_t^i$, $y_t^C$ and $y_t^U$, that expectations of future values of $y_t^C$ will be functions of $y_t^C$ and $y_t^U$, and that expectations of future values of $y_t^U$ will be functions of current and past values of $y_t^U$. Hence, the triangular structure of the VAR representation in equation (5.2) will remain the same.

A similar argument can be made with respect to omitted variables. Suppose a domestic variable that is important for the propagation mechanism of the shocks is left out of the empirical model. In this case it is effectively included in the structural error term. In a larger model including the additional variable would still have the triangular form of both (5.1) and (5.2). Eliminating the additional variable from the system by direct substitution would lead to a model in which the first element of the 'structural' error in (5.1) would now contain the structural errors in both of the lower blocks of the system. The structural errors in these lower blocks would remain the same, however. A consequence of this would be that our method of identification of the elements of $(y_t^i, y_t^C, y_t^U)'$ will lead to an overestimate of the important of domestic shocks in the system.

If some element of $y_t^U$ has been left out of the model, a similar argument implies that the structural errors in the $y_t^U$ equations will be a linear function of the true errors in these equations and the error in the left-out equation. But the triangular structure of VAR would be preserved, including the property that VAR errors of the higher-ordered variables will be a linear combination of both their own and lower-ordered shocks whereas the VAR errors corresponding to the lowest-ordered variables, $y_t^U$, will be functions only of their own shocks.

### The data

Quarterly data on all variables were generously provided by Stefan Gerlach, and they are thus a subset of those used in Gerlach *et al.* (2003). The consumer price and real GDP series were seasonally adjusted in Eviews using the X-12 option. Quarterly growth rates were calculated as 1st differences of the natural logarithm of the corresponding levels. The sample period is 1990:1 to 2002:4.

Estimation and calculations of variance decompositions and historical decompositions were carried out in RATS 6.0.

*Table 5.3* Countries and variables used in the VAR analysis

| Symbol | Country | Variables included |
|--------|---------|--------------------|
| $y^i$ | i = {Hong Kong, Korea, Malaysia, Philippines, Singapore, Taiwan, Thailand} | – CPI inflation<br>– Real GDP growth<br>– Money market interest rate |
| $y^C$ | China | – CPI inflation<br>– Real GDP growth<br>– CPI inflation |
| $y^C$ | United States | – Real GDP growth<br>– Federal Funds Rate |

### The results

The discussion will focus on the decomposition of forecast error variances to answer the question what proportions of the forecast error variances of inflation and growth in country i can be ascribed to shocks in the US, in China, and in the local economy. This will reveal whether there are differences among the countries in the degree of dependence on external shocks and to gauge the relative importance of China and the USA as the source of these shocks.

By definition forecast errors are the consequences of shocks occurring between the time of the forecast and the realization of the outcome. The variance of the forecast errors can thus be attributed to the variance of the underlying shocks and provided the shocks are uncorrelated with each other, it is possible to decompose the total variance into the contribution of each of the shocks. As explained above, the restrictions imposed on the VAR permits a decomposition according to the country of origin of the shocks but not to the market origin. Table 5.4 presents the results obtained for forecast horizons of 8 and 16 quarters for the inflation rates and the real growth rates.[14]

Several aspects of the results are noteworthy. First, foreign shocks are generally very important for these countries. For the two countries with arguably the most stable exchange rate vis-à-vis the US dollar, Hong Kong and Malaysia, over seventy per cent of the forecast error variance (FEV) of inflation at a horizon of sixteen quarter is explained by external shocks. For the other countries, the proportion accounted for by external shocks is close to or exceeds one half. This means that even if conventional models of inflation – i.e. models in which the output gap, the real interest rate, and the real exchange rate are the proximate determinants – are applicable to the economies in our sample, it is important to realize that the driving variables in these models are themselves heavily influenced by external forces.

In view of the small size of the economies, their substantial openness to trade, and their proclivity to conduct monetary with a view towards stabilizing the nominal exchange rate, it is not surprising that external sources of shocks should be so important. It is perhaps more surprising that only a relatively small part of the external effects can be associated with shocks originating in China. Shocks to the

*Table 5.4* Decomposition of the forecast error variance[a]

|  |  |  | Inflation | of which due to mainland China | Real growth | of which due to mainland China |
|---|---|---|---|---|---|---|
| 4 LAGS | 8 Quarters | Singapore | 67.57 | 3.14 | 50.07 | 13.44 |
|  |  | Malaysia | 66.95 | 15.19 | 65.89 | 3.74 |
|  |  | Hong Kong | 54.17 | 8.19 | 54.52 | 4.56 |
|  |  | Taiwan | 42.85 | 24.28 | 54.3 | 11.98 |
|  |  | Korea | 42.34 | 6.82 | 46.55 | 1.63 |
|  |  | Philippines | 41.93 | 8.5 | 35.78 | 7.4 |
|  |  | Thailand | 32.13 | 3.24 | 56.22 | 10.13 |
|  | 16 Quarters | Hong Kong | 77.64 | 10.39 | 56.46 | 4.87 |
|  |  | Malaysia | 70.98 | 19.96 | 67.49 | 4.09 |
|  |  | Singapore | 69.97 | 2.91 | 51.34 | 12.84 |
|  |  | Taiwan | 50.85 | 23.73 | 60.16 | 12.56 |
|  |  | Philippines | 50.08 | 8.27 | 39.14 | 6.99 |
|  |  | Korea | 47.05 | 6.29 | 49.47 | 1.77 |
|  |  | Thailand | 45.74 | 7.26 | 58.61 | 9.99 |

Note: [a] Baseline model with three US variables (CPI inflation, Real GDP growth, Federal Funds Rate), one Mainland China variable (CPI inflation), and two local variables (CPI inflation and real GDP growth). The equations contained 4 lags of each of the variables as well as a constant term.

US variables generally account for the largest part of the external effects, even if in Hong Kong, Malaysia, and Taiwan the proportion of the FEV accounted for by mainland China is significant.[15] It should be kept in mind that these results are based on relationships estimated for the entire period from 1990 to 2003. It is likely that China has become more important over time in the region as trade and financial linkages have grown. To capture such effects one would have to rely on econometric techniques that allow for time-varying coefficients, a potentially fruitful area of future research.

It bears emphasizing that even if mainland China is not an important source of shocks, it is quite possible that it constitutes an important mechanism of transmission of shocks coming from elsewhere. In fact, given the fixed exchange rate between the RMB and the USD for much of the sample, one would expect the Chinese economy to be influenced importantly by developments in the United States, and in view of China's strong trade links to the other countries in the region, the shocks originating elsewhere would affect them as well. If this result holds up to further scrutiny, it implies that it is misleading to look at relationships between China and the other countries in the region without controlling for the influence of the United States.

The third striking result in Table 5.4 is the differences between Hong Kong, Malaysia, and Singapore on the one hand and Korea, Philippines, Taiwan, and Thailand on the other with respect to the importance of external influences for the forecast error variance of CPI inflation. At the 16 quarter horizon the share accounted for by external shocks is about 70 per cent for the former group of countries whereas it is 'only' around 50 per cent for the latter. My interpretation of this difference is that it reflects a greater independence of monetary/exchange-rate policy in Korea, Philippines, Taiwan, and Thailand than in the other countries.[16]

Finally it is interesting to note that there is much less difference between the countries with respect to the decomposition of the forecast error variance of the real growth rates. If my interpretation is correct, this means that monetary independence can provide some control of domestic price developments but that this is less the case for output fluctuations.

### *Extensions*

The VAR analysis has uncovered interesting similarities and differences across the countries in the sample, and I have suggested that these may be related to differences in monetary/exchange rate policies they have adopted. It is not possible to test this suggestion formally within the system of equations that I have estimated, however. One way to do so would be to estimate policy reaction functions together with equations for inflation and output growth, and to simulate the counterfactual situation where all countries are assumed to react in the same way to the external shocks. This approach would require a higher-dimension VAR as well as the imposition of additional restrictions to identify the structural policy reaction equation.

Extending the dimension of the VAR system quickly leads to problems of degrees of freedom. To deal with this it may be interesting to adopt a Bayesian procedure as implemented by Sims and Zha (1998) which involves combining prior assumptions about the structure of the interactions with information in the data. If the same prior is used for all countries, this approach could be useful in highlighting differences between them that really stand out in the data.

Another approach to dealing with the problem of degrees of freedom would be to estimate a panel VAR system in which differences among countries are introduced by having separate monetary policy reaction functions for each one. The panel structure may also allow the estimation to be carried out on a shorter sample which would make coefficient instability due to structural changes less of an issue.

Finally it would be interesting to explore to what extent periods of deflation (i.e. negative inflation rates) generate different dynamic behaviour of the endogenous variables than periods of inflation. To do so would however require different estimation methods, for example a threshold VAR approach.

## Summary and conclusions

Countries in East Asia have experienced a significant and persistent reduction in inflation in the past fifteen years. This paper has investigated (i) the role of world-wide factors in the determinants of inflation rates in the region, (ii) whether China has had a particularly important role to play, and (iii) why the inflation experiences have different between countries.

Empirical analysis of these issues has been carried using vector autoregression models for seven small economies: Hong Kong, Malaysia, Korea, Philippines, Singapore, Taiwan, and Thailand. The models have a semi-structural interpretation due to its recursive structure of interactions between the United States, China and the small economies in the region. While some of the results are expected, for example that external shocks are very important for inflation and GDP growth in these small countries, others are less in line with conventional views. Shocks originating in China do not appear to be as important as might be gleaned from the literature. Instead developments in the world economy in general, represented in the empirical analysis by the United States, are by far more important sources of external shocks. This does not rule out China as an important conduit of such shocks to the other countries. In fact, this is what one would expect given the fixed exchange rate policy of China.

The results also point to interesting differences in the responses of individual countries to the same external shocks. It is argued that some of these differences can be ascribed to differences in monetary/exchange rate policies, but the evidence is more circumstantial than based on estimated policy reactions. It is suggested that extensions of the empirical framework may be able to uncover direct evidence for differences among countries.

## Acknowledgement

The author is Executive Director (Research) at the Hong Kong Monetary Authority on leave from the Graduate Institute of International Studies in Geneva Switzerland where he is Professor of International Economics. The first version of this paper prepared for the Third BIS Annual Conference, Understanding Low Inflation and Deflation, Brunnen, Switzerland, 18–19 June 2004.

## References

Ahearne, A., J. Gagnon, J. Haltimaier, S. Kamin *et al.* (2002) 'Preventing deflation: lessons from Japan's experience in the 1990s', Federal Reserve Board International Finance Discussion Papers, No. 729, June.

Borio, Claudio and Andrew J Filardo (2004) 'Back to the future? Assessing the deflation record', BIS Working Papers, No. 152. Basel, BIS, March.

Bryant, Ralph C., Peter Hooper and Catherine L. Mann (1993) *Evaluating Policy Regimes, New Research in Empirical Macroeconomics*, Washington, D.C.: The Brookings Institution Press.

Cushman, David O. and Tao Zha (1997) 'Identifying Monetary Policy in a Small Open Economy under Flexible Exchange Rates', *Journal of Monetary Economics*, 39: 45–65.

Disyatat, Piti (2003) 'Asia in a Low Inflation Environment: Facts, Origins, and Implications for Policy', Bank of Thailand Discussion Paper DP/03/2003, March.

Fung B., G. Ma and R. McCauley (2003) 'Deflation and its challenges to monetary policy in Asia', unpublished BIS working paper.

Genberg, Hans (2003) 'Foreign versus domestic factors as sources of macroeconomic fluctuations in Hong Kong', Hong Kong Institute for Monetary Research, Working Paper, No. 17.

Genberg, Hans and Laurent Pauwels (2004) 'Wage-Price Dynamics and Deflation in Hong Kong', *Pacific Economic Review*, forthcoming.

Genberg, Hans, Michael K. Salemi, and Alexander K. Swoboda (1987) 'Foreign and Domestic Disturbances as Sources of Aggregate Economic Fluctuations: Switzerland 1964–1981', *Journal of Monetary Economics*, 19: 45–67.

Gerlach, Stefan, Raphael Lam, and Wenshen Peng (2003) 'Disinflation and Deflation in Asia: A Panel Data Study', mimeo, November 28.

Gerlach-Kristen, Petra (2004) 'Internal and external shocks in Hong Kong: Empirical evidence and policy options', mimeo, University of Hong Kong.

Hoffmaister, Alexander and Jorge Roldós (1997) 'Are Business Cycles Different in Asia and Latin America?' Working Paper WP/97/9, International Monetary Fund.

Ito, Takatoshi and Tomoko Hayashi (2004) 'Inflation Targeting in Asia', vKIMR Occasional Paper, No. 1. Hong Kong: HKIMR.

Kumar, Manmohan S., Taimur Baig, Jörg Decressin, Chris Faulkner-MacDonagh, and Tarhan Feyzioglu (2003) 'Deflation: Determinants, Risks, and Policy Options', IMF Occasional Paper 221. Washington, D.C.: International Monetary Fund, June.

Schellekens, Philip (2003) 'Deflation in Hong Kong SAR', IMF Working Paper WP/03/77. Washington, D.C.: International Monetary Fund.

Sims, Christopher A. and Tao Zha (1998) 'Bayesian Methods for Dynamic Multivariate Models', *International Economic Review*, 39(4), Symposium on Forecasting and Empirical Methods in Macroeconomics and Finance: 949–968.

# 6    External balances in five Asian countries

*Jaewoo Lee*

## Introduction

Following the Asian crisis, the current account balances for many Asian countries turned from deficit to surplus. For example, Korea and Thailand, which used to run current account deficits in most years over the 1980–1996 period, have run current account surpluses in all post-crisis years. The surplus continued into 2005 in most countries, and moreover, at a relatively high level in some countries, including China. The continued surplus in these countries led some to suspect persistent exchange rate undervaluation as a means of stimulating exports while suppressing imports. Combined with the rapid accumulation of international reserves in the region since 2000, this suspicion gained force (see Aizenman and Lee (2005) for a summary of the debate on new mercantilism).

Common assertions notwithstanding, the nexus between the exchange rate and the current account has not been established firmly in international economics. Earlier efforts to establish a robust correlation produced mixed results (Rose 1991). From a macroeconomic perspective, both the current account and exchange rate are endogenous variables that are influenced by a myriad of shocks, and there is no a priori reason to expect the two variables to exhibit a stable unconditional correlation. In the literature, the elasticities of the current account (or trade balance) to the exchange rate that are estimated from macroeconomic data are much smaller than those estimated from disaggregated data (Bergin 2006).

The difficulty of affirming a strong empirical relationship between the exchange rate and current account (or the trade balance part of it) has sometimes cast doubt on the role of the exchange rate in international adjustment, christened as 'elasticity pessimism' (Obstfeld 2004). One version of the elasticity pessimism, related to the pricing-to-market behaviour, has made its way to the current debate on the pros and cons of the flexible exchange rate regime (see Duarte and Obstfeld 2004; Engel and Devereux 2006, for example).

It is thus not clear how much of the ongoing current account surplus in Asia is an indication of the undervalued exchange rate. To understand the role of the exchange rate in the evolution of current account surpluses in recent years, this paper takes a semi-structural approach that was applied by Lee and Chinn (2006) to advanced economies. In particular, decomposing the shocks that hit the current account and the exchange rate depending on whether they have permanent effects on the exchange rate or not, Chinn and Lee (2005) estimated the role of the exchange rate in current account developments in G3 economies (namely the United States, Japan, and the Euro area). This paper applies the same methodology to five 'emerging-market' countries in Asia, in an attempt to uncover the role of the exchange rate undervaluation in their current account surpluses of recent years.

The estimates suggest that the exchange rate depreciation – which is consistent with undervaluation – accounts for part, but not all, of the current account surplus in recent years. The relative importance of exchange rate depreciation in driving current account surplus has changed over time. In many countries, the exchange rate depreciation indeed appears to have been an important part of the surge in current account surplus following the Asian crisis. By the middle of the current decade, however, only a small part of the remaining current account surplus appears to be associated with a depreciated exchange rate.

The rest of the paper is organized as follows. Section 2 examines the time series properties of the current account in a univariate context, concentrating on the stationary aspect of the current account. The results indicate that the recent current account surplus may indeed exceed the level consistent with the intertemporal budget constraint. Section 3 considers the current account and exchange rate jointly, using the bivariate structural VAR. We estimate how much of the recent current account surplus is driven by shocks that, in turn, are associated with a depreciated exchange rate. Section 4 concludes.

## Univariate Approach

What is the appropriate level of current account? The answer varies with the circumstances of each country, but there is no reason why the zero balance should be the answer. Viewing the current account balance as the difference between savings and investment, it is desirable that countries do not keep their savings and investment identical. It is economically efficient for countries with a greater capacity for savings to provide funds to countries with a greater need for investment. Countries that provide funds out of their larger savings will run current account surplus, and countries that receive funds for their investment will run current account deficit. Both surplus and deficit in current accounts can be an efficient outcome, and improve the global allocation of resources.

The concern, however, lies with the possibility that current account imbalance implies a systematic misallocation of resources. In particular, concerns arise that the basic budget constraint is being violated. Trehan and Walsh (1991) and Taylor (2001) showed that the stationarity of the current account offers one test for whether the current account satisfies the intertemporal budget constraint.

We can write the intertemporal budget constraint for current account as follows.

$$b_t = \rho b_{t-1} + nx_t, \qquad (6.1)$$

where $b$ denotes net external assets, $nx$ denotes the trade balance and $\rho$ denotes the growth adjusted rate of return – the rate of return minus growth rate and assumed to be constant for brevity. Iterating the budget constraint forward:

$$b_{t-1} = -\sum_{j=0}^{\infty} \rho^{-(j+1)} E_{t-1}(nx_{t+j}) + \lim_{j\to\infty} \rho^{-(j+1)} E_{t-1}(b_{t+j}). \tag{6.2}$$

The long-run budget constraint requires that the last term equal zero:

$$\lim_{j\to\infty} \rho^{-(j+1)} E_{t-1}(b_{t+j}) = 0. \tag{6.3}$$

According to Trehan and Walsh (1991), a sufficient condition for this restriction to hold is that the ratio of the current account to GDP is stationary.

Such has also been the implication of the intertemporal view of the current account (Sheffrin and Woo 1990). Combining the intertemporal budget constraint and the consumption decision of a forward-looking consumer, they show that the current account can be represented as the discounted present value of net output.

$$ca_t = -\sum_{s=1}^{\infty} \left(\frac{1}{1+r}\right)^i E_t(\Delta NO_{t+s}), \tag{6.4}$$

where *NO* refers to net output (output minus investment and government spending). This equation implies that a country will run current account surplus when it expects its future income to decline. In addition, since the growth in net output is stationary, the current account itself – the present value of net output growth – is predicted to be stationary.

Testing for the stationarity of the current account to GDP ratio, the panel-based test easily rejects the null hypothesis of unit root in current accounts. However, unit root tests applied to each country show that current accounts, though stationary, are highly persistent series. The KPSS tests of the null hypothesis that the current account is stationary is not rejected at 1 per cent level, but rejected at 5 per cent level for China, Indonesia, and Korea (upper panel of Table 6.1).

One possibility is a structural shift in these countries. Probably by more than coincidence, China and Korea have both accumulated very high levels of international reserves since the late 1990s, largely through current account surplus. While some viewed such accumulation of reserves as prima facie evidence for mercantilist intervention, Aizenman and Lee (2005) viewed that they were more likely to have been driven by the heightened precautionary demand following the Asian crisis. The current account surplus of recent years, during the phase of rapid accumulation in reserves, may then be viewed as a transitory aberration. Failing to account for the unusual nature of current account imbalances in recent years, unit root tests will find the current account balance to be less stationary than otherwise.

Such interpretation finds support in the results of unit root tests conducted for a shorter sample, covering the period prior to the crisis. The lower panel of Table 6.1 reports the results of KPSS tests for the five countries for the sample ending in 1997. The null of stationary current account can be rejected at 10 per cent significance

*Table 6.1* Testing for stationarity of current account balances

| KPSS Unit Root Test | | |
|---|---|---|
| Over the whole sample<br>Null Hypothesis: CA to GDP ratio is stationary<br>Exogenous :Constant<br>Bandwidth:2(Fixed using Bartlett kernel) | | |
| | | LM-Stat. |
| Kwiatkowski-Phillips-Schmidt-Shin test statistic | | |
| China | | 0.561 |
| India | | 0.177 |
| Indonesia | | 0.480 |
| Korea | | 0.710 |
| Thailand | | 0.411 |
| Asymptotic critical values[a]: | 1% level | 0.739 |
| | 5% level | 0.463 |
| | 10% level | 0.347 |
| Over the subsample (until 1997) | | |
| Kwiatkowski-Phillips-Schmidt-Shin test statistic | | |
| China | | 0.177 |
| India | | 0.387 |
| Indonesia | | 0.086 |
| Korea | | 0.439 |
| Thailand | | 0.269 |
| Asymptotic critical values*: | 1% level | 0.739 |
| | 5% level | 0.463 |
| | 10% level | 0.347 |

Note: [a]Kwiatkowski-Phillips-Schmidt-Shin (1992, Table 1).

level for Korea, and cannot be rejected for the other four countries. The contrast between the upper and lower panels of Table 6.1 suggests that the current account surpluses in recent years – since 2000 – may indeed have exceeded the level consistent with the intertemporal budget constraint.

Hence, statistical evidence suggests that the current account series of five Asian countries are stationary and thus that a large part of the recent current account imbalance will dissipate over time. This, however, leaves two questions open: To what level will the current account balances of these countries revert? Would they revert to zero balance, surplus, or deficit? Next, as they return to a stationary level, what exchange rate adjustment will accompany them? Would the decline in the current account surplus involve a large exchange rate depreciation? We now turn to a bivariate approach that analyzes jointly the current account and the real exchange rate to answer these questions.

## Bivariate approach

To explore the role of the exchange rate in the recent developments in the current account, we decompose the source of current account developments according to their long-term effect on the real exchange rate. Numerous shocks buffet the current account and the exchange rate and their effects cannot be easily signed or quantified. Rather than trying to control for shocks of all possible varieties – an attempt likely to be unattainable given the data limitation –we group different shocks by a criterion that relates to the persistence of their effects on the exchange rate.

Some shocks will have permanent (long-term) effects on the exchange rate, while others have only transitory effects. The stationarity of current account implies that neither shock has a permanent effect on the current account, and that their current account effects will wear out over time. (The speed with which they wear out will differ across countries). In the process of unwinding their effects on the current account, shocks that have permanent effects on the real exchange rate will involve no further exchange rate adjustment. In contrast, shocks that have only transitory effects on the real exchange rate will reverse their impact effects as their effects on the current account wear out.

Shocks can be divided into two such groups by adopting the econometric identification scheme of Blanchard and Quah (1989). Two fundamental shocks are distinguished by their long-run effects on the real exchange rate. One type of shocks has a permanent effect on the real exchange rate, while the other has only a transitory effect. Consider the following bivariate VAR, estimated for the current account ($ca_t$) and the first-differenced real exchange rate ($\Delta q_t$).

$$\begin{bmatrix} ca_t \\ \Delta q_t \end{bmatrix} = B(L) \begin{bmatrix} ca_t \\ \Delta q_t \end{bmatrix} + \begin{bmatrix} \eta_t^{ca} \\ \eta_t^{q} \end{bmatrix} = B(L) \begin{bmatrix} ca_t \\ \Delta q_t \end{bmatrix} + B(0) \begin{bmatrix} \varepsilon_t^{T} \\ \varepsilon_t^{P} \end{bmatrix} \tag{6.5}$$

where country-specific transitory shocks are denoted as $\varepsilon_t^{T}$, and permanent shocks as $\varepsilon_t^{P}$. When $\varepsilon_t$ denotes the vector of these transitory and permanent shocks, the following standard assumptions are made: $E(\varepsilon_t) = 0$, $E(\varepsilon_t \varepsilon_t') = I$, and $E(\varepsilon_t \varepsilon_s') = 0$ when $t \neq s$.

We can obtain MA representation of this dynamic system, and the long-run responses of the exchange rate to each shock. The identification assumption that temporary shocks have no long-run effect on the real exchange rate translates into the condition that the matrix of long-run responses, $(1 - B(1))^{-1} B(0)$, is lower triangular. Combined with an additional sign restriction to ensure that the covariance matrix is positive semi-definite, the matrix $B(0)$ can be uniquely determined and the structural shocks can be uncovered.

If we were to identify the system by Choleski factorization that assumes a lower triangular matrix for $B(0)$, the real exchange rate innovation is assumed to have no contemporaneous effect on the current account. It is very difficult, however, to find a theoretical model that is consistent with zero restrictions on the contemporaneous correlation between the exchange rate and the current account.

In contrast, the Blanchard and Quah approach enables us to identify the system on the basis of a criterion that is consistent with a wide spectrum of intertemporal open macro models. Transitory shocks are defined as those shocks that have no long-run effect on the exchange rate. On the downside, transitory and permanent shocks identified here cannot necessarily be interpreted as shocks to the exchange rate and current account, because estimated innovations to the exchange rate and current account ($\eta_t$) are linear combinations of transitory and permanent shocks.[1] As the result, our own discussion of the decomposition results will not be able to associate the estimated shocks with easily observable counterparts, and instead provide suggestive evidence on the identity of corresponding shocks.

Before we turn to the data, a caveat is in order. Faust and Leeper (1997) have noted that the bivariate VAR based on long-run identification restrictions can be subject to aggregation bias and large standard errors. This caveat applies no less strongly to our sample countries which have gone through rapid structural changes during the sample period, including China in particular. Indeed, some of the results remind us of this caveat and call for caution in interpreting the econometric results.

### Data and estimation results

The current account and real exchange rate data are obtained from the *International Financial Statistics* at annual frequency.[2] For all five countries, the real effective exchange rates (based on consumer price index) and current accounts from 1981 to 2005 were used for estimation. The current account is measured by the ratio of its dollar value to the dollar-denominated nominal GDP. The real exchange rate is the first-differenced log of the real effective exchange rate index based on consumer price index and is defined in such a way that a numerical increase represents an appreciation in the effective exchange rate.

The VAR system was estimated with two lags, allowing sufficiently long lags considering the large persistence in the current account process of these countries. Estimation results are reported in Table 6.2. The current account equation is estimated with high values of $R^2$ and F-statistic. In the real exchange rate equation, no variable carries as strong statistical significance as in the current account equation, and the overall fit is also weaker, with the $R^2$ being less than that of the current account equation (except Korea).

Figure 6.1 shows two exemplary impulse-responses that are obtained for China and India. The overall pattern for all five countries first can be summarized as follows. With the exception of China, two different types of shocks, with transitory versus permanent effects on the real exchange rate, are found to bring about opposite correlations between the real exchange rate and current account. A real depreciation caused by transitory shocks is found to be accompanied by an improvement in the current account, consistent with the usually suspected effect of the exchange rate on the current account, whereas permanent shocks improve the current account and real exchange rate simultaneously.

The effects of permanent shocks are similar for all five countries and the earlier results for G7 countries by Lee and Chinn (2006). Permanent shocks are found to bring about real appreciation and an improvement in the current account. A prime candidate for this shock is the shock to preference between home and foreign goods. A permanent shift in preference in favour of home goods would improve home country's terms of trade and the real exchange rate permanently, accompanied

Table 6.2 VAR estimation results

| | China | | India | | Korea | | Indonesia | | Thailand | |
|---|---|---|---|---|---|---|---|---|---|---|
| | CA2Y | DRE | CA2Y | DRE | CA2Y | DRE | CA2Y | DRE | CA2Y | DRE |
| CA2Y(−1) | 0.610 | 0.499 | 1.136 | 1.751 | 0.398 | 2.028 | 0.968 | 1.729 | 0.853 | 0.098 |
| | (0.277) | (1.435) | (0.275) | (2.006) | (0.340) | (0.711) | (0.233) | (1.953) | (0.277) | (0.277) |
| CA2Y(−2) | −0.179 | −0.492 | −0.624 | 0.989 | −0.039 | −0.545 | −0.254 | 1.055 | −0.093 | 0.015 |
| | (0.268) | (1.391) | (0.289) | (2.109) | (0.374) | (0.783) | (0.254) | (2.130) | (0.249) | (0.355) |
| DRE(−1) | 0.056 | 0.350 | −0.020 | 0.385 | −0.126 | 0.404 | −0.012 | −0.355 | −0.269 | 0.314 |
| | (0.046) | (0.238) | (0.033) | (0.244) | (0.153) | (0.320) | (0.030) | (0.251) | (0.195) | (0.279) |
| DRE(−2) | 0.021 | 0.145 | 0.039 | −0.123 | −0.068 | −0.026 | −0.012 | −0.196 | 0.251 | −0.074 |
| | (0.049) | (0.256) | (0.031) | (0.228) | (0.089) | (0.186) | (0.026) | (0.220) | (0.169) | (0.242) |
| C | 0.012 | −0.021 | −0.006 | 0.005 | 0.009 | −0.023 | −0.002 | −0.043 | −0.003 | −0.013 |
| | (0.007) | (0.036) | (0.003) | (0.019) | (0.008) | (0.016) | (0.005) | (0.042) | (0.009) | (0.014) |
| $R^2$ | 0.42 | 0.21 | 0.54 | 0.38 | 0.38 | 0.52 | 0.65 | 0.26 | 0.67 | 0.09 |
| F-statistic | 3.23 | 1.18 | 5.37 | 2.76 | 2.70 | 4.84 | 8.70 | 1.70 | 9.78 | 0.48 |
| Log likelihood | 58.84 | 20.97 | 81.17 | 35.47 | 47.99 | 30.98 | 59.87 | 8.82 | 46.66 | 38.11 |
| AIC | −4.68 | −1.39 | −6.62 | −2.65 | −3.74 | −2.26 | −4.57 | −0.32 | −3.47 | −2.76 |
| SC | −4.43 | −1.14 | −6.38 | −2.40 | −3.49 | −2.01 | −4.33 | −0.07 | −3.23 | −2.51 |
| Log likelihood | 80.18 | | 117.17 | | 90.64 | | 72.20 | | 89.84 | |
| AIC | −6.10 | | −9.32 | | −7.01 | | −5.18 | | −6.65 | |
| SC | −5.61 | | −8.83 | | −6.52 | | −4.69 | | −6.16 | |

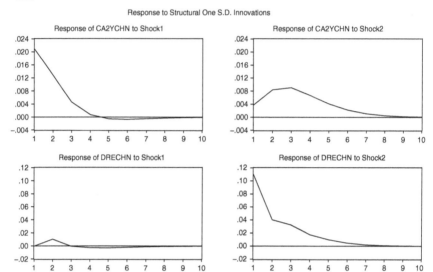

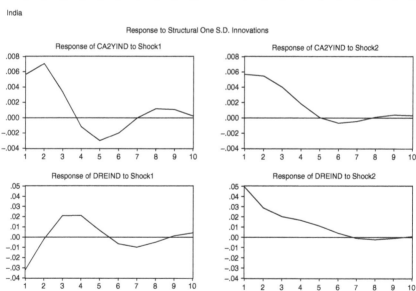

*Figure 6.1* Sample impulse and responses: China and India.

by an improvement in trade balance. The combination of the real appreciation and an improvement in the current account can also be caused by a negative productivity shock, if their effect on the terms of trade is strong enough to dominate the Balassa-Samuelson effect.

Temporary shocks, which bring about a negative association between the real exchange rate and current account, can be viewed as nominal demand shocks. The estimated response to temporary shocks can be generated by a monetary shock that depreciates the real exchange rate, bringing about an improvement in the current account balance. Some of temporary real shocks, which have no long-run effect on the real exchange rate, would also be captured as temporary shocks. An important point for our exercise is that, regardless of their exact identity, these temporary shocks involve an exchange rate adjustment as their effects on the current account wear out.

However, one contrast appears, relative to the results for advanced economies. As depicted in the impulse response for India (similar patterns apply to the impulse responses of Indonesia, Korea, and Thailand). The responses to shocks exhibit non-monotonic patterns over time. While the impact effect is consistent with the pattern just discussed, the dynamic effect over time is much more diverse and not necessarily consistent.

Moreover, in China's case, the temporary shocks have a muted effect on the real exchange rate while they have significant effect on the current account. A transitory shock is found to lead to a delayed appreciation followed by depreciation, while improving the current account at impact. This is a contrast not only to the other four Asian countries in this paper, but also to G7 countries that were studied in Lee and Chinn (2006). In addition to the fundamental difficulty of VAR to do justice to China's structural transformation over the past two decades, this result suggests that the effect of temporary shocks on the real exchange rate may have been particularly small in China. For example, the limited role of monetary policy during much of the sample period may have led to such a result.

Considering these anomalies, the bivariate VAR does not provide stand-alone evidence for the contribution of real depreciation to current account movements. Nevertheless, the portion of the current account driven by permanent shocks will get resolved without accompanying further exchange rate effects. The decomposition of the current account balances into those induced by transitory and permanent shocks offers one measure of how large a portion of the current account imbalances will entail an exchange rate adjustment.

### *History and prospects*

Having estimated the structural matrix (matrix $B(0)$ in equation (6.1)), we can decompose the residuals from the VAR into the transitory and permanent shocks. We can then uncover the contribution of transitory and permanent shocks to the past movements in the current account and the real exchange rate, subject to the initial conditions. The initial conditions, determined by the values of the current account and the real exchange rate at the beginning of the sample, are viewed as deterministic factors for the purpose of our decomposition exercise.

The decompositions for all five countries are presented in Figure 6.2. The upper panel refers to the current account to GDP ratio, and the lower panel refers to the log of the real exchange rate index. In both panels, the solid lines denote the actual

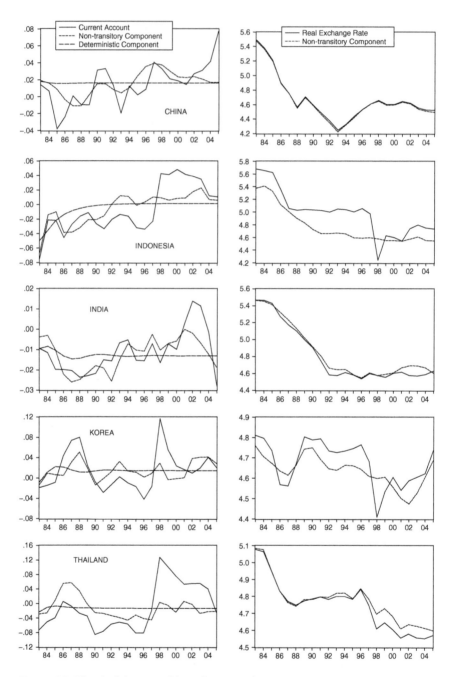

*Figure 6.2* Historical decomposition – five countries.

values and the dotted lines denote the contribution of permanent shocks – including the contribution of initial conditions. In the current account panel, the broken lines denote the contribution of the initial conditions and the estimated constant term. This corresponds to the level of current account that will have prevailed, free from both permanent and transitory shocks that hit these economies during our sample period (circa 1981).

China's current account appears to have been influenced largely by permanent shocks prior to 2000. For most of the 1980s and 1990s, permanent shocks account for most of the movements in the current account and the exchange rate. The real effective exchange rate depreciated from a highly appreciated level prior to economic liberalization, which is captured by the VAR. The current account balance turned from an average deficit in the 1980s to surplus in the late 1990s, driven by permanent shocks. In the past couple of years, however, the permanent shocks predict a much more modest level of current account surplus than the actual value, implying that the bulk of the very high level of current account surplus over the recent years can be attributed to transitory shocks.

The associated exchange rate adjustment, however, is estimated to be small, for the transitory shocks are not found to generate a large exchange rate adjustment. The relatively small magnitude of exchange rate adjustment, which contrasts with the evidence for the other four countries or advanced economies (as in Lee and Chinn 2006), may reflect the difficulty of capturing underlying economic changes by the bivariate VAR. Despite large uncertainty implied by our decomposition exercise, typical experience of other countries suggests that substantial exchange rate adjustment may not be precluded, when the large surplus caused by transitory shocks unwinds itself.

India's current account balance had two large swings – a prolonged deficit in the 1980s until the early 1990s, and a sharp and short surpluses in the early 2000s. According to the VAR decomposition, the deficits in the 1980s and the early 1990s were largely driven by permanent shocks, while a substantial part of the large surplus in the early 2000s was caused by transitory shocks. Over the latter period, transitory shocks are found to have contributed to keeping the exchange rate at a more depreciated level than is implied by permanent shocks alone. In 2005, transitory shocks have played a role in the deepening of the current account deficit.

In both China and India, permanent shocks are found to have been the main driving force behind the movement in their current account balances until the early 2000s. It is particularly noteworthy that transitory shocks did not play a significant role in their current account balances through the Asian crisis period. In the remaining three economies that experienced the full-blown crisis around 1997, transitory shocks are estimated to have played much more prominent roles during the late 1990s surrounding the crisis period.

Indonesia's current account balance had a sharp turnaround from deficit to surplus following the Asian crisis in 1998, and the bulk of it is attributed to transitory shocks. The estimated VAR implies that transitory shocks played a critical role in both the sustained deficit in the years prior to the crisis and the sharp pickup in surplus following the crisis. All through the post-crisis years, transitory shocks contributed to a larger surplus than is implied by non-transitory (permanent) shocks alone. On the exchange rate side, transitory shocks led to a sharp depreciation in the immediate aftermath of the crisis in 1998, and have since contributed to the recovery in the exchange rate. It thus provides little case for a further exchange rate appreciation that will unwind the effect of transitory shocks.

Much of Korea's current account surplus over the past couple of years is caused by permanent shocks, and the current account surplus in 2005 is close to the deterministic part of the VAR. Historically, transitory shocks have played a very large role in the current account balance. During the years leading up to the crisis (from the mid-1990s to 1996/7), transitory shocks generated a sizable appreciation in the real exchange rate and deterioration in the current account balance. Immediately following the crisis, transitory shocks contributed to a sharp depreciation in the real exchange rate and improvement in the current account. Subsequently, during the current decade, the role of transitory shocks in the current account and exchange rate movements has declined.

In the decomposition of Thailand's current account balance, the most distinct phase is the years following the crisis, when a large current account surplus was generated by transitory shocks. The real effective exchange rate was also more depreciated than was implied by the contribution of permanent shocks. And the transitory shocks are found to have played an important role in the current account deficit of the mid-1990s (before the crisis). By 2005, however, the contribution of transitory shocks to the current account appears much more limited.

It is tempting to speculate what particular shocks could have been behind the transitory shocks uncovered by our decomposition. One possibility is the over-investment that was driven by demand shocks, including monetary shocks. For Indonesia and Korea in the early and mid-1990s, transitory shocks are estimated to have kept the real exchange rate levels higher than the level consistent with permanent shocks alone, while pushing the current account deficit to a relatively high level.

However, there is a limit to naming the shocks on the basis of the bivariate VAR, as mentioned in the beginning of this section. More important for our decomposition exercise is the fact that temporary shocks were found to have played a significant role around the crisis period for the three crisis-hit countries, consistent with the short-lived crisis experience of these countries. While our methodology finds that transitory shocks played a prominent role around the time of the Asian crisis, transitory shocks are found to account for a much smaller portion of the current account surplus of Indonesia, Korea, and Thailand in 2005.

## Conclusion

Applying the time-series approach to five Asian economies, we find that there was a substantial role played by transitory shocks in the evolution of the current account in recent years. For all countries, transitory shocks are found to have driven the sharp rise in the current account surplus following the Asian crisis. In three countries that experienced a full-blown crisis, transitory shocks are found to have played a critical role in the prolonged deficit prior to the crisis, too. However, by 2005, the VAR evidence suggests only limited evidence for exchange rate depreciation that will accompany the correction of current account imbalances. In four economies except China, much of the 2005 values of the current account is caused by the permanent shocks, implying little room for exchange rate depreciation.

## Acknowledgement

I appreciate comments received from Yin-Wong Cheung, but am solely responsible for all errors and misinterpretations. The views expressed in this paper are those of the author and should not be attributed to the International Monetary Fund, its Executive Board, or its management.

## References

Aizenman Joshua and Jaewoo Lee (2005) 'International Reserves: Precautionary and Mercantilist Views, Theory and Evidence', *Open Economies Review*, 18 (2): 191–214.

Bayoumi Tamim, Jaewoo Lee and Sarma Jayanthi (2006) 'New Rates from New Weights', *IMF Staff Papers*, 53 (2): 272–305.

Bergin Paul (2006) 'How Well Can The New Open Economy Macroeconomics Explain the Exchange Rate and Current Account?' *Journal of International Money and Finance*, forthcoming.

Blanchard Olivier and Daniel Quah (1989) 'The Dynamic Effects of Aggregate Demand and Supply Disturbances', *American Economic Review*, 79 (4): 655–673.

Chinn Menzie D. and Jaewoo Lee (2005) 'Three Current Account Balances: Semi-Structuralist Approach', NBER Working Paper, No. 11853.

Devereux Michael B. and Charles Engel (2006) 'Expectations and Exchange Rate Policy', University of Wisconsin, mimeo.

Duarte Margarida and Maurice Obstfeld (2004) 'Monetary Policy in the Open Economy Revisited: The Case for Exchange-Rate Flexibility Restored', University of Berkeley, mimeo.

Faust J. and E. M. Leeper (1997) 'When Do Long-Run Identifying Restrictions Give Reliable Results?', *Journal of Business and Economic Statistics*, 15 (3): 345–53.

Lee Jaewoo and Menzie D. Chinn (2006) 'Current Account and Real Exchange Rate Dynamics in the G7 Countries', *Journal of International Money and Finance*, 25: 257–74.

Obstfeld Maurice (2004) 'External Adjustment', *Review of World Economics*, 140 (4): 541–68.

Obstfeld Maurice and Kenneth Rogoff (1996) *Foundations of International Macroeconomics*, Cambridge, MA: MIT Press.

Rose Andrew (1991) 'The Role of Exchange Rates in a Popular Model of International Trade', *Journal of International Economics*, 30: 301–16.

Sheffrin Steven M. and Wing Thye Woo (1990) 'Present Value Tests of An Intertemporal Model of the Current Account', *Journal of International Economics*, 29: 237–53.

Taylor Alan (2001) 'A Century of Current Account Dynamics', *Journal of International Money and Finance*, 21 (6): 725–48.

Trehan Bharat and Carl E. Walsh (1991) 'Testing Intertemporal Budget Constraints: Theory and Application to U.S. Federal Budget and Current Account Deficits', *Journal of Money, Credit, and Banking*, 23 (2): 206–23.

# 7 What drives business cycle correlation in the Pacific Rim?

*Jakob de Haan, Richard Jong-A-Pin and Mark Mink*

## Introduction

This chapter examines to what extent business cycles in the Pacific Rim countries are correlated and what factors cause these correlations to change over time. The degree of business cycle correlation is important for policy makers for various reasons. First, as pointed out by Crosby (2003), the domestic economy may react to disturbances in economies in close geographic proximity, or to larger but perhaps more distant economies such as the United States. Second, as pointed out by Genberg (2006), the increased trade integration among economies in the region has led to calls for coordination of exchange rate policies (or even currency unions)[1] lest competitive depreciations lead to artificial distortions in competitiveness, disruptions of trade, and dislocation of production. Referring to the experience of Europe, it is often argued that such exchange rate cooperation is necessary now that the degree of integration of at least some countries in the region has reached levels close to that in Europe at the time the Exchange Rate Mechanism was introduced. However, monetary integration requires that business cycles of countries participating in a system of fixed exchange rates or a currency union are sufficiently aligned.

Some recent studies examine business cycle correlation for various countries that we consider. For instance, Moneta and Rüffer (2006) estimate dynamic common factor models for output growth of ten East Asian countries and find that, except for China and Japan, all countries share a significant common factor. The degree of correlation has fluctuated over time, with an upward trend particularly evident for the newly industrialized countries. Girardin's (2005) analysis of ten East Asian countries for 1975–2002, based on a Markov-switching trivariate vector autoregressive (VAR) system, suggests that correlations with Japan are almost uniformly negative. However, when transmission variables are taken into account, positive correlations appear during rapid-growth regimes for China, Malaysia, Singapore, Taiwan, and South Korea.

Some other studies have examined the factors determining business cycle correlation in the region. For instance, Crosby (2003) analyzes a sample of Asia–Pacific countries and finds that trade is not strongly associated with higher business cycle correlations. Structural similarity between countries turns out to be positively associated with business cycle correlation. Similarly, Shin and Wang (2004) find that for 12 Asian economies increasing trade is not necessarily associated with an increased correlation of business cycles. Intra-industry trade, rather than inter-industry trade or the volume of trade itself, turns out to be the major channel through which business cycles become more correlated.

Using data for 17 Pacific Rim countries, we first examine to what extent business cycles of these countries are aligned using the correlation between detrended GDP series. We find no clear trend towards increased bilateral business cycle correlation over time. In the second part of the paper we analyze what factors cause business cycles in the region to become more correlated. As pointed out by Baxter and Kouparitsas (2005: 114), 'despite the theoretical and empirical analyses to date, it seems fair to say that there is no consensus on the important determinants of business cycle co-movement. The difficulty is that there are many potential candidate explanations'. Baxter and Kouparitsas (2005) therefore apply the Extreme Bounds Analysis (EBA) of Leamer (1983) to assess to what extent variables are robustly related to business cycle correlation. They conclude that bilateral trade is robust, but other variables that previous studies found to be important – including specialization and currency unions – are not robustly related to business cycle correlation. Inklaar *et al.* (2008) extend the analysis of Baxter and Kouparitsas (2005), using Sala-i-Martin's (1997) variant of the EBA, as the EBA as proposed by Leamer (1983) is extremely restrictive. We follow the methodology of Inklaar *et al.* (2008) and examine factors driving business cycle correlation that have been suggested in previous studies. We conclude that trade intensity is robustly related to business cycle correlation, but financial integration is not; the evidence on specialization is mixed. We also find a few other variables to be related to business cycle correlation, notably bilateral correlation between inflation rates.

The remainder of the chapter is structured as follows. Section 2 examines how business cycle correlation between the countries in our sample developed over time. Section 3 outlines our method to identify the determinants of business cycle correlation, while Section 4 describes the data we used. Section 5 presents the empirical results, and the final section offers some concluding comments.

## Business cycle correlation over time

Various measures have been suggested in the literature to measure business cycle alignment. Most of these measures are judged by their characteristics and not so much by economic reasoning. An exception is the work by Kalemli-Ozcan *et al.* (2001), who argue that a natural measure of asymmetry quantifies the potential loss of welfare due to asymmetric GDP fluctuations in the absence of risk sharing mechanisms. They compare utility under autarky, where the consumption possibilities are constrained by the country's own GDP, and under full cross-country risk sharing. In the latter case, consumption possibilities are equal to a fraction of total GDP of the area with risk sharing. Moving from autarky to full risk-sharing will generally bring utility gains and Kalemli-Ozcan *et al.* (2001)

derive the following measure for these gains when assuming log-utility:

$$G_i = \frac{1}{\delta}\left(\frac{1}{2}\sigma^2 + \frac{1}{2}\sigma_i^2 - \text{cov}_i\right) \tag{7.1}$$

where $\delta$ is the intertemporal discount rate. This measure states that the gains from risk-sharing for country $i$ will be larger when the standard deviation of GDP growth in country $i$ is larger, when the standard deviation of GDP growth in the rest of the risk-sharing area is larger, and when the covariance between country $i$ and the rest of the area is smaller. The interpretation of this negative sign on the covariance is straightforward as joining an area with largely unrelated fluctuations will provide more insurance by stabilizing aggregate output. Furthermore, the higher the standard deviations of growth, the more is gained by risk sharing.

Following most of the literature, we use the correlation between detrended GDP series to measure the degree of business cycle alignment.[2] The countries included in this exercise are Australia, Canada, Chile, China, Hong-Kong, Indonesia, Japan, Korea, Malaysia, Mexico, New Zealand, Peru, Philippines, Singapore, Thailand, the United States, and Vietnam. We calculate correlations for three periods: 1960–1974, 1975–1989 and 1990–2004. Although it would be preferable to use data at a quarterly frequency, we resort to using yearly observations as for many countries statistics on quarterly economic activity are not available. We obtained GDP statistics from the Groningen Growth and Development Centre, which are all constructed using the same definition of economic activity and which do not contain any breaks that might complicate statistical inference. The cyclical component of the series is extracted by means of the band-pass filter developed by Christiano and Fitzgerald (2003). We configured the filter in such a way that only fluctuations with a duration of between 2 and 8 years are allowed to pass. Finally, we modified the correlation coefficients that we calculated on the basis of the filtered data by means of the Fisher transformation.[3] Applying this transformation is a necessity when using correlation coefficients as a dependent variable in a regression analysis since their value is bounded between $-1$ and 1. As a result, it is unlikely that the error terms are normally distributed, which complicates reliable inference. David (1949) shows that the transformed correlation coefficient does not suffer from this problem.

Figure 7.1 reports (untransformed) bilateral correlations calculated for 1960–1974 and 1990–2004. Data points above the diagonal line indicate country-pairs for which cycle correlation has risen over time. There is a trend towards decreased bilateral cycle correlation over time (the average correlations are: 0.33 for 1960–1974, 0.13 for 1975–1989, and 0.17 for 1990–2004). When we consider correlations with the US and Japan, both important export markets and potential currency anchors, we find somewhat mixed results. Average correlations with the US are decreasing over time (per-period averages equal 0.46, 0.14, and 0.08), while for Japan an increase in correlation seems to have taken place during the later years of the sample (per-period averages equal 0.20, $-0.22$, and 0.27). Even though the

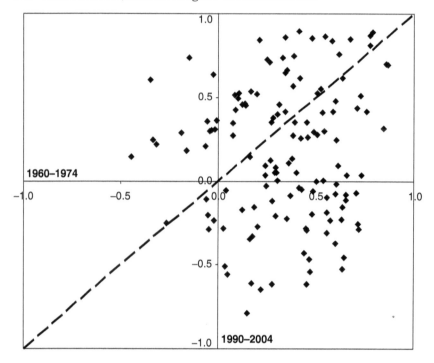

*Figure 7.1* Bilateral business cycle correlation: 1960–74 and 1990–2004.

causes of these developments remain unclear yet, these findings suggest that not all countries in the sample would benefit from pegging their currency to the Yen or the US dollar as there are substantial differences in patterns of economic activity within the region.

Figure 7.2 provides some more insight in the magnitude of these differences by presenting the ten country-pairs with the highest and the lowest business cycle correlations. It is quite remarkable that the ten country pairs with the lowest correlation during 1990–2004 all had a positive correlation in the period 1960–1974.

## Estimation method

Apart from trade, the literature has suggested many other variables that may be related to business cycle correlation. We follow Baxter and Kouparitsas (2005) and apply an Extreme Bounds Analysis (EBA) to examine which variables are robustly related to business cycle correlation in the Pacific Rim. However, we employ the EBA as suggested by Sala-i-Martin (1997) since Leamer's (1983) EBA is extremely restrictive. In addition, we employ robust estimators to control for possible outliers.[4]

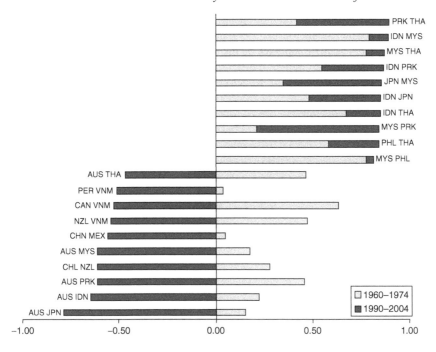

*Figure 7.2* Largest and smallest bilateral business cycle correlations in the Pacific Rim.

The EBA can be exemplified as follows. We estimate equations of the following general form:

$$Y = \alpha M + \beta F + \gamma Z + u \tag{7.2}$$

where $Y$ is the dependent variable (in our case: business cycle correlation); $M$ is a vector of 'standard' explanatory variables (that may be empty); $F$ is the variable of interest; $Z$ is a vector of up to three (here we follow Levine and Renelt 1992) possible additional explanatory variables, that – according to the literature – may be related to the dependent variable; and $u$ is an error term. In our analysis we only include trade intensity in the $M$ vector as many studies find that this variable is related to business cycle correlation.[5] Leamer's extreme bounds test for variable $F$ says that if the lower extreme bound for $\beta$ – i.e. the lowest value for $\beta$ minus two standard deviations – is negative, while the upper extreme bound for $\beta$ – i.e. the highest value for $\beta$ plus two standard deviations – is positive, the variable $F$ is not robustly related to $Y$.

Sala-i-Martin (1997) rightly argues that the test applied in this EBA is too strong for any variable to really pass it. If the distribution of the parameter of interest has some positive and some negative support, then one is bound to find a regression for which the estimated coefficient changes sign if enough regressions are run.

Instead of focusing on the extreme bounds of the estimates of the coefficient of a particular variable, Sala-i-Martin (1997) suggests to analyze the entire distribution of the estimates of the parameter of interest. Broadly speaking, if the averaged 90 per cent confidence interval of a regression coefficient does not include zero, Sala-i-Martin classifies the corresponding regressor as a variable that is strongly related to $Y$.

Following Sturm and De Haan (2005), we report the percentage of the regressions in which the coefficient of the variable $F$ is significantly different from zero at the 5 per cent level as well as the outcomes of the cumulative distribution function (CDF(0)) test. The CDF(0) test is based on the fraction of the cumulative distribution function lying on each side of zero. CDF(0) indicates the larger of the areas under the density function either above or below zero; in other words, regardless of whether this is CDF(0) or 1–CDF(0). So CDF(0) will always be a number between 0.5 and 1.0. In our analysis, we consider a variable to be robust if the CDF(0) test statistic is larger than 0.95.[6]

Apart from model uncertainty, there is another important problem in this line of research that has been neglected, namely the role of outliers.[7] Temple (2000) suggests using so-called robust estimation techniques to deal with this problem. Robust estimators can be thought of as trying to seek out the most coherent part of the data, which is the part best approximated by the model that is estimated. These estimators will not be led astray by outliers. Following Barnett and Lewis (1994: 316) we define an outlier as an observation 'lying outside' the typical relationship between the dependent and explanatory variables revealed by the remaining data. For instance, point A in Figure 7.3(a) is clearly an outlier. Outliers in the dependent variable – i.e. in the $y$-direction – often possess large positive or large negative residuals, which are easy to detect by plotting the residuals.[8] Observations may be outliers for several reasons. The most obvious one involves problems with the quality of the data. Outliers in the explanatory variables may be more problematic than outliers in the dependent variable. As Figure 7.3(b) shows, an unusual observation in the $x$-direction (B) can actually tilt the OLS regression line. In such a case we call the outlier a (bad) leverage point. Note that looking

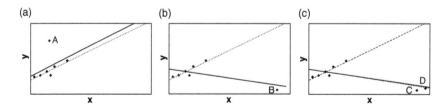

*Figure 7.3* Outlying observations and bad leverage points.
Source: Sturm and De Haan (2005)

Note: The solid lines represent the OLS estimates including the unusual observation(s). The dotted lines represent the OLS estimates without the unusual observations A, B, or C. The dashed line represents the OLS estimate without observations C and D.

at the OLS residuals cannot discover bad leverage points. If a leverage point tilts the regression line, deleting the points with the largest OLS residuals implies that some 'good' points would be deleted in stead of the 'bad' leverage point.

Basically, there are two ways to deal with outliers: regressions diagnostics and robust estimation. Diagnostics are certain statistics mostly computed from the OLS regression estimates with the purpose of pinpointing outliers and leverage points (see, for instance, Belsley *et al.* 1980). Often the unusual observations are then removed or corrected after which an OLS analysis on the remaining observations follows. When there is only one unusual observation, some of these methods work quite well. However, single-case diagnostics are inadequate in the presence of multiple outliers or leverage points (Temple, 2000).

Take for instance Figure 7.3(c). Deleting either of the two outliers will have little effect on the regression outcome and will therefore not be spotted by the single-case diagnostics. The potential effect of one outlying observation is clearly masked by the presence of the other. Testing for groups of observations to be influential might solve this masking effect problem. However, a serious problem in the multiple observation case is how to determine the size of the subset of jointly influential observations. Suppose we are interested in detecting all subsets of size $m = 2, 3, \ldots$ of observations that are considered to be jointly outliers and/or high-leverage. A sequential method might be useful, but where to stop? In the multiple observation case the number of possible subsets for which each diagnostic measure of interest can be computed is: $\dfrac{n!}{m!(n-m)!}$ where $n$ is number of observations. For $m = 5$ and $n = 80$ this results in over 24 million diagnostics. Therefore we prefer so-called robust regression techniques that employ estimators that are not strongly affected by (groups of) outliers.

Two closely related methods are the Least Median of Squares (LMS) and Least Trimmed Squares (LTS) introduced by Rousseeuw (1984). LMS minimizes the median of the squared residuals. LTS typically minimizes the sum of squares over half the observations, the chosen half being the combination which gives the smallest residual sum of squares. According to Temple (2000), LTS is generally thought preferable to LMS. However, because of its low finite-sample efficiency LTS is not suited for inference. As proposed by Rousseeuw (1984), this can be resolved by using reweighted least squares (RWLS). A simple, but effective, way is to put weight zero if the observation is an outlier and weight one otherwise.

Temple (2000: 195) has argued to use robust estimation techniques when applying the EBA:

> It is well known in the statistics literature that the presence of a few influential outliers can either hide a relationship, or create the appearance of one where none exists ... This suggests that any good approach to model uncertainty should ideally be robust to observations that are measured with error, or drawn from a different regime ... I propose using a simple variant of EBA in which each regression is first estimated by robust methods.

This is the approach that we use in this chapter.

## Data description

Although *trade integration* plays a central role in the theory on Optimum Currency Areas, its impact on business cycle correlation is ambiguous from a theoretical point of view. First, as changes in domestic income usually have an impact on the demand for foreign goods as well, trade integration could induce spillover of demand shocks between countries and thereby lead to correlation of business cycles. However, standard trade theory predicts that openness to trade can also induce specialization and inter-industry trade flows. In this case, if business cycles are dominated by industry-specific shocks, the increase in specialization will render these shocks more asymmetric amongst countries and therefore reduces cycle correlation. Only if intra-industry rather than inter-industry trade relations are sufficiently strong, such shocks can spill over to other countries and thereby increase cycle correlation.

The literature suggests several measures to quantify trade intensity between a pair of countries (see De Haan *et al.* 2008 for a survey). Frankel and Rose (1998), for instance, scale total trade (measured as the sum of exports $X$ and imports $M$) between two countries $(i, j)$ by the sum of both countries' GDP or by the sum of both countries' total trade. Otto *et al.* (2001) suggest to scale by the lowest of both countries' GDP levels, while Clark and Van Wincoop (2001) use a measure proposed by Deardorff (1998), which involves scaling by the product of GDP levels and multiplying the result by world GDP. We thus end up with four indicators of trade intensity that will all be used in the analysis to check to what extent conclusions on the role of trade in business cycle correlation depend on the measure chosen. We obtain the data on international trade flows from Feenstra *et al.* (2005). Figure 7.4 shows that overall trade intensity, measured as bilateral trade over GDP, has increased substantially over time.

Another factor influencing business cycle correlations is *specialization*. After all, not only will economies producing the same type of goods be hit by the same type of industry-specific shocks, they are likely to react in a similar way to aggregate shocks as well. Indeed, Imbs (2004) finds that similarities in economic structure lead to increased cycle correlation. To take these effects into account, we define three measures of specialization. The first two are based on differences in import and export patterns, the third on intra-industry trade.[9]

Following Baxter and Kouparitsas (2005), we calculate the import specialization measures as follows:

$$\sum_{n=1}^{N} \left| s_t^{in} - s_t^{jn} \right|$$

where $s_t^{in}$ equals the share of product category $n$ in total imports of country $i$ at time $t$. The industry shares are calculated on basis of 3-digit SITC data, obtained from Feenstra *et al.* (2005). We also calculated the squared differences – instead of the absolute difference – as well as the correlation between the shares. Our first measure of specialization is the first principal component of these import dissimilarity measures. The second specialization measure is the first principal

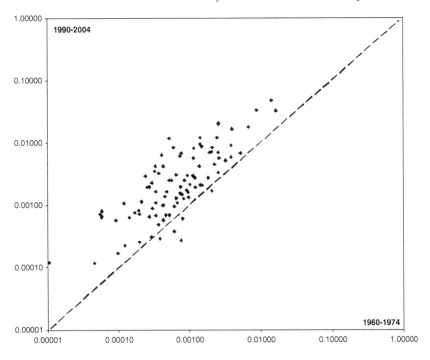

*Figure 7.4* Bilateral trade intensity in the Pacific Rim (in log), 1960–74 vs. 1990–2004.

component of the export dissimilarity measures. Figures 7.5 and 7.6 show that for the overall majority of country pairs, differences in import and export patterns have declined over time. The correlation in import shares for the various periods are 0.31, 0.36, and 0.47, while for export shares these numbers equal 0.09, 0.12 and 0.23. Hence, the increase in trade intensity reported above does not seem to have induced an increase in specialization patterns.

Following Inklaar *et al.* (2007), our third specialization indicator captures the share of bilateral trade that can be attributed to intra-industry trade.[10] After all, as pointed out before, if trade is primarily of an intra-industry nature, industry specific shocks could in fact increase business cycle correlation. Following Grubel and Loyd (1971), the measure is calculated as:

$$1 - \frac{\sum_{n=1}^{N} \left| E_t^{ij,n} - E_t^{ji,n} \right|}{\sum_{n=1}^{N} \left( E_t^{ij,n} + E_t^{ji,n} \right)}$$

where $E_t^{ij,n}$ denotes exports corresponding to product category $n$ from country $i$ to country $j$ at time $t$. Again, we use 3-digit SITC data from Feenstra *et al.* (2005).[11]

According to Imbs (2004), *financial integration* can have an impact on business cycle correlation as well, although the sign of this effect is again ambiguous. First, financial linkages can result in a higher degree of cycle correlation by generating

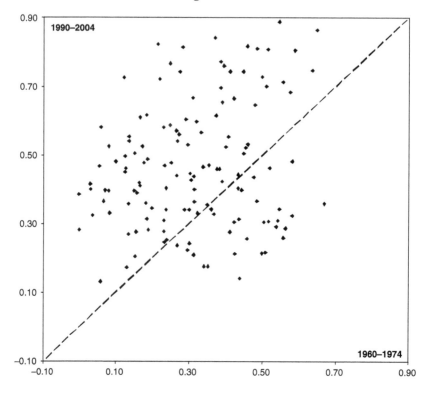

*Figure 7.5* Bilateral import share correlations in the Pacific Rim, 1960–74 vs. 1990–2004.

large demand side effects or through contagion effects. However, in addition, two channels exist through which financial integration might impede business cycle correlation. After all, increasing capital mobility can allow for easier reallocation of capital in a manner consistent with countries' competitive advantages and thereby promote the abovementioned specialization in production patterns. In addition, Kalemli-Ozcan *et al*. (2004) argue that specialization is also more likely to occur if capital markets are sufficiently integrated to use risk diversification in order to prevent output fluctuations from inducing fluctuations in income as well. In order to empirically examine which effect dominates in our sample, we include two indicators of financial integration that have been suggested by Imbs (2004). First, we include a dummy for capital account restrictions which equals one if at least in one of the two countries such restrictions are in place. We construct this variable on the basis of the Lane and Milesi-Ferretti (2001) database, updated with statistics from the IMF Annual Reports on Exchange Arrangements and Exchange Restrictions (AREAER). Our second variable is calculated as:

$$\left|\left(NFA/GDP\right)_{it} - \left(NFA/GDP\right)_{jt}\right|$$

where *NFA* is the net foreign asset position of country *i* or *j* as calculated by Lane and Milesi-Ferretti (2001) on the basis of current account statistics. The indicator

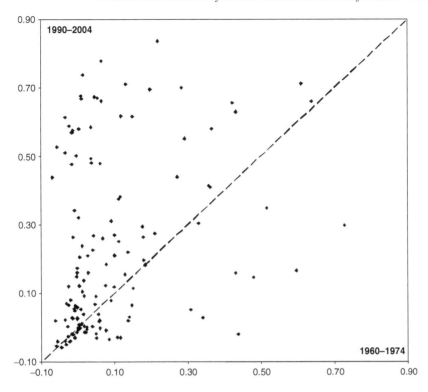

*Figure 7.6* Bilateral export share correlations in the Pacific Rim, 1960–74 vs. 1990–2004.

will have a high value if countries have diverging external positions, which implies they will be more likely to lend to or borrow from each other than countries with similar external positions.

There is little agreement on whether *monetary policy* might have an impact on business cycle correlation. On the one hand, similar monetary policies will be less of a source of asymmetric shocks and can thereby lead to higher business cycle correlation. In addition, a currency union will promote trade (Rose, 2000), which can have either a positive or a negative effect on cycle co-movement. Furthermore, if floating exchange rates are considered a shock absorbing mechanism, a common currency may lead to less business cycle correlation if the countries in the monetary union face asymmetric shocks. After all, in face of an external shock, a fixed exchange rate regime requires the central bank to follow a policy so as to maintain the peg, forcing all the adjustment to take place in the real economy rather than the exchange rate. To empirically asses this issue, we follow De Haan *et al.* (2002) and include the standard deviations of changes in the bilateral exchange rate in our model. Additionally, we follow Camacho *et al.* (2006) by including the correlation of inflation rates. We obtained the data for both variables from the Penn World Tables version 6.2.

*Table 7.1* EBA results using OLS/WLTS with total trade scaled by sum of trade in M-vector and intra-industry trade and import dissimilarity as specialization measures

|  | Lower bound | Upper bound | % significant | CDF(0) |
|---|---|---|---|---|
| In M-vector: | | | | |
| Trade | −0.66 | 9.14 | 99 | 1.00 |
| Other variables: | | | | |
| Std. dev. exchange rate | −0.27 | 0.29 | 15 | 0.68 |
| Correlation of inflation | −0.09 | 0.34 | 87 | 0.98 |
| Abs. differences savings rate | −0.01 | 0.01 | 42 | 0.85 |
| Abs. differences government share in GDP | −0.01 | 0.02 | 9 | 0.71 |
| Average openness | 0.00 | 0.00 | 33 | 0.84 |
| Absolute difference NFA positions | −0.15 | 0.18 | 12 | 0.81 |
| Common legal family dummy | −0.06 | 0.20 | 64 | 0.96 |
| Capital account restrictions | −0.12 | 0.21 | 5 | 0.77 |
| Import dissimilarity | −0.13 | 0.00 | 96 | 1.00 |
| Intra-industry trade | −0.53 | 0.87 | 27 | 0.78 |

We also include a number of other variables in our model that have been suggested in the literature to capture *structural differences* between countries. In particular, we take account of

1    the absolute difference between the savings rates (suggested by Camacho *et al.* 2006)
2    the absolute difference between the government's share of GDP (suggested by Clark and van Wincoop, 2001)
3    the average openness of the two countries (suggested by Baxter and Kouparitsas, 2005), and
4    a dummy for common legal origin (suggested by Otto *et al.* 2001).

We obtained data for the first three of these variables from the Pen World Tables version 6.2, while for the last variable we used La Porta *et al.* (1998). The data appendix describes all data used and their sources in some detail. All data used are available on request.

## Results

Tables 7.1–7.4 show the estimation results for the EBA using LTS/RWLS. In our analysis we only include trade in the *M* vector as many authors conclude that this variable is robustly related to business cycle correlation (see Inklaar *et al.* 2008). When testing for robustness, we did not include our import and our export dissimilarity measures at the same time. As we have four different indicators of trade, in all this gives us eight different sets of results. We do not report all of them in order to save space (they all point to the same conclusions), but the omitted tables are available on request.

*Table 7.2* EBA results using OLS/WLTS with total trade scaled by sum of trade in M-vector and intra-industry trade and export dissimilarity as specialization measure

|  | Lower bound | Upper bound | % significant | CDF(0) |
|---|---|---|---|---|
| In M-vector: |  |  |  |  |
| Trade | −0.14 | 8.09 | 99 | 1.00 |
| Other variables: |  |  |  |  |
| Std. dev. exchange rate | −0.24 | 0.29 | 13 | 0.72 |
| Correlation of inflation | −0.09 | 0.37 | 87 | 0.97 |
| Abs. differences savings rate | −0.01 | 0.01 | 48 | 0.87 |
| Abs. differences government share in GDP | −0.01 | 0.02 | 12 | 0.68 |
| Average openness | 0.00 | 0.00 | 29 | 0.80 |
| Absolute difference NFA positions | −0.15 | 0.18 | 11 | 0.78 |
| Common legal family dummy | −0.04 | 0.21 | 81 | 0.98 |
| Capital account restrictions | −0.12 | 0.21 | 6 | 0.73 |
| Export dissimilarity | −0.12 | 0.05 | 64 | 0.94 |
| Intra-industry trade | −0.38 | 0.87 | 36 | 0.85 |

*Table 7.3* EBA results using OLS/WLTS with total trade scaled by GDP in M-vector and intra-industry trade and import dissimilarity as specialization measures

|  | Lower bound | Upper bound | % significant | CDF(0) |
|---|---|---|---|---|
| In M-vector: |  |  |  |  |
| Trade | −4.24 | 33.91 | 98 | 1.00 |
| Other variables: |  |  |  |  |
| Std. dev. exchange rate | −0.29 | 0.25 | 15 | 0.73 |
| Correlation of inflation | −0.09 | 0.32 | 80 | 0.98 |
| Abs. differences savings rate | −0.01 | 0.01 | 36 | 0.83 |
| Abs. differences government share in GDP | −0.01 | 0.02 | 6 | 0.80 |
| Average openness | 0.00 | 0.00 | 13 | 0.68 |
| Absolute difference NFA positions | −0.16 | 0.18 | 2 | 0.64 |
| Common legal family dummy | −0.06 | 0.20 | 55 | 0.95 |
| Capital account restrictions | −0.10 | 0.20 | 1 | 0.77 |
| Import dissimilarity | −0.12 | 0.02 | 92 | 0.99 |
| Intra-industry trade | −0.40 | 0.82 | 25 | 0.83 |

In Table 7.1 our trade indicator is bilateral trade using total trade as scaling factor. The indicators of specialization are import dissimilarity and intra-industry trade, while in Table 7.2 we replace the first by export dissimilarity. It is clear that trade intensity is robustly related to business cycle correlation since the CDF(0) statistic exceeds 0.95. This result is in line with the findings of many previous studies but differs from those of Crosby (2003).

Unlike Imbs (2004) and Inklaar *et al.* (2008), we only find mixed evidence for our indicators of specialization. Only the import dissimilarity measure passes the CDF(0) test. Whereas Baxter and Kouparitsas (2005) do not find that import

*Table 7.4* EBA results using OLS/WLTS with total trade scaled by GDP in M-vector and intra-industry trade and export dissimilarity as specialization measure

|  | *lower bound* | *upper bound* | *% significant* | *CDF(0)* |
|---|---|---|---|---|
| In M-vector: |  |  |  |  |
| Trade | −4.40 | 53.82 | 100 | 1.00 |
| Other variables: |  |  |  |  |
| Std. dev. exchange rate | −0.23 | 0.22 | 13 | 0.76 |
| Correlation of inflation | −0.09 | 0.34 | 79 | 0.98 |
| Abs. differences savings rate | −0.01 | 0.01 | 43 | 0.86 |
| Abs. differences government share in GDP | −0.01 | 0.02 | 10 | 0.80 |
| Average openness | 0.00 | 0.00 | 15 | 0.68 |
| Absolute difference NFA positions | −0.16 | 0.18 | 2 | 0.61 |
| Common legal family dummy | −0.04 | 0.20 | 68 | 0.97 |
| Capital account restrictions | −0.11 | 0.20 | 1 | 0.74 |
| Export dissimilarity | −0.12 | 0.06 | 64 | 0.90 |
| Intra-industry trade | −0.41 | 0.82 | 29 | 0.85 |

similarity is robustly related to business cycle correlation, our results clearly point in the other direction. This difference may be explained by the use of a different EBA, as Baxter and Kouparitsas employ Leamer's version of the EBA. Tables 7.1 and 7.2 also show the outcomes of this test, even though we consider this test to be too strong. According to Leamer's test, all variables that we consider to be robust should be regarded as fragile.

Also our indicators of financial integration do not survive the CDF(0) robustness test. This result is in line with the findings of Inklaar *et al.* (2008) for OECD countries, but not with those of Imbs (2004). Interestingly, two other variables pass the robustness test in Tables 7.1 and 7.2: the inflation correlation, and the legal family variable. Although Camacho *et al.* consider the inflation correlation as a proxy for similar monetary policy, the significant relationship between this variable and business cycle correlation may also reflect that inflation is, to some extent, determined by cyclical conditions. Otto *et al.* (2001) argue that legal systems may underlie different economic structures; as a consequence, there may be different effects of common shocks, both with respect to the initial response and the propagation of these shocks, in countries with different legal systems. Our results support this view.

In Tables 7.3 and 7.4 the trade indicator is total bilateral trade scaled by GDP. In Table 7.3 the indicators of specialization are import dissimilarity and intra-industry trade, while in Table 7.4 we replace the first by export dissimilarity. All results are the same as before. We also employed minimum GDP and the product of GDP as scaling factors for our trade variable. With one exception, this again gave the same results. The exception is that export dissimilarity passes the CDF(0) test in these specifications. We therefore conclude that the evidence on the impact of specialization on business cycle correlation is mixed: the intra-industry trade variable is never robust, the import dissimilarity measure is always robust, while the export dissimilarity measure is sometimes robust.

## Conclusions

Using data for 17 Pacific Rim countries for 1960–1974, 1975–1989 and 1990–2004 we examine (1) whether business cycles in the region have become more similar, and, (2) what factors drive business cycle correlation in these countries. We find no clear trend towards increased bilateral business cycle correlation for Pacific Rim countries over time. We analyze factors driving business cycle correlation that have been suggested in previous studies using Extreme Bounds Analysis and robust estimators.

We conclude that trade intensity is robustly related to business cycle correlation, but financial integration is not; the evidence on specialization is mixed. We also find a few other variables to be related to business cycle correlation, notably inflation correlation.

## Acknowledgement

The views expressed here are solely those of the authors and do not reflect the position of De Nederlandsche Bank.

## References

Barnett V. and Lewis T. (1994) *Outliers in Statistical Data*, New York: John Wiley and Sons.

Baxter M. and Kouparitsas M. (2005) 'Determinants of Business Cycle Comovement: A Robust Analysis', *Journal of Monetary Economics*, 52: 113–157.

Belsley D. A., Kuh E. and Welsch R .E. (1980) *Regression Diagnostics*, New York: John Wiley and Sons.

Camacho M., Perez-Quiros G. and Saiz L. (2006) 'Are European Business Cycles Close Enough to Be Just One?', *Journal of Economic Dynamics and Control*, 30(9/10): 1687–1706.

Cheung Y. and Yuen J. (2005) 'The Suitability of a Greater China Currency Union', *Pacific Economic Review*, 10(1): 83–103.

Christiano L. and T. J. Fitzgerald (2003) 'The Band-Pass Filter', *International Economic Review*, 44: 435–65.

Clark T. E. and van Wincoop, E. (2001) 'Borders and Business Cycles', *Journal of International Economics*, 55: 59–85.

Crosby M. (2003) 'Business Cycle Correlations in Asia–Pacific', *Economics Letters*, 80: 35–44.

David F. N. (1949) 'The Moments of the z and F Distributions', *Biometrika*, 36: 394–403.

Deardorff A. V.(1998) 'Determinants of bilateral trade: does gravity work in a neoclassical world?', in Frankel, J.A. (ed.), *The Regionalization of the World Economy*, Chicago: University of Chicago Press. pp. 7–22.

De Haan J., Inklaar R. and Sleijpen, O. (2002) 'Have Business Cycles Become More Synchronized?', *Journal of Common Market Studies*, 40 (1): 23–42.

De Haan J., Inklaar R. and Jong-A-Pin, R.M. (2008) 'Will Business Cycles in the Euro Area Converge? A Critical Survey of Empirical Research', *Journal of Economic Surveys*, 22(2): 243–273.

Feenstra R. C., Lipsey R. E., Deng H., Ma A. C. and Mo H. (2005) 'World Trade Flows: 1962–2000', NBER Working Paper, No. 11040.

Frankel J. A. and Rose A. K. (1998) 'The Endogeneity of the Optimum Currency Area Criteria', *The Economic Journal*, 108: 1009–1025.

Genberg H. (2006) 'Exchange Rate Arrangements and Financial Integration in East Asia: On a Collision Course?', Austrian Central Bank Working Paper, No. 122.

Girardin E. (2005) 'Regime-Dependent Synchronization of Growth Cycles between Japan and East Asia', *Asian Economic Papers*, 3(3): 147–176.

Grubel H.G. and Lloyd P. J. (1971) 'The Empirical Measurement of Intra-Industry Trade', *Economic Record*, 47 (120): 494–517.

Gruben W. C., Koo J. and Millis E. (2002) 'How Much Does International Trade Affect Business Cycle Synchronization?', Federal Reserve Bank of Dallas Working Paper, No. 0203.

Heston A. R., Summers S. and Aten, B. (2006) Penn World Table Version 6.2, Center for International Comparisons, University of Pennsylvania, Philadelphia.

Imbs J. (2004) 'Trade, Finance, Specialization and Synchronization', *Review of Economics and Statistics*, 86: 723–734.

Inklaar R., Jong-A-Pin R. and De Haan J. (2008) 'Trade and Business Cycle Synchronization in OECD Countries, A Re–examination', *European Economic Review*, 52(4): 646–666.

Kalemli-Ozcan S., Sørensen B. E. and Yosha, O. (2001) 'Economic Integration, Industrial Specialization, and the Asymmetry of Macroeconomic Fluctuations', *Journal of International Economics*, 55: 107–137.

——— (2004) 'Asymmetric Shocks and Risk Sharing in a Monetary Union: Updated Evidence and Policy Implications for Europe', CEPR Discussion Paper, No. 4463.

Lane P. R. and Milesi-Ferretti G. M. (2001) 'The External Wealth of Nations: Measures of Foreign Assets and Liabilities in Industrial and Developing Countries', *Journal of International Economics*, 55(2): 263–294.

La Porta R., Lopez-de-Silanes F., Shleifer A. and Vishny, R. W. (1998) 'Law and Finance', *Journal of Political Economy*, 106(6): 1113–1155.

Leamer, E. E. (1983) 'Let's Take the Con Out of Econometrics', *American Economic Review*, 73(3): 31–43.

Levine R. and Renelt D. (1992) 'A Sensitivity Analysis of Cross-country Growth Regressions', *American Economic Review*, 82: 942–963.

Mink M., Jacobs J. and De Haan J. (2007) 'Measuring Synchronicity and Co-movement of Business Cycles with an Application to the Euro Area', CESIfo Working Paper, No. 2112.

Moneta F. and Rüffer R. (2006) 'Business Cycle Synchronisation in East Asia', ECB Working Paper, No. 671.

Otto G., Voss G. and Willard L. (2001) 'Understanding OECD Output Correlations', Reserve Bank of Australia Research Discussion Paper, No. 2001–5.

Rose A. (2000) 'One Money, One Market: The Effect of Common Currencies on Trade', *Economic Policy*, 30: 7–46.

Rousseeuw P. J. (1984) 'Least Median of Squares Regression', *Journal of the American Statistical Association*, 79: 871–880.

Sala-i-Martin X. (1997) 'I Just Ran Two Millions Regressions', *American Economic Review*, 87(2):178–183.

Sala-i-Martin X., Doppelhofer G. and Miller R. I. (2004) 'Determinants of Long-term Growth: A Bayesian Averaging of Classical estimates (BACE) Approach', *American Economic Review*, 94(4): 813–835.

Shin K. and Wang. Y. (2004) 'Trade Integration and Business Cycle Synchronization in East Asia', *Asian Economic Papers*, 2(3): 1–20.

Sturm J. E. and De Haan J. (2005) 'Determinants of Long–term Growth: New Results Applying Robust Estimation and Extreme Bounds Analysis', *Empirical Economics*, 30:1–22.

Temple J. (2000) 'Growth Regressions and What the Textbooks Don't Tell You', *Bulletin of Economic Research*, 52 (3): 181–205.

**Data Appendix**

| Variable: | Suggested by: | Source: | Explanation: |
|---|---|---|---|
| *Dependent variable* | | | |
| Correlation between output gaps in real GDP | Frankel and Rose (1998) | GGDC (Groningen Growth and Development Centre) | Output gaps are computed using the Christiano-Fitzgerald filter with an upper bound of eight years |
| *Financial integration* | | | |
| Capital account controls | Imbs (2004) | IMF Annual Reports on Exchange Arrangements and Exchange Restrictions | Dummy variable which equals 1 if at least one of the countries has controls in place |
| Absolute difference between net foreign asset positions | Imbs (2004) | Lane and Milesi-Ferretti (2001) | Net foreign asset positions are expressed as percentages of GDP |
| *Monetary integration* | | | |
| Exchange rate volatility | Otto et al. (2001) | Heston et al. (2006) | Standard deviation of the change in the natural logarithm of the exchange rate |
| Correlation between inflation rates | Camacho et al. (2006) | Heston et al. (2006) | Inflation rates are computed as the percentage change in the CPI |
| *Trade integration* | | | |
| Bilateral trade scaled by GDP | Frankel and Rose (1998) | Feenstra et al. (2005) | Bilateral trade divided by the sum of both countries' GDP |
| Bilateral trade scaled by minimum GDP | Otto et al. (2001) | Feenstra et al. (2005), GGDC, IMF (for the US GDP deflator) | Bilateral trade divided by the smallest of both countries' GDP |
| Bilateral trade scaled by the product of GDP | Clark and van Wincoop (2001) | Feenstra et al. (2005), GGDC, IMF (for the US GDP deflator) | Bilateral trade multiplied by world GDP and divided by two times the product of both countries' GDP |
| Bilateral trade scaled by trade | Frankel and Rose (1998) | Feenstra et al. (2005) | Bilateral trade divided by the sum of both countries' total trade |

**Data Appendix**

| Variable: | Suggested by: | Source: | Explanation: |
|---|---|---|---|
| *Specialization* | | | |
| Sum of the absolute differences between export shares | Baxter and Kouparitsas (2005) | Feenstra et al. (2005) | Export shares are calculated at the SITC3 level and are expressed as percentages of GDP |
| Sum of the squared differences between export shares | Baxter and Kouparitsas (2005) | Feenstra et al. (2005) | Export shares are calculated at the SITC3 level and are expressed as percentages of GDP |
| Correlation between export shares | Baxter and Kouparitsas (2005) | Feenstra et al. (2005) | Export shares are calculated at the SITC3 level and are expressed as percentages of GDP |
| *First principal component of these three export measures* | | | |
| First principal component of three import measures (defined in the same way as the export similarity measures above) | Baxter and Kouparitsas (2005) | Feenstra et al. (2005) | Import shares are calculated at the SITC3 level and are expressed as percentages of GDP |
| Bilateral intra-industry trade | Gruben et al. (2002) | Feenstra et al. (2005) | $1 - \sum_k \left| X_{i,j} - M_{i,j} \right| / \sum_k \left( X_{i,j} + M_{i,j} \right)$ where $i$ and $j$ denote countries and k denotes the SITC3 category |
| **Structural characteristics** | | | |
| Absolute difference between savings ratios | Camacho et al. (2006) | Heston et al. (2006) | Savings are expressed as percentages of GDP |
| Average Openness | Baxter and Kouparitsas (2005) | Heston et al. (2006) | Openness is defined as the sum of a country's exports and imports scaled by its GDP level |
| Absolute difference between the government's share of GDP | Clark and van Wincoop (2001) | Heston et al. (2006) | |
| Common legal origin | Otto et al. (2001) | La Porta et al. (1998) | Dummy variable which equals 1 when countries share a common legal origin |

# Part III
# Foreign exchange rates

# 8 Have exchange rate regimes in Asia become more flexible post crisis?

## Re-visiting the evidence

*Tony Cavoli and Ramkishen S. Rajan*

## Introduction

There is a broad consensus that the soft US dollar pegs operated by a number of Asian countries prior to 1997 contributed to the regional financial crisis of 1997–8. There is, however, much less agreement on the types of exchange rate regimes operated by many Asian countries since the crisis. To be sure, among the crisis-hit countries, the Malaysian ringgit has been unambiguously fixed to the US dollar (at 3.80 Malaysian Ringgit per US dollar) since September 1998. In contrast, the four other crisis-hit countries, viz. Indonesia, Korea, the Philippines and Thailand, officially proclaimed to have floated their exchange rates while adopting a monetary policy strategy based on inflation targeting (see Table 8.1 and Cavoli and Rajan, 2005).

There is a burgeoning literature documenting that there can be a significant divergence between *de facto* and *de jure* exchange rate policies and regimes. Just how flexible have exchange rates in Asia become post-crisis? Can they still be characterized as soft US dollar pegs as suggested by Calvo and Reinhart (2002), Fukuda (2002) and McKinnon (2001), or have they become genuinely more flexible as suggested by Baig (2001), Hernández and Montiel (2001), Kawai (2002) and others.[1]

At a first glance, Figure 8.1 reveals that exchange rates appear to have become more flexible in recent years for all the countries except Malaysia. Even if the Asian currencies have become more flexible, what form has the flexibility taken, i.e. free floating, managed floating, basket pegging, etc? The extent and form of flexibility of Asian currencies post-crisis is not solely of academic interest, being directly related to the ongoing debate on the need for global macroeconomic adjustments and the manner in which such adjustments are to be attained (Rajan 2004).

This paper revisits the evidence regarding the extent of exchange rate flexibility in the five Asian countries post-crisis using alternative methodologies and data up to mid-2004. Different measures of *de facto* regimes inevitably capture different characteristics of any regime. As such, using a number of methodologies is critical as a robustness exercise – the existence of similar results from alternative methods allows us to form conclusions about exchange rate regimes with significantly greater confidence than if only one method was employed.

*Table 8.1* Highlights of inflation targeting regimes in selected Asian countries

| Country | Date | Target price index | Target horizon | Escape clauses | Accountability | Target set by | Publication and accountability |
|---|---|---|---|---|---|---|---|
| Indonesia | May 1999 | Core CPI (excluding food and energy) | 1–2 years | none | None, but parliament can request reports at any time | Central Bank | Quarterly Inflation report, Annual report to public |
| Philippines | Dec 2001 | Core CPI (excluding food and energy) | 2 years | Yes, in the event of oil price shocks, food supply shocks | Public explanation of the nature of the breach and steps to address it | Central Bank | Quarterly inflation report, publication of monetary policy meetings |
| Thailand | Apr 2000 | Core CPI (excluding food and energy) | Indefinite | None | Public explanation of breach and steps taken to address it | Central Bank in consultation with Government | Inflation Report, inflation forecasts and publication of models used |
| Korea | Jan 1998 | Core CPI (excluding non-cereal agricultural products and petroleum products) | indefinite | Changes caused by major force | None | Central Bank in consultation with Government | Inflation report and submission to parliament, publication of monetary policy meetings |

Sources: Compiled by authors from Bank of Korea, Bank Indonesia, Bank of Thailand, Bangko Sentral ng Pilipinas websites

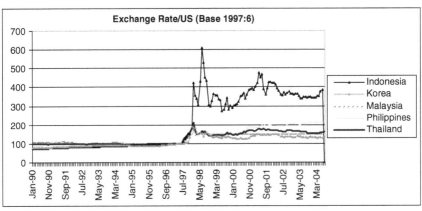

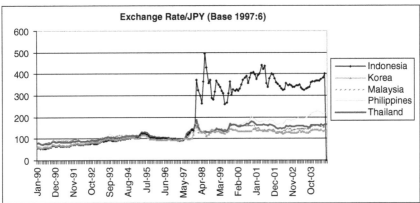

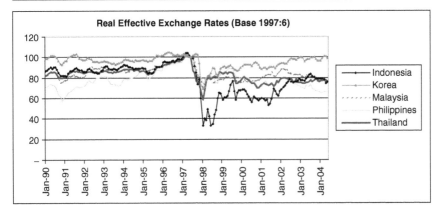

*Figure 8.1* Exchange rates 1990–2004.
Sources: IMF International Financial Statistics CD-ROM and ADB-ARIC.

An important caveat is in order before proceeding. There are a number of recent papers on the topic of *de facto* regime classification – for instance, see Bénassy-Quéré *et al.* (2004), Bubula and Otker-Robe (2002; 2003), Frankel *et al.* (2001), Calvo and Reinhart (2002), Kim (2003), Levy-Yeyati and Sturzenegger (2002), Reinhart and Rogoff (2002) and Shambaugh (2004). This paper does not concern itself with the methodology of actually classifying exchange rate regimes but instead concentrates on detecting possible regime changes in the five Asian countries pre- and post-crisis.

The remainder of the paper is organized as follows. Section 2 examines the *de facto* regimes by investigating the unconditional volatilities of exchange rates, interest rates and international reserves using monthly data for the period January 1990 to July 2004. It also conducts more formal tests to ascertain the degree of exchange rate flexibility and the extent of intervention employed to control the volatility of the currency for the same period. The focus is on the difference in the variability of exchange rates, interest rates and international reserves in each Asian country pre- and post-crisis, as well as between the Asian countries and noted 'floaters' (Australia, New Zealand, Canada, UK and US) post-crisis.[2] Section 3 computes a set of exchange market pressure (EMP) indices to provide a summary measure of the degree of flexibility (or inversely, the degree of intervention). Section 4 presents more formal tests on the extent to which each of the currencies examined have been pegged to the US dollar and to the Japanese yen using an extension of the methodology pioneered by Frankel and Wei (1994). Section 5 offers a summary and some concluding remarks.

### Pre and post crisis behaviour of exchange rates, interest rates and reserves

We attempt to do two things in this section. One, we investigate the behaviour of exchange rates, interest rates and reserves for the crisis-affected countries using monthly data for the period 1990–2004. The nexus between the volatilities of exchange rates, interest rates and reserves is important from a policy perspective in that it offers some insight into whether central banks used interest rates or reserves to manage currency movements. Two, in order to assist with the comparison we split the sample into the pre crisis and post-crisis sub-samples. The volatilities of exchange rates, interest rates and reserves for the pre and post-crisis samples are compared for each country and between the crisis-hit countries and the known 'floaters' of Australia, New Zealand, Canada, UK and US (as defined by Calvo and Reinhart, 2002).

### Standard deviations of exchange rates, interest rates and reserves

Figures 8.2a–c present annual (calendar year) standard deviations of monthly percentage changes in exchange rates for the crisis-affected countries.[3]

The extreme volatility of the exchange rates during the crisis of 1997–8 notwithstanding, the exchange rate volatilities in Korea, Thailand and Indonesia

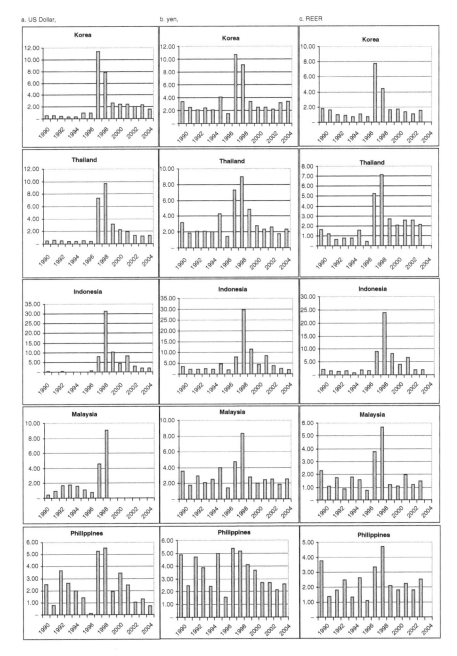

*Figure 8.2* Standard deviations of local exchange rates per:
Source: IMF IFS. Calculated as calendar year standard deviations of percentage first differences (Exchange rates, and reserves/lagged money base), first differences (Interest rates).

are significantly higher in the post-crisis period, while there is no volatility of the ringgit against the US dollar, as would be expected (Figure 8.1). The differences in variability for the Philippines seem economically insignificant when eyeballing the data. Exchange rate volatility of the regional currencies against the yen does not appear to have increased discernibly pre and post-crisis, except possibly for Indonesia (Figure 8.2b). The results for the real effective exchange rates (REERs) show similar but not as marked differences between the two periods compared to the volatilities of local currencies per US dollars (Figure 8.2c). Overall, the exchange rate volatilities offer some indicative initial evidence to support the claim that exchange rate regimes in Korea, the Philippines and Thailand have become more flexible post-crisis.

It is well known that unconditional exchange rate volatility alone cannot adequately describe the currency regime adopted by a country. This is because central banks could use interest rates and reserves as policy instruments to help actively manage or influence currency movements. Accordingly, in order to present a more complete account of the possible change of regime (i.e. degree of conditional exchange rate flexibility), the volatilities of interest rates and reserves must also be taken into account. Specifically, a regime considered to be less flexible will have relatively low exchange rate volatility, *ceteris paribus*.[4] If, in the event of relatively low exchange rate volatility and where reserve volatility is high but interest rate volatility is low, then it might be posited that reserves are the primary policy instrument (i.e. exchange rate intervention). If reserve volatility is low but interest rate volatility is high, then plausibly, interest rates might be the primary instrument for stabilizing the currency (Reinhart 2000).[5]

Figure 8.3 examines the money market interest rates in annual standard deviation of monthly first differences. As is apparent, interest rates are clearly less volatile after the crisis, particularly for Korea, Thailand and the Philippines.[6]

Figure 8.4 shows the annual standard deviations of the monthly deviation of foreign reserves (net foreign assets) scaled by lagged base money from its Hodrick-Prescott (HP) filtered trend. This adjustment for trend is made to remove the effects of possible reserve accumulation by central banks that do not specifically related to day-to-day exchange rate management. Specifically, it is common knowledge that Korea and other Asian countries (except the Philippines) have been accumulating reserves since 1998, a reflection of the fact that the currencies have been undervalued (Kim *et al.* 2004; Hernández and Montiel 2001). However, here we are principally interested in the management of volatility as opposed to the management of the value of the exchange rate. In addition, reserves are scaled by lagged domestic monetary base in order to compare the magnitude of the reserve change in relation to the stock of money base in the system. Since reserves are used to alter relative monies, scaling the change in reserves offers some information about the proportion of the money base that is being used for intervention. From Figure 8.4, it can be seen that the differences in reserve volatility between the pre- and post-crisis periods are not easily detectable for most countries. Korea is a notable exception where it seems that reserves

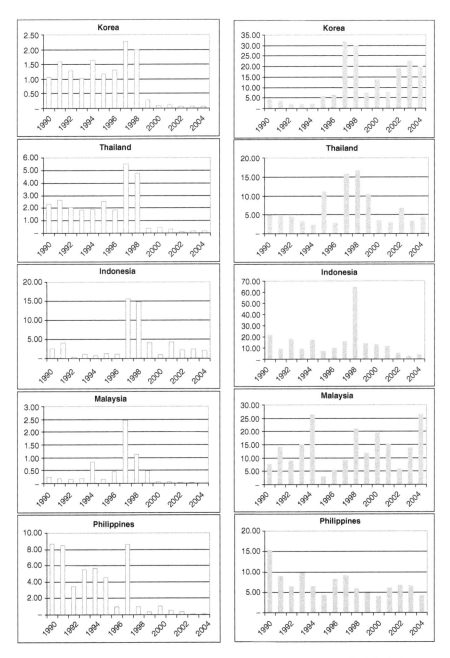

*Figure 8.3* Interest rate standard deviations.   *Figure 8.4* Reserve standard deviations.
Source: IMF IFS. Interest Rate standard deviations are calculated as the annual standard deviation
of monthly first differences. Reserve standard deviations are calculated as annual standard deviation
of monthly deviations of net foreign assets from their Hodrick-Prescott trend, then scaled by lagged
base money.

volatility has increased significantly post-crisis (also see Willett 2004). There is also evidence to suggest that reserve volatility for Indonesia may have diminished after the crisis.

Comparing Figures 8.2a and 8.2c, it can be seen, at least for the local currency per US dollar and the REERs, that exchange rate volatility is higher post-crisis and that interest rates have become less volatile. The implication regarding the volatility of reserves is harder to categorically determine. The conclusion is that the exchange rate regimes for Korea, Thailand, Indonesia and the Philippines have become more flexible post-crisis. The reverse is true for Malaysia. However, this conclusion is clouded somewhat by the volatility of reserves, where there is little evidence to support a conclusion of increased flexibility. In fact, Korea seems to be using reserves more aggressively after the crisis than before, while the volatility of international reserves does not appear to have materially decreased post-crisis for Thailand and the Philippines.

### Pre versus post crisis volatilities and comparison with known floaters

Table 8.2 presents the standard deviations of exchange rates, interest rates and reserve changes as before for the five Asian countries and for the known floaters for the pre and post-crisis sample periods. We define the pre crisis sample as spanning the period 1990:1 to 1997:3, while the post-crisis sample period is 1999:6 to 2004:6.[7] We aim to do two things here. First, we compare the relative volatilities in a single country over the two sample periods. Second, we compare the post-crisis samples of the five Asian countries with the known floaters.

A comparison of each sample confirms the conclusions of the previous section. Irrespective of how the exchange rate is expressed (i.e. vis-à-vis the US dollar, yen or REER), its volatility after the crisis increased for Korea, Thailand and Indonesia, decreased for Malaysia, and remained more-or-less stable (with a bias to a slight decrease) in the Philippines. Correspondingly, interest rate and reserve volatility decreased after the crisis for the most part, although there are a few important exceptions. The first relates to interest rates in Indonesia. Unlike in the other countries, they have become more variable after the crisis. Along with a post-crisis reduction in reserve volatility, this suggests that interest rates are possibly used more frequently as a policy instrument.[8] The second exception is the increase in reserve volatility in Korea. Is this an indication of some desire to continue to use reserves as an exchange rate management tool?

As in Baig (2001) and Calvo and Reinhart (2002) and others, we compare the post-crisis volatilities for the Asian countries and the known floaters. For the most part the exchange rate variation is lower for those countries in the Asian sample than for the floaters. The interest rate volatility in the floaters is also lower, suggesting that they are less inclined to intervene using interest rate policy. (Interest rate smoothing appears to be a more important objective among industrial countries). With regard to the volatility of reserves, it appears that New Zealand is an outlier here, and that the floaters possess less variation in reserves.[9]

Table 8.2 Standard deviations pre and post crisis

| | ER/US | | ER/Yen | | REER | | Non market rate | | [(NFA-Hp Trend)/MB(-1)] | |
|---|---|---|---|---|---|---|---|---|---|---|
| | Pre | Post | Pre | Post | Pre | Post | Pre | Post | Pre | Post |
| Indonesia | 0.24 | 6.09 | 2.87 | 6.42 | 1.57 | 4.88 | 1.97 | 2.67 | 23.74 | 14.31 |
| Korea | 0.79 | 2.29 | 2.69 | 2.89 | 1.15 | 1.48 | 1.28 | 0.10 | 7.81 | 21.51 |
| Philippines | 2.24 | 2.17 | 3.82 | 3.11 | 2.33 | 2.05 | 5.68 | 0.60 | 11.83 | 7.23 |
| Thailand | 0.50 | 2.11 | 2.57 | 3.01 | 1.08 | 1.37 | 2.26 | 0.25 | 10.61 | 5.79 |
| **Average** | **0.94** | **3.17** | **2.99** | **3.86** | **1.53** | **2.45** | **2.80** | **0.91** | **13.50** | **12.21** |
| Malaysia | 1.25 | – | 2.80 | 2.45 | 1.58 | 1.46 | 0.41 | 0.06 | 23.62 | 30.28 |
| Australia | 2.06 | 3.25 | 3.67 | 3.63 | 2.10 | 2.08 | 0.32 | 0.15 | 5.79 | 9.13 |
| Canada | 1.22 | 1.91 | 2.85 | 4.09 | 1.25 | 1.39 | 0.56 | 0.21 | 6.02 | 5.05 |
| New Zealand | 1.57 | 3.55 | 3.20 | 2.94 | 1.43 | 2.15 | 0.71 | 0.16 | 43.43 | 22.63 |
| UK | 3.25 | 2.29 | 3.87 | 2.86 | 1.76 | 1.22 | 0.64 | 0.82 | 10.77 | 3.46 |
| USA | – | – | 2.87 | 2.45 | 1.64 | 1.78 | 0.18 | 0.21 | 1.25 | 0.38 |
| **Average** | **2.03** | **2.75** | **3.29** | **3.19** | **1.64** | **1.73** | **0.48** | **0.31** | **13.45** | **8.13** |

Sources: IMF IFS and ADB-ARIC data, monthly observations.

Note: Standard deviations for exchange rates are calculated from percentage first differences for interest rates, first differences and for net foreign assets, the deviation from the HP Trend is taken and divided by lagged money base. Pre sample period: 1990:1 to 1997:3. Post Crisis data: 1999:6 2004:6 (except REER for East Asian countries, 1999:6 to 2004:5)

The simple analysis undertaken thus far leads to the conclusion that, with the exception of Malaysia, the Asian countries have moved towards more flexible exchange rates. However, the Asian currencies are clearly far less flexible than the known floaters, suggesting some degree of continued market intervention to stabilize the exchange rate.[10] Results of this nature have led many to hypothesize about a possible "Fear of Floating" in some emerging market economies (for instance, see Baig, 2001 and Calvo and Reinhart, 2002).

## Exchange market pressure (EMP) indices

### *Defining the indices*

As discussed, it is important to simultaneously consider the three variables (namely exchange rates, interest rates and reserve changes) to obtain a proper perspective on the extent of exchange rate flexibility (or inversely, the extent of intervention). One way of incorporating all of these variables would be to compute an exchange rate pressure (EMP) index. This section presents two sets of simple EMP indices based on Baig (2001), Bayoumi and Eichengreen (1998), Glick and Wihlborg (1997) and Calvo and Reinhart (2002):[11]

$$Index\ 1 = \sigma_{ER}/(\sigma_{ER} + \sigma_{NFA}) \tag{8.1}$$

$$Index\ 2 = \sigma_{ER}/(\sigma_{ER} + \sigma_{NFA} + \sigma_{IR}) \tag{8.2}$$

where $\sigma_{ER}$ is the annual standard deviation of monthly (log) percentage difference in the exchange rate, $\sigma_{IR}$ is the annual standard deviation of monthly first differences in money market rates, and $\sigma_{NFA}$ is the annual standard deviation of the monthly deviation of reserves from its HP trend (and scaled by lagged Money Base). All standard deviations are calculated as in the previous sections.

While there are a number of different types of EMP indices (for instance, see Guimãeres and Karacadag 2004), the particular set of indices were chosen because they are easily aligned with the discussion of the previous section about the role of interest rates and/or reserves as policy instruments. For instance, a low index value in this instance may imply less exchange rate flexibility or a higher level of intervention. Other things being equal, higher reserve volatility will reduce the index value, possibly suggesting that reserves are being employed as a monetary policy tool in order to limit exchange rate flexibility.

Index 1 measures the possible effects of reserve intervention but ignores the effects of interest rates. Baig (2001) and Bayoumi and Eichengreen (1998) are primarily concerned with this type of index as interest rate movements contain market as well as policy determinants.[12] While this is true, the same can be said of reserves data – which are not cleansed of currency valuation changes.[13] It may be worth evaluating the effects of interest rate based intervention in light of the move by some Asian central banks towards inflation targeting and the use of interest rate rules (Cavoli and Rajan, 2005). Hence, Index 2 is a generalized index capturing both reserve and interest rate intervention. By construction, each index presents values bounded by 0 and 1, and the weights attributable to each variable in the denominator of the index are equal.[14]

### Interpreting the results

As in the previous section, three measures of the exchange rate are used, namely local against the US dollar, the yen, and the REER. The results are presented in Figures 8.5 and 8.6. Figures 8.5a–8.5c show Index 1 for the US dollar, yen and

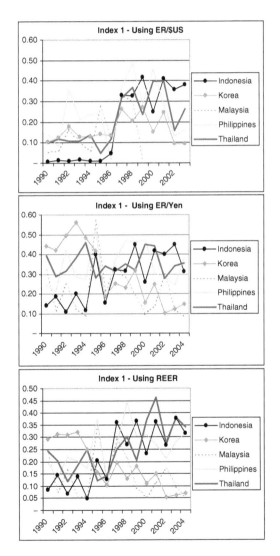

*Figure 8.5* Flexibility index 1.
Sources: IMF IFS and ADB-ARIC

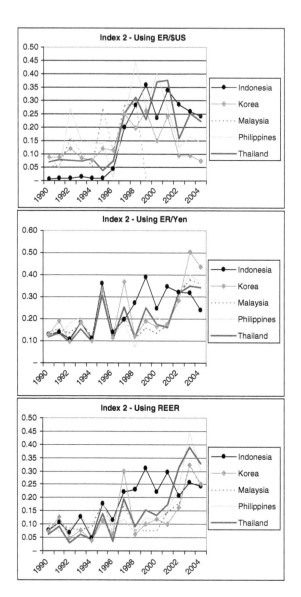

*Figure 8.6* Flexibility index 2.
Source: IMF IFS and ADB-ARIC

REER, respectively. Figures 8.6a–8.6c show Index 2 for the US dollar, yen and REER, respectively.

Focusing on Index 1, an examination of Figures 8.5a–8.5c tends to confirm that pre-crisis, there was a greater inclination on the part of central banks to intervene in the market against the US dollar, most so in the case of Indonesia and Thailand.

Both these countries appear to have become fairly flexible post-crisis, as evidenced by the rise in their respective EMPs, especially vis-à-vis the US dollar. Less obvious results are obtained in the case of the Philippines, while the Malaysian ringgit has become completely inflexible vis-à-vis the US dollar. Somewhat surprisingly, after a period of some flexibility, the Korean won appears to be becoming somewhat less flexible against the US dollar.

Looking at the local currency per yen, pre crisis the regional currencies appeared to have been fairly flexible vis-à-vis the yen. This suggests that local central banks allowed their currencies values relative to the yen to be determined by the yen/US rate, so-called 'third currency phenomenon'. Thus, prior to 1997, if regional countries had given greater weight to the yen in their baskets pre crisis, there would have been lower degrees of regional real exchange rate overvaluations following the nearly 50 per cent nominal appreciation of the US dollar relative to the yen between June 1995 to April 1997 (which in turn led to a rise in the value of the regional currencies relative to the yen) (Bird and Rajan 2002; Rajan 2002). Post-crisis, while there does not appear to be any discernible change in the degree of flexibility of the Indonesian rupiah, the Philippine peso, the Thai baht and the Malaysia ringgit vis-à-vis the yen post-crisis, while the Korean won has become relatively less flexible vis-à-vis the yen post-crisis.[15]

Based on the foregoing analysis, as would be expected, while the Thai baht has become more flexible in REER terms, the won seems to have become less so. Indeed, comparing Figures 8.5a–8.5c, it is apparent that while the EMP of the Korean won vis-à-vis the US dollar was lower than the yen or the REER pre crisis, post-crisis its EMP vis-à-vis the REER was equivalently low for all three. This suggests that while the won may have been heavily managed relative to the US dollar prior to the crisis, there is some evidence to suggest it has become more managed relative to a basket (involving the yen and US dollar), such that the won's REER is relatively stable.

How robust are these results? If one examines Figures 8.6a–8.6c (using Index 2), we reach the same conclusion that the regional currencies with the exception of the Malaysian ringgit have become more flexible vis-à-vis the US dollar post-crisis. As discussed above, it appears as though the Korean won is reverting to a soft dollar peg. Interestingly, however, the further conclusion that the won may be more heavily pegged to the REER than the US dollar post-crisis no longer holds. The reason for this is the rise in the Korean won's EMP post-crisis relative to the yen compared to the previous conclusion of a decline (compare Figure 8.5b and 8.6b). However, the finding that the Thai baht has become relatively more flexible in general (relative to the US dollar, the yen and in REER terms) continues to hold.

## Extent of the influence of the US dollar and the yen in Asian currencies

One of the main results from the previous two sections is that the extent of intervention in the US dollar has decreased for the most part, but there appears to be evidence supporting a reversion to a US dollar peg in some instances, particularly in the case of Korea. However, there is some degree of uncertainty as to whether the Korean won is following (pegged to?) the yen more closely post-crisis. This section presents two sets of formal tests (OLS and Kalman Filter based estimates) to ascertain the degree to which local currencies have been and continue to be influenced by the US dollar and by the yen.

### *Influence of the US dollar and yen – time invariant results*

The first set of tests is based on the well-known work by Frankel and Wei (1994). The method essentially involves conducting an OLS test of the local currency on other currencies that are considered to influence the former. Each currency is expressed in terms of an 'independent' numeraire. The equation examined is as follows:

$$ER_t = \alpha + \beta_1 US_t + \beta_2 JP_t + \mu_t \tag{8.3}$$

where *ER* refers to the local currency. All currencies are expressed in log differences and the numeraire currency used is the Swiss franc.[16] As with the empirical results in the previous section, the pre crisis sample is 1990:1 to 1997:3 and the post-crisis sample is 1999:6 to 2004:6.

Table 8.3 presents the pre and post-crisis values of $\beta_1$ and $\beta_2$ for Korea, Thailand, Indonesia, and the Philippines.[17] Only the pre crisis regressions are presented for Malaysia given the country's stated post-crisis rigid fix to the US dollar. The coefficient values are interpreted as the degree of influence of the US dollar and yen, respectively, on the local currency. A larger $\beta$ value is suggestive of a high degree of influence of the US dollar and hence possible intervention in the market for that currency. This said, it is important to note that a large positive and significant coefficient on $\beta_1$ does necessarily imply strong US dollar pegs. As Hernández and Montiel (2001) observe '(such) results are consistent either with a tight peg against the U.S. dollar … or with a much looser currency link to the dollar combined with tight economic links to the dollar area and a relative absence of independent shocks during the sample period'.

The results based on the simple OLS in Table 8.3 reveal that the value of $\beta_1$ has fallen after the crisis. By and large, this validates the results from the previous sections in that the degree of flexibility against the US dollar has increased after the crisis. Not only has the value fallen, but the level of significance has declined as well, possibly an indication of a reduction in the tightness of the peg to the US dollar. Also noteworthy is the increase in the degree of influence of the yen after the crisis. This is noticeable across-the-board. It should be noted though that the significance levels are lower for the yen than for the US dollar. This is broadly consistent with the results in Section 3, whereby the EMPs of the currencies using the US dollar have generally risen post-crisis and have fallen relative to the yen, but the former still exceeds the latter.

*Table 8.3* OLS estimates using Frankel and Wei (1994) method

Equation: $ER_t = \beta_0 + \beta_1 US_t + \beta_2 JP_t + \mu_t$

| | Korea | | Thailand | | Indonesia | | Malaysia | Philippines | |
|---|---|---|---|---|---|---|---|---|---|
| | *Pre* | *Post* | *Pre* | *Post* | *Pre* | *Post* | *Pre* | *Pre* | *Post* |
| $\beta_0$ | 0.00 | −0.00 | 0.00 | 0.00 | 0.00 | 0.00 | −0.00 | 0.00 | 0.01 |
| | (0.84) | (−0.02) | (2.16)** | (0.88) | (14.78)† | (1.69)* | (−0.55) | (0.67) | (2.61)† |
| $\beta_1$ | 0.93 | 0.70 | 0.84 | 0.68 | 0.99 | 0.13 | 0.89 | 1.10 | 0.75 |
| | (36.59)† | (4.74)† | (101.22)† | (5.23)† | (95.87)† | (0.36) | (21.27)† | (16.32)† | (5.53)† |
| $\beta_2$ | 0.11 | 0.45 | 0.11 | 0.20 | 0.02 | 0.44 | 0.09 | −0.03 | 0.06 |
| | (3.13)† | (3.80)† | (14.27)† | (1.83)* | (3.15)† | (1.64) | (1.81)* | (−0.37) | (0.51) |
| $R^2_{adj}$ | 0.97 | 0.72 | 0.99 | 0.60 | 0.99 | 0.31 | 0.89 | 0.75 | 0.54 |
| DW | 1.91 | 1.74 | 2.06 | 1.98 | 1.97 | 2.01 | 1.80 | 1.92 | 2.20 |
| Obs | 87 | 61 | 87 | 61 | 97 | 61 | 87 | 87 | 61 |

Note: * (**)(†), 10% (5%)(1%) significant levels, respectively. Malaysia post crisis regressions not included. Korea pre crisis and post crisis results contained serial correlation. To correct for this and to reduce the incidence of biased parameter estimates, Korea pre crisis and Indonesia post crisis model includes ARMA(1,1) terms and Indonesia post crisis includes ARMA(3,3) terms.

*Influence of the US dollar and yen – time varying coefficients*

The relative degree of significance between the US dollar and the yen can be explored further by applying the Kalman Filter to the regressions. Such regressions allow for the coefficient's evolution to be tracked over the entire sample. The model used is as follows:

$$ER_t = \alpha + \beta_t X_t + \mu_t \tag{8.4}$$

$$\beta_t = \beta_{t-1} + \varepsilon_t \tag{8.5}$$

Equation (8.4) once again describes the measurement equation of the system ($X_t = [US_t, JP_t]$), but each coefficient ($\beta_t = [\beta_{1t}, \beta_{2t}]$) is assumed to vary over time, the evolution of which is given by Equation (8.5). This particular simple version of the Kalman Filter method applies a recursive algorithm that uses a log likelihood function to estimate the value of each $\beta_t$ at each iteration. The likelihood function is used to update the state estimates, $\beta_t$ and the estimated state covariance, $P_t$ conditional on information obtained at time $t - 1$.[18] The result is that the evolution of each $\beta$ can be examined for the pre crisis and post-crisis periods without the need to split the sample.[19]

One of the advantages of the Kalman Filter technique over the simple Frankel-Wei OLS tests is that the volatility of a coefficient can be observed over time. This may offer us greater insight into central bank behaviour. A smooth time path of the coefficient might imply that the central bank intervenes to maintain the influence of one currency over the other. A high but erratic coefficient value possibly implies a strong correlation that is not necessarily brought about by central bank behaviour. Rather, it could imply a strong correlation that occurs naturally in the market for that particular currency pair, driven by market conditions, trader behaviour or noise.

Figure 8.6 shows the one-step ahead forecasts of $\beta_1$ and $\beta_2$ (for the US dollar and the yen) at each iteration over the sample period 1990:1 to 2004:6 for the five Asian countries. As with the EMP indices, the crisis period is easy to detect for both the US dollar and the yen. The results lend weight to those of the previous section in that the won, baht, and rupiah are all seemingly less influenced by the US dollar after the crisis. For Korea and Thailand, the value of $\beta_1$ is more volatile post-crisis. Volatility of the coefficient values over time might possibly be interpreted as a loosening of the degree of influence of a particular currency over the local currency – perhaps a reflection of a loosening of a peg to that currency. This is consistent with Kim and Lee (2004) who find that Thai and Korean interest rates have become less sensitive to US interest rates post-crisis, suggesting greater flexibility of these currencies relative to the US dollar.

As expected, the $\beta_1$ coefficient for Malaysia is 1 after the crisis. Interestingly, the influence of the yen ($\beta_2$) is more volatile after the crisis for Thailand and higher in value for Korea and Indonesia, but also more volatile, especially for Korea. The results for the Philippines accord to those in the last section. There appears to be

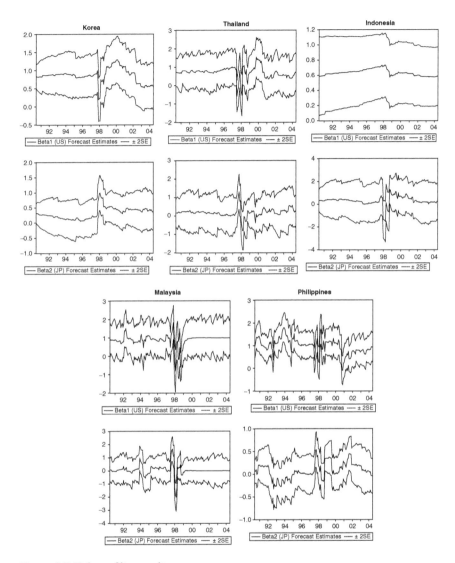

*Figure 8.7* Kalman filter results.

little difference in the influence of the US dollar or the yen between the pre and post-crisis periods.

Figure 8.7 presents the time variation of $\beta_1$ and $\beta_2$ on the same graph for each country. It can be seen here that, in general, the influence of the US dollar has decreased after the crisis, but that the influence of the yen has increased. For Korea, there is a sizeable difference between the influence of the dollar and that of the yen before the crisis. After the crisis there is evidence of convergence, as

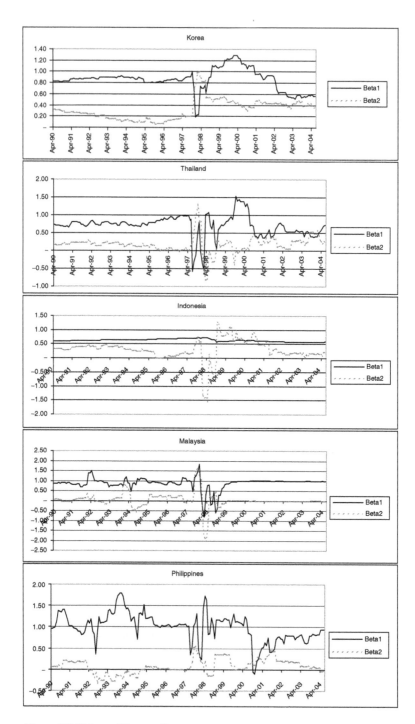

*Figure 8.8* Kalman filter results.

the coefficient for $\beta_1$ has decreased and $\beta_2$ increased. This is consistent with the conclusions drawn based on the EMP using Index 1, but not Index 2. The extent to which the baht is driven by the dollar is more erratic post-crisis and is matched by the yen. This is in line with the conclusions in the previous section which suggest that the baht may have become more flexible vis-à-vis both the yen and the US dollar post-crisis. Indonesia's coefficient for the US dollar is relatively smooth compared to the yen, suggesting a possible inclination to continue to fix to the US dollar. The comparative results for the Philippines show that while the degree of influence of the US dollar may be high, it is not smooth. This is representative of a scenario where a high correlation does not necessarily imply a peg. The yen maintains a small influence over the Philippine peso. Needless to say, the results for Malaysia are as expected, the ringgit being influenced entirely by the US dollar post-crisis.

## Concluding remarks

This paper has reviewed the pre and post-crisis exchange rate regimes for Korea, Thailand, Indonesia, Malaysia and the Philippines. The *de jure* regimes for Korea, Thailand and Indonesia seem to suggest that exchange rates underwent a transition from soft US dollar pegs to floating exchange rates (cum inflation targeting) after the crisis. Malaysia's regime reverted to a fully fixed exchange rate vis-à-vis the US dollar since September 1998. The Philippines, which was least impacted by the crisis, maintained its status as operating a 'dirty' floating exchange rate regime.

We return to our basic question posed in the Introduction, namely have the Asian countries (except Malaysia) moved to more flexible exchange rate regimes, or have they reverted to soft US dollar pegs post-crisis? From the various measures of *de facto* regimes presented in this paper, it appears that there is definitely an increase in exchange rate flexibility after the crisis in the case of Thailand. There is some evidence of a possible reversion to a US dollar peg for Indonesia (also see Siregar and Rajan 2003). The results for Korea are arguably most interesting in that they suggest that while there is still a significant and possibly increasing degree of influence by the US dollar on local currencies after the crisis, the influence of the yen has increased materially post-crisis. However, the variability of this influence has also increased. As such, it is unclear whether the Korean monetary authorities are consciously placing more weight to the yen in managing the Korean won as suggested by Taguchi (2004), or they have genuinely let the currency float and the market has caused a higher co-movement between local currencies and the yen. This is an area for future research.[20]

## Acknowledgement

Valuable comments by Mark Spiegel and seminar participants at the University of Adelaide are gratefully appreciated. The usual disclaimer applies.

# References

Baig T. (2001) 'Characterizing Exchange Rate Regimes Post-Crisis East Asia', IMF Working Paper, No.01/152. Washington, DC.

Bayoumi T. and Eichengreen B. (1998) 'Exchange Rate Volatility Intervention: Implications of the Theory of Optimum Currency', *Journal of International Economics*, 45: 191–209.

Bénassy-Quéré A., Coeuré B. and Mignon, V. (2004) 'On the Identification of De Facto Currency', unpublished working paper. CEPII, mimeo, November.

Bird G. and Rajan R. S. (2002) 'Optimal Currency Baskets and the Third Currency Phenomenon: Exchange Rate Policy in Southeast Asia', *Journal of International Development*, 14(8): 1053–1073.

Bubula A. and Otker-Robe I. (2002) 'The Evolution of Exchange Rate Regimes Since 1990: Evidence from De Facto Policies', IMF Working Paper, No.02/155. Washington, DC.

——(2003) 'Are Pegged and Intermediate Exchange Rate Regimes More Crisis Prone?' IMF Working Paper, No.03/223. Washington, DC.

Calvo G. and Reinhart C. M. (2002) 'Fear of Floating', *Quarterly Journal of Economics*, 117(2): 379–408.

Cavoli T. and Rajan R. S. (2005) 'Inflation Targeting and Monetary Policy Rules for Small and Open Developing Economies: Simple Analytics with Application to Thailand', Working Paper, No.SPP-05-05, School of Public Policy, National University of Singapore.

Cuthbertson K., Hall S. and Taylor M. (1992) *Applied Econometric Techniques*, UK: Harvester Wheatsheaf.

Eichengreen B. (2004) 'Monetary and Exchange Rate Policy in Korea: Assessments and Policy Issues', prepared for a symposium at the Bank of Korea, Seoul, August.

Frankel, J. and Wei S. J. (1994) 'Yen Bloc or Dollar Bloc? Exchange Rate Policies The East Asian Economies', in Ito T. and Krueger A. (eds*.), Macroeconomic Linkage: Savings, Exchange Rates, and Capital Flows*, Chicago: University of Chicago Press, pp. 295–333.

Frankel J., Fajnzylber E., Schmukler S. and Servén, L. (2001) 'Verifying Exchange Rate Regimes', *Journal of Development Economics*, 66(2): 351–386.

Fukuda S. (2002) 'Post-Crisis Exchange Rate Regimes in East Asia', mimeo, November.

Girton L. and Roper D. (1977) 'A Monetary Model of Exchange Market Pressure Applied to the Post-war Canadian Experience', *American Economic Review*, 67(4): 537–48.

Glick R. and Wihlborg, C. (1997) 'Exchange Rate Regimes and International Trade', in P. Kenen and B. Cohen, (eds), *International Trade and Finance: New Frontiers for Research*, Cambridge University Press, pp. 125–151.

Guimãeres R. F. and Karacgdag C. (2004) 'The Empirics of Foreign Exchange Intervention in Emerging Market Countries: The Cases of Mexico and Turkey', IMF Working Paper, No. 04/123, Washington, DC.

Hernández L. and Montiel P. (2001) 'Post-Crisis Exchange Rate Policy in Five Asian Countries: Filling in the 'Hollow Middle?' IMF Working Paper, No.01/170, Washington, DC.

Kawai M.(2002) 'Exchange rate arrangements in East Asia: Lessons from the 1997–98 currency crisis, Bank of Japan, Institute for Monetary and Economic Studies', *Monetary and Economic Studies*, 20(S–1, December): 167–204.

Kim S. (2003) 'Monetary Policy, Foreign Exchange Intervention, and the Exchange Rate in a Unifying Framework', *Journal of International Economics*, 60: 355–386.

Kim C. J. and Lee J. W. (2004) 'Exchange Rate Regime and Monetary Independence in the Post-Crisis East Asia: An Application of Regime-Switching Model with Endogenous Explanatory Variables', mimeo, November.

Kim J. S., Li Jie, Ozon S., Rajan R.S. and Willett, T. D. (2004) 'Reserve Adequacy in Asia Revisited: New Benchmarks Based on the Size and Composition of Capital Flows', Conference Proceedings No. 04-03, KIEP (Seoul, Korea), December.

Levy-Yeyati E. and Sturzenegger F. (2002) 'Classifying Exchange Rate Regimes: Deeds vs. Words', Working Paper, Department of Economics, Universidad Torcuato di Tella.

McKinnon R. (2001) 'After the Crisis, the East Asian Dollar Standard Resurrected: An Interpretation of High-Frequency Exchange-Rate Pegging', in J. Stiglitz and S. Yusuf (eds), *Rethinking the East Asian Miracle*. World Bank and Oxford University Press, pp. 197–246.

Oh J. (2004) 'Exchange Rate Disparities and Needs of Policy Cooperation in East Asia', paper presented at the WEAI conference, Vancouver, June 20–July 3.

Ouyang A., R. S. Rajan and T. D. Willett (2007) 'Managing the Monetary Consequences of Reserve Accumulation in Emerging Asia', mimeo, June.

Pentecost E. J., Van Hooydonk C. and Van Poeck A. (2001) 'Measuring and Estimating Exchange Market Pressure in the EU', *Journal of International Money and Finance*, 20(3): 401–418.

Rajan R. S. (2002) 'Exchange Rate Policy Options for Post-Crisis Southeast Asia: Is there a Case for Currency Baskets?' *The World Economy*, 25(1): 137–163.

———(2004) 'The US Current Account Deficit, Exchange Rate Flexibility and Asian Reserves', RIS Policy Brief, No.11, New Delhi, January.

Rajan R. S. and Siregar R. (2002) 'Choice of Exchange Rate Regime: Currency Board (Hong Kong) or Monitoring Band (Singapore)?' *Australian Economic Papers*, 41(4): 538–556.

Reinhart C. M. (2000) 'Mirage of Floating Exchange Rates', *American Economic Review*, 90: 65–70.

Reinhart C. M. and Rogoff, K. (2004) 'The Modern History of Exchange Rate Reinterpretation', *Quarterly Journal of Economics*, 119(1): 1–48.

Shambaugh J. (2004) 'The Effect of Fixed Exchange Rates on Monetary Policy', *Quarterly Journal of Economics*, 119(1): 301–352.

Siregar R. and Rajan R.S. (2003) 'Exchange Rate Policy and Reserve Management in Indonesia in the Context of East Asian Monetary Cooperation', mimeo, December.

Taguchi H. (2004) 'The Post-crisis Exchange Rate Management in Selected East Asian Countries: Flexibility of Exchange Rate and Sensitivity', Working Paper, No. 8, COE-CAS, Waseda University.

Tanner E. (2001) 'Exchange Market Pressure and Monetary Policy: Asia and Latin America in the 1990s', IMF Staff Papers 47: 311–333.

Willett T. D. (2004) 'Assessing Korea's Post Crisis Managed Float', prepared for a symposium at the Bank of Korea, Seoul, August.

# 9   The evolution of the East Asian currency baskets – still undisclosed and changing

*Gunther Schnabl*

## More exchange rate flexibility in East Asia?

Before the 1997/98 Asian crisis, the East Asian countries China, Hong Kong, Indonesia, Korea, Malaysia, the Philippines, Singapore, Taiwan, and Thailand pursued a common exchange rate peg to the US dollar. This (informal) East Asian dollar standard (McKinnon and Schnabl 2004a) was beneficial for growth in the region for several reasons. First, it ensured macroeconomic stability by bringing the domestic rates of inflation close to the US level. Second, the joint peg to the dollar provided low transaction costs not only for trade with the US but also for intra-regional trade flows, which make up about 50 per cent of overall East Asian trade. Third, exchange rate stability provided low transaction costs for short-term and long-term international capital flows.

After the onset of the East Asian crisis, the East Asian dollar standard fell apart. While China, Hong Kong, Singapore, and Taiwan kept their exchange rates stable against the dollar, the currencies of the crisis countries Indonesia, Korea, Malaysia, the Philippines, and Thailand depreciated. The post-crisis policy recommendations for the exchange regimes in East Asia have been of diverse natures. Associating exchange rate stability against the dollar with overly low risk premia on volatile capital inflows, the IMF recommended (more) exchange rate flexibility (Fischer 2001). In contrast, McKinnon and Schnabl (2004a; b) argue that exchange rate stabilization per se is not a reason for overinvestment and, even post-crisis, due to the high degree of 'dollarization' of international transactions in the region exchange rate stabilization against the dollar is fully rational.

A third strand of literature has proposed maintaining exchange rate stability in the region, while at the same time pegging to more than one anchor currency. According to Williamson (2000; 2005), currency basket arrangements would be beneficial for the East Asian countries as they stabilize the nominal effective exchange rates. To maintain intra-regional exchange rate stability, Ogawa and Ito (2002) have proposed to coordinate the currency baskets in the region. Kawai (2006) argues that such coordinated currency baskets based on the dollar, yen and euro can be a first step on the path towards an Asian monetary union.

While post-crisis East Asian exchange rate volatility against the dollar by and large declined (close) to the pre-crisis level, since the year 2005 exchange rate volatility against the dollar has increased. This may be due to either rising exchange rate flexibility or due to higher exchange rate stability against the yen and the euro.

## The rationale for exchange rate stabilization in East Asia

Despite policy recommendations to pursue more exchange rate flexibility, fully flexible exchange rates such as between the dollar and the euro are unlikely in East Asia. This is because stable exchange rates in East Asia have proved to be beneficial for international trade, macroeconomic stability, and international capital flows in the region.

### *International trade*

Building upon Ricardo, the welfare gains originating in the international partition of labour are widely acknowledged. The policy implication is to remove exchange rate volatility to foster international trade and welfare. As the growth performance in East Asia has been strongly based on international and intra-regional trade, exchange rate stability has played a prominent role for economic policy making.

The impact of exchange rate volatility on trade has both a micro- and macroeconomic dimension. From a microeconomic perspective (high frequency) exchange rate volatility – for instance measured as day-to-day or week-to-week exchange rate fluctuations – is associated with higher costs for international goods and capital transactions because uncertainty is high and hedging foreign exchange risk is costly. Indirectly, fixed exchange rates enhance international price transparency as consumers can compare prices in different countries more easily. If exchange rate volatility is reduced or eliminated, international goods arbitrage enhances efficiency, productivity and welfare.

These microeconomic benefits of exchange rate stabilization were, for instance, an important motivation of the European (monetary) integration process (European Commission 1990) which can be seen as a role model for East Asian monetary integration (Kawai 2006). In East Asia, before and after the Asian crisis, the East Asian countries strongly controlled day-to-day exchange rate fluctuations as shown in Figure 9.1. Compared to the freely floating euro/dollar rate the daily fluctuations of the East Asian currencies against the dollar were kept – except for the Asian crisis period – at a significantly lower levels than the benchmark freely floating euro against the dollar.

The macroeconomic dimension arises from the fact that long-term exchange rate fluctuations – for instance measured as monthly or yearly changes of the exchange rate level – affect the competitiveness of domestic export and import competing industries. In small open economies the growth performance can be strongly influenced by long-term fluctuations of the exchange rate level. Even large, comparatively closed economies such as the euro area and Japan have proved to be sensitive to large exchange rate swings, in particular in the case of appreciation. For instance, McKinnon and Ohno (1997) show for Japan that

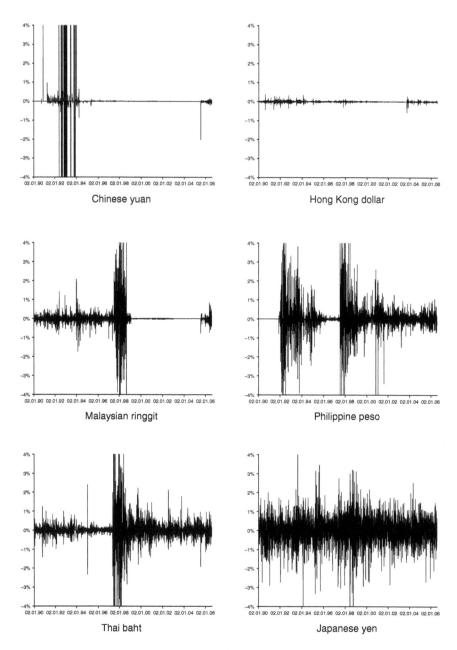

*Figure 9.1* Exchange rate volatility against the US dollar, 1990:01–2006:08 (Daily).
Source: Bloomberg. Volatility is measured in daily percentage changes against the dollar.

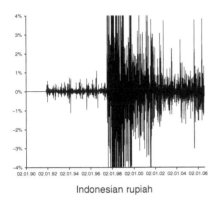

Indonesian rupiah

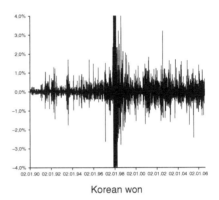

Korean won

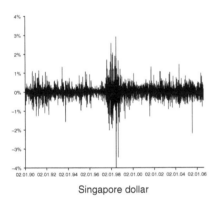

Singapore dollar

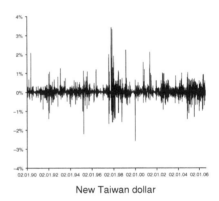

New Taiwan dollar

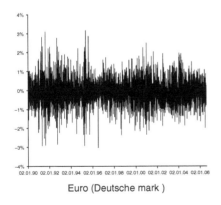

Euro (Deutsche mark )

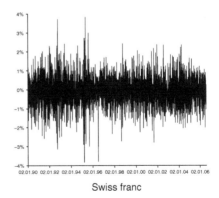

Swiss franc

*Figure 9.1* (Continued)

since the early 1970s when the yen became flexible against the dollar, growth has been strongly slowed down by the appreciation of the Japanese currency.

## *Macroeconomic stability*

While exchange rate fluctuations can influence the macroeconomic stability in open economies significantly through the trade channel, there are also direct linkages inter alia via monetary policy making. As put forward by McKinnon (1963) pegged exchange rates are an important tool for macroeconomic stabilization in small open economies. Assuming that for small economies the international price level is given and traded goods make up a high share of the domestically consumed goods, exchange rate volatility translates into domestic price level fluctuations. The welfare effect of stable exchange rates originates in macroeconomic stability which provides a favourable environment for investment and consumption.

Furthermore, emerging markets and developing countries mostly do not have a history of central bank independence and macroeconomic stability. As monetary policy is often a tool to finance government expenditure, inflation and depreciation are the result. In this context pegged exchange rates provide an important tool to contain inflation tax via both a commitment towards exchange rate stability and a disciplining effect on monetary growth (Crocket and Goldstein 1976).

As stressed by McKinnon and Schnabl (2004a) before the Asian crisis the East Asian countries pinned down their price levels close to the level of the US by pegging their exchange rates commonly to the US dollar. These tight dollar pegs are shown in Figure 9.2. International and intra-regional goods market arbitrage further enhanced the low inflation environment which can be seen as a crucial determinant of the (pre-crisis) East Asian economic miracle.

## *Financial markets*

After the Asian crisis, financial markets have gained an increasing role in the discussion about the pros and cons of exchange rate stabilization (McKinnon and Schnabl 2004a; b; De Grauwe and Schnabl 2008). There is both a short-term (microeconomic) and a long-term (macroeconomic) perspective which are based on the fact that underdeveloped capital markets (as they are prevalent in emerging markets and developing countries) make financials institutions vulnerable to exchange rate fluctuations (Eichengreen and Hausmann 1999).

With domestic foreign exchange markets being small and illiquid, most international short-term payment transactions are denominated in international currency. An active forward market in foreign exchange does not exist.[1] For this reason the foreign exchange risk of short-term capital transactions typically remains un-hedged. Monetary authorities can provide an informal hedge for private short-term capital transactions by minimizing daily exchange rate fluctuations. In practice, formal or informal limits to daily exchange rate fluctuations (Figure 9.1) defined in terms of per cent exchange rate changes are established (Chmelarova and Schnabl 2006). These allow private banks and enterprises to repay (reclaim)

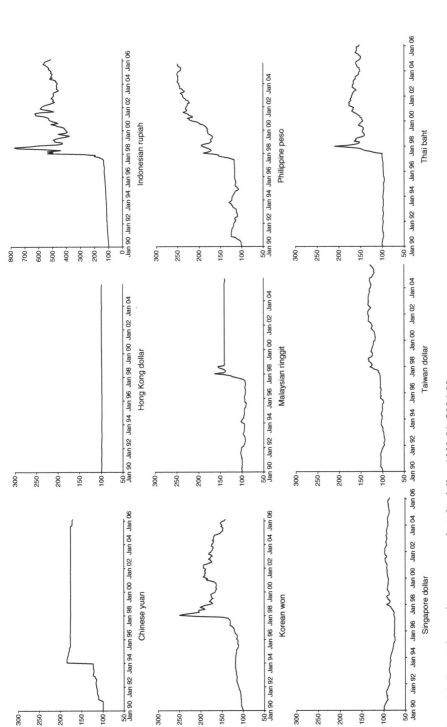

*Figure 9.2* East Asian exchange rates against the dollar, 1990:01–2006:08.

Source: IMF: IFS, Central Bank of China.

Note: Index 1990.01 = 100. Note different scale for Indonesia.

their short-term foreign currency liabilities (assets) with minimal exchange rate risk.

At low frequencies of exchange rate volatility, the rationale for exchange rate stabilization in debtor countries originates in liability and asset dollarization. If net debt is denominated in foreign currency, sharp depreciations increase the liabilities in terms of domestic currency. The probability of default and crisis increases. (Long-term) exchange rate stabilization is equivalent to reducing default risk on balance sheets (Eichengreen and Hausmann 1999; McKinnon and Schnabl 2004a).

Also emerging market creditor countries such as China, Taiwan and Russia have an incentive to stabilize exchange rates as international assets tend to be denominated in international currency. When East Asian investors accumulate assets in US dollars, an appreciation of the domestic currency against the dollar would reduce the value in terms of the domestic currency. The consequence is 'fear of appreciation', foreign exchange intervention and reserve accumulation (McKinnon and Schnabl 2004b).

## Currency diversification in international reserves and currency baskets

Given the rationale for exchange rate stabilization in East Asia as discussed above, it seems unlikely that East Asian countries will pursue fully flexible exchange rates. This will be the case as long as they have not found a way of intra-regional exchange rate stabilization which allows them to float commonly against the euro and the dollar. Instead, they will tend to stabilize exchange rates in the form of tight or soft pegs based on smoothing daily, monthly and yearly exchange rate fluctuations.

McKinnon and Schnabl (2004a) have shown that post-Asian crisis most East Asian countries have returned to their pre-crisis exchange rate stability against the dollar, at least at high frequencies (i.e. day-to-day or week-to-week exchange rate fluctuations). As shown in Figure 9.3, also measured in arithmetic averages of month-to-month per cent exchange rate changes post-crisis exchange rate volatility against the dollar has declined gradually up to the year 2004. This finding is in line with the McKinnon (2005) hypothesis of network externalities in favour of the world dollar standard.

### *The risk of one-sided dollar pegs*

Although the dollar remains the most important anchor currency in the region, Figure 9.3 also suggests that East Asian exchange rate volatility against the dollar was on the rise in 2005 and 2006 and is now in average more than exchange rate volatility of the (South) Eastern and Central European currencies (emerging Europe) against the euro. This may indicate either a general increase in exchange rate volatility as advocated by the IMF (Fischer 2001) or a (gradual) change in the anchor currencies. The main alternative anchor currencies are the euro, the Japanese yen or both.

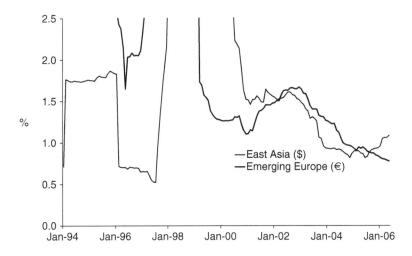

*Figure 9.3* Exchange rate volatility in East Asia and emerging Europe.
Source: IMF. Regional exchange rate volatility defined as arithmetic averages of two year rolling standard deviations.

Frankel and Chinn (2005) and Galati and Wooldrige (2006) argue that the role of the dollar as an international currency may be challenged by the euro, depending on the long-term inflation expectations for the US economy. In East Asia, the degree of macroeconomic stabilization, which is achieved via exchange rate pegs, hinges not only on domestic efforts to keep the exchange rate stable against the anchor currency but also on the monetary policy in the anchor country.

While low and stable US inflation has been a crucial prerequisite for the rise of the dollar as an international currency, the degree of US price stability has fluctuated over time. Since the late 1960s, the US dollar has experienced several phases of rising inflation and sustained depreciation pressure. During these periods a relatively loose US monetary policy was transmitted via reserve accumulation into rising inflationary pressure in countries stabilizing their currencies against the US dollar.

Back in the late 1960s and early 1970s, an expansionary fiscal and monetary stance in the US contributed to a world-wide increase in inflation, which finally triggered the breakdown of the Bretton Woods system. While the European currencies were de-linked from the dollar (thereafter stabilizing their exchange rates against the German mark), most countries outside of Europe, for instance those in East Asia, continued to peg their currencies more or less tightly to the dollar. The international role of the dollar was enhanced by its dominant role as an invoicing currency for international trade, the deepness of US capital markets, and the lack of alternative international currencies (McKinnon 2005). This has led Dooley *et al.* (2004) to argue that the United States is at the centre of what they have called a revived (informal) Bretton Woods system.

Reminiscent of the early 1970s, in the new millennium an exceptionally loose fiscal and monetary stance under the Bush administration has triggered a discussion about the impact of fast reserve accumulation in the countries stabilizing their exchange rates against the dollar. When the Federal Reserve kept the interest rate at historically low levels from 2001 to 2004, the dollar came under strong depreciation pressure. As many countries continued to stabilize exchange rates against the dollar, they accumulated (and continue to accumulate) large amounts of dollar reserves. Figure 9.4 shows the substantial degree of reserve accumulation in East Asia, which has accelerated in many countries since 2001, most dramatically in China, Korea, Malaysia, and Japan.

While fast reserve accumulation has the benefit of strengthening the credibility of the exchange rate pegs, it has two main downsides. First, as under fixed exchange rates the scope for sterilization of foreign exchange intervention is limited, the East Asian countries have experienced fast monetary expansion. Although inflation has been contained in most countries so far, the fast growth of monetary aggregates has contributed to surging stock and real estate prices. An eventual burst of such 'bubbles', for instance in China, may result in cumbersome recessions like those experienced after the Asian crisis and in Japan since the early 1990s.

Second, as outlined above for countries with sustained current account surpluses, rising world inflation has a negative impact on the real value of export revenues and international assets. If, as in the case for many commodity exporting countries, export revenues are earned in dollars and spent on imports from the euro area, dollar depreciation against the euro erodes the real purchasing power of dollar denominated earnings. For international creditor countries, such as Japan, China, Russia and Taiwan the appreciation of domestic currencies reduces the value of these assets in terms of domestic currencies as well as in terms of purchasing power in third currencies.

The upshot is that, between 2001 and 2004, private and public investors reacted asymmetrically to the sustained dollar depreciation. As the sharply rising US current account deficit went along with rising current account surpluses in countries stabilizing their exchange rates against the dollar, private investors tended to convert dollar positions into domestic currencies, bringing their domestic currencies under appreciation pressure. In contrast, the monetary authorities in many emerging markets in East Asia, the Middle East, Latin America, and the CIS tended to resist this appreciation pressure via foreign exchange intervention. From the perspective of the monetary authorities, this 'leaning against the wind' via the build-up of international assets was fully rational because it shields export industries against appreciation and maintains the nominal value of the large stocks of international dollar assets. Both factors contribute to (short-term) macroeconomic stability.

In the longer-term, however, the monetary authorities of East Asian countries may change their exchange rate targets. If they expect the depreciation of the dollar to continue, they may consider reducing their dependency on the dollar as an anchor and reserve currency (Chinn and Frankel 2005; Eichengreen 2005).

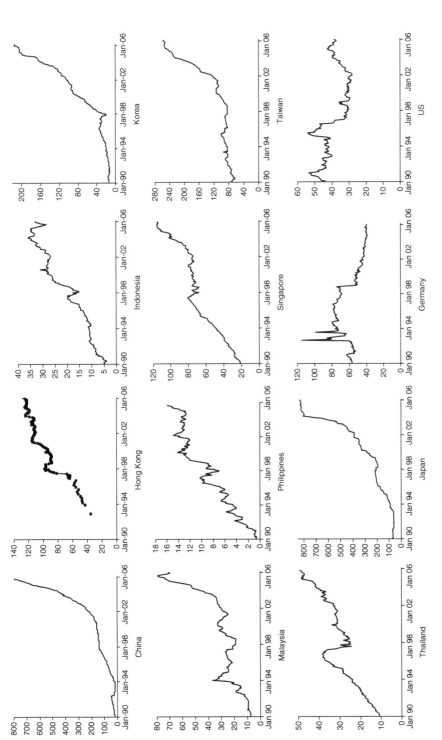

*Figure 9.4* Official foreign exchange reserves in billions of dollars, 1980:01–2006:02 (Monthly).
Source: IMF: IFS.

Note: Billion dollars. Note different scales on the y-axis.

The current expectations about the future value of the US dollar hinge on the expected macroeconomic policies in the US. Starting from 2004, the interest rate increases of the Federal Reserve helped to sustain the value of the dollar, which appreciated against most currencies during 2005. Yet if the US fiscal deficit and the low private savings rate are expected to continue, as the burst of the current 'real estate bubble' seems to trigger new interest rate cuts, the future federal funds rate may be expected to decline again. The implication would be a higher level of US inflation and further depreciation pressure on the dollar.

### *Diversification of risk*

If central banks around the world that have in the past used the dollar as the predominant anchor and reserve currency see a significant probability of a sustained dollar decline, they will consider reducing their dependency on the US currency (Eichengreen 2005). In contrast to former periods of dollar depreciation such as in the 1970s, today the euro has become a viable competitor as an anchor and reserve currency (Chinn and Frankel 2005; ECB 2005; Lim 2006). Although the integration of the European financial markets is still lagging behind the US, deep and liquid euro capital markets provide a broad variety of investment opportunities (Galati and Wooldrige 2006). In addition, the European Central Bank may be perceived as more inflation-averse than the Federal Reserve, which would further strengthen the attractiveness of the euro as an international currency.[2]

Instead of solely pegging to the dollar, the East Asian countries may peg to a basket of currencies for several reasons. Williamson (2000; 2005) has proposed that a currency basket for the East Asian countries should reflect the direction of trade (rather than the currency denomination of trade). The benefits would be nominal effective exchange rate stability[3] and lower fluctuations of overall nominal trade (Gudmundsson 2005). The weights of such a currency basket would closely reflect the trade structure of the respective countries, giving substantial weights to the dollar, the yen, and the euro as well as to smaller East Asian currencies such as the Korean won, the Malaysian ringgit, and the Chinese yuan.[4]

In particular, Japan is one of the most important trading partners of the smaller East Asian countries and an important competitor in third markets for the more advanced economies such as Korea and Taiwan. For instance, the strong depreciation of the Japanese yen against the dollar after 1995 (when the smaller East Asian countries kept their exchange rates tightly pegged to the dollar) contributed to the Asian crisis (McKinnon and Schnabl 2003).

For this reason, Kawai (2002) has proposed that the yen should be given a prominent weight in the East Asian currency baskets in order to maintain intra-East Asian exchange rate stability. Ogawa and Ito (2002), reflecting the argument of McKinnon and Schnabl (2004a) that the common peg of the East Asian currencies to the dollar contributed to the stabilization of intra-regional exchange rates and thereby fostered intra-regional trade, have proposed a coordination of the

East Asian currency baskets. This could be achieved by Williamson's (2005) and Kawai's (2006) proposition that dollar, yen, and euro should be (by and large) treated equally in the East Asian exchange rate strategies.

In addition to this purely trade-oriented approach, there is also a case for basket pegging from the point of view of macroeconomic stabilization. As shown above, since 2001 the tight pegs to the dollar in East Asia have contributed to a fast accumulation of foreign reserves. With underdeveloped capital markets and free capital flows, the scope for sterilization of foreign exchange intervention is limited. The respective expansion of the money supply may be regarded as a threat to price and macroeconomic stability. Asset market bubbles may emerge (Schnabl and Hoffmann 2007).

Given exchange rate stabilization, the domestic price level can be regarded as a function of the price level of the anchor country. In the case of a currency basket, the domestic price level would be a function of the price levels of all anchor countries which are represented in the basket. From this perspective the East Asian countries would be inclined to give a higher weight to currencies which are regarded as particularly stable. The Japanese yen may not qualify as an anchor currency as long as the (close to) zero interest rate policy and deflation continue. The euro certainly would.

Furthermore, the expectations about the longer-term stability of specific anchor currencies will also have an impact on the choice of the currency composition of foreign reserves. In the past, the foreign reserves of the East Asian countries were widely considered to be denominated mostly in US dollars, as international transactions in East Asia were dollarized and exchange rates were stabilized against the dollar with the dollar as the intervention currency. Network externalities matter as governments tend to hold reserves in the currency in which they intervene.

Nevertheless, if the East Asian central banks expect a further depreciation of the dollar, they may wish to diversify their portfolio of international currencies (Eichengreen 2005). Then it may be worth tolerating slightly less market liquidity in the euro capital markets in return for the benefits of more diversification. This would imply that higher weights are given to the euro. This can be achieved with the help of two strategies. First, while pegging against the US dollar continues (causing foreign reserves to be accumulated in US dollars), dollar reserves can be converted into euro reserves.[5] Although the peg against one anchor currency would be compatible with a diversification of reserves, the downside of this strategy is that dollar sales would put further depreciation pressure on the dollar and therefore would require additional foreign exchange intervention. This effect could be avoided if the restructuring of the currency structure of official foreign reserve holdings were to take place in times of dollar appreciation, as it was the case in 2005.

Although there is no direct need to give different currencies similar proportions as anchor and reserve currencies, countries may strive to 'harmonize' the currency structure of the foreign assets with the weights of the currencies in their intervention baskets. Gudmundsson (2005) argues that many central banks use a minimum variance analysis to determine their reserve compositions. This implies that reserve structures mirror intervention basket structures in order to reduce nominal fluctuations of the value of the international reserves. For instance, Russia had given the dollar a weight of 60 per cent in foreign reserves and 65 per cent in the currency basket in mid-2005, giving the euro weights of 33 per cent and 35 per cent respectively (Schnabl 2006).

To this end, the desire to diversify the currency denomination of international reserves may enhance the role of the euro in possible basket strategies. This implies a causal relation between policy goals concerning the reserve composition and the desired exchange rate target. Exchange rate stabilization based on basket strategies also would allow full hedging of the foreign exchange risk of international payments flows, as uncertainty only originates in the exchange rate fluctuations between the dollar, the euro, and the yen. For these exchange rate fluctuations, the highly developed capital markets in Japan, the US, and the euro area provide sufficient tools for hedging the foreign exchange risk.

## Estimation of baskets structures

Has the structure of the East Asian currency baskets changed recently as suggested by Kawai (2006)? Frankel and Wei (1994) have proposed an OLS estimation which allows the tracking of the structures of undisclosed currency baskets as they prevail in East Asia. The empirical analysis of the currency basket structures in East Asia proceeds in two stages. First, we test for the basket structures before the Asian crisis, which are expected to reveal a strong US dollar weight. Second, based on a rolling window approach, possible changes in basket structures are identified.

Following Frankel and Wei (1994), an 'outside' currency – the Australian dollar[6] – is used as a numéraire for measuring exchange rate volatility in the East Asian currencies (except the yen). This volatility can be partitioned into movements in major currencies against the Australian dollar. For example, if changes in the Korean won against the Australian dollar are largely explained by changes in the US dollar against the Australian dollar, the US dollar has very high weight in the Korean currency basket. The exchange rates of each of the nine East Asian currencies are regressed on the US dollar, the Japanese yen, and the euro[7] with the Australian dollar as numéraire:

$$e_{EastAsiancurrencyAUD} = \alpha_1 + \alpha_2 e_{DollarAUD_t} + \alpha_3 e_{YenAUD_t} + \alpha_4 e_{EuroAUD} + u_t \tag{9.1}$$

The multivariate OLS regression[8] is based on first differences of logarithms in the exchange rate $e$. The residuals are controlled for heteroscedasticity. The daily data are compiled from Bloomberg. The $\alpha$ coefficients represent the weights of the respective currencies in the currency basket. If the East Asian currency is closely fixed to one of the major currencies appearing on the right hand side of (9.1), the corresponding $\alpha$ coefficient will be close to unity. If a coefficient is close to zero, there is no exchange rate stabilization against that particular currency.

## The pre-crisis currency baskets

First, as in McKinnon and Schnabl (2004a) we estimate the composition of East Asian countries' currency baskets for the pre-Asian crisis period, which starts in February 1994 when China unified its foreign exchange market and ends in May 1997 before the first major turbulence of the Asian crisis (869 observations). Table 9.1 reports the results, showing the high weights of the dollar in the East Asian currency baskets. The estimates for $\alpha_2$ are all close to unity, ranging from 0.82 for the Singapore dollar up to 1.00 for the Chinese yuan, the Hong Kong dollar, and the Indonesian rupiah. The correlation coefficients ($R^2$) being close to unity indicate that fluctuations of the East Asian currencies' exchange rates against the Australian dollar can almost fully be explained by fluctuations of the dollar against the Australian dollar.

The results show that high dollar weights also can be achieved under a downward crawling peg arrangement, as in Indonesia before May 1997. The $\alpha_2$ coefficients of the Korean won, the Philippine peso, and the Taiwan dollar are very close to unity with lower, but still large, t-statistics. For the Thai baht and the Malaysian ringgit, the $\alpha_2$-coefficients are still close to 0.9, with some small weight for the yen as measured by $\alpha_3$.

Singapore shows the lowest weight for the dollar (82 per cent) and smaller (but highly statistically significant) weights for the yen (14 per cent) and the German mark (8 per cent). There is some evidence of small weights for the yen in the

*Table 9.1* Pre-Asian crisis East Asian currency basket structures (1.1.1994–30.5.1997)

|  | Constant $\alpha_1$ | Dollar $\alpha_2$ | Yen $\alpha_3$ | DM $\alpha_4$ | $R^2$ |
|---|---|---|---|---|---|
| Chinese yuan | −0.00 | 1.01∗∗∗ | −0.01 | −0.02 | 0.97 |
|  | (−1.15) | (158.63) | (−1.48) | (−1.70) |  |
| Hong Kong dollar | 0.00 | 1.00∗∗∗ | 0.00 | −0.01 | 1.00 |
|  | (0.30) | (454.79) | (0.25) | (−1.36) |  |
| Indonesian rupiah | 0.00 | 1.00∗∗∗ | −0.01 | 0.01 | 0.97 |
|  | (3.19) | (144.93) | (−0.92) | (0.85) |  |
| Korean won | 0.00 | 0.97∗∗∗ | 0.06∗∗∗ | 0.01 | 0.93 |
|  | (1.42) | (66.27) | (3.31) | (0.29) |  |
| Malaysian ringgit | −0.00 | 0.88∗∗∗ | 0.09∗∗∗ | 0.01 | 0.90 |
|  | (−1.48) | (54.80) | (5.30) | (0.45) |  |
| Philippine peso | −0.00 | 0.97∗∗∗ | 0.02 | −0.01 | 0.86 |
|  | (−0.34) | (43.34) | (0.74) | (−0.45) |  |
| Singapore dollar | −0.00 | 0.82∗∗∗ | 0.14∗∗∗ | 0.08∗∗∗ | 0.86 |
|  | (−1.32) | (34.37) | (4.83) | (2.97) |  |
| New Taiwan dollar | 0.00 | 0.98∗∗∗ | 0.03∗∗ | −0.01 | 0.93 |
|  | (0.84) | (57.30) | (1.38) | (−0.54) |  |
| Thai baht | −0.00 | 0.92∗∗∗ | 0.08∗∗∗ | −0.01 | 0.95 |
|  | (−0.61) | (81.25) | (5.17) | (−0.35) |  |

Source: Datastream.

Notes: Daily data. T-Statistics in Parentheses. ∗∗ significant at the 5% level. ∗∗∗ significant at the 1% level. 869 observations. White heteroscedasticity-consistent standard errors and covariance.

pre-crisis East Asian currency baskets of Korea (6 per cent), Malaysia (9 per cent), Singapore (14 per cent), Taiwan (3 per cent) and Thailand (8 per cent). However, except for Singapore there is no evidence of exchange rate stabilization against the German mark. All in all, before the Asian crisis East Asia can be characterized as adhering to an informal dollar standard (McKinnon 2005).

### Changing currency structures

As outlined above, after the Asian crisis it has been recommended to increase the weight of the Japanese yen in the East Asian currency baskets to minimize macroeconomic turbulence caused by bilateral exchange rate fluctuations against the Japanese yen. There may be a rationale to include the euro into the currency basket, not only because of trade linkages with the European Union but primarily because of the wish to diversify international reserves. The years 2005/06 would have been an optimal time for reshuffling the currency structure of international reserves as the dollar was strong against the euro due to rising US interest rates. In times of dollar appreciation, dollar sales would not trigger a run out of the dollar which would devalue the remaining dollar assets.

Using rolling regressions, the country panels in Figure 9.5 summarize the dollar's weight in each East Asian currency basket since the early 1990s. Based on daily data, the rolling 130-day $\alpha_2$ coefficients are plotted for each of the East Asian countries (except Japan). A window of 130 days corresponds to an observation period of six months (5 observations per week). The first window starts on January 1, 1990 and ends on June 29, 1990. The $\alpha_2$ coefficient is calculated for the first period. Then the window is shifted by one day and the coefficient is calculated again, up to August 2006. A value of unity stands for a 100 per cent weight of the respective currency in the respective currency basket.

Figure 9.5 shows the time path of the dollar weights in the East Asian currency baskets. For all countries, as suggested by Table 9.1, the weight of the dollar has been very high and (close to) unity before the Asian crisis. The Asian crisis is marked by a sharp decline of the $\alpha_2$ coefficient in many East Asian countries (except China and Hong Kong). This phenomenon represents the crisis and (strong) depreciations of the East Asian currencies. Post-crisis, it seems that the weights of the dollar in the East Asian currency baskets have evolved differently.

First, China and Hong Kong have very stable dollar weights (close to unity). Officially shifting toward a currency basket regime in July 2005, China seems to have decreased the weight of the dollar in its basket only slightly since then. The sudden decline of the coefficient in the second half of 2005 is due to the one-time 2.1 per cent appreciation of the yuan against the dollar (and other currencies) on July 21st 2005. This effect fades out after the July 21st value leaves the estimation window in early 2006. Since then, the weight of the dollar seems to have decreased only very marginally.

In contrast, in Malaysia, which has allowed for more exchange rate flexibility since July 2005, the weight of the dollar seems to have declined significantly.

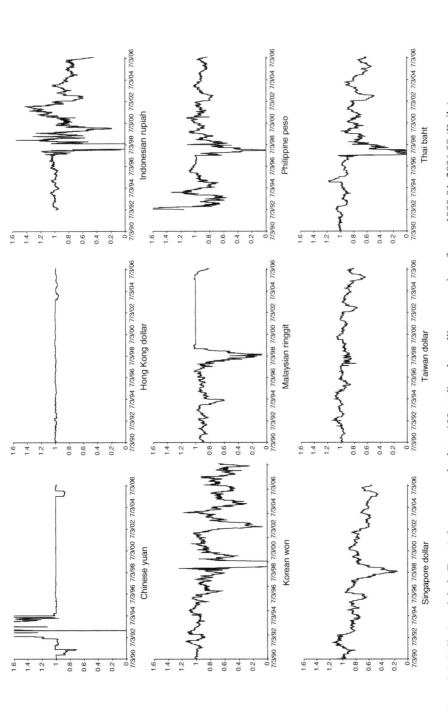

*Figure 9.5* Dollar's weight in East Asian currency baskets: 130-trading-day rolling regressions for $\alpha_2$, 1990:01–2006:08 (Daily).
Source: Bloomberg. 1 corresponds to 100%.

Note: A $\alpha_2$-coefficient close to unity shows 100% weight for the dollar in the currency basket.

The estimated weight of the dollar declined from 100 per cent in early 2005 down to about 80 per cent in August 2006. The trend seems to point further downward. For Indonesia, Korea and the Philippines the coefficients are rather volatile. This may indicate either high volatility in the foreign exchange market or sudden exchange rate changes. Nevertheless, particularly in Korea the weight of the dollar in the currency baskets exhibits a strong downward trend. While in the early 1990s the weight of the dollar was close to unity, in the year 2006 the weight seems to have declined to about 50 per cent. This may indicate a shift in the basket structure rather than more exchange rate flexibility, because at the same time the stock of Korean foreign reserves increased considerably (Figure 9.4)

Also for Singapore, Taiwan and Thailand, there seems to be a clear downward trend of the dollar weights in the respective currency baskets. While for all three countries the weight was close to unity in the early 1990s, by 2006 it was around 80 per cent in Taiwan, 70 per cent in Thailand and 60 per cent in Singapore. For all three countries the trend is pointing downwards. To this end, Figure 9.5 provides evidence that – although the dollar remains the prominent anchor currency in East Asia – its role seems to decrease. There is no evidence that this downward trend has faded out recently. As the dollar weights in the East Asian currency baskets have become rather heterogeneous, intra-regional exchange rate volatility in East Asia is increasing.

The appreciation of the dollar in 2005 provided a good occasion to shift the structure of the currency baskets away from the dollar toward the yen or the euro. Estimating the rolling weights of both currencies in the East Asian currency baskets are complementary tests for possible changing structures. Figure 9.6 shows the results for the Japanese yen. As shown by McKinnon and Schnabl (2003) one major reason for the Asian crisis has been the depreciation of the Japanese yen against the US dollar and the East Asian currencies which were pegged to the dollar. To avoid a decline of competitiveness against Japanese exporters in the domestic and third markets, the East Asian countries may increase the weights of the Japanese yen to reduce long-term exchange rate fluctuations against the Japanese currency.

Figure 9.6 provides evidence in favour of a growing role of the Japanese yen in the East Asian currency baskets.[9] Although the $\alpha_3$ coefficients are rather volatile there is a clear upward trend for Korea, Singapore, Taiwan and Thailand. In these countries, the yen seems to have gained weights between 20 and 30 per cent by 2006. In Malaysia the weight of the yen seems to have increased from zero in July 2005 to about 10 per cent in August 2006. In China despite the tight peg to the dollar a very small weight seems to be given to the Japanese yen very recently.[10] For Indonesia and the Philippines no clear trend can be recognized although for Indonesia the $\alpha_3$-coefficients are significantly higher for the yen after the Asian crisis than before. Hong Kong clearly adheres to its tight dollar peg.

All in all, Figure 9.6 provides evidence of a growing role for the Japanese yen as anchor currency in East Asia. The motivation is likely to be driven by strong trade linkages with Japan, concerns about competition in third markets (US) and rising attempts to achieve East Asian monetary integration.[11]

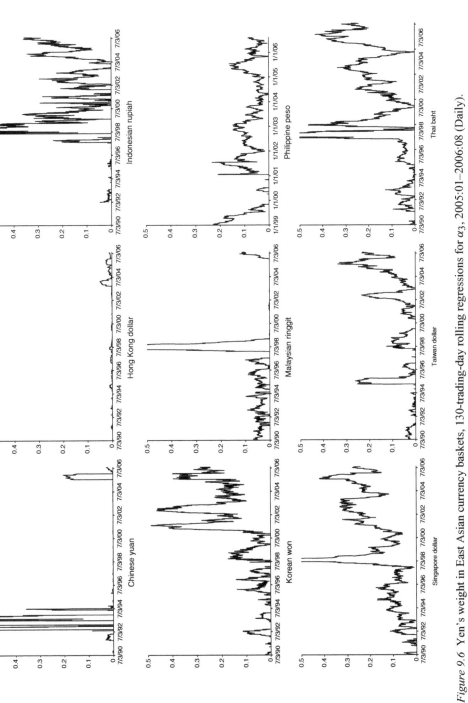

*Figure 9.6* Yen's weight in East Asian currency baskets, 130-trading-day rolling regressions for $\alpha_3$, 2005:01–2006:08 (Daily).
Source: Bloomberg.

Note: 1 corresponds to 100%.

Finally, the role of the euro in the East Asian currency baskets is traced. In Figure 9.7, the time scale starts in the 1999 when the euro was introduced. Before 1999, as shown in Table 9.1 (with the exception of Singapore) the German mark did not play a major role as an anchor currency in East Asia (McKinnon and Schnabl 2004a). Also after January 1999, the rolling window estimations do not reveal a specific trend as it is observed for the Japanese yen. For three countries, China, Hong Kong and Malaysia, the euro seems not to play any role for the exchange rate policies at all.

For all other countries there are spikes in the coefficients, which after a certain time period fade out again. This may allow two interpretations. First, the spikes represent a certain weight of the euro in some East Asian currency baskets. This hypothesis is most likely for Singapore where the coefficient is comparatively stable and the German mark turned out significant in previous estimations (Table 9.1). For the other currencies the evidence seems less robust. The spikes may represent temporary euro purchases (to change the currency structure of foreign reserves) but not changes in the structure of the currency baskets itself.

Finally, to obtain a comprehensive picture of the structure of currency baskets in East Asia, we calculate arithmetic averages of the weights of the dollar, the yen, and the euro in the currency baskets of the nine East Asian countries (except Japan) during 2005. The result as shown in Figure 9.8 implies a rising weight in the East Asian currency baskets for the Japanese yen but less for the euro.

## Conclusion

Before the 1997/98 East Asian crisis, the East Asian countries (except Japan) pegged their currencies tightly to the dollar, forming an informal dollar standard. As the motivations for pegging to the dollar – i.e. macroeconomic stabilization, dollar denomination of international trade, intra-regional trade, and international capital flows—remained unchanged after the crisis, the East Asian countries (except Japan) have returned to their dollar pegs.

However, the sustained depreciation pressure on the US dollar, which can be linked to the US twin deficit, has led to rising reserve accumulation in US dollars, which constitutes a risk for macroeconomic stability. While the successive US interest rate increases since 2004 have put a hold on this trend, meanwhile the interest rate peak seems to be reached. Expectations about new decline of US interest rates and a further decline of the dollar may create an incentive to further diversify the risk of one-sided dollar pegs based on basket strategies.

In East Asia, the yen and the euro may enter the currency baskets for (partially) different reasons. As Japan is a more important trading partner than the euro area and an important competitor in third markets, the yen may enter the currency basket to equilibrate intra-East Asian competitiveness. In contrast, trade matters less for the euro area, but the role of the euro as a macroeconomic anchor and international store of value is growing. While our estimations did not find robust evidence in favour of a (growing) role of the euro in the East Asian currency baskets the role of the euro as a reserve currency in East Asia may be increasing.

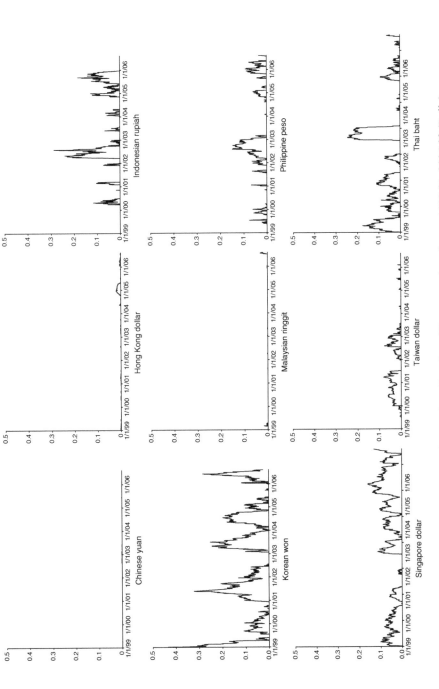

*Figure 9.7* Euro's weight in East Asian currency baskets: 130-trading-day rolling regressions for $\alpha_4$, 1999:01–2006:08 (Daily).

Source: Bloomberg.

Note: 1 corresponds to 100%.

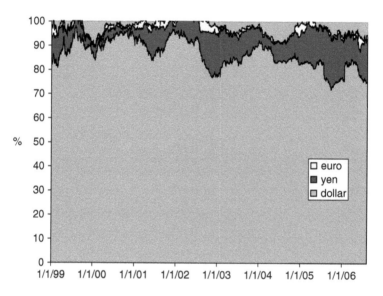

*Figure 9.8* The East Asian currency structure, 1999–2006.
Source: Bloomberg.

Note: Arithmetic averages of the $\alpha$-coefficients.


## Acknowledgements

The author thanks Adrian Höhl, Axel Löffler und Ulrike Mühler for excellent research assistance.


## References

Chinn M. and Frankel J. (2005) 'Will the Euro Eventually Surpass the Dollar as Leading International Reserve Currency?' NBER Working Paper, No. 11510.

Chmelarova, V. and Schnabl G. (2006) 'Exchange Rate Management in Developed and Underdeveloped Capital Markets', European Central Bank Working Paper, No. 636.

Crockett A. and Goldstein M. (1976) 'Inflation under Fixed and Flexible Exchange Rates', IMF Staff Papers, No. 23: 509–544.

De Grauwe P. and Schnabl G. (2005) 'Nominal versus Real Convergence with Respect to EMU Accession – EMU Entry Scenarios for the New Member States', *Kyklos*, 58 (4): 481–499.

——— (2008) 'Exchange Rate Stability, Inflation and Growth in the (South) Eastern and Central Europe', *Review of Development Economics*, Forthcoming.

Dooley M., Folkerts-Landau D. and Garber P. (2004) 'The Revived Bretton Woods System: The Effects of Periphery Intervention and Reserve Management on Interest Rates and Exchange Rates in Center Countries', NBER Working Paper, No.10332.

Eichengreen B. (2005) 'Sterling's Past, Dollar's Future: Historical Perspectives on Reserve Currency Competition', NBER Working Paper, No. 11336.

Eichengreen B. and Hausmann R. (1999) 'Exchange Rates and Financial Fragility', NBER Working Paper, No. 7418.

European Central Bank (ECB) (2005) *Review of the International Role of the Euro*, Frankfurt December 2005.

European Commission (1990) 'One Market, One Money: An Evaluation of the Potential Benefits and Costs of Forming an Economic and Monetary Union', *European Economy*, 44.

Fischer S. (2001) 'Exchange Rate Regimes: Is the Bipolar View Correct?' *Journal of Economic Perspectives*, 15: 3–24.

Frankel J. and Wei S. -J. (1994) '"Yen Bloc or Dollar Bloc?" Exchange Rate Policies in East Asian Economies', in Ito Takatoshi and Krueger Anne (eds), *Macroeconomic Linkages: Savings, Exchange Rates, and Capital Flows*, Chicago. pp. 295–329.

Galati G. and Wooldrige P. (2006) 'The Euro as a Reserve Currency: a Challenge to the Pre–Eminence of the US Dollar?' BIS Working Paper, No. 218.

Gudmundsson M. (2005) 'The Role of the Effective Exchange Rate in Monetary Frameworks', The International Experience, mimeo.

Kawai M. (2002) 'Exchange Rate Arrangements in East Asia: Lessons from the 1997/98 Currency Crisis', *Monetary and Economic Studies*, 20: 167–204.

——— (2006) 'Toward a Regional Exchange-Rate Regime in East Asia', mimeo.

Lim E. -G. (2006) 'The Euro's Challenge to the Dollar: Different Views from Economists and Evidence from COFER and Other Data', IMF Working Paper, No. 06/153.

McKinnon R. (1963) 'Optimum Currency Areas', *American Economic Review*, 53: 717–25.

——— (2005) *Exchange Rates under the East Asian Dollar Standard: Living with Conflicted Virtue*, Cambridge, Massachusetts: MIT Press.

McKinnon R. and Ohno K. (1997) *Dollar and Yen: Resolving Economic Conflict between the United States and Japan*, Cambridge, Massachusetts.

McKinnon R. and Schnabl G. (2003) 'Synchronized Business Cycles in East Asia and Fluctuations in the Yen/Dollar Exchange Rate', *The World Economy*, 26 (8): 1067–1088.

——— (2004a) 'The East Asian Dollar Standard, Fear of Floating, and Original Sin', *Review of Development Economics*, 8 (3): 331–360.

——— (2004b) 'A Return to Exchange Rate Stability in East Asia? Mitigating Conflicted Virtue', *International Finance*, 7 (2): 169–201.

Ogawa E. and Ito T. (2002) 'On the Desirability of a Regional Basket Currency Arrangement', *Journal of the Japanese and International Economies*, 16 (3): 317–334.

Schnabl G. (2006) 'The Russian Currency Basket. The Rising Role of the Euro for Russia's Exchange Rate Policies', *Intereconomics*, 41 (3): 135–141.

Schnabl G. and Hoffmann A. (2007) 'Monetary Policy, Vagabonding Liquidity and Bursting Bubbles in New and Emerging Markets – An Overinvestment View', *CESifo Working Paper*, No. 2100.

Williamson J. (2000) *Exchange Rate Regimes for Emerging Markets: Reviving the Intermediate Option*, Washington D.C., Institute for International Economics.

——— (2005) 'A Currency Basket for East Asia, Not Just for China. Institute for International Economics', Policy Briefs in International Economics 05(1).

# 10 Implications of refined renminbi effective exchange rates with Asian entrepôt and intra-regional trade

*San Sau Fung, Marc Klau, Guonan Ma and Robert McCauley*

## Introduction

Discussion of exchange rate policy in Asia can benefit from more appropriate measures of exchange rates on a multilateral basis. Estimates of effective exchange rate (EER) can serve as a useful analytical tool and indicator for this purpose in several ways. They can be deployed, in ascending order of centrality, as a summary measure of external competitiveness, as an element in indices of monetary and financial conditions, as a reference for foreign exchange intervention policy, or even as an operating target for exchange rate policy. Looking across economies, perceptions of effective exchange rates, correct or otherwise, can affect how each economy reacts to its trading partners' exchange rate changes. If policy makers consider a calculated effective exchange rate as a useful reference in policy discussions, then a proper measure is needed. Better measures of effective exchange rates could thus play their assigned role more appropriately and could even make inappropriate responses to currency movements less likely.[1]

The measurement of effective exchange rates in Asia, however, faces two challenges. First, trade relationships within Asia and between Asia and the rest of the world are veiled by the entrepôt trade of Hong Kong SAR's (Hong Kong hereafter) and Singapore's entrepôt trade. The importance of these trade hubs challenges the statistician to look through the veil to discern the bilateral trade flows. Secondly, intra-regional trade is growing fast in Asia, particularly trade with China. This development challenges the statistician to use updated data to generate relevant measures of the EER. Fung *et al.* (2006) have made a systematic effort to refine the calculation of the EERs of the renminbi (RMB) and other Asian exchange rates, to make allowances for Hong Kong's role as an entrepôt and to reflect the fast-growing intra-regional trade.

Following Fung *et al.* (2006), this paper explores some of the policy implications of refined measures of Asian effective exchange rates. The next section briefly summarises the main results of our refined construction of Asian EERs. The following three sections use the refined EERs to analyze three policy topics. First, we show how the RMB's bilateral exchange rate stability translated into instability of the EER and draw the implications of a counterfactual of EER stability for the volatility of bilateral exchange rates. Second, we analyze the EER basket for the RMB that has been suggested by the People's Bank of China (PBC), showing how our results can be used to set weights on the named currencies. Finally, we discuss possible interactions among Asian currencies, and how the differences between our base and refined EER measures might condition such interaction differently. The last section summarizes the main findings of the paper.

## Refining the RMB and other Asian effective exchange rates

Starting from a base scenario, Fung *et al.* (2006) and Klau and Fung (2006) refine the calculation of the Asian effective exchange rates by adjusting for Hong Kong's re-export trade and updating the base year. These two refinements bear significantly on the determination of weights and the construction of the actual EERs of the RMB and other Asian currencies. To gauge the effects of these two refinements, the trade weights and actual EER indices under the base scenario without any refinements are compared to the refined scenario. We will first discuss the two refinements and then summarize the impact on the calculated EERs for the RMB and other Asian currencies.

### Two refinements in calculation of Asian effective exchange rates

First, significant entrepôt trade flows confound the measurement of Asia's patterns of trade that are used to construct EER measures. In particular, the official trade data published by both China and its trading partners give a distorted view of their underlying trade relationships, because a substantial portion of China's two-way trade with the rest of the world takes the form of Hong Kong's re-exports. If one parts the veil of Hong Kong, then the trade weights for both China and its trading partners look different. In particular, in the RMB EER basket, a naïve weight on Hong Kong overstates the flow of manufactured goods from China destined for final sale in Hong Kong and understates their flow to China's other trading partners. At the same time, from these other trading partners' point of view, naïve trade data overweight Hong Kong and underweight China. In particular, substantial transhipment flows (which do not even register in Hong Kong trade data) between mainland China and Taiwan, China (Taiwan hereafter) take place via Hong Kong, and this further overweights Hong Kong and underweights Taiwan in the RMB EER basket. Fung *et al.* (2006) and Klau and Fung (2006) apply insights from the body of work that attempts to reconcile the Chinese and US data on the scale of the bilateral trade imbalance[2] to construct trade weights for the currencies of China's major trading partners in Asia.

Second, China's external trade has grown rapidly and has shifted towards manufacturing. In the process, China's imports have increasingly come from the rest of Asia while much of its exports have gone to the US market, highlighting China's emergence as a major link in the global supply chain. Given this rapid evolution of trade patterns, use of weights based on decade-old trade patterns runs the risk of overweighting Europe and North America and underweighting Asia.

*Table 10.1* Trade weights in the EER basket of the Chinese renminbi[a] (in %)

| | Unadjusted trade data and base period = 1991 | Adjusted trade data and base period = 1999–2001 |
|---|---|---|
| | *Base scenario* | *Refined scenario* |
| **Asia** | **54.8** | **46.5** |
| Hong Kong SAR | 34.7 | 4.8 |
| India | 0.0 | 0.4 |
| Indonesia | 0.9 | 0.6 |
| Japan | 13.7 | 20.7 |
| Korea | 2.5 | 7.1 |
| Malaysia | 0.5 | 1.3 |
| Singapore | 1.3 | 2.8 |
| Taiwan (China) | 0.3 | 7.2 |
| Thailand | 0.8 | 1.3 |
| **North America** | **21.8** | **28.7** |
| United States | 20.1 | 26.7 |
| **Euro area** | **17.3** | **17.2** |
| **Other Europe** | **4.3** | **4.6** |
| **Others** | **1.8** | **3.0** |
| *Memo:* | | |
| Asia excl. HK | *20.1* | *41.7* |
| Asia excl. HK and JP | *6.4* | *21.0* |
| Narrow dollar bloc[b] | *54.8* | *31.5* |
| Broad dollar bloc[c] | *55.9* | *34.7* |

Notes: [a] Based on bilateral weighting scheme. [b] Comprising US and Hong Kong SAR. [c] Comprising the narrow dollar bloc and Brazil, Chile, Malaysia, Mexico and the Philippines.

Thus, to accommodate these rapid changes, Fung *et al.* (2006) update the trade weights and effective exchange rate indices over time.

### Refining the RMB effective exchange rate

A most striking result from these two refinements is that the combined trade weight on Asia (including Japan) in the RMB EER basket decreases substantially, from 55 per cent under the base scenario to 47 per cent under the refined scenario (Table 10.1). Within Asia, the decline of the Asian weight is due to the sharp reduction in the weight of Hong Kong (from 35 per cent to only 5 per cent). This reduction overwhelms the increase in the weights on all the other Asian economies in the basket. Asia's weight falls as the weight on the United States increases by 7 percentage points in the Chinese RMB basket. The weight of the euro area remains about the same.

A second contrast is that while the refined scenario preserves the weight on the US, it reduces the weight on the US dollar in the RMB EER basket. This is true in relation to a narrow 'dollar bloc' comprising only the US and Hong Kong, with the latter's pegged currency. In the RMB EER basket, the weight on this dollar bloc would be almost halved, from 55 per cent under the base scenario to just 32 per cent, owing to the redistribution of Hong Kong's trade weight to economies other than the US. This is also true in relation to a broader 'dollar bloc' including the Malaysia (into mid-2005), Philippines, and Latin America (Brazil, Chile and Mexico) as well. We return to this issue in Section 4 below.

The actual indices of the RMB EERs under the base and refined scenarios show similarities and differences (Fung *et al.* 2006). On the one hand, the RMB effective exchange rates broadly follow similar movements under the two scenarios, with a correlation coefficient of above 95 per cent for the monthly EER movements. On the other hand, the EER indices under these two scenarios sometimes diverged by several percentage points, especially during the Asian financial crisis. This is consistent with the decreased dollar bloc weight in the refined scenario, because some Asian currencies that gain weight in China's basket (eg the Korean won and New Taiwan dollar) depreciated against the dollar during the crisis.

Overall, the refined RMB EERs are more volatile than those under the base scenario (Fung *et al.* 2006). The most important reason behind the increased EER volatility as measured under the refined scenario is the sharply reduced dollar bloc weight in the RMB EER basket. Given the history of the RMB's tight dollar link, an RMB EER basket assigning a smaller dollar bloc weight will translate fluctuations in the bilateral dollar rates of other trading partners' currencies into an increase in the effective volatility of the RMB.[3] This finding again underscores the importance of properly measuring the trade weights in the effective basket, since an overweighting of the dollar bloc conveys an exaggerated impression of currency stability under a dollar peg.

### *Refining the effective exchange rates of other Asian currencies*

Taking account of Asia's entrepôt and rising intra-regional trade matters not only for the effective exchange rate of the RMB but also for those of other Asian currencies. In the previous sub-section, we saw how this data adjustment tends to redistribute the trade weights in the RMB EER basket away from Hong Kong and toward other trading partners. From the standpoint of the trading partners, this same adjustment tends to redistribute trade weights away from Hong Kong and toward China. When the RMB and the HK dollar were closely linked to the US dollar, this redistribution did not matter much. Not so since July 2005 when the distribution of weights as between Hong Kong and China begins to make a difference.

Thus, one salient comparison is between the trade weights for China and Hong Kong with and without the adjustment. Table 10.2 displays the weights on China and Hong Kong in the baskets of other Asian currencies. The weight on China under the refined scenario is a multiple of the weight under the base scenario for all of Asia save Hong Kong. Conversely, the weight on Hong Kong is lower under the refined scenario than under the base scenario for all of Asia save India. In short, without an adjustment for re-exports/transshipment via Hong Kong, China

*Table 10.2* Weights on China and Hong Kong in the baskets of Asian currencies

*In per cent*

| Basket of | Weight on China | | | Weight on Hong Kong | | |
|---|---|---|---|---|---|---|
| | *Base scenario*[a] | *Refined scenario*[2] | *Official* | *Base scenario*[a] | *Refined scenario*[b] | *official* |
| China | . | . | . | 34.7 | 4.8 | ... |
| Hong Kong SAR | 33.5 | 19.4 | 42.0 | . | . | . |
| India | 0.0 | 3.6 | 6.7 | 3.6 | 3.9 | 4.1 |
| Indonesia | 3.5 | 5.0 | 0 | 2.3 | 1.4 | 0 |
| Japan | 4.3 | 13.6 | 7.1 | 4.5 | 1.7 | 6.3 |
| Korea | 2.6 | 12.9 | ... | 4.6 | 2.3 | ... |
| Malaysia | 1.2 | 3.8 | ... | 3.2 | 1.9 | ... |
| Philippines | 1.2 | 2.7 | 0 | 5.9 | 2.1 | 0 |
| Singapore[c] | 1.6 | 5.3 | 6.9 | 4.8 | 2.2 | 7.0 |
| Taiwan (China) | 0.1 | 13.5 | ... | 12.3 | 2.6 | ... |
| Thailand | 2.0 | 5.7 | ... | 3.9 | 1.9 | ... |

Source: Hong Kong Monthly Digest of Statistics December 2001, Hong Kong Census and Statistics Department; Reserve Bank of India, Bank of Japan, Bangko Sentral ng Philipinas; IDEAGlobal, BIS calculations.

Notes: [a] 1991 trade data, unadjusted for re-exports/transshipment via Hong Kong. [b] 1999–2001 trade data, adjusted. [c] The 'official' weights shown for Singapore refer to the estimates by Malcolm (2004). See also Graph 8. "." denotes not applicable and "..." denotes not available.

tends to be underweighted and Hong Kong to be overweighted, in many cases by 50 per cent.

As for the resulting EER indices, however, such a misallocation of trade weights had little effect before July 2005, given both RMB's and Hong Kong dollar's tight links to the US dollar (Fung *et al.* 2006). This can be verified from the observation that the EERs for other Asian economies (except Hong Kong and Singapore) are broadly the same under both scenarios (Fung *et al.* 2006). As long as the Hong Kong dollar and the RMB tracked the US dollar closely, the practical importance of distinguishing them was limited. Since July 2005, the Chinese renminbi has slowly trended up against the dollar over time (Frankel and Wei 2007).

The following three sections use the refined measures of Asian effective exchange rates in three policy settings. We illustrate the distinction between bilateral and effective exchange rate stability for the RMB; we analyze the RMB basket as suggested by the PBC; and we discuss the interaction of currencies managed for effective exchange rate stability.

## Currency stability: bilateral versus effective

Currency stability, or its converse, currency volatility, matters to policy makers to varying degrees. For ten years prior to the July 2005 RMB policy move, for example, the Chinese government *seemed* to have put a big premium on stability.

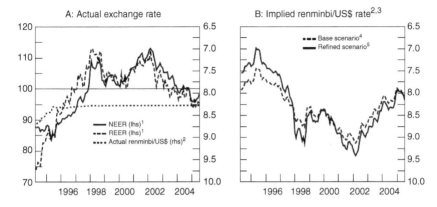

*Figure 10.1* Actual and implied exchange rates for the Chinese renminbi.
Source: BIS calculations.

Notes: [1]Sample average=100. [2]Inverted scale. [3]By fixing NEER to the ex-post average between Apr 1994 and Jun 2005. [4]Unadjusted 1991 trade data. [5]Adjusted 1999–2001 trade data.

However, the question of how currency stability should be defined and measured must be posed. Currency stability can be interpreted in bilateral or multilateral terms. Indeed, in the case of the Chinese renminbi, bilateral dollar stability was achieved at the expense of effective stability (Panel A of Figure 10.1).

Several considerations can incline policy-makers to bilateral exchange rate stability. If an economy's corporate sector or government has extensive US dollar liabilities, then policy-makers may seek to maintain bilateral stability against the dollar to keep these debts from expanding relative to income. This consideration, however, does not seem to be a large one in China (Prasad *et al.* 2005). Regarding the other side of the balance sheet, however, there may be concern that the prospect of RMB weakness against the dollar could lead to deposit shifts from RMB to US dollars. This was not a far-fetched concern in the years following the Asian financial crisis (Ma and McCauley 2002), but at current levels of deposit dollarization in China – well less than 5 per cent since late 2006 – it would not seem a big one. Another consideration is to maintain competitiveness in dollar bloc markets, especially the US. This consideration is often seen to gain importance from the fact that a high fraction of China's trade (perhaps over 90 per cent) is dollar-invoiced. It must be asked, however, whether dollar invoicing of imports from Europe means that prices should not be expected to rise in the wake of substantial euro appreciation against the dollar. In sum, it is easy to overstate the benefit of the stability of the bilateral dollar exchange rate.

A number of considerations argue more strongly for effective exchange rate stability. Despite the dollar invoicing, China's global competitiveness is better gauged by effective exchange rates, since China trades globally. Price stability is another important consideration.[5] Experience has shown that domestic price stability is not necessarily well served by bilateral stability. China imported deflation when the dollar was strong (Ha *et al.* 2003) and has been importing inflation since the dollar began to weaken in 2002, amid rising global prices for food and energy. Effective exchange rate stability (or a Singapore-style policy of managing an appreciation in effective terms) would have damped some of these cross-border price pressures. (From the standpoint of avoiding the import of deflation or inflation, however, even a basket with a too-small weight on non-dollar currencies would represent an improvement on a pure dollar peg.) Thus, an effective exchange rate framework may better serve the considerations of competitiveness and price stability.

Such considerations make the following experiment relevant. What path would the bilateral RMB/USD exchange rate have followed, if effective stability had been pursued? In other words, how much volatility of the bilateral RMB/USD rate would have been necessary to maintain the effective stability of the RMB? We conduct a simulation to address this counterfactual question, on the assumption that the RMB nominal EER (NEER) level was targeted to the ex-post average between April 1994 and June 2005, and that the dollar exchange rates of all the other currencies in the RMB EER basket followed their observed paths against the dollar, not responding to the hypothetical shifts in the RMB/USD rate. Panel B of Figure 10.1 presents the implied RMB/USD rates under both the base and refined scenarios, suggesting that the RMB would have depreciated against a strong US dollar in the 1995–2001 period but would have appreciated vis-à-vis a weakening dollar since 2002.

This result is intuitive: given the substantial weight on the USD and the dollar bloc in the RMB EER basket, an appreciation (depreciation) of the dollar vis-à-vis other major currencies would require an implied offsetting depreciation (appreciation) of the RMB against the dollar, if a constant NEER is to be maintained. In fact, a comparison of Panel A and B in Figure 10.1 reveals that the implied RMB/USD rate under a hypothetical NEER target is the inverse of the RMB NEER under a de facto dollar link.

Moreover, the smaller the dollar weight, the larger the compensating implied changes in the RMB/USD rate would be required to maintain a given NEER. As discussed earlier, Hong Kong and thus some version of the dollar bloc is easily overweighted in the RMB EER basket if the veil of Hong Kong is not seen through. An excessive dollar share in a RMB EER basket, in turn, leads to RMB/USD movements that do not suffice to maintain effective stability. With a much smaller weight on the dollar bloc under the refined scenario, a more volatile RMB/USD rate would be needed to maintain a steady NEER. Intuitively, with a reduced dollar bloc weight, a more volatile bilateral RMB/USD rate with effective stability and a more volatile NEER with bilateral dollar stability are just two sides of the same coin.[6]

Indeed, one way to characterise the exchange rate regime shift since July 2005 is to examine the bilateral volatility of the Chinese RMB relative to its effective volatility. As reported in Table 10.3, the ratio of bilateral to effective volatility has clearly risen over time, an indication that the Chinese RMB has taken on greater

*Table 10.3* Bilateral versus effective volatility of the renminbi[a]

|  | Bilateral USD (1) | | NEER (refined scenario) (2) | | Ratio (1)/(2) | |
|---|---|---|---|---|---|---|
|  | *weekly data* | *monthly data* | *weekly data* | *monthly data* | *weekly data* | *monthly data* |
| Aug 2005–Dec 2005 | 0.1 | 0.1 | 1.3 | 2.5 | 0.08 | 0.04 |
| Jan 2006–Dec 2006 | 0.4 | 0.6 | 1.4 | 3.2 | 0.29 | 0.19 |
| Jan 2007–Oct 2007 | 0.5 | 0.8 | 0.9 | 1.9 | 0.55 | 0.42 |

Source: Fung *et al.* (2006): National data; BIS calculations.

Notes: [a] Standard deviation of annualised percentage changes. Effective exchange rate is the refined measure.

effective orientation. This observation holds on the basis of the refined NEER index with its smaller weight on the dollar.

## Major currency blocs in the renminbi basket

How might our refinements help shed lights on appropriate weight assignments in the RMB basket following the 21 July 2005 exchange rate regime shift? At the time, the Chinese policymakers announced a new renminbi exchange rate regime of a managed float 'with reference to a basket of currencies'. There have been no official statements about the precise composition and weights of this renminbi basket, though eleven currencies were named as part of the basket: four 'major currencies' (the US dollar, euro, yen and Korean won) and seven 'other currencies' (the Singapore dollar, British pound, Malaysian ringgit, Russian ruble, Australian dollar, Thai baht and Canadian dollar). Informally, it is an '11-currency PBC basket'.

Our refined estimates of RMB EER based on a broader, 33-currency basket may be useful to Chinese policymakers on two fronts. First, Chinese policymakers may improve the weight allocation across the 11 trading partners included in the PBC basket by taking into consideration of entrepôt and large intra-regional trade in Asia, as discussed above. Second, policymakers could make allowance for some of China's important trading partners in our broader RMB basket that are excluded from the 11-currency PBC basket, notably Hong Kong and Taiwan. Their influence, as well as that of other important trading partners excluded in the PBC basket, could be captured by using our refined trade weights and by incorporating the estimated co-movements of such excluded currencies with the three major currencies of the dollar, yen and euro. This is based on the notion that in a three-currency world (Williamson 1999), effective weights on the dollar, yen and euro blocs may exceed the weights on the US, Japan and the euro area, because of the exchange rate co-movements between the three main currencies and other currencies. A narrower basket can therefore to some extent approximate a broader basket.

Most would agree that even the weight on a narrowly-defined dollar bloc in an RMB EER basket would exceed that on the US alone, mainly because of Hong Kong and until July 2005, Malaysia. If East Asia sat squarely in the dollar bloc, then the overall weight on the yen in the RMB's effective exchange rate would be no higher than the trade weight on Japan. However, since the 1997 Asian financial crisis, currencies in the region have moved in greater sympathy with the yen. Before the crisis, it was rare for a regional currency to share more than 20 per cent of the yen's movement against the dollar (McCauley 1997). During the crisis, amid much idiosyncratic variation, one could discern a more substantial co-movement between yen and regional currencies (Galati and McCauley 1998). Hence the effective weight on the yen bloc in an RMB basket easily exceeds that on Japan if one takes into consideration of co-movements between non-Japan Asian currencies and the yen.

Similarly for the euro bloc: the euro area picks up weight first of all by the tendency of pound sterling, the Swiss franc, and the Nordic currencies to move with the euro against the dollar. In addition, the euro gains from the strong correlation of the antipodean currencies with the euro after its inception. Before that, the Australian and New Zealand dollars were actually as well as nominally part of the dollar bloc. Similarly, the Canadian dollar now shows a considerable euro and yen echoes in its trading against the US dollar. In East Asia, the euro's movements, as distinct from the yen's movements, are most evident in the Singapore dollar, but this relationship adds less weight to the euro than does Switzerland.

Therefore, Chinese policymakers can capture the weights on some of the currencies absent in the 11-currency PBC basket and allocate them to those on the dollar, yen and euro by estimating their co-movements with these big three currencies (Kawai, 2002). For Hong Kong, one could simply add its entire weight to the US dollar in the PBC basket, given the currency board arrangement. The appropriate Hong Kong weight to be added to the dollar is our refined weight in Table 10.1 to ensure that the weight on the dollar bloc is not too heavy. For the TWD and other currencies not included in the 11-currency PBC basket, Appendix 1 shows the estimation of the coefficients of their co-movement (the betas) with the three major currencies, using the following equation:

$$(X/\$) = \alpha + \beta_{\text{jpy}}(\yen/\$) + \beta_{\text{eur}}(\euro/\$) \tag{10.1}$$

where X=domestic currency of the specific economy (all variables are daily percentage changes).

Using the refined weights on Japan, the euro area and other trading partners in Table 10.1 and the estimated average responses (betas) of non-Japan Asian currencies (as well as the Canadian dollar, British pound and Swiss franc) to the yen-dollar and euro-dollar movements in the appendix, we calculate their contributions to the so-called 'yen bloc' and 'euro bloc' in the RMB EER basket. These contributions raise the effective weights on the yen and euro blocs beyond the refined weights on Japan and the euro area. The remaining weights of the currencies absent in the 11-currency PBC basket can then be assigned to the 'dollar bloc'.

In this manner, the weights assigned to the yen, euro and dollar blocs capture the influence of the currencies that are included in our basket but not in the PBC 11-currency basket.

Table 10.4 compares the results of these exercises. Column (1) reports the refined estimates of weights in our RMB basket. If we simply take the 11 currencies mentioned for the PBC basket as given and normalize their weights, the weights on the 11 currencies in the PBC basket would be shown in column (2). However, if we assign the refined and much reduced Hong Kong weight to the dollar, and allocate the weights of the TWD and other excluded currencies to the dollar, yen and euro according to their respective co-movements with these major currencies, the appropriate weights of the 11 currencies in the PBC basket would look like those in column (3). Thus, Chinese policymakers can use a smaller basket to reasonably represent a broader basket and in setting the reference weights, avoiding excessive

*Table 10.4* Weight distributions under different baskets

|  | The refined estimated of 33-currency basket (1) | The PBC basket (normalized) (2) | The PBC basket (adjusted) (3) | The three-currency basket (4) |
|---|---|---|---|---|
| **USD** | **26.7** | **31.6** | **39.0** | **53.6** |
| **JPY** | **20.7** | **24.5** | **21.8** | **24.5** |
| **EURO** | **17.2** | **20.3** | **19.2** | **21.9** |
| TWD | 7.2 | — | — | — |
| *KRW* | *7.1* | *8.4* | *7.1* | — |
| *HKD* | *4.8* | — | — | — |
| **SGD** | **2.8** | **3.3** | **2.8** | — |
| **GBP** | **2.6** | **3.1** | **2.6** | — |
| **CAD** | **2.1** | **2.5** | **2.1** | — |
| **AUD** | **1.3** | **1.5** | **1.3** | — |
| **THB** | **1.3** | **1.5** | **1.3** | — |
| **MYR** | **1.3** | **1.5** | **1.3** | — |
| SEK | 0.7 | — | — | — |
| IDR | 0.6 | — | — | — |
| CHF | 0.6 | — | — | — |
| INR | 0.4 | — | — | — |
| PHP | 0.4 | — | — | — |
| DKK | 0.4 | — | — | — |
| NOK | 0.3 | — | — | — |
| **RUB** | **1.5** | **1.8** | **1.5** | — |
| *Memo* | | | | |
| **PBC basket** | 84.6 | 100.0 | 100.0 | 100.0 |

Source: Appendix, Fung et al (2006) and authors' estimates.

Notes: The first column is refined trade weights from Fung *et al.* (2006) for a basket of 33 currencies. Russia is not included in this 33-currency basket and is assumed to take the weights of Brazil, Chile, Mexico and New Zealand. The second column normalises the weights of the 11 currencies named for the PBC basket in the first column as 100. The third column is derived from the effective weights on the dollar, yen and euro block and the refined weights on the other nine currencies in the PBC basket (see Appendix). The fourth column is the effective weights on the three major currency blocks for a basket based solely on three major currencies (see Appendix).

over- or under-weighting the currencies included in a relatively small basket for the RMB.

To go one step further, suppose that the hypothetical basket for the RMB were even narrower and were solely based on the three major currencies of dollar, yen and euro, excluding all the other nine currencies in the PBC basket. In this case, the appropriate weights on them should be the respective effective weights on these three currency blocs that take into consideration of both the refined weights and the related exchange rate co-movements. As indicated by column (4) of Table 10.4, the effective yen and euro bloc weights reach 25 per cent and 22 per cent, respectively, in the 3-currency basket for the RMB, compared with more like 15 per cent each under the base scenario. The implied dollar bloc weight in this RMB EER basket would seem less appropriately at 70 per cent than around 50 per cent.

## Effective exchange rates as a mechanism for cross-border reactions

The finding that the conventionally measured RMB effective exchange rate over-weights the dollar has several implications. The first implication is for Chinese policy. Since the Chinese authorities shifted from a dollar orientation to a basket orientation in July 2005, there is a risk of their assigning an insufficient weight to non-dollar currencies. The cost of this underweighting would be a very mild version of the cost of the dollar orientation prior to July 2005, as argued above: a tendency to domestic deflation in a market environment of a strong dollar globally, and a tendency toward inflation in a market environment of a weak dollar. This insight is based on the fact that, given China does not only trade with the US, the EER would be more comprehensive than the bilateral dollar rate in assessing the 'exchange rate channel' for transmission of cross-border price pressure.

The second implication arises from the symmetrical effect that Chinese trading partners' weight on China could be too small, and their weight on Hong Kong could be correspondingly too big, as discussed earlier (Table 10.2). Prior to July 2005, with both the RMB and the Hong Kong dollar closely aligned with the dollar, the relative weighting of the two made little difference. Similarly, were both China and Hong Kong to adopt the same basket orientation, it would again matter little that trading partners had the relative weights wrong.[7] Since the orientations of the RMB and Hong Kong dollar have begun to diverge, however, the weights do matter. Let us consider the effect of China's adoption of a basket orientation, while Hong Kong's dollar is assumed to remain linked to the US dollar.

Consider the case of Singapore, which manages its currency against a trade-weighted basket. If it gives weight to Hong Kong in its basket that really belongs to China, it would under-react to China's adoption of a basket orientation. To see this, note that, were the RMB to be managed against a basket, the management of the Singapore dollar would tilt away from the dollar. However, the under-weighting of China in Singapore's basket would mean that Singapore's incremental

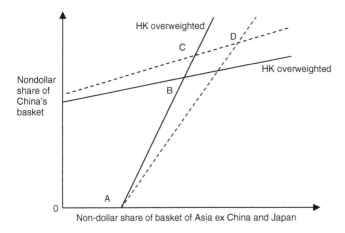

*Figure 10.2* Response of the rest of Asia to China's shift to a broad basket.

weight on the non-dollar currencies would be too small. This result is clearest for Singapore, with its explicit basket orientation, but it would hold more broadly in East Asia to the extent that regional currencies are more implicitly managed against their respective baskets and that the weights on China are too low, as suggested above.

   Stepping back, these two implications work in the same direction. In the spirit of Ogawa and Ito (2002), Figure 10.2 depicts a stylized policy reaction function of East Asia in response to hypothetical changes in the non-dollar weight of the RMB EER basket. Their reaction function, the solid line ABC, is upward sloping since it is optimal for East Asia to reduce its dollar weight if the dollar bloc in the RMB EER basket shrinks. For its part, the RMB reaction function (the other upward-sloping solid line) reflects the response of the Chinese currency to movements in the Korean won or other East Asian currencies. As these currencies move more in tandem with the yen, euro or RMB, the RMB moves less in tandem with the US dollar.

   Suppose China manages the RMB against a basket, and thus abandons the initial status quo of a dollar peg suggested by point A on the diagram. These choices would leave China and the rest of Asia at point B. Point B is not directly above point A to the extent that Asia excluding Japan and China, puts weight on the RMB. Were the RMB to begin to move with non-dollar currencies, then other Asian currencies would in effect show a higher weight on the yen and euro. In this case, the RMB also moves further away from the dollar in response to the reaction to its own basket orientation by the currencies of other East Asian economies.

   If neither the Chinese authorities nor others see through the veil of Hong Kong, then they will overweight the US dollar and thus put too little weight on non-dollar currencies. If China saw through the veil of Hong Kong and used the improved trade weights we propose above in Sections 2 and 4, the outcome would rather be point C. And if China's trading partners also see through the veil of Hong Kong, then their own responses to China's adoption of a basket would be larger. In particular, a more appropriate weight on China would result in the dotted line reaction function to the right of AB. A proper weighting of China in the management of regional currencies thus would leave the outcome at D. Comparing points B and D, misapprehensions arising from Hong Kong's status as an entrepôt for the China trade could contribute to keeping the dollar element in East Asian exchange rates more prominent than it might otherwise be.

## Concluding remarks

The measurement of effective exchange rates in Asia faces two challenges. First, trade relationships in Asia and between Asia and the rest of the world are veiled by Hong Kong's entrepôt trade. While the effect of Hong Kong's entrepôt role in obscuring trade relationships within Asia and between Asia and the rest of the world is at some level understood by policy-makers and market analysts, we are not aware of a systematic effort to adjust measures of effective exchange rates for entrepôt trade. Secondly, intra-regional trade is growing very fast in Asia, particularly trade with China. Our earlier work has refined the measurement of Asian EERs by taking account of Hong Kong's entrepôt trade and updating the base year (Fung *et al.* 2006).

This paper builds on our earlier efforts to explore the implications for policy of using improved measurement of effective exchange rates. In particular, we have discussed several applications of improved measurements of effective exchange rates in policy discussion, including currency stability in multilateral as opposed to bilateral terms, the proper weight allocation within the RMB EER basket, and interactions among regional currencies in East Asia. The refinements also matter for macroeconomic analysis. For example, as implied by the improved measure, the deflationary shock to China during the Asian financial crisis, when the RMB was tightly linked to the dollar, was much sharper, owing to the heavier weight on many depreciating Asian currencies (and correspondingly, a lighter weight on the Hong Kong dollar). That is, the renminbi appreciated much more in effective terms than otherwise measured during that episode.

The most important message is that effective exchange rates constructed without our proposed refinements would overweight the dollar bloc, narrowly or broadly defined, in the RMB EER basket. Therefore, as the Chinese authorities have moved to adopt some effective orientation in their exchange rate policy, the relative weights in the basket need to be determined more carefully than just looking at simple trade flows. Symmetrically, without our refinements, the effective exchange rates of other Asian currencies would underweight the RMB relative to the Hong Kong dollar, which would also in effect overweight the US dollar.

This underweighting of the RMB would matter more if the orientations of the RMB and Hong Kong dollar diverge further.

## Acknowledgement

The views expressed in this papers are those of the authors only and do not necessarily reflect those of the BIS. We are grateful for the comments by David Archer, Claudio Borio, Yin-Wong Cheung, Michael Chui, Gabriele Galati and the participants of the Hong Kong Institute of Monetary Research seminar in April 2005 in Hong Kong and the Asia Pacific Economic Association 2006 Annual Conference in July 2006 in Seattle. Corresponding author is Guonan Ma, Bank for International Settlements Centralbahnplatz 2, CH-4002 Basel Switzerland. Tel: +852 2878 7015, Fax: +852 2878 7123, Email: Guonan.ma@bis.org .

## References

Buldorini L., Makraydakis S. and Thimann C. (2002) 'The effective exchange rates of the euro', *European Central Bank Occasional Paper Series,* No. 2, February.

Calvo G. and C Reinhart, C. (2002) 'Fear of floating', *Quarterly Journal of Economics,* 117 (May): 379–408.

Cooper R. (1971) 'Currency devaluation in developing countries', *Princeton Essays in International Finance,* No. 86, June.

Feenstra R., Hai W., Woo W. and Yao S. (1999) 'Discrepancies in international data: an application to China–Hong Kong entrepôt trade', *American Economic Review Papers and Proceedings,* 89(2): 338–343.

Frankel J. and Wei S. (2007) 'Assessing China's exchange rate regime', NBER Working Papers, No. W13100, May.

Fung K. and Lau L. (1998) 'The China–US bilateral trade balances: how big is it really?' *Pacific Economic Review,* 3(1): 33–47.

Fung S., Klau M., Ma G. and McCauley R. (2006) 'Estimation of Asian effective exchange rates: a technical note', BIS Working Papers, No. 217, October.

Galati G. and McCauley R. (1998) 'The yen/dollar exchange rate and fluctuations in Asia–Pacific currencies', *BIS Quarterly Review,* November: 13–15.

Goldstein M. and P. Turner (2005) *Controlling Currency Mismatches.* Institute for International Economics, Washington.

Ha J., Fan K. and Shu, C. (2003) 'The causes of inflation and deflation in mainland China', *Hong Kong Monetary Authority Quarterly Bulletin,* September (36): 23–31.

Hargreaves D. and Strong C. (2003) 'JPMorgan effective exchange rates: revised and modernised', JPMorgan Global Data Watch, May, New York.

Ho C., Ma G. and McCauley R. (2005) 'Trading Asian currencies', *BIS Quarterly Review,* March: 49–58.

Ho C. and McCauley R. (2003) 'Living with flexible exchange rates', BIS Working Papers, No. 130.

Kawai, M. (2002) 'Exchange rate arrangements in East Asia: Lessons from the 1997–98 currency crisis', Bank of Japan, Institute for Monetary and Economic Studies, *Monetary and Economic Studies,* 20(S-1), December.

Klau M. and Fung S. (2006) 'The new BIS effective exchange rate indices', *BIS Quarterly Review*, March: 51–65.

Lardy N. (1996) *China in the World Economy*, Institute for International Economics, Washington, DC.

Latter T. (2004) 'Hong Kong's exchange rate regimes in the twentieth century: the stories of three regime changes', Hong Kong Institute of Monetary Research Working Paper, No. 17, September.

Leahy M. (1998) 'New summary measures of the foreign exchange rate value of the dollar', *Federal Reserve Bulletin*, October: 811–818, Washington DC.

Ma G. and McCauley R. (2002) 'Rising foreign currency liquidity of banks in China', *BIS Quarterly Review*, September: 67–74.

McCauley R. (1997) 'The euro and the dollar', *Princeton Essays in International Finance*, No. 205, November.

McKinnon R. and Schnabl G. (2003) 'The East Asian dollar standard, fear of floating and original sin', unpublished mimeo, September.

Ogawa E. and Ito T. (2002) 'On the desirability of a regional basket currency arrangement', *Journal of the Japanese and International Economies*, 16, (3): 317–334.

Suttle P. and Fernandez D. (2005) 'Emerging Asia's monetary future', *JPMorgan Global issues*, January.

US Department of Commerce (1995) 'Comparison of 1992–93 merchandise trade statistics of the United States and the People's Republic of China', *Commerce News*, Bureau of Census.

Williamson J. (1999) 'The Case for a common basket peg for East Asian currencies', in Collingnan S., Pisani-Ferry J. and Park Y., (eds.), *Exchange Rate Policies in Emerging Asian Countries*, London: Routledge. pp. 327–343.

## Appendix: Response of selected currencies to the yen/$ and euro/$ rates

The following table presents the results of simple OLS regressions:

$$(X/\$) = \alpha + \beta_{jpy}(\yen/\$) + \beta_{eur}(\text{€}/\$)$$

where $X$ = domestic currency of the specific economy. All variables are daily percentage changes. The table shows only the included regressors.

*Beta estimation and currency bloc weights in the renminbi basket: %*

| | Trade weight[a] | Yen bloc | | Euro bloc | |
|---|---|---|---|---|---|
| | | $\beta_{jpy}$ | Contribution to the yen bloc[b] | $\beta_{eur}$ | Contribution to the euro bloc[b] |
| Japan | 20.7 | 1 | 20.7 | | |
| Asia and Oceania | | | 3.6 | | 1.2 |
| Australian dollar | 1.3 | 0.17 | 0.2 | 0.51 | 0.7 |
| | | (5.33) | | (16.89) | |
| Indian rupee | 0.4 | 0.03 | 0.0 | 0.01 | 0.0 |
| | | (3.56) | | (1.78) | |
| Indonesian rupiah | 0.6 | 0.25 | 0.2 | −0.11 | −0.1 |
| | | (4.37) | | (−2.58) | |
| Korean won | 7.1 | 0.21 | 1.5 | −0.01 | −0.1 |
| | | (15.09) | | (−0.53) | |
| New Zealand dollar | 0.2 | 0.16 | 0.0 | 0.54 | 0.1 |
| | | (5.02) | | (16.97) | |
| Philippine peso | 0.4 | 0.05 | 0.0 | 0.07 | 0.0 |
| | | (2.15) | | (2.26) | |
| Singapore dollar | 2.8 | 0.20 | 0.6 | 0.09 | 0.3 |
| | | (18.00) | | (9.58) | |
| New Taiwan dollar | 7.2 | 0.12 | 0.9 | 0.03 | 0.2 |
| | | (13.4) | | (4.19) | |
| Thai baht | 1.3 | 0.17 | 0.2 | 0.04 | 0.1 |
| | | (8.96) | | (2.56) | |
| **Euro area** | 17.2 | | | 1 | 17.2 |
| **Others** | | | **0.4** | | **3.5** |
| Canadian dollar | 2.1 | 0.08 | 0.2 | 0.15 | 0.3 |
| | | (4.28) | | (5.69) | |
| British pound | 2.6 | 0.06 | 0.2 | 0.53 | 1.4 |
| | | (3.50) | | (29.9) | |
| Swiss franc | 0.6 | 0.05 | 0.0 | 0.95 | 0.6 |
| | | (4.86) | | (68.29) | |
| Danish krone | 0.4 | | | 1 | 0.4 |
| Norwegian krone | 0.3 | | | 0.82 | 0.2 |
| | | | | (56.76) | |
| Swedish krona | 0.7 | | | 0.84 | 0.6 |
| | | | | (53.87) | |
| **Total effective weights** | | | **24.6** | | **21.9** |

Notes: [a] The trade weights refer to those under 'refined scenario' in Table 10.1. [b] Effective weight defined as trade weight multiplied by the corresponding betas estimated over the period from 5 Jan 1999 to 28 Feb 2005. The beta estimation is for the sample period of 5 January 1999 and 28 February 2005. White heteroskedasticity t-value in parentheses. We assume that the Danish Krona is pegged to the euro.

# Part IV
# Financial markets

# 11 Foreign bank lending and bond underwriting in Japan during the lost decade

*Jose A. Lopez and Mark M. Spiegel*

## Introduction

During the 1980s, the Japanese financial markets grew dramatically in scale and importance and clearly established Tokyo as a world financial centre. Many foreign financial institutions began to establish or greatly expand their presence in these markets. This paper examines the subsequent path of foreign intermediation activity during the so-called 'lost decade' of Japan in the 1990s. We examine both lending activity by foreign commercial banks in Japan and underwriting activity in the international yen-denominated bond sectors by foreign firms during this period.

At a first pass, it may seem that the connection between these two types of intermediation activities is tenuous, as the act of originating a loan and carrying it on your balance sheet is quite distinct from that of bond underwriting, where the intermediaries attempt to place the debt securities with other investors. However, financial intermediation in all of its forms involves the acquisition of knowledge. While bond underwriters do not directly carry much of the risk associated with their borrowers on their balance sheets, they do carry exposure to the reputation effects of the outcomes of the bonds that they underwrite. Because of this, bond underwriting also involves the costly monitoring of the expected quality of bond issues.

Intermediation takes on special characteristics when the financial intermediary is operating in a foreign market. A potentially important reason is that special regulatory restrictions are often placed on foreign firms. Foreign financial intermediaries also often possess information sets that differ from their domestic competitors, both regarding the prospects of potential borrowers as well as access to investors who desire to take on a certain type of exposure. This implies that foreign financial intermediaries may behave differently than their domestic counterparts, even where they stand on an equal regulatory footing. Moreover, foreign firms may be exposed to different shocks than domestic firms. For example, Peek and Rosengren (2000) show that Japanese bank lending in the US contracted during the Japanese economic downturn, suggests that foreign bank activity may be sensitive to home country conditions.

In this paper, we examine the impact of domestic economic conditions on foreign intermediation activity. We concentrate on the same episode as that examined by Peek and Rosengren – the Japanese economic boom of the 1980s and subsequent downturn after the bursting of the asset price bubble in 1992 – but ask how it affected the behaviour of foreign intermediaries operating in Japan. For foreign investment banks, the Japanese downturn implied deteriorated demand conditions by borrowers, but also deteriorated the financial strength of potential domestic competitors.

The net impact on intermediation activity of this shock would then be likely to depend on the relative importance of these two impacts. In the case of lending by foreign banks, we would expect to see the first impact, the downturn in domestic conditions, dominate. On the other hand, in the case of underwriting activity, especially in the international yen-denominated markets, we would expect the second impact, the increase in the potential competitive advantage of foreign underwriters, to have the dominant effect as financing was extended to borrowers outside Japan.

We find that the share of foreign bank lending in Japan fell sharply subsequent to bursting of the asset price bubble in the beginning of the 1990s, and again subsequent to the launch of the 'quantitative easing' policy by the Bank of Japan in 2001. This finding seems logical as the decline in funding demand would be paramount for foreign banks making loans that they intended to keep on their books.

Our results do not necessarily imply that foreign banks exacerbate the volatility of credit extension. While we do confirm that foreign bank lending in Japan exhibited more volatility than lending by domestic banks, we find that the imperfect correlation between foreign and domestic bank lending implied that the presence of foreign banks reduced the overall volatility of total bank lending relative to domestic bank lending alone.

We then turn to bond underwriting. While foreign firms began their underwriting activities in the domestic Japanese market by the mid-1990s, we examine their international yen-denominated bond-underwriting activities, such as those in the euro-yen and 'samurai' bond markets, where regulation played a much smaller role. Underwriting in these markets does not constitute foreign lending to Japan, as borrowers are primarily foreign. Nevertheless, it constitutes foreign intermediation activity in the Japanese financial markets, as foreign firms bring to bear their expertise both in locating potential investors and in assessing borrower quality.

Issuance of these bonds exhibited an upturn in 2000 and into the quantitative easing period for various reasons, such as the growing spreads between Japanese and emerging-market country interest rates contributing to 'carry trade' interme-diation towards those countries. We demonstrate that foreign investment banks played a large role in underwriting this activity and gained market share over the course of the so-called lost decade. While other changes, such as regulatory innovations, also contributed to the increase in foreign participation in Japanese underwriting activity, we argue that the increased share of foreign underwriting was also encouraged by the financial difficulties faced by domestic competitors during this period.

Our analysis therefore indicates that foreign financial activity in Japan responded to changes in the Japanese environment differently, depending on the nature of the activity. In the case of formal bank lending, the deterioration in local Japanese borrowing capacity and the increase in the interest rate differential between the US and Japan in the wake of 'quantitative easing' efforts by the Bank of Japan diminished the abundance of profitable lending opportunities. In contrast, these same interest rate movements encouraged foreign financial market participation in the international yen-denominated bond underwriting activity, as foreign underwriting efforts eased foreign access to low Japanese lending rates, while the deterioration in local borrowing conditions had little impact.

The remainder of this paper is organized into five sections. The next section reviews the literature on foreign intermediation, which is dominated by analyses of the impact of foreign banks on the domestic banking sector. The following section examines the experience of foreign banks in Japan during the lost decade. Section 4 examines the experience of foreign underwriters in international yen-denominated bond markets, and Section 5 concludes.

## Literature on foreign intermediation activity

The literature on the impact of foreign competitors on the domestic financial sector has primarily stressed the case of sophisticated and large developed-country foreign banks operating in emerging-market economies. A primary issue in this literature is whether or not the presence of foreign banks enhances the stability of the domestic financial system. Loosely, the argument in favour of this contention is that foreign banks can rely on home markets for credit during local downturns, while their domestic counterparts will find their credit sources more constrained. The primary argument on the other side stresses the fact that foreign banks are likely to be less committed to operations in the emerging market economy, and therefore will reduce their activity more abruptly during downturns, exacerbating the volatility of the supply of credit.[1]

Overall, the evidence appears to be mixed. Galindo *et al.* (2004) find that well-diversified foreign banks are prone to respond quickly and decisively to changes in the relative attractiveness of opportunities in a foreign host country. Arena *et al.* (2006) find that foreign banks are less sensitive to local monetary conditions. They also find that the lending and deposit rates offered by foreign banks tend to be modestly smoother during periods of financial distress, although the differences are not statistically significant. Goldberg (2002) looks at the volatility of US bank claims on foreign countries. She finds that US foreign claims seem to respond to source country conditions. However, she does not find that foreign claims of US banks are correlated with foreign real interest rates, and overall, the economic importance of local macroeconomic conditions on US bank lending is found to be minimal.

Other studies examine banking efficiency. Claessens and Glaessner (1998) find that the costs of financial services in eight developing Asian economies are decreasing in those countries' financial openness. However, they find that a subset of foreign banks can overcome this disadvantage because of specialized knowledge of the host country in question, for example, of a former colony of its source country. Berger *et al.* (2000) find that foreign institutions are generally less efficient than their domestic counterparts.

Despite the fact that the bulk of international lending takes place between developed nations, there is less evidence concerning the patterns of foreign lending in developed countries. In a series of papers, Peek and Rosengren (1997; 2000) have documented supply shocks to the extension of credit by Japanese banks in the US subsequent to the sharp decline in equity values experienced in that nation. Peek and Rosengren (1997) find decreased lending by US branches of Japanese banks subsequent to these equity declines, while Peek and Rosengren (2000) finds a negative impact of this decreased Japanese bank activity on real activity in the US.

This paper examines the opposite question, namely the degree to which foreign bank activity in Japan responded to host country conditions. A close antecedent to this paper is Goldberg (2007), which examines the pattern of US bank lending in Europe. Goldberg finds weak evidence that US bank flows to Europe are pro-cyclical, with US bank loans to Europe increasing in European GDP and decreasing in European interest rates, although the first result is not statistically significant.

Since bank lending is typically the main external funding source for borrowers, the term 'financial intermediation' almost always refers to banking activities.[2] However, capital markets activities, especially the issuance of financial securities, also provide borrowers with external financing, although with important differences in such areas as monitoring and corporate governance.

The international bond market in a given currency is commonly divided into three segments

- domestic bonds;
- foreign bonds; and
- Eurobonds.

Domestic bonds are mainly issued by domestic entities, in the domestic currency, under domestic regulations, and sold predominantly to domestic residents. Foreign bonds are issued by foreign borrowers within the domestic market of the currency of denomination and again under domestic regulation, which can be quite different than that for domestic bonds. Finally, Eurobonds are issued mainly outside of domestic regulations and are issued by borrowers of various nationalities. While these bonds may be purchased by domestic investors, a significant percentage of the bonds are purchased by investors domiciled in other countries.

The extant literature on the impact of foreign competitors on bond underwriting by a currency's domestic institutions is quite small and typically limited to specific episodes. Balder *et al.* (1991) examined Eurobond underwriting in the late 1980s and found that underwriters had a competitive advantage in issues denominated in their home currency. Similar results were found by McCauley and White (1997) and McCauley (1999). However, Kollo (2005) found that this advantage had been in decline since 1993.

A few studies have examined the effect of the introduction of the euro on the Eurobond market. Studies by Galati and Tsatsaronis (2003), Santos and Tsatsaronis (2003), and Kollo (2005) found increased competition in Eurozone underwriting markets.

Focusing on Japan, several papers have examined the impact of increased competition in the domestic bond markets arising from the securities subsidiaries of Japanese commercial banks. In April 1993, Japan's Financial System Reform Act removed most barriers between commercial and investment banking, thus allowing commercial banks to underwrite securities. As reported in Hamao and Hoshi (2000), their share of bond issues as lead managers rose from 9 per cent in the first quarter of 1994 to 42 per cent in the first quarter of 1995 and to 85 per cent by the end of 1997. With respect to the percentage of funds raised, the values went from 7 to 34 to 82%, respectively. Hamao and Hoshi (2000) argue that these new underwriters were successful in capturing market share, even in light of the potential conflicts of interest arising from banking ties between issuers and the subsidiaries' parent firms. Takaoka and McKenzie (2004) document that the entry of these competitors lowered underwriting commissions. Yasuda (2005) shows that borrowers with lending relationships were offered even lower underwriting fees. However, McKenzie and Takaoka (2006) demonstrate that borrowers switched away from using these new underwriters on their subsequent bond issues. In fact, as documented by Hamao and Hoshi (2000), many securities subsidiaries were merged or liquidated a few years after their creation.

## Foreign bank lending in Japan during the lost decade

We concentrate on two questions: First, to what extent do foreign bank lending levels in Japan respond to domestic conditions, i.e. how cyclical is foreign bank lending in Japan? Second, how does the presence of foreign lending affect the overall volatility of credit conditions in Japan?

Figure 11.1 depicts the total and share of foreign bank lending in Japan over our 24 year sample period. The data demonstrate that foreign lending levels appear to be pro-cyclical to some extent, although the share of foreign bank lending in the overall Japanese bank lending package has remained surprisingly stable in the range of 1.5 to 3 per cent of overall Japanese bank lending. Troughs in the share of foreign lending occurred after the equity market crash in 1995 and at the height of the quantitative easing period around 2005 in which Japanese commercial banks were flooded with excess reserves by the Bank of Japan to encourage lending. These troughs appear to correspond to poor economic fundamentals in the first case, and low domestic interest rates in the latter. Still, there are glaring exceptions. A trough in the share of foreign bank lending occurred in 1990, during the height of the Japanese boom. It is therefore unclear how cyclical foreign lending is relative to domestic lending.

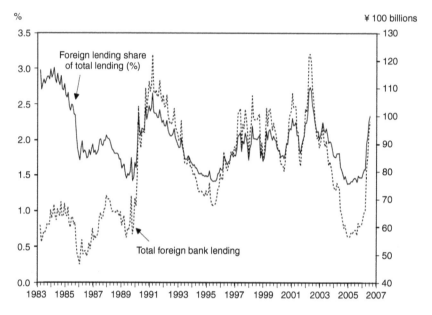

*Figure 11.1* Foreign bank lending in Japan (1983–2006).
Source: Bank of Japan.

Foreign bank lending in Japan also has been extremely volatile. Figure 11.2 depicts annual year-on-year growth in foreign and domestic lending in percentage terms. It is clear that in percentage terms, foreign lending has been much more volatile than domestic lending over our sample period. Moreover, if one looks carefully, it is clear that growth in foreign bank lending is positively correlated to growth in domestic bank lending. Over our complete sample, the correlation coefficient is 0.30.

To formally gauge the impact of foreign lending on the volatility of bank credit in Japan, we calculated Sharpe ratios for domestic and foreign lending from the beginning of 1983 through the second quarter of 2006, defined as the sample average divided by the sample standard deviation. We obtain a Sharpe ratio of 4.46 for foreign bank lending over the sample period, but one of 4.78 for domestic bank lending, implying that foreign lending was indeed more volatile than domestic lending over the period. Perhaps more surprisingly, because foreign lending was positively correlated with domestic lending, the Sharpe ratio for domestic lending alone was modestly greater than that for domestic plus foreign lending, which came in at 4.80. This suggests that while the univariate foreign lending series was more volatile than its domestic lending counterpart, it appears to have modestly reduced the volatility of credit extension over this period as it was imperfectly correlated with domestic lending.

Some caveats should be mentioned concerning this result: First, in the absence of the foreign banks, much of their lending activity would have likely been undertaken

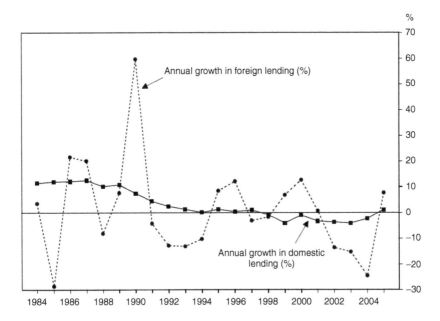

*Figure 11.2* Foreign and domestic bank lending in Japan, growth (1983–2006).

by domestically chartered banks. Second, intermediation services by foreign and domestic Japanese banks are substitutable only to a limited degree; a significant portion of lending by foreign banks in Japan is engaged in servicing subsidiaries of home-country firms.

We next examine parametric evidence concerning the determinants of foreign and domestic bank lending in Japan. We posit that lending decisions respond to perceived relative opportunities. As such, we condition on both Japanese and US interest rates, where the latter is taken as indicative of the 'world' rate of interest, or the rates of return available for lending abroad, as well as measures of local and foreign economic conditions. Japanese economic conditions are proxied for by the growth of GDP measured in log differences. As a measure of home country conditions for the foreign banks, we take the growth in the total level of GDP for the original 20 OECD countries net of Japan, again measured in log differences.[3] Our base specification therefore follows Goldberg (2002; 2007) in assessing the relative sensitivity of foreign and domestic Japanese banks to local and home economic conditions. We estimate:

$$L_t = \alpha + \beta_1 t + \beta_2 \log\left(r_t^J\right) + \beta_3 \log\left(r_t^{US}\right) + \beta_4 gGDP_t^J + \beta_5 gGDP_t^{CC}$$
$$+ \beta_6 BOOM_t + \varepsilon_t \tag{11.1}$$

where $t$ represents a linear time trend; $r_t^J$ is the 3-month Japanese interest rate at time $t$, $r_t^{US}$ is the 3-month US interest rate at time $t$, $gGDP_t^J$ represents real

*Table 11.1* Volatility of foreign and domestic lending (¥ 100 billion)

|  | Standard deviation | Sharp ratio ($\mu/\sigma$) |
|---|---|---|
| Foreign Lending | 18.40 | 4.43 |
| Domestic Lending | 854.89 | 4.73 |
| Foreign + Domestic | 866.87 | 4.76 |
| Correlation Coefficient | 0.65 | |

Source: Bank of Japan.

GDP growth in Japan at time $t$, $gGDP_t^{CC}$ represents real GDP growth in potential creditor countries at time $t$, measured as the percentage growth in the sum of the 20 original OECD countries, excluding Greece, Ireland, and Japan itself; $BOOM_t$ is a zero-one dummy identifying the boom portion of the sample, with value one for all year prior to 1992 and value zero afterwards; and $\varepsilon_t$ is an independent and identically disturbed disturbance term. We estimate the specification using ordinary least squares with White's heteroskedasticity correction.

Our results are shown in Table 11.2. It can be seen that both with and without the inclusion of a linear time trend, foreign and domestic bank lending in Japan is increasing in Japanese interest rates and decreasing in US interest rates as expected, usually at statistically significant levels. The exception is that Japanese bank lending appears to be insensitive to US interest rates. It can also be seen that foreign bank lending in Japan seems to be more sensitive to Japanese interest rates than domestic bank lending, confirming the results above that foreign bank lending appears to be more volatile.

The results for GDP growth, both in Japan and abroad, are weaker. We do obtain the expected result that foreign bank lending in Japan is measurably declining in growth in creditor countries' home markets, at a 5 per cent confidence level when the linear time trend is included, and at a 10 per cent confidence level when the linear time trend is excluded. The impact on Japanese bank lending has the same sign, but the coefficient estimates are smaller than those on the foreign banks and are statistically insignificant. The evidence therefore suggests that foreign bank lending in Japan is more sensitive to external conditions than domestic bank lending.

Concerning domestic economic conditions, we obtain an unexpected negative coefficient for both domestic and foreign bank lending in Japan, with the point estimates for foreign bank lending again exhibiting greater sensitivity. This result is surprising, as one would expect greater lending during good times. The result may be indicative of a demand effect, where in good times borrowing firms have access to alternative financing sources, such as commercial paper. Alternatively, it could reflect the easy monetary policy that pervaded Japan during the latter 1990s, although the latter explanation conflicts with our results for Japanese interest rates above. We similarly obtained a negative and significant coefficient on the $BOOM_t$ dummy, suggesting that bank lending was greater during the post-boom era.

*Table 11.2* Determinants of foreign and domestic bank lending

|  | Foreign banks | Japanese banks | Foreign banks | Japanese banks |
|---|---|---|---|---|
| Constant | 11.129*** | 14.897*** | 11.517*** | 15.440*** |
|  | (0.426) | (0.255) | (0.057) | (0.056) |
| Time | 0.002 | 0.003** | — | — |
|  | (0.003) | (0.001) |  |  |
| Japan 3 month | 8.103*** | 6.669*** | 7.680*** | 6.077*** |
| interest rate | (1.607) | (1.008) | (1.812) | (1.115) |
| US 3 month | −3.698** | −2.083 | −4.712*** | −3.501*** |
| interest rate | (1.515) | (1.373) | (1.097) | (1.315) |
| GDP growth | −0.483** | −0.197* | −0.566*** | −0.314*** |
| Japan | (0.187) | (0.116) | (0.182) | (0.112) |
| GDP growth | −0.906** | −0.415 | −0.817* | −0.291 |
| creditor Ctys. | (0.413) | (0.320) | (0.436) | (0.352) |
| Boom | −0.181* | −0.337*** | −0.225*** | −0.399*** |
|  | (0.094) | (0.080) | (0.081) | (0.081) |
| # of Obs. | 88 | 88 | 88 | 88 |
| $R^2$ | 0.383 | 0.570 | 0.374 | 0.550 |
| F-value | 12.24 | 19.56 | 13.31 | 22.55 |

Notes: Dependent Variable: log of lending.
Standard errors in parentheses. Ordinary least squares estimates with White's heteroskedasticity-corrected standard errors. GDP growth rates calculated as log differences. * Significant at 10% confidence level. ** Significant at 5% confidence level. *** Significant at 1% confidence level.

To mitigate estimation problems stemming from potential unit root issues in our time series, we next differenced the data and used the following specification

$$\Delta L_t = \beta_1 + \beta_2 \Delta \log\left(r_t^J\right) + \beta_3 \Delta \log\left(r_t^{US}\right) + \beta_4 \Delta gGDP_t^J + \beta_5 \Delta gGDP_t^{CC}$$
$$+ \beta_6 BOOM_t + v_t \tag{11.2}$$

Note that the constant term would now be interpreted as $\beta_1$, the coefficient estimate on the linear time trend. We also ran the specification with and without the $BOOM_t$ dummy, which drops out after first-differencing in equation (11.1), but captures the possibility of a shift in the linear growth trend around the end of the boom period.

Our results are shown in Table 11.3. It can again be seen that both foreign and domestic banks respond to Japanese interest rates, with changes in foreign bank lending being much more responsive than their domestic counterparts. Looking at US interest rates, we again see that foreign bank lending is sensitive to these rates at statistically significant levels. The results for Japanese banks are mixed, as US rates enter insignificantly without the inclusion of the $BOOM_t$ dummy, but significantly with the incorrect positive sign with the dummy variable included. In either specification, the coefficients on foreign bank lending are substantially more negative, suggesting as expected that foreign lending rates in Japan are more sensitive to home country conditions than domestic bank lending rates are to foreign conditions. For the remaining variables, we fail to find any statistically

*Table 11.3* Determinants of changes in foreign and domestic bank lending

|  | Foreign banks | Japanese banks | Foreign banks | Japanese banks |
|---|---|---|---|---|
| Constant | 0.004 | 0.031*** | −0.020 | −0.010*** |
|  | (0.019) | (0.006) | (0.022) | (0.003) |
| Δ Japan 3 month | 6.873*** | 0.977** | 6.486*** | 0.292 |
|   interest rate | (1.866) | (0.457) | (1.730) | (0.340) |
| Δ US 3 month | −3.501*** | −0.379 | −2.950** | 0.596*** |
|   interest rate | (1.104) | (0.463) | (1.128) | (0.145) |
| Δ GDP growth | −0.174 | −0.038 | −0.162 | −0.017 |
|   Japan | (0.245) | (0.080) | (0.244) | (0.034) |
| Δ GDP growth | −0.429 | 0.023 | −0.355 | 0.152 |
|   creditor Ctys. | (0.477) | (0.153) | (0.487) | (0.112) |
| Boom | — | — | 0.060 | 0.107*** |
|  |  |  | (0.038) | (0.006) |
| # of Obs. | 87 | 87 | 87 | 87 |
| $R^2$ | 0.201 | 0.035 | 0.226 | 0.833 |
| F-value | 4.46 | 1.15 | 4.59 | 104.87 |

Notes: Dependent Variable: difference in log of lending.
Standard errors in parentheses. Ordinary least squares estimates with White's heteroskedasticity-corrected standard errors. GDP growth rates calculated as log differences. * Significant at 10% confidence level. ** Significant at 5% confidence level. *** Significant at 1% confidence level.

significant relationship between changes in GDP growth and changes in lending rates for either domestic or foreign bank lending.

In summary, our results suggest that foreign bank lending are generally more sensitive to both domestic and foreign interest rates, as would be expected. This is consistent with our earlier finding that foreign bank lending in Japan during this period was more volatile. However, it should be stressed that this does not necessarily imply that the presence of foreign banks exacerbates the overall volatility of bank activity in Japan, as foreign and domestic lending rates are imperfectly correlated.

## Foreign activity in yen-denominated bonds

In this section, we examine the role that foreign securities firms played in international yen-denominated bond underwriting during the 1990s. In Japan, the foreign bond market is known as the 'samurai' bond market. The market was controlled quite closely by the Ministry of Finance using regulations targeted at the eligibility of issuers, underwriters and investors (Hoschika 2005). Most of these controls were not fully removed until the broader financial market deregulation of 1998. The Euro-yen bond market, which dates back to at least 1977, was also subject to related controls, as detailed in Hoshi and Kashyap (1999), that were also removed in the late 1990s.

Figure 11.3 presents nominal issuance in the samurai and Euro-yen bond markets from 1992 through 2005, based on annual summary data from the

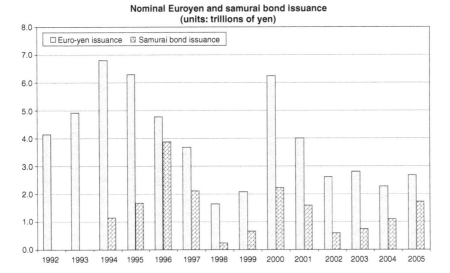

*Figure 11.3* Issuance of international yen-denominated bonds.
Source: Author calculations based on year-end data from the International Financing Review.

*International Financing Review.*[4] Issuance in these two markets has clearly followed the overall pattern of the Japanese banking crisis. Samurai bond issuance rose up through 1996, but then dropped to a low in 1998. Subsequent issuance has been driven primarily by the level of yen interest rates and yen-related swap rates. According to Claessens *et al.* (2007), yen-denominated Eurobonds over the period from 1980–2000 accounted for 13 per cent of issues and about 8.25 per cent of nominal issuance values. Issuance in the Euro-yen market peaked in 1994 before dropping sharply to a low in 1998. Again, subsequent issuance, except for 2000 when many US corporates issued debt, has been in line with the level of yen interest rates and yen-related swap rates.

Bond underwriting in the international yen sector follows the general procedures used in the Eurobond markets; see Claes *et al.* (2002) for a more detailed description. The financial firm that is the principal player in a bond underwriting transaction is known as the bookrunner. The bookrunner initiates the transaction with the borrower and is responsible for organizing the underwriting syndicate (if one is used), pricing the bond and placing of the issue, either directly with investors or in the primary market.[5] The former are known as 'bought' deals, where the underwriting syndicate purchases the entire issue and distributes it to their clients. A reasonably large amount of Eurobond issuance is 'bought' deals. The latter requires the bookrunner to make a market in the bond in order to support initial trading and placement at the specified price.

Either way, the bookrunner specifically and the syndicate in general take on substantial risk since they have taken the bond issue onto their own books for a period of time. The underwriters hope to quickly remove the issue from their books and place it with investors. A common measure of compensation is the underwriter spread, defined as the gross fees charged by the underwriter as a percent of the issuance size. While default risk is a component of that compensation, Eurobond market issuers generally carry a higher credit profile, For example, less than one percent of the financial firms in Kollo and Sharpe (2006) are below investment grade.

Overall, underwriting activity in the Eurobond markets is very competitive, with few barriers to entry and low underwriter concentration. Among yen-denominated bonds, the Eurobond markets are less concentrated than the domestic market, where the first foreign underwritten issue was not recorded until 1995. The degree of concentration in the international yen bond markets has also decreased more rapidly.

The bookrunner's role is quite informationally intensive. In particular, the bookrunner must convince a borrower to issue in a particular sector and currency denomination. He must have a viable investor clientele to purchase the bond issue. He is expected to construct a syndicate, if needed, to place the issue. He must be capable of supporting the bond issue in the primary market. Finally, since 70 per cent of Eurobond issuance is said to be swap-driven, as reported by Claes *et al.* (2002), the bookrunner must be able to manage this component of the financing in an effective manner.

Domestic underwriters might have a comparative advantage as well, including superior information concerning domestic economic fundamentals and/or from superior access to investors wishing to invest in the domestic currency. They might also be protected by national regulation, as was the case in Japan, where the securities subsidiaries of Japanese banks were not allowed to underwrite bonds until 1992 and all restrictions on underwriters were removed by 1998.

However, due to their different skills and information sets, foreign firms may still be able to compete. Foreign firms could bring to market their own rosters of borrowing clients or expand their services to domestic borrowers. Foreign firms may use their rosters of domestic and international investors to place the bonds. Similarly, the foreign firm could be better able to execute currency swaps, either due to their superior market presence, or to better pricing due to their credit ratings. This might have been the case during the late 1990s, when many Japanese financial institutions experienced distress. The foreign firm might also be able to introduce a financial innovation, as in the case of the Merrill Lynch introduction of dual currency bonds to the Japanese samurai bond market discussed below.

We examine the activity of foreign underwriters by using the IFR league tables for both the samurai and Euro-yen markets from 1992 through 2005. The league tables are constructed by assigning the appropriate share of a bond issue to its bookrunner(s). For example, a sole bookrunner receives a 100 per cent share, whereas two co-bookrunners receive a 50 per cent share.

*Table 11.4* Euro-yen league tables for 1995 and 2005

| Rank | 1995 | | | 2005 | | |
|---|---|---|---|---|---|---|
| | Underwriter | Total | Share (%) | Underwriter | Total | Share (%) |
| 1 | Nomura International | 1,181,854 | 18.81 | Nomura | 575,843 | 21.5 |
| 2 | Daiwa Europe | 941,190 | 14.98 | Citigroup | 575,117 | 21.5 |
| 3 | Nikko Europe | 679,769 | 10.82 | Deutsche Bank | 368,193 | 13.8 |
| 4 | IBJ International | 518,620 | 8.25 | Merrill Lynch | 163,827 | 6.1 |
| 5 | Merrill Lynch | 472,699 | 7.52 | Daiwa Secs SMBC | 147,608 | 5.5 |
| 6 | Yamaichi International | 412,704 | 6.57 | Barclays Capital | 147,320 | 5.5 |
| 7 | Sanwa International | 367,658 | 5.85 | Morgan Stanley | 114,608 | 4.3 |
| 8 | Fuji International | 321,942 | 5.12 | UBS | 108,526 | 4.1 |
| 9 | Morgan Stanley | 228,020 | 3.63 | Mizuho FG | 101,035 | 3.8 |
| 10 | Daichi Kangyo Bank | 189,524 | 3.02 | Lehman Bros | 74,905 | 2.8 |
| Total | | 5,313,979 | 84.57 | | 2,376,983 | 88.90 |

Source: International Financing Review. Issuance is measured in million yen.

The bookrunners are then ranked by their total issuance in that market for the year. The IFR publishes the league tables consisting of the top ten bookrunners for each year; see Table 11.4 for an example of the Euro-yen league tables for 1995 and 2005. Note that in most cases the top ten bookrunners account for less than 100 percent of issuance in that market sector for that year. Nevertheless, we assume that the league tables capture the majority of underwriting activity.

We follow Kollo (2005) in estimating underwriters' market shares by using their market shares in the top ten league tables.[6] Figures 11.4 and 11.5 present the percentage of issuance in the samurai and Euroyen sectors, respectively, by Japanese and American bookrunners in the top ten league tables for the years 1992 through 2005. Both charts clearly present the declining share of underwriting by Japanese firms in both sectors of the international yen bond market. The decline is most pronounced in the Euro-yen sector (see Figure 11.5), where the share declined from 93 per cent in 1992 to 30 per cent in 2005. The US share rose from 6 to 35 per cent during this period. A reason for the relatively smooth decline of the Japanese share is that the Euro-yen sector is only lightly regulated.[7] Hence, competition for underwriting mandates was more open and permitted the foreign firms to use any of their available comparative advantages to full effect.

In contrast, the decline in the Japanese share of the samurai bond underwriting market starts abruptly in 1998. The first samurai bond for which a foreign firm was the bookrunner was issued only in 1995. A key reason for this dominance was regulation of the market for both issuers and borrowers. For example, prior to 1993, securities firms affiliated with Japanese banks were prohibited from underwriting any bonds. Also, prior to 1996, the Ministry of Finance had in place credit rating eligibility requirements that prevented low rated and unrated borrowers from

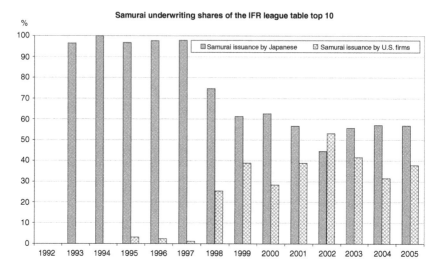

*Figure 11.4* National shares of Samurai bond issuance.
Source: Author calculations based on year-end data from the International Financing Review.

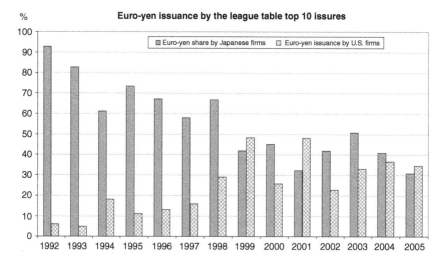

*Figure 11.5* National shares of Euro-yen bond issuance.
Source: Author calculations based on year-end data from the International Financing Review.

issuing in the samurai market. The prohibition on samurai underwriting by foreign bank-affiliated securities firms was removed in 1997, and it was in 1998 that the US share of samurai bond issuance increased markedly from a few percentage points to 25 per cent.

Our ability to explain the change in underwriting shares by US and foreign securities firms is limited by our lack of data on individual bond issues. However, anecdotal evidence gleaned from weekly IFR reports provides some market-specific insights. There appear to be several examples of issues by foreign firms that bring to market their own rosters of domestic and international borrowers. One example is the increased issuance by US corporations in 2000 due primarily to changes in US accounting rules. Most of these issues had US bookrunners, although often with Japanese firms as equal partners. Similarly, various press accounts of US firms leading underwriting syndicates for Japanese firms cite both their long-term business relationships in the overseas markets and innovative financing structures.

A potentially important informational difference between Japanese and foreign firms is the set of end investors. Of course, securities firms work to establish relationships with various types of institutional investors, but the degree of success in uncertain. The anecdotal evidence weakly supports the notion that Japanese firms may have placed more of their issuance with Japanese investors than foreign firms, but even the Japanese firms are found to place roughly 80 per cent of their issuance overseas.

Much clearer evidence on the impact of investor information sets arises from the introduction of dual-currency samurai bonds issued by lower quality sovereign borrowers. Dual-currency bonds have their interest and principal payments denominated in different currencies and were introduced to the samurai market by Merrill Lynch in 1996. Aside from the innovation in financing structure, an important innovation with these issues was that they were targeted to retail investors, which was possible after deregulation by the Ministry of Finance allowed these retail transactions. While Merrill had some retail clientele in Japan, they were able to market the securities on a larger scale by coordinating their distribution network with those of smaller Japanese brokerage firms. This highlights how foreign underwriters can use their knowledge and expertise in alternative funding methods to their advantage.

Finally, the swap driven element of their bond issues seems to provide foreign firms with some advantages in the international yen market for two reasons. First, borrowers with multi-currency relationships with a foreign underwriter would feel comfortable with them in yet another currency. Of course, this element would also be present for Japanese firms with established relationships. More compelling is the development of the 'Japan premium' in 1995 and for a few years afterward. Anecdotally, this rise in funding costs hurt Japanese underwriters in their perceived ability to absorb the underwriting risks and hence provide funding at a competitive rate.[8]

In summary, the behaviour of foreign securities firms in the international yen-denominated bond markets has been impacted by Japanese domestic economic conditions, but seemingly less so than in the domestic banking sector. While issuance has primarily been driven by yen interest rates and swap rates, the participation of foreign firms has been increasing, particularly due to the deregulation of these markets. However, the weakening, and even failure, of Japanese firms also allowed foreign firms to capture market share.

## Conclusion

Our results show quite a contrast between the behaviour of lending by foreign commercial banks and underwriting activity by foreign investment banks in Japan over our sample period. In the case of lending activity, we found that foreign bank lending was very sensitive to domestic Japanese conditions, particularly Japanese interest rates, more so than their domestic Japanese bank counterparts. In the case of underwriting activity, however, we saw marked growth in the activity over the so-called lost decade in Japan.

A key explanation for these differing outcomes is the difference in borrower clienteles. The banking sector lends primarily to Japanese domestic borrowers, whose financing needs and performance are directly tied to the Japanese economy. For underwriters in the international yen-denominated sectors, the borrowers are mainly foreign firms with a specific need for yen funding or with an opportunity to swap their yen funding for another source of funding. While these borrowers would not be immune to the state of the Japanese economy and associated exchange rates, their financing needs are based on a wider set of economic and financial factors.

We should stress that our analysis for the specific Japanese case is potentially confounded by a number of other potential factors. Most notably, we have to acknowledge that the regulatory reforms that occurred in Japanese bond markets are likely to have played a large role in encouraging the increase in foreign underwriting market share in Japan in the 1990s. However, we can point to the second sharp decline in foreign bank activity, namely that subsequent to the adoption of the zero interest rate policy, as evidence that distinctions exist independent of the regulatory impact. Over this period, reduced interest rates on Japanese loans discouraged lending by foreign banks while the same low rates were a catalyst for bond underwriting activity identified with the so-called 'carry trade' based on borrowing cheaply in Japan and lending abroad.

## Acknowledgement

Christopher Candelaria provided excellent research assistance. This paper was prepared for the 2006 APEA conference proceedings. The views expressed are solely those of the authors and do not necessarily reflect those of the Federal Reserve Bank of San Francisco or the Federal Reserve Board of Governors.

## References

Arena M., Reinhart C. and Vázquez F. (2006) 'The Lending Channel in Emerging Economies: Are Foreign Banks Different?' NBER Working Paper, No.12340.

Balder J., Lopez J. A. and Sweet L. M. (1991) 'Competitiveness in the Eurocredit Market', in Spindler J. A. (ed.), *International Competitiveness of U.S. Financial Firms: Products, Markets and Conventional Performance Measures*. A Staff Study by the Federal Reserve Bank of New York. pp. 26–41.

Berger A. N., DeYoung R., Genay H. and Udell G.F. (2000) 'Globalization of Financial Services: Evidence from Cross-Border Performance', *Brooking Papers on Financial Performance*, 2000: 23–158.

Carter R. and Manaster S. (1990) 'Initial Public Offerings and Underwriter Reputation', *Journal of Finance*, 45(4): 1045–1068.

Claes A., De Ceuster M. J. K. and Polfiet R. (2002) 'Anatomy of the Eurobond Market: 1980–2000', *European Financial Management*, 8: 373–386.

Claessens, S., Klingebiel D. and Schmukler, S. (2007), 'Government Bonds in Domestic and Foreign Currency: The Role of Macroeconomic and Institutional Factors', *Review of International Economics*, 2(15): 370–413.

Claessens S. and Glaessner T. (1998) 'Internationalization of Financial Services in Asia', Policy Research Working Paper, No.1911, World Bank.

Galati, G. and Tsatsaronis, K. (2003) 'The impact of the euro on Europe's financial markets', *Financial Markets, Institutions and Instruments*, 12(3): 165–222.

Galindo A., Micco A. and Powell A. (2004) 'Loyal Lenders or Fickle Financiers: Foreign Banks in Latin America', Manuscript, Inter-American Development Bank.

Goldberg L. (2002) 'When is Foreign Bank Lending to Emerging Markets Volatile?' in Edwards S. and Frankel J. (eds), *Preventing Currency Crises in Emerging Markets*. NBER and University of Chicago Press. pp. 171–198.

—— (2007) 'The International Exposure of U.S. Banks: Europe and Latin America Compared', in Edwards S. (ed.) *Capital Controls and Capital Flows in Emerging Economies: Policies, Practices and Consequences*. NBER and University of Chicago Press, 203–232.

Gorton G. and Winton A. (2003) 'Financial Intermediation', in Constantinides G., Harris M. and Stultz R., (eds.) *Handbook of the Economics of Finance, Volume 1A*. Elsevier North-Holland. Chapter 8, 431–552.

Hamao Y. and Hoshi T. (2000) 'Bank-Owned Securities Subsidiaries in Japan: Evidence after the 1993 Financial System Reform', in Masohiko A. and Saxonhouse G. R. (eds) *Finance, Governance and Competitiveness in Japan*. Oxford: Oxford University Press. pp. 105–117.

Hoschka T. C. (2005) 'Developing the Market for Local Currency Bonds by Foreign Issuers: Lessons from Asia', Working Paper Series, No. 63, Economics and Research Department, Asian Development Bank.

Hoshi T. and Kashyap A. (1999) 'The Japanese Banking Crisis: Where Did it Come from and How Will it End?' in Bernanke B. S. and Rotemberg J. (eds), *NBER Macroeconomics Annual*: 129–201.

Kollo M. G. (2005) 'Underwriter Competition and Gross Spreads in the Eurobond Market', Working Paper Series, No.550, European Central Bank.

Kollo M. G. and Sharpe I. G. (2006) 'Relationships and Underwriter Spreads in the Eurobond Floating Rate Market', *Journal of Financial Research*, 29(2): 163–180.

McCauley R. N. and White W. R. (1997) 'The Euro and European Financial Markets', Working Paper, No. 41, Bank for International Settlements.

McCauley R. N. (1999) 'The Euro and the Liquidity of European Fixed Income Markets', in *Market Liquidity: Research Findings and Selected Policy Implications*, Bank for International Settlements, Committee on the Global Financial System, Publication, No. 11.

McKenzie C. R. and Takaoka S. (2006) 'Underwriter Switching in the Japanese Corporate Bond Market', manuscript, Keio University.

Megginson W. and Weiss K. (1991) 'Venture Capitalist Certification in Initial Public Offerings', *Journal of Finance*, 46(3): 879–904.

Peek J. and Rosengren E. S. (1997) 'The International Transmission of Financial Shocks: The Case of Japan', *American Economic Review*, 87(4): 495–505.

—— (2000) 'Collateral Damage: Effects of the Japanese Bank Crisis on Real Activity in the United States', *American Economic Review*, 90(1): 30–45.

—— (2001) 'Determinants of the Japan Premium: Actions Speak Louder than Words', *Journal of International Economics*, 53(2): 283–305.

Santos, J. and Tsatsaronis, K. (2003) 'The cost of barriers to entry: evidence from the market for corporate euro bond underwriting', BIS Working Paper no. 134, September.

Takaoka S. and McKenzie C. R. (2006) 'The Impact of Bank Entry in the Japanese Corporate Bond Underwriting Market', *Journal of Banking and Finance*, 30(1): 59–83.

Yasuda A. (2005) 'Do Bank Relationships Affect the Firm's Underwriter Choice in the Corporate-Bond Underwriting Market?' *Journal of Finance*, 60(3): 1259–1292.

# 12 The core-AMU denominated Asian bonds for local investors in East Asia

*Eiji Ogawa and Junko Shimizu*

## Introduction

In August 2003, the ASEAN+3 (Japan, China, and Korea) Financial Ministers have established Asian Bond Markets Initiative (ABMI), which aimed to develop efficient and liquid bond markets in Asia. The ABMI has been promoting to issue local currency denominated bonds to contribute to mitigation of currency and maturity mismatches in financing regional borrowers. To further contribute to the development of deeper and more liquid regional bond markets, the Financial Ministers agreed to take some measure at the ASEAN+3 Finance Ministers' Meeting in May 2005 in Istanbul, Turkey. One of the agreements is to launch a study on Asian currency basket bond.

At the same time, the Executive Meeting of East-Asia Pacific central banks (EMEAP) has promoted the Asian Bond Fund (ABF) Initiative to enhance efficiency of capital movements in the region by deepening regional domestic bond markets. The first stage was to establish the so-called ABF 1, which was a kind of fund to invest in US dollar denominated bonds issued by sovereign and quasi-sovereign entities in the EMEAP member countries. The second project is to establish the so-called ABF 2. The ABF 2 is a fund that compose of local currency denominated bonds of eight EMEAP countries.[1] This is a kind of fund of bond funds, which is a similar concept of currency basket denominated bonds.

In Ogawa and Shimizu (2005), we proposed an Asian Monetary Unit (AMU) as a regional common currency unit that is a weighted average of the thirteen East Asian currencies (ASEAN+3) in order that the monetary authorities should monitor intra-regional exchange rate in their surveillance process in East Asia. At the second stage, create a core-AMU currency basket, which is composed of some core currencies in the region, should be created. We recommend using it as a denomination currency of Asian bond in order to reduce mismatching of assets and liabilities in terms of currency. The AMU should be composed of the thirteen East Asian currencies because it is supposed to be used as a surveillance indicator in ASEAN+3 Finance Ministers' Meeting. However, it is not adequate as a denomination currency of Asian bond for private sector's uses. For a practical use, we need to create a core-AMU, which is composed of only the Asian currencies with convertibility in both the current and capital accounts.

Then, we expect that local investors as well as foreign ones would freely make cross-boarder transactions in terms of a core-AMU in the regional bond markets.

In this chapter, we have two objectives. First, we decide criteria to choose core-AMU currencies among the East Asian currencies. We expect that the criteria will promote further coordinated efforts to deregulate their capital and foreign exchange controls in order to join in the core-AMU currencies. Second, we create a core-AMU denominated Asian bond to investigate their return and risk profiles for local investors in East Asian countries. In addition, we calculate a correlation matrices among the core-AMU denominated Asian bond, the US Treasury, and the euro denominated bond for local investors in East Asian countries.

The remainder of this paper consists of the following sections. Section 2 overviews the current progress of Asian bond markets. Section 3 discusses the role of AMU and the choice of composition currencies. Section 4 proposes a core-AMU currency basket as a denomination currency of Asian bond and decides criteria to choose core-AMU currencies. Section 5 simulates a core-AMU denominated Asian bond and investigates their return and risk profiles for local investors in the region. Section 6 calculates a correlation matrices among the core-AMU denominated Asian bond, the US Treasury, and the euro denominated bond for local investors in East Asian countries. The final section summarizes the concluding remarks.

## The current progress of Asian bond markets in East Asia

Most countries in East Asia have actively developed their local bond markets after the Asian currency and financial crises since the governments of the countries recognized the importance of strengthening their financial sectors for prevention and management of currency and financial crises. As a part of the Asian Bond Market Initiative, the Asian Development Bank (ADB) launched the Asian Bond Online (http://asiabondonline.abd.org) as a website on Asian bond markets, in May 2004 to disseminate information on the region's bond markets. From the website, we can easily show the current progress of Asian bond markets in the region.

Figure 12.1 shows the movement of domestic outstanding issuance from 1997 to 2005. Among the eight East Asian countries, the domestic bond markets in South Korea and China are constantly expanding. In other countries, their sizes are still very small although their trends are upward. Table 12.1 shows the size of local currency bond market in 1999 and 2005. We found that the local currency bond markets in each Asian country were still extremely small except for Japan, South Korea and China in 2005. However, the ratios of local currency bond markets to GDP also have increased rapidly in some countries.

Table 12.2 shows the cross-boarder portfolio flows among the areas in the world in 2003. It indicates that share of intra-regional portfolio flow in East Asia was 4.9 per cent, which was much lower than those in the EU 15 (63.5 per cent) and NAFTA (15.8 per cent). According to Asian Bond Monitor 2005 by the ADB (2005), China, Singapore and Malaysia invested a higher portion of their total cross-border portfolio assets in other East Asian market in 2003 (17.2 per cent, 22.9 per cent and 47.2 per cent, respectively). In contrast, Japan only invested

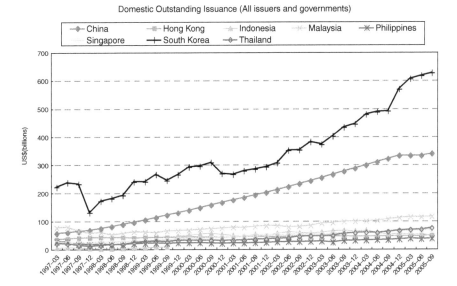

*Figure 12.1* Domestic outstanding issuance (all issuers and government).
Source: The BIS International Financial Statistics 2005.

*Table 12.1* Size of local currency bond market in 1999 and 2005

|  | as of December 1999 | | as of December 2005 | |
| --- | --- | --- | --- | --- |
|  | as a Percentage of GDP(%) | in USD billions | as a Percentage of GDP(%) | in USD billions |
| China | 21.7 | 215.0 | 27.3 | 606.8 |
| Hong Kong | 35.6 | 57.1 | 48.0 | 85.6 |
| Indonesia | 32.0 | 49.3 | 18.0 | 50.5 |
| Japan | 131.8 | 6, 356.0 | 194.0 | 8, 855.2 |
| South Korea | 59.6 | 265.6 | 83.4 | 656.4 |
| Malaysia | 83.6 | 66.1 | 94.8 | 124.0 |
| Philippines | 30.3 | 23.0 | 41.2 | 40.6 |
| Singapore | 45.2 | 37.4 | 70.2 | 81.9 |
| Thailand | 27.0 | 33.1 | 45.9 | 81.0 |

Source: Asiabond Online website: http://asianbondsonline.adb.org/regional/regional.php.

1.3 per cent of its total cross-borer portfolio flows in East Asian assets. It also reported that East Asian investors invested into a significant amount of the US dollar and the euro denominated debts issued in East Asia. These facts indicate that there might be much room for expanding cross-border portfolio flows especially for the Japanese investors.

*Table 12.2* Cross-border portfolio flows in 2003

|  | *(% of Total)* | | |
| --- | --- | --- | --- |
| *Investment to* | *Investment from* | | |
|  | *NAFTA* | *EU15* | *East Asia* |
| Total portfolio investment | | | |
| NAFTA | 15.8 | 18.6 | 33.5 |
| EU15 | 46.7 | 63.5 | 36.1 |
| East Asia | 13.7 | 4.4 | 4.9 |
| Rest of World | 23.8 | 13.5 | 25.5 |
| Total Global | 100.0 | 100.0 | 100.0 |
| Long-term debt securities | | | |
| NAFTA | 21.4 | 15.3 | 34.1 |
| EU15 | 45.4 | 69.0 | 38.2 |
| East Asia | 5.9 | 1.9 | 2.7 |
| Rest of World | 27.3 | 13.8 | 24.9 |
| Total Global | 100.0 | 100.0 | 100.0 |
| Equity securities | | | |
| NAFTA | 13.4 | 23.7 | 34.7 |
| EU15 | 44.8 | 53.6 | 27.8 |
| East Asia | 18.0 | 9.3 | 10.9 |
| Rest of World | 23.9 | 13.3 | 26.5 |
| Total Global | 100.0 | 100.0 | 100.0 |

Source: Asia Bond Monitor 2005, ADB.

## The role of the AMU and the choice of composition currencies

Under the high intra-regional trade linkage, the internal stability of exchange rates in the region is very important for growth and stability of the regional economy. Therefore, the coordinated exchange rate policies should be necessary for stability of intra-regional exchange rates among the East Asian countries. Ogawa and Shimizu (2005) proposed an AMU as a surveillance indicator in the Economic Review and Policy Dialogue of the ASEAN+3 Finance Ministers' Meeting. Accordingly, we need to monitor deviation of each East Asian currency based on a weighted average of East Asian currencies such as the AMU.[2]

Conditions to be a composition currency of a common currency basket like the AMU depends on purposes for what we use it. The AMU should include all of ASEAN+3 currencies for the surveillance regardless to their convertibility (and inconvertibility) in both current and capital accounts. Because of its role of a benchmark (or numéraire) for regional currencies in East Asia, the AMU should include all regional currencies of East Asian countries even if the weights of some minor currencies are very small. However, more than half of them actually have a lot of barriers to conduct transactions freely in foreign exchange markets due to their monetary authorities' regulation. Therefore, it is not practical to use the

AMU as a denomination currency of regional bonds that should be freely traded at the cross-boarder transactions.

Dammers and McCauley (2006) and Iwata (2005) indicated that development in private ECU in the financial field begun in the early 1980s and developed rapidly. In the same way, we expect that the AMU would be used not only by the monetary authorities but also by the private sector. In the future, the AMU would be used as a denomination currency of regional economic transactions (trade and capital transactions) and asset stocks (foreign exchange reserves and cross-border bonds) as the ECU was used as a denomination currency in the EU under the EMS. Iwata (2005) indicated that there were still rooms for the private ACU (Asian Currency Unit) composed of main Asian currencies to develop.[3] In addition, he suggested that the relatively small size of domestic bond market and the shortage of its liquidity might render ACU bond market comparative advantage.

The AMU as a common denomination currency would contribute to increasing of the liquidity in the Asian bond market or deepening the Asian Bond Market. In the history of the ECU, the 'private' ECU was created by the commercial banking system.[4] We learn the experiences of the private ECU to decide criteria to choose core-AMU currencies in the next section.

## Criteria to choose core-AMU currencies

We should start an AMU composed of only core currencies in the region if we expect an AMU as a same role like the ECU. We name it core-AMU. Because we expect a core-AMU as a denomination currency of Asian bond, which will be traded in a secondary market, a core-AMU basket currency needs to meet two different conditions as follows. At first, the credit rating of local currency sovereign bond should be similar among core-AMU currencies in order to issue an Asian bond denominated in terms of a core-AMU basket currency. We investigate each latest credit rating of long-term local currency sovereign bond by S&P for nine East Asian countries.[5] The second column of Table 12.3 shows the results. Among the nine East Asian countries, the highest credit rating is AAA/Stable for Singaporean sovereign bond, and the lowest is BB/Positive for Indonesian sovereign bond. We regard the first criterion for a core-AMU currency should be above single A rating. We choose six countries, which are Japan, Hong Kong, Korea, Singapore, Thailand, and Malaysia.

Second, composition currencies of a core-AMU currency basket also should be freely traded in the inter-bank foreign exchange market. Among East Asian currencies, the Japanese yen, the Singapore dollar, and the Hong Kong dollar have already ensured convertibility in both current and capital accounts and liberalized capital and foreign exchange controls. On one hand, the other East Asian countries have liberalized only the current account related transaction of foreign exchange while they have not yet opened the capital account related transactions of foreign exchange by keeping capital and foreign exchange controls. In this situation, it is necessary for us to focus on foreign exchange transaction, or 'foreign exchange convertibility' as a criterion in order to decide composition currencies of a core-AMU currency basket.

When we consider the foreign exchange convertibility, we have to check it in two different markets. One is a spot market and the other is a forward swap market. Additionally, we classify foreign exchange transactions into two categories, current account related transaction and capital account related transaction. We suppose currencies, which has no restriction of foreign exchange transaction related to both current and capital account in both the markets, as a composites of a core-AMU currency basket. However, we could loose our criteria select composites of a core AMU to a condition of no restriction on current account related transaction only. It is because this might be enough if a monetary authority agrees to regard the foreign exchange transactions backed with Asian bond as a kind of trade demand. Further, we add possible transaction in forward swap market within one year as a criterion to be a composite of core-AMU currency basket, because forward swap is one of most popular measures to hedge foreign exchange risks. Needless to say, the liquidity conditions of both spot and forward swap markets have to be checked. We use the published reports about the actual foreign exchange market liquidity by Deutsche Bank, which recognized the market condition into three categories, such as good, average and poor.[6] We add the calculated bid-ask spread of one month forward swap (against the US dollar) to indicate a market liquidity, in the same way of Ogawa and Shimizu (2004) and Shimizu and Ogawa (2005) just for a reference.[7]

Columns three to six of Table 12.3 show the current situation of foreign exchange transaction in East Asia and core-AMU qualification. As mentioned above, the Japanese yen, the Hong Kong dollar, and the Singapore dollar are fully convertible for both current and capital accounts related foreign exchange transactions. In forward swap markets, their bid-ask spread is the smallest level among the sampled currencies. Thus we could select these three currencies as composites of 'hard' core-AMU currencies. The South Korean won, the Thai baht, and the Indonesian rupiah have no restriction on current account related foreign exchange transaction in spot market. Although their regulatory in capital account related foreign exchange transactions in spot market and in forward swap market are still left in some cases, we are able to make a forward swap transaction of these currencies within a certain amount. Their market liquidity conditions also are above average.

After we considered these two criteria, we selected the Japanese yen, the Hong Kong dollar, the South Korean won, the Singapore dollar, and the Thai baht to create a core-AMU currency basket. The Chinese yuan could not be selected since their sovereign credit rating is below single A at the moment and they are still strictly restricted even in spot market. According to the latest reports, the central bank of China has not given any timetable toward full convertibility of the Chinese yuan when it will lift restrictions on inflows and outflows of money for investment purposes, or the capital account. Hong Kong also will keep the existing regime for at least five years. On the other hand, Korea recently announced that it will move up the target date of its plan to fully liberalize its capital account to 2009 from 2011.

Table 12.3 The core-AMU qualification

| Country | Sovereign credit rating (S&P)[a] | FX spot market | | | FX forward swap market | | | Core-AMU qualification |
|---|---|---|---|---|---|---|---|---|
| | | Regulatory on current account[b] | Regulatory on capital account[b] | Liquidity[c] | Regulatory[b] | Liquidity within 1 year[c] | 1 month swap bid-ask spread in May 2006[d] (%) | |
| Japan | AA−/Positive | O | O | Good | O | Good | 0.01 | Yes |
| Hong Kong | AA−/Stable | O | O | Good | O | Good | 0.02 | Yes |
| Korea | A+/Stable | O | △ | Good | △ | Good | 0.11 | Yes |
| Singapore | AAA/Stable | O | O | Good | △ | Good | 0.03 | Yes |
| Thailand | A/Stable | O | △ | Good | △ | Good | 0.1 | Yes |
| Malaysia | A+/Stable | △ | △ | Good | △ | Good | 0.19 | No |
| Philippines | BB+/Negative | △ | O | Good | △ | Average | 0.19 | No |
| Indonesia | BB/Positive | O | O | Good | △ | Average | 0.79 | No |
| China | BBB+/Positive | × | × | Good | × | Poor | — | No |

Notes: [a] The dates of Sovereign Credit Rating (S&P) are from the website of Aisabondsonline. Each credit rating and outlook is for each Long-term Local Currency Sovereign Bond. [b] Each country's regulatory information is from its central bank and monetary authority website. O means no restrictions. △ means some restriction, and × means transactions are restricted for non-residents. [c] Each market liquidity information is from Asian Currency Handbook 2005 (Deutsche Bank). [d] Each 1 month swap bid-ask swap spread in May 2006 is calculated by the same procedure of Ogawa and Shimizu (2004). All spot rates and forward rates are collected from Bloomberg currency composite rates and Prebon Yamane Asia Region pages on sample days.

## Return and risk profiles of core-AMU denominated Asian bond

At first, we create a core-AMU currency basket which is composed of the six East Asian currencies which include the Japanese yen, the Hong Kong dollar, the South Korean won, the Singapore dollar, and the Thai baht. In order to determine the core-AMU basket weights, we refer to Ogawa and Shimizu (2005; 2006), which explain the details of way to calculate the AMU. The basket weights of the AMU are based on both the trade share and the share of GDP measured at PPP. In addition, we have to take into account the current condition of bond issuance in local markets to create a core-AMU basket currency. In this paper, we use the data of 'International Bonds and Notes by residence of issuer' of Table 14b in BIS Annual Report. Accordingly, the basket weights of core-AMU are based on the average share of three different categories as follows:

- each county's respective share of GDP measured at PPP in 2005[8]
- each country's respective share of trade volumes (the sum of exports and imports of the core-AMU countries with ASEAN+3 countries)[9]
- each county's respective share of International Bonds and Notes by residence of issuer as of December 2005.

Table 12.4 shows the basket weights of each of the five East Asian currencies for the core-AMU. The Japanese yen has the highest share of the core-AMU (58.0%). The Hong Kong dollar and the South Korean won have more than 10 per cent of share, which are 14.15 per cent, and 16.55 per cent, respectively. The share of the Thai baht is 6.54 per cent. The smallest share is the Singapore dollar (4.76%) since both the trade volume and the GDP measure at PPP of Singapore are the smallest among the five countries. Figure 12.2 shows movements of the core-AMU compared with those of the AMU, which is composed of the thirteen East Asian currencies. Both the core-AMU and the AMU move almost similarly while the core-AMU seems to be more volatile than the AMU. It is because the basket weight of the Japanese yen in the core-AMU is much higher than that in the AMU (27.8%).

Next, we use yield data of local government bonds to calculate the core-AMU denominated Asian bond in order to investigate the risk properties of the core-AMU denominated Asian bond for regional investors.[10] It is supposed to be a portfolio investment into the local government bonds with same basket weights of the core-AMU.

We suppose that local investors in the East Asian countries who evaluate their returns of the core-AMU denominated Asian bond in terms of their local currencies. Returns on investing in the bonds for one month are calculated as follows: the investors exchanges an initial fund of a local currency into the core-AMU at the relevant exchange rate, purchases the core-AMU denominated Asian bonds at a price in terms of the core-AMU, holds them for one month, sells them at their price in terms of the core-AMU one month later, and exchanges the revenue in terms

*Table 12.4* Core-AMU basket weights of East Asian currencies (benchmark year = 2000/2001)

| Country | Share of trade volume[a] % | Share of GDP measured at PPP[b] % | Share of Int'l bonds and notes by residence of Issuer[c] % | Arithmetic average shares %, (a) | Benchmark exchange rate[d] (b) | AMU weights (a)/(b) |
|---|---|---|---|---|---|---|
| Hong Kong | 22.79 | 3.81 | 15.84 | 14.15 | 0.1328 | 1.0650 |
| Japan | 61.76 | 67.10 | 45.14 | 58.00 | 0.0091 | 63.7683 |
| Korea | 7.90 | 17.70 | 24.07 | 16.55 | 0.0009 | 191.9798 |
| Singapore | 0.58 | 2.14 | 11.55 | 4.76 | 0.5912 | 0.0805 |
| Thailand | 6.97 | 9.25 | 3.39 | 6.54 | 0.0246 | 2.6548 |

Notes: Author's calculation. [a] The data of trade volume are calculated as the average of total export and import volumes in 2001, 2002 and 2003 taken from DOTS(IMF). [b] The data GDP measured at PPP are in 2005 taken from the World Development Report, April 2006, World Bank. [c] The data of international Bonds and Notes by Residence of Issuer are as of December, 2005 from BIS Annual Report Trade 14b. [d] The Benchmark exchange rate ($-euro/Currency) is the average of the daily exchange rate in terms of US$-euro in 2000 and 2001.

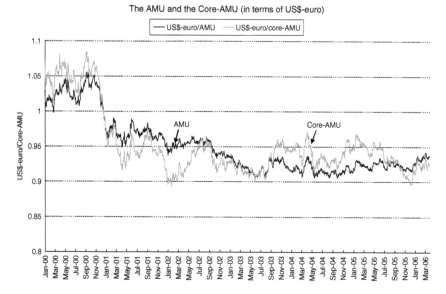

*Figure 12.2* The AMU and the core-AMU in terms of US$-euro.
Source: Authors calculation.

of the core-AMU into a local currency.[11, 12] The returns are then divided into interest rate (bonds yield) returns and foreign exchange returns.[13] Our formula to calculate the value of a core-AMU denominated Asian bond in terms of a local currency for a one month investment is represented as follows:

Core-AMU denomianted Bond return (local currency equivalent)

= Core-AMU denomiante Bond return (in terms of the Core-AMU)

+ Foreign exchange return

$$= \frac{Bond_t - Bond_{t-1}}{Bond_{t-1}} \cdot \frac{E_t}{E_{t-1}} \times 100 + \frac{E_t - E_{t-1}}{E_{t-1}} \times 100$$

where $Bond_t$ is the closing price of bond in terms of the core-AMU at month $t$ and $E_t$ is the closing foreign exchange rate vis-à-vis the core-AMU at month $t$.[14] We suppose the East Asian investors in the ASEAN5 plus Japan, South Korea, China, and Hong Kong to compare their risk properties of returns on the core-AMU denominated Asian bond from January 2000 to March 2006.

Table 12.5 shows the analytical results. The average 1-month return of the core-AMU denominated Asian bond was minus 0.02 per cent. It was very small since it is dominantly composed of the Japanese government bonds, whose returns were very low during the sample period. However, its standard deviation

Table 12.5 Month bond value of core-AMU denominated Asian bonds (Jan 2000–March 2006)

| | China | Indonesia | Japan | Korea | Malaysia | Philippines | Singapore | Thailand | Hong Kong |
|---|---|---|---|---|---|---|---|---|---|
| (1 month Core-AMU denominated Bond Return in terms of each local currencies[a], %) | | | | | | | | | |
| Max | 4.23 | 11.69 | 2.37 | 5.16 | 4.25 | 8.86 | 3.35 | 3.23 | 4.24 |
| Min | −5.69 | −15.53 | −3.20 | −4.35 | −5.65 | −4.52 | −3.71 | −3.46 | −5.69 |
| Average ($\mu$) | −0.17 | 0.27 | 0.03 | −0.34 | −0.16 | 0.22 | −0.17 | −0.06 | −0.13 |
| Std. Dev. ($\sigma$) | 2.08 | 3.65 | 1.12 | 1.73 | 2.07 | 2.37 | 1.44 | 1.61 | 2.04 |
| $\mu/\sigma$ | −0.08 | 0.07 | 0.03 | −0.19 | −0.08 | 0.09 | −0.12 | −0.04 | −0.06 |
| Total return through the whole period[b] | −13.09 | 16.29 | 1.86 | −22.84 | −12.50 | 15.70 | −12.34 | −5.38 | −10.72 |
| (1 month core-AMU denominated bond return[c], %) | | | | | | | | | |
| Max | | | | | 0.92 | | | | |
| Min | | | | | −1.96 | | | | |
| Average ($\mu$) | | | | | −0.02 | | | | |
| Std. Dev. ($\sigma$) | | | | | 0.29 | | | | |
| $\mu/\sigma$ | | | | | −0.06 | | | | |
| (Foreign exchange return in each local currencies vis-à-vis the core-AMU[d], %) | | | | | | | | | |
| Max | 4.24 | 11.60 | 2.04 | 5.16 | 4.25 | 8.84 | 3.40 | 3.28 | 4.25 |
| Min | −5.69 | −15.32 | −2.70 | −4.23 | −5.66 | −4.52 | −3.73 | −3.52 | −5.69 |
| Average ($\mu$) | −0.15 | 0.29 | 0.05 | −0.32 | −0.14 | 0.24 | −0.15 | −0.04 | −0.11 |
| Std. Dev. ($\sigma$) | 2.06 | 3.62 | 1.01 | 1.76 | 2.05 | 2.35 | 1.44 | 1.64 | 2.03 |
| $\mu/\sigma$ | −0.07 | 0.08 | 0.05 | −0.18 | −0.07 | 0.10 | −0.10 | −0.03 | −0.06 |

Notes: Author's calculation. [a] 1 month Core-AMU denominated Bond Return and 1month foreign exchange return in each local currencies vis-à-vis the Core-AMU. [b] Total return through the whole period is the return which investors by core-AMU denominated bond at the beginning of Jan 2000, hole it for the whole period, and sell it ate the end of March 2006. [c] 1 month Core-AMU denominated Bond Return is calculated by Core-AMU denominated bond value. The bond value for 1month is the weighted bond value in each core-AMU country's with the same basket share of Core-AMU for 1month. [d] Foreign exchange returns are actual ex-post foreign exchange related returns which are uncovered by forward transaction at the beginning of period.

also was very small. Thus, the core-AMU denominated Asian bond itself is low risk asset. The main factor of the core-AMU denominated Asian bond returns equivalent of each local currency depends on each foreign exchange return. It means that the fluctuations of each East Asian currency vis-à-vis the core-AMU affect the volatilities of each East Asian investor's return on the core-AMU denominated Asian bond.

In fact, total returns of each East Asian investor through the whole period were completely different. We suppose that the total return is the return which investors buy core-AMU denominated Asian bond at the beginning of January 2000, hold it for the whole period, and sell it at the end of March 2006. The calculation results largely depend on the exchange rates both at the beginning and the end of the period. For example, the Japanese yen vis-à-vis the core-AMU does not move a lot since the share of the Japanese yen of the core-AMU is larger than a half. Therefore the bond returns of the Japanese investors are very small but stable. The Chinese yuan, the Malaysian ringgit, the South Korean won, the Singapore dollar, and the Hong Kong dollar appreciated vis-à-vis the core-AMU in this period. Therefore, the bond returns of these countries' investors who hold the core-AMU denominated Asian bond were minus. On the other hand, the Indonesian rupiah and the Philippine peso wee depreciated vis-à-vis the core AMU while their returns were positive.

When we compare the standard deviations of 1-month core-AMU denominated Asian bond returns among the East Asian countries, we find that those of the core-AMU member countries are basically lower than those of the other East Asian countries except for Indonesia. It suggests that the risks of core-AMU denominated Asian bond returns for local investors could be lower if a country joins in the core-AMU member countries.

These results show that the core-AMU denominated Asian bond is a stable investment choice especially for Japanese investors. Thus, we expect that they will play an important roll to create and promote a core-AMU denominated Asian bond market at the first stage.

## Correlation between core-AMU, US dollar and euro denominated bonds

In this section, we calculate correlation coefficient matrices among the returns on the core-AMU denominated Asian bond, the US Treasury, and the euro denominated bond for local investors in East Asian countries. International portfolio diversification has been widely practiced by international investors who seek to reduce their investment risks. However, it is said that the monetary authorities in East Asian countries hold most of their international reserves in US treasury bonds. If the returns of the core-AMU denominated Asian bond in terms of each local currency are negatively or less correlated with the returns of the US dollar denominated bond in terms of each local currency, we suggest for them to hold the core-AMU denominated Asian bond in order to mitigate their foreign exchange risks.

Table 12.6 shows the analytical results. For China, Malaysia, and Hong Kong, their correlation coefficients between the US dollar denominated bond and the core-AMU denominated Asian bond are not negative though very small. For Indonesia, South Korea, the Philippines, Singapore, Thailand, and Japan, those were negative. These results indicate that the core-AMU denominated Asian bond should be a beneficial asset to diversify their international portfolio and to reduce their foreign exchange risks. Accordingly, we suggest that the core-AMU denominated

*Table 12.6* Correlation matrix of US bond, euro bond and core-AMU denominated bond

China

|  | US bond | euro bond | Core-AMU |
|---|---|---|---|
| US bond |  |  |  |
| euro bond | −0.0953 |  |  |
| Core-AMU | 0.0976 | −0.2912 |  |

Hong Kong

|  | US bond | euro bond | Core-AMU |
|---|---|---|---|
| US bond |  |  |  |
| euro bond | −0.3462 |  |  |
| Core-AMU | 0.0339 | −0.2737 |  |

Indonesia

|  | US bond | euro bond | Core-AMU |
|---|---|---|---|
| US bond |  |  |  |
| euro bond | −0.8132 |  |  |
| Core-AMU | −0.5369 | −0.5638 |  |

South Korea

|  | US bond | euro bond | Core-AMU |
|---|---|---|---|
| US bond |  |  |  |
| euro bond | 0.4425 |  |  |
| Core-AMU | −0.2666 | −0.2336 |  |

Malaysia

|  | US bond | euro bond | Core-AMU |
|---|---|---|---|
| US bond |  |  |  |
| euro bond | −0.1138 |  |  |
| Core-AMU | 0.0405 | −0.2968 |  |

Philippines

|  | US bond | euro bond | Core-AMU |
|---|---|---|---|
| US bond |  |  |  |
| euro bond | 0.5399 |  |  |
| Core-AMU | −0.4317 | −0.4173 |  |

Singapore

|  | US bond | euro bond | Core-AMU |
|---|---|---|---|
| US bond |  |  |  |
| euro bond | −0.0497 |  |  |
| Core-AMU | −0.0156 | −0.0934 |  |

Thailand

|  | US bond | euro bond | Core-AMU |
|---|---|---|---|
| US bond |  |  |  |
| euro bond | 0.2710 |  |  |
| Core-AMU | −0.3041 | −0.1915 |  |

Japan

|  | US bond | euro bond | Core-AMU |
|---|---|---|---|
| US bond |  |  |  |
| euro bond | 0.4223 |  |  |
| Core-AMU | −0.3125 | −0.4916 |  |

Notes: Author's calculation. All bond returns are 1 month bond returns in terms of each local currency.

Asian bond would play an important role for international diversification in the region.

## Conclusion

In this chapter, we have two objectives. The first is to determine the criteria to select core-AMU currencies among the East Asian currencies. The other is to create a core-AMU denominated Asian bond to investigate their return and risk profiles for local investors in East Asian countries.

Because we expect the core-AMU currency basket as a denomination currency of Asian bond, which will be traded in a secondary market, a core-AMU currency basket also should be freely traded in the inter-bank foreign exchange market. Thus, we focused on the convertibility as a criterion to be one of composition currencies. As a result, we selected the five East Asian currencies, which include the Japanese yen, the Hong Kong dollar, the South Korean won, the Singapore dollar, and the Thai baht to create the core-AMU currency basket. We calculated the core-AMU with the basket weights based on the trade share, the share of GDP measured at PPP, and the share of International Bonds and Notes by residence of issuer. The core-AMU moves more volatile than the AMU because the core-AMU's basket share on the Japanese yen is 58.9 per cent, which was much higher than the AMU (27.8%).

We found that the core-AMU denominated Asian bond, was a kind of low risk asset. The main factor of the core-AMU denominated Asian bond returns equivalent of each local currency depends on each foreign exchange return. It means that the fluctuations of each East Asian currency vis-à-vis the core-AMU affect the volatilities of each East Asian investor's return on the core-AMU denominated Asian bond. Comparison of their standard deviations among the East Asian countries showed that those of the core-AMU member countries were basically lower than those of the other East Asian countries except for Indonesia. It implies that the risks of the core-AMU denominated Asian bond returns for local investors could be lower if a country joined in the core-AMU member countries.

Calculation of correlation coefficient matrices among the core-AMU denominated Asian bond, the US Treasury, and the euro denominated bond for each local investor obtains the following results. For China, Malaysia, and Hong Kong, their correlation coefficients between the US bond and the core-AMU denominated Asian bond are not negative, but very small. For Indonesia, South Korea, Philippines, Singapore, Thailand, and Japan, those are negative. These results indicate that the core-AMU denominated Asian bond is an asset that can contribute to reducing their foreign exchange risks.

Accordingly, we suggest that the core-AMU denominated Asian bond should play an important role for international diversification in the region. Since the core-AMU denominated Asian bond is supposed to be a stable investment choice especially for the Japanese investors, we expect that the Japanese investors might play an important role to create and promote a core-AMU denominated Asian bond market at the first stage.

## Acknowledgements

This paper is a revised version of the paper that was presented in the Korea and the World Economy IV at Korea University, Seoul, Korea on July 7–8, 2006. The authors appreciate Doo Yong Yang for his useful comments.

## References

Deutche Bank (2005) *Asian Currency Handbook.*

Dammers, Clifford R. and Robert N. McCauley (2006) 'Basket weaving: the euromarket experiences with basket currency bonds', *BIS Quarterly Review*, March 2006: 79–92.

Iwata, Kenji (2005) 'Formation of Regional Financial and Currency Area: Some Lessons from Europe to Asia', 3rd Conference of EUSA-AP, 10 December 2005.

Ogawa, Eiji and Junko Shimizu (2004) 'Bond Issuers' Trade-off for Common Currency Basket Denominated Bonds in East Asia', *Journal of Asian Economics*, 15: 719–738.

—— (2005) 'AMU Deviation Indicator for Coordinated Exchange Rate Policies in East Asia', *RIETI Discussion Paper*, No.05-E-017.

—— (2006) 'AMU Deviation Indicator for Coordinated Exchange Rate Policies in East Asia and its Relation with Effective Exchange Rates', *RIETI Discussion Paper*, No.06-E-002.

Shimizu, Junko and Eiji Ogawa (2005) 'Risk properties of AMU denominated Asian bond', *Journal of Asian Economics*, 16 (4): 590–611.

# 13 A new framework for analyzing adequate and excessive reserve levels under high capital mobility

*Jie Li, Ozan Sula and Thomas D. Willett*

## Introduction

We use adequate and excessive reserve levels in our title rather than the traditional 'optimal' levels of reserves for a specific theoretical reason. Traditional models of optimal reserve holdings focus on the equation of the marginal costs and benefits of holding a particular level of reserves. In our analysis we focus as well on the costs of acquiring and reducing reserve levels. Often these costs can be quite important and as a result there can be a wide range over which deviations of reserve levels from their optimal values should induce no action by the countries to adjust its reserve levels.

The addition of under high capital mobility in the title is also important. The initial models of optimal reserve holdings focused on a world of low capital mobility and the chief benefit of reserves was to avoid the need for balance of payments adjustment or to reduce its costs by allowing adjustment to be spread out more smoothly over time. In a world of substantial international capital mobility, additional important considerations come into play.

One of the strongest statistical correlates of recent currency crises in emerging market economies is low levels of international reserves.[1] In the first generation crisis models higher reserves can only postpone not prevent crises. In second generation models, however, a country's international liquidity position can be important. Higher reserves will reduce the probability of crises for countries with fundamentals that are neither very good nor very bad, i.e. in the vulnerable zone. Thus, in contrast to the assumption of the early models, balance of payments flows may not be independent of reserve levels. Thus we need to model two rather than one function of reserve. Where prevention fails, the traditional role of reserves to finance payments deficits retains its importance.

Furthermore, in a world of capital account crises, the variability of payments flows during normal periods may not give a good indication of financing needs during a crisis. Sula and Willett (2006) have found that the variability of the capital account during periods of inflow is not a good predictor of the size of capital flow reversals or sudden stops during crises. Thus we replace the traditional variability of payments term with estimates of the size of potential capital outflows during crises such as can be based on evidence from recent crises (see Kim *et al.* 2004).

This paper is structured as follows. Section 2 briefly discusses the buffer stock models in the traditional demand for international reserves literature as well as some other newly developed literature. Section 3 provides a discussion of high capital mobility and optimal reserves. An analytical model is introduced in Section 4 as a suggested framework to analyze adequate or excessive levels of reserves under high capital mobility. Section 5 concludes.

## A brief review of the literature

Moving beyond the traditional way of treating reserve adequacy as a simple number of months worth of imports, there was a wave of literature in the 1960s and 1970s devoted to the cost-benefit analysis of the demand for international reserves.[2] With the widespread adoption of more flexible exchange rates, the study of international reserves fell out of favour, but the rash of currencies in the 1990s and the rapid accumulation of reserves in their wake have generated a new stream of studies. While some studies sought to explain these accumulations as optimal responses,[3] others suggested that the accumulations were often excessive, especially after 2000 or so.[4]

An important consideration missing in the traditional literature of the demand for international reserves is the adjustment cost a country has to bear when it wants to lower its reserve levels. In the terminology of Cohen (1966), the traditional reserves literature looked at the permanent cost of different reserve levels and ignored the transitional costs of adjusting form one reserve level to another except for the case where a country was running cost of reserves. This issue was relatively unimportant in Asia in the past when reserve holdings were small, but it came to the fore as Asian countries continued to accumulate seemingly greater than optimal levels of reserves after the Asian financial crises. When adjustment costs are large relative to the cost of holding extra reserves, there is no incentive for those countries to reduce their reserve holdings.

An earlier, informal, literature does focus on these adjustment costs in the context of the reserve accumulation by countries such as Germany and Japan during the 1960s and the general explosion of international liquidity that accompanied the breakdown of the Bretton Woods system in the early 1970s.[5] While global monetarists argued that there was little sterilization and such reserve increases were consequently a major source of the global inflation of the 1970s, economists such as Fritz Machlup argued that the potential incentives facing governments differed substantially from those assumed by the global monetarists' analysis of reserve optimizing governments. Studies such as Laney and Willett (1982) showed that there was a good deal of sterilization by surplus countries and that there was little correlation between the countries that had the biggest reserve increases and those that had the highest inflation. Claassen (1975) illustrated an optimization procedure of reserve management that explains less frequent balance of payments adjustment policies above the target level of reserves than below it. He showed that the maximum level of reserves that nations hold is three times higher than their target level. Willett (1980) provided a public choice analysis of the incentives facing central banks and governments with respect to reserve policy and concluded that because of high adjustment costs the labelling of some countries such as Germany and Japan as 'reserve sinks' during the 1960s and 1970s was quite justified.

Today much of Asia seems to be in a similar situation. Hence our basic argument is that because of such adjustment costs, there will be a range of reserve holdings within which the monetary authorities are reluctant to adjust to the 'optimal' level of reserves. We call this range the 'inaction zone' of reserve holdings.

## Capital surges, sudden stops and optimal reserves

Before formalizing the existence of an inaction zone that would prevent the adjustment to the optimal level of reserves, we would like to discuss the consequence of high capital mobility on the optimal level. As the emerging economies liberalized financial capital flows during the 1990s, most of these countries become far more exposed to the risk of sudden stops or outright capital reversals. Furthermore, empirical studies show that currency crisis associated with sudden stops of capital flows tend to cause deeper recessions (Calvo 1998; Hutchison and Noy 2002). In this section we consider the effects of the degree of capital mobility and in particular the behaviour of capital flows on optimal levels of reserves.

Large capital inflows increase the size of optimal levels of reserves in two ways. First they increase the probability of sudden stops and currency crises.[6] Persistent and large capital inflows tend to cause appreciation of the real exchange rate, widening of current account deficits and domestic credit booms. In addition, causes of surges in capital inflows may also imply their eventual reversal. For example, imperfect information may cause investors to over-invest creating surges in capital inflows to emerging markets. If the true information is revealed, a sudden stop or a currency crisis becomes very likely. Thus while a balance of payments surplus due primarily to the current account should typically reduce calculations of optimal reserve levels through making currency crisis less likely, a payments surplus due to a surge of capital inflows would typically raise expectations of the probability of a crisis due to the increased likelihood of a sudden stop. This raises the optimal level of reserves.

Second, if there have been large inflows of financial capital, the expected size of outflows in the case of a crisis is increased. Since the costs to the economy of a crisis are a positive function of the size of capital outflows minus the amount offset by reserve financing, the optimal level of reserves also increases in order to reduce the cost of a crisis if it should occur. We cannot, of course, say exactly how much optimal reserve levels should change in response to capital inflows, but recent research that we summarize below gives us some important clues.

Table 13.1 presents the size of reversals during several recent currency crises.[7] A reversal is measured as the difference of the size of inflows between the crisis year and the previous year divided by GDP. In the first two rows, average values for 38 emerging markets and the Asian crises countries are given. The rest of

*Table 13.1* Net capital flows reversals during crises as a percentage of GDP

|  | Total flows: % | FDI: % | Private loans: % | Portfolio: % |
|---|---|---|---|---|
| All Emerging markets | 1.6 | −0.4 | 1.6 | 1.1 |
| Asian crises | 8.2 | 0.0 | 6.4 | 1.7 |
| Indonesia 97 | 5.1 | 0.7 | 1.4 | 3.4 |
| Korea 97 | 5.9 | −0.1 | 6.9 | 0.1 |
| Malaysia 97 | 7.2 | −0.1 | 7.5 | 0.0 |
| Philippines 97 | 5.7 | 0.4 | 0.1 | 5.6 |
| Thailand 97 | 17.0 | −0.8 | 16.2 | −0.5 |
| Mexico 94 | 4.3 | −1.6 | 0.6 | 5.0 |
| Russia 98 | 2.8 | 0.4 | 0.4 | 2.2 |
| Turkey 94 | 7.3 | 0.0 | 5.6 | 1.5 |
| Turkey 01 | 9.8 | −1.0 | 8.1 | 2.3 |

the rows are for some of the recent well-known crisis episodes. We present these values for total capital flows as well as three other major types of capital flows: Foreign direct investment (FDI), portfolio flows and private loans.

We see that except for FDI, all types of capital flows display large reversals during crises. During the Asian crises the fall in capital inflows is largest for private loans. Other emerging market crises witness similar falls in both portfolio and loan flows. The data also suggest that FDI usually does not reverse.[8] On the contrary, it increases in some of the episodes. During the Asian crises, the largest outflows were from the private loan category, presumably bank loans. Thailand, for example, experienced a fall in capital inflows of 17 per cent of GDP and almost all of this fall was in private loans. Reversals in Indonesia and Philippines were predominantly from portfolio investors. Both crises in Turkey were associated with reversals in private loans, while the reversals in Russia and Mexico were mainly portfolio flows. There is no clear-cut conclusion in terms of reversal sizes across different crises episodes for private loans and portfolio flows. When all reversals are averaged across emerging markets, reversal sizes are fairly similar for these different types of flows.

What are the implications of this simple table for the optimal levels of reserves? First of all, the large swings in capital flows during crisis necessitate substantial levels of reserves in order to keep such reversals from imposing large costs on domestic economies. Optimal reserves calculations should be based on customized coverage ratios. While we do not provide actual coverage ratios in this paper, we can conclude that a country that has large inflows of FDI require lower levels of reserves compared to a country that is exposed to high levels of portfolio and loan inflows.

Table 13.2 presents the size of capital outflows during the Asian crisis scaled up to 2002 and 2003 values and the actual reserve holdings in five Asian economies. Based on the various combinations of types of capital flows, the maximum sizes of outflows during the Asian crisis are scaled up to 2002 and 2003 values. We use M2 (which grew more than GDP for all five countries), GDP and the short-term

*Table 13.2* Scaled-up figures of capital outflows in year 2002 and year 2003
(US $ billions)

| | 2002 | | | | 2003 | | |
|---|---|---|---|---|---|---|---|
| | *Scaled by M2* | *Scaled by GDP* | *Scaled by STD* | *Actual reserve holdings* | *Scaled by M2* | *Scaled by STD* | *Actual reserve holdings* |
| Indonesia | −18.58 | −17.85 | −13.74 | 30.97 | −21.21 | −20.92 | 34.96 |
| Korea | −107.99 | −56.6 | −36.51 | 121.35 | −114.58 | −59.35 | 155.28 |
| Malaysia | −4.81 | −4.35 | −3.48 | 34.22 | −5.26 | −4.73 | 44.52 |
| Philippines | −3.31 | −3.17 | −2.41 | 13.14 | −3.28 | −3.29 | 13.46 |
| Thailand | −35.05 | −28.56 | −10.2 | 38.05 | −40.71 | −34.03 | 41.08 |

debt as basis for scaling. These calculations suggest that by 2003 all five countries had already built up more than adequate reserve levels to handle a repeat of the actual capital outflows that occurred during the 1997–98 scaled up to current values.[9]

Table 13.2 shows that Asian economies have been accumulating more than sufficient reserves to offset potential capital flow reversals. Furthermore, we see that these reserves are more than 'adequate' by all traditional standards.[10] It seems that these Asian countries are not eager to adjust their reserve levels down to optimal ones. Why? The following section shows that the existence of adjustment costs can substantially increase the incentives to allow reserves to remain above the optimal levels suggested by traditional model.

## The model[11]

A central bank tries to minimize the total costs of both expected output loss due to a currency crisis and the opportunity costs of holding reserves.

$$\underset{R}{Min}\ C = C_1 P + C_2 R \tag{13.1}$$

where $C_1$ is the cost of a currency crisis; P is the probability of the currency crisis; $C_2$ is the unit cost of holding reserves and R is the level of reserve holdings.

### Discussion of assumptions

One of the most important lessons learned from Asian financial crises is the significant role of the ratios of short-term external debt to international reserves or M2 to reserves in predicting the occurrence of currency crises.[12] Of course, reserve holdings are not the only determinant of crises. Other solvency and liquidity variables as well as the fundamentals of an economy (including political, financial considerations, exchange rate and current account positions) tend to affect the probability of crises too. In the first generation crisis models, the role of reserves is very limited: if the fundamentals[13] of a country are sufficiently bad, a currency crisis is inevitable regardless the levels of reserve holdings. The only role that reserve hoarding can play is to postpone the crisis. But in the second generation models, the role for reserves in the prevention of currency crises is substantially increased. A sound level of reserves signals the capability of a government to defend its currency, which gives those speculators second thoughts about the potential successfulness of currency attacks. Thus, reserve hoarding may help deter speculative attacks for countries whose fundamentals are in the vulnerable zone. Therefore, we assume that the probability function P is a decreasing function of reserve holdings. The higher are the reserve holdings; the lower is the probability of currency crises.

The virtues of holding reserves are two fold. First, they reduce the probability of a currency crisis. Second, if one occurs, they can shrink the cost of a crisis ($C_1$) by offering a cushion to partially offset the effects of capital flight since the net effects on the foreign exchange and domestic financial markets will be the quantity of speculative outflows minus the amount that these are financed by the running down of reserves. Recent crises in emerging markets have often imposed economic costs for greater than merely reducing domestic GDP to reduce payments deficits. The combination of high interest rates and depreciating currencies generated deep recession, sometimes resulting in as much as 5–10 per cent of lost GDP over a period of several years. Thus the benefits of avoiding such crises can be quite high, especially for countries with financial system problems and high levels of foreign currency denominated debt. The cost function ($C_1$) should be a decreasing function of reserve holdings. For simplicity, we will start the analysis from the assumption of a constant value of $C_1$.

$C_2$, the unit cost of reserve holdings, is often interpreted as opportunity cost proxied by the spread between borrowing rate of external debts and T-bill rates in US or the spread between the marginal rate of capital in emerging markets and T-bill rates. The first kind of proxy comes from the understanding that reserves could be used to pay back external debts instead of investing them in the low-yield T-bills. In order to keep a certain level of liquidity, a government has to bear the costs of paying higher interest on external debts relative to that received on its reserve holdings. The second proxy comes from the argument that instead of accumulating reserves, the government of an emerging economy could make use of reserves to increase the domestic investments so that the country earns the marginal rate of return on capital, typically a much higher return compared to the T-bill rates.[14] Thus, the government has to forgo the higher yield from the domestic use of capital to hold extra international liquidity in terms of reserves.

The cost of acquiring or reducing reserves will vary under different scenarios. For example, the unit cost of acquiring reserves is much smaller when an economy is in recession than when it is over heated. Actions to generate a current account surplus such as devaluation will normally have a desirable simulative effect on the domestic economy via the Keynesian multiplier. Furthermore, these would be no need to sterilize the resulting reserve increases as expansionary monetary policy would also be desirable. On the other hand if the domestic economy was overheated, both of these developments would worsen the situation.

Even if the domestic economy is in equilibrium, there is a strong incentive not to disturb this by balance of payments adjustments, unless its reserve levels become quite low. As long as a country can effectively sterilize, the political cost of continuing to accumulate reserves is likely to be low even when this is not optimal from a purely economic point of view. As capital mobility increases, however, sterilization becomes increasingly difficult and eventually impossible.[15] Then a government faces a more difficult choice of inflation or revaluation. Of course, capital controls prevent another type of option, although their effectiveness over the longer term has frequently been questioned. On the other hand, if the economy is in recession and the government wants to use expansionary monetary policy to stimulate the domestic economy anyway, then it would not want to sterilize the enlarged monetary base while accumulating reserves. In this case, the cost of reserve accumulation is low (or perhaps even negative)[16] and the sterilization cost will not occur. Thus, the unit cost of acquiring or reducing reserves may be different depending on the status of an economy.

To illustrate the discussion above, Figure 13.1 describes different costs of adjusting reserves under different states of the economy. The horizontal line represents levels of reserves. R* is the optimal level. Any reserve levels to the right of R* are too much while any levels to the left of R* are too little. The vertical line represents the status of economy. S* describes the normal situation. Any points higher than S* stand for overheated economy and vice verse. If the economy is located in either Quadrant I or III, the costs of adjusting reserves are low or negative. In quadrant I, the economy is overheated with too much reserves. The government can undertake appreciation of domestic currency to cool down the economy as well as reduce the current account surplus which in turn, limits the growth of reserves. Thus, the two adjustment objectives are consistent. In quadrant III, the

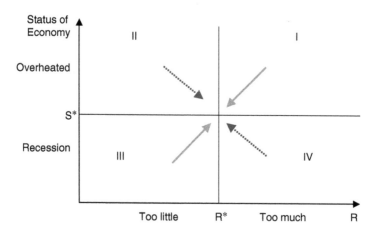

*Figure 13.1* Costs of adjustment under different internal states of the economy.

economy is in recession with too little reserves. The government should depreciate its currency to boost exports in order to accumulate more reserves and stimulate economic growth. The two adjustment objectives are again consistent.

But in quadrants II and IV, the two adjustment objectives are inconsistent. In quadrant II, if the government wants to boost its reserve holding to a normal level, it has to depreciate which will push up inflation. In quadrant IV, if the government wants to deflate its reserve holdings, it has to undergo appreciation which will lead the economy into more recession.

Figure 13.2 illustrates the different adjustment costs with two (in)consistent policy objectives. The horizontal line represents the reserve holdings with R* the optimal level. The status of exchange rates is plotted against the vertical line. Any points higher than E* describe overvaluation of the home currency and vice versa.

Quadrant II and IV contain all the combinations where adjustment costs are low or negative. In quadrant II, there exists overvaluation of domestic currency and too little of reserve accumulation. The only policy response to this situation is to depreciate which will move the objectives toward the optimal one (R*, E*). In quadrant IV, appreciation of domestic currency will remove the disequilibrium too.

However, in either quadrant I or III, the adjustment will be harder.

Table 13.3 summarizes the different adjustment costs under various situations. We take into account three kinds of disequilibria simultaneously: the status of the economy (recession and overheated), exchange rates (undervalue and overvalue) and reserves (too little and too much). The red zone shows the inconsistency of the three disequilibria which indicates greater adjustment costs for reserves. The green zone indicates the lower adjustment costs area. For example, in cell (1), the undervalued currency requires appreciation in order to restore equilibrium. However, appreciation of domestic currency will reduce reserves accumulation which exacerbates the 'too little' situation.

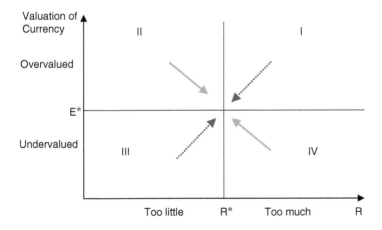

*Figure 13.2* Costs of adjustment under different external states of the economy.

*Table 13.3* Adjustment costs under different situations

| Exchange rates, status of economy and reserves | Recession | | Overheat | |
|---|---|---|---|---|
| | Too little | Too much | Too little | Too much |
| Undervalue | High (1) | High (2) | High (3) | Low (4) |
| Overvalue | Low (5) | High (6) | High (7) | High (8) |

The unit cost of reducing reserves may depend on the status of exchange rates arrangement as well. In general, the cost of reducing a unit of reserves is higher when the exchange rate is undervalued than when the exchange rate is overvalued. When speculative attacks are invited by an overvalued currency, the cost of reducing reserve holdings is negligible since the reserves are utilized to defend the currency from prospective or actual attacks. But when the currency is undervalued, reducing reserve holding typically requires exchange rate changes.

When a country is following a sticky exchange rate regime such as an adjustable peg, the economic and political costs of a substantial appreciation are likely to be seen by the government as quite high. This seems to describe the case of China today. Note that resistance to currency appreciation can come from many sources other than old fashioned mercantilist belief that it was important to have trade or current account surpluses. In general we would expect a country's reluctance to appreciate its currency despite above optimal reserve holdings to be greater, the more important is export growth to the economy, the greater is its general mercantilist orientation and/or the political influence of export interests, the greater is the concern about domestic unemployment, the less flexible is its exchange rate, and the less flexible is its economy.

This last point deserves some elaboration. As the literature on optimal currency areas emphasizes, an inflexible domestic economy increases the costs of a fixed exchange rate. It also, however, raises the costs of exchange rate adjustments, where they are used to correct a disequilibrium rather than to prevent one from emerging. With a highly flexible economy the recessionary effects of a revaluation could relatively easily be offset by expansionary domestic policies. If the domestic economy is initially in equilibrium than a revaluation should still be accompanied by more expansionary domestic macro policies even if the economy is relatively inflexible. In this case, however, there will be greater transitional costs unless the expansionary domestic policies can especially target the sectors that will be particularly hurt by revaluation. Agriculture in China is an example.

To sum up, $C_2$ can vary substantially under different scenarios. We can investigate the effects of these variations on the government's decision making. However, to start with, we will assume a constant unit cost of holding reserves.

Similar to the recent studies by Garcia and Soto (2004) and Li and Rajan (2006), we assume that the probability function $P$ is a function of the level of reserves.

A higher level of reserves signals a better cushion when a country faces Balance of Payments (BOP) disequilibrium. It makes a country more capable to defend its currency when the country faces speculative attacks on its currency. Thus, the probability of a currency crisis would be lower with higher reserve holdings, at least when its fundamentals are in the vulnerable rather than the bad zone as depicted in second generation crisis models.

### An illustration of the model

The vertical axis of Figure 13.3 represents the total cost of the economy while the horizontal axis stands for the reserve levels. With the assumptions of the constant crisis cost ($C_1$) and the linear probability function (P), $TC_1$ (CR*) is drawn to represent the expected total cost from a currency crisis.[17] The negative slope of the $TC_1$ is derived from the negative slope of the probability function (P) with respective to reserve levels. $TC_2$ (OB) is a schedule representing the cost of holding reserves. With the assumption of the constant value of $C_2$, the schedule becomes a straight line (OB) with the slope $C_2$. As long as the absolute value of the slope of $TC_1$ is greater than the slope of $TC_2$, the point minimizing the total cost (TC, the darkened curve) is where $TC_1$ cuts the horizontal axis. Thus, R* is the optimal level of reserves which minimizes the total costs summing from $TC_1$ and $TC_2$.[18] Meanwhile, if we drop the assumption of linearity of the probability function, R* can be found wherever the slope of $TC_1$ meets that of $TC_2$.[19]

There are several characteristics of TC that are worth mentioning. First, the AB part of TC is overlapping with $TC_2$ since $TC_1$ drops out after point A. Second, there is an asymmetry of TC with the dividing point A. The part of the TC right to the point A rises much more gradual than the left part of the TC declines. This is due to the sharp contrast between the cost of a currency crisis and that of holding reserves. The asymmetry of TC interestingly leads to one of our main findings later on: the asymmetry of an inaction zone.

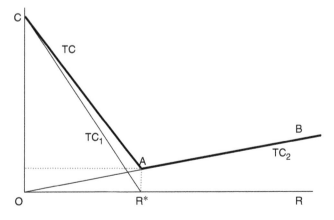

*Figure 13.3* Total costs and reserve holdings.

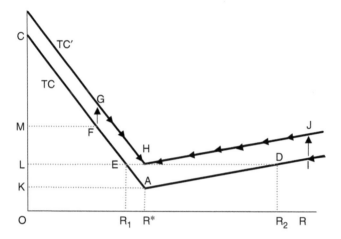

*Figure 13.4* Fixed adjustment cost of reserves.

In the discussion of $C_2$ in the previous subsection, we combined the opportunity cost and adjustment cost as the costs of holding reserves. If we decompose the cost into the opportunity cost and adjustment cost, we can draw Figure 13.4. Taking $C_2$ as the sole opportunity cost, point A is still the optimal point which minimizes the total costs. Assume that there is a fixed adjustment cost if the government wants to deviate from the current reserve level.[20] We will discuss the case when the adjustment cost is variable later on.

Once the government decides to change its reserve level, it will incur a fixed cost due to the policy changes needed to accomplish the change. This shifts the total cost curve from TC to TC'. Any point along the TC curve between point D and E forms an inaction zone in which the government has no incentive to deviate from its current reserve level. Because of the adjustment costs, the lowest total cost along TC' is L which is higher than any point in the inaction zone. If the starting point is any one beyond the inaction zone, then the government will adjust its reserve level to the optimal one with total cost L. For an instance, if the current reserve level is at point F this brings the total cost to M. Since M is greater than L, the government will adjust. The dynamics is from point F through G to H. The jump from F to G reflects the fixed adjustment cost. The process from G to H represents the trajectory the government seeks to minimize total costs. Meanwhile, if the starting point is at I, then the adjustment process will be from I through J to H. Therefore, the inaction zone in terms of the range of reserves is from $R_1$ to $R_2$.

Under the assumption of perfect foresight the fixed costs of adjustment would include the cost of two adjustments, the first to initiate a changing flow of reserves and the second to stop the new flow once the optimum level was achieved. Thus, not only the current state of the economy, but estimates of future states and exogenous developments in payments flows would be relevant. Because of a combination of under certainty and heavy discounting of the future, we expect that these other considerations will frequently be given relatively little weight, however.

As noted earlier, the inaction zone displays an asymmetric feature. In the inaction zone, the range when the reserve level is higher than the optimal level $(R_1 R^*)$ is much greater than the range when the reserve level is lower than the optimal one $(R^* R_2)$. This asymmetry is due to the uneven costs between a crisis and holding excessive reserves. The cost of holding extra reserves is much lower than the cost of a crisis. Therefore, a government has more incentive to increase reserve holdings when they are insufficient than to reduce reserve holding when they are above optimal.

The size of the inaction zone is related to the slopes of TC curves. Figure 13.5 shows the comparison of two inaction zones with two different slopes of TC curves. The original zone from TC lies between $R_1$ and $R_2$ while the inaction zone from TC$'$ is given by $R_3$ $R_4$. The later zone is greater than the first one in terms of the size, which indicates that as the ratios of crisis and reserve holding costs to the adjustment cost become smaller, the government has less incentive to adjust. This leads to an enlargement of the inaction zone.

An important factor that would affect the size of the inaction zone is high capital mobility. An increase in the inflow of financial capital to an emerging market increases both the probability of a currency crisis and its magnitude if it occurs. This makes the slope of the left side of the TC curve steeper, causing more asymmetry of the inaction zone.

Furthermore, greater capital inflow makes the accumulation of reserves less costly. In a world of low capital mobility, the accumulation of reserves typically comes primarily from the trade surplus. Turning a trade deficit to a trade surplus might require a substantial depreciation of domestic currency. The existence of J curves makes it harder for such exchange rate policy to be effective in the

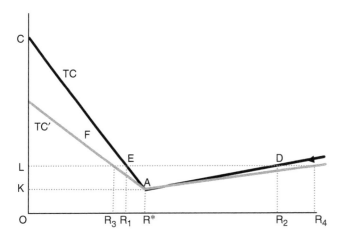

*Figure 13.5* Comparison of two inaction zones.

short term. But in the world of high capital mobility, international investors seek investment opportunities in emerging markets and make investment through FDI, portfolio flows or bank loans. These inflows combined with various motivations to limit appreciation can easily push up the reserve levels with little costs. This would make the slope of the right hand side of the TC curve flatter, causing more asymmetry of the inaction zone around the optimal level of reserves.

A natural extension is to take into account expectations of future balance of payments developments. The current level of reserves, state of economy, and exchange rates arrangements are not the only determinants of whether the government should adjust or not. On the surplus side, the government should adjust sooner if it perceives that the current surplus situation will persist. It should delay adjustment if it thinks the current surplus situation is only temporary. Thus, the shape of the inaction zone will, in turn, depend on the expectations of future balance of payments developments.

## Concluding remarks and future research

For whatever reasons recent history has shown financial capital flows to emerging markets to be subject to surges and sudden stops. Thus, it is likely wise policy to sterilize some portion of large rapid inflows and to accumulate increased international reserves to both reduce the probability of sudden large reversals and to help cushion the economy in the case that they do occur. We argue that wise reserve policy should involve forward looking active management of this type and should not rely just on historical variability as assumed in most models of optimal reserve holdings. Of course, in implementing such a strategy the estimation or 'guestimation' of parameters for how much to sterilize and by what fraction to increase reserves are crucial. We have no illusion that such optimal parameters can be estimated precisely, but we believe that the framework outlined here gives us a valuable framework for analysis.

We also argue that because of (often substantial) adjustment costs, the range over which countries reserve levels may vary without inducing nationally optimal corrections is likely to be quite considerable. This zone of optimal inaction will typically be much greater above than below the optimal level calculated without regard to adjustment costs. It will also vary with the state of the domestic economy. We argue that the biggest national interest argument for surplus countries to take adjustment actions will be to help to avoid the overheating of the domestic economy.

From the standpoint of strictly short-run national interests, the analysis suggests the wisdom of countries with above optimal accumulations to diversify an increasing portion of their accumulations into higher return, less liquid assets. This leaves untouched, however, the problem that large continuing global imbalances may generate for the future stability of the global system. In contrast to the benign view of the current situation as Bretton Woods II offered by Dooley *et al.* (2003), we are struck by the rapidity with which international financial markets can change directions and thus derive only limited comfort from arguments that the financial markets are not currently signalling that they see serious problems on the horizon. Our analysis of international financial flows over the last several decades suggests that optimism today can quickly turn to pessimism tomorrow and with both views being correct with respect to short-term outlooks. The need is for longer term perspectives. In our judgment a laissez-faire approach to the current global imbalances runs very great risks. It is in this context rather than just narrow short-run national interests that issues of large reserve accumulations should be addressed.

Officials should carefully follow the changes in the capital account and accumulation of capital flows. Especially large and fast increases in capital inflows may require an immediate adjustment of the optimal reserve level. Recent crisis episodes showed that these types of increases can reverse sharply, especially if the real exchange rate is appreciated and the current account is in a large deficit.

Fortunately such surges are frequently accompanied by over all payments surpluses, making it easy to accumulate additional reserves. Thus in the phase of capital inflow surges, it would seem wise for governments to offset a nontrivial portion of these inflows with sterilized intervention in the foreign exchange market, adding the resultant accumulations of foreign currency to liquid reserves.

## Acknowledgement

An earlier version of this paper was presented at the 2006 Annual Meetings of the Asian Pacific Economics Association. Valuable comments from the participants, especially Joshua Aizenman and Ronald McKinnon are gratefully acknowledged. This paper is a part of collaborative projects on international capital flows and reserve adequacy undertaken by the Claremont Institute of Economic Policy Studies at Claremont Graduate University and the Research Center for Foreign Reserves at the Central University of Finance and Economics. The fundings from China's Ministry of Education and CUFE (project QBJ0706) are also acknowledged.

## References

Aizenman J. (1998) 'Buffer Stocks and Precautionary Savings with Loss Aversion', *Journal of International Money and Finance* 17(6): 931–947.

Aizenman J. and Marion N. (2003) 'The High Demand for International Reserves in the Far East: What's Going On?' *Journal of Japanese and International Economics*, 17(1): 370–400.

Aizenman J., Lee Y. and Rhee Y. (2007) 'International Reserves Management and Capital Mobility in a Volatile World: Policy Considerations and a Case Study of Korea', *Journal of the Japanese and International Economies*, 21(1): 1–15.

Bar-Ilan A., Marion N. and Perry, D. (2007) 'Drift Control of International Reserves', *Journal of Economic Dynamics and Control*, 31(9): 3110–3137.

Bird G. and Rajan R. (2003) 'Too Much of a Good Thing? The Adequacy of International Reserves in the Aftermath of Crises', *The World Economy*, 26(6): 873–891.

Bussiere M. and Mulder C. (1999) 'External Vulnerability in Emerging Market Economies: How High Liquidity Can Offset Weak Fundamentals and the Effects of Contagion', IMF Working Paper, No. 99/88. Washington, DC.

Calvo G. (1998) 'Capital Flows and Capital-Market Crises: The Simple Economics of Sudden Stops', *Journal of Applied Economics*, 1(1): 35–54.

Cheung Y-W. and Ito H. (2006) 'Cross-sectional Analysis on the Determinants of International Reserve Accumulation', Manuscript, APEA annual conference, Seattle, July 29–30.

Claassen E. M. (1975) 'Demand for International Reserves and the Optimum Mix and Speed of Adjustment Policies', *American Economic Review*, 65(3): 446–453.

—— (1976) 'The Optimizing Approach to the Demand for International Reserves: A Survey', in Classen E. M. and Salin P. (eds), *Recent Issues in International Monetary Economics*, Amsterdam: North Holland. pp. 73–116.

Cohen B. J. (1966) *Adjustment Costs and the Distribution of New Reserves*, Princeton, N.J.: Department of Economics, Princeton University.

Dooley M., Folkerts-Landau D. and Garber, P. (2003) 'An Essay on the Revived Bretton Woods System', NBER Working Paper, No. 9971.

Edison H. (2003) 'Are Foreign Reserves in Asia too High?' World Economic Outlook, IMF.

Edison H., Guimarães-Filho R., Kramer C. and Miniane J. (2007) 'Sterilized Intervention in Emerging Asia: Is It Effective?' Presented at conference on *Capital Flows, Macroeconomic Management and Regional Cooperation in Asia*, November 30, 2007, Washington D.C.

Garcia P. and Soto C. (2004) 'Large Hoarding of International Reserves: Are They Worth it?' Working Papers Central Bank of Chile, No. 299.

Hutchison M. and Noy I. (2002) 'Sudden Stops and the Mexican Wave: Currency Crises, Capital Flow Reversals and Output Loss in Emerging Markets', *Journal of Development Economics*, 79 (1): 225–248.

Jeanne O. and Ranciere R. (2006) 'The Optimal Level of International Reserves for Emerging Market Countries: Formulas and Applications', IMF Working Paper, No. 06/229. Washington, DC.

Kim J. S., Li J., Sula O., Rajan R. and Willett T. D. (2005) 'Reserve Adequacy in Asia Revisited: New Benchmarks Based on the Size and Composition of Capital Flows', Conference Proceedings, Monetary and Exchange Rate Arrangement in East Asia, Seoul: Korea Institute for Economic Policy.

Laney L. and Willett T. D. (1982) 'The International Liquidity Explosion and Global Monetary Expansion: 1970–72', *Journal of International Money and Finance*, 2: 141–152.

Li J. (2007) 'Examining the Interactions of High Reserves and Weak Fundamentals in Currency Crises', *Applied Economics Letters*, 14(8): 617–621.

Li J. and Rajan R. (2006) 'Can High Reserves Offset Weak Fundamentals: A Simple Model of Precautionary Demand for Reserves', *Economia Internazionale*, 59(3): 317–328.

Ouyang A., Rajan R. and Willett T. (2007) 'China as a Reserve Sink: The Evidence from Offset and Sterilization Coefficients', Presented in the conference on *Capital Flows, Macroeconomic Management and Regional Cooperation in Asia*, November 30, 2007, Washington D.C.

Sachs J., Tornell A. and Velasco A. (1996) 'Financial Crises in Emerging Markets: the Lessons from 1995', *Brookings Papers on Economic Activity*, 1: 147–215, Brookings Institution.

Sula O. and Willett T. D. (2006) 'Measuring The Reversibility of Different Types of Capital Flows', Working Paper, Claremont Graduate University.

Sula O. (2006) 'Surges and Sudden Stops of Capital Flows to Emerging Markets', Working Paper, Claremont Graduate University.

Willett T. D. (1980) 'International Liquidity Issues', American Enterprise Institute, Washington D.C.

Willett T. D., Nitithanprapas E., Nitithanprapas I. and Rongala S. (2005) 'The Asian Crises Reexamined', Asian Economic Papers, 3: 32–87.

# 14 Financial liberalization and corporate debt maturity in Thailand, 1993–97

*Federico Guerrero and Elliott Parker*

## Introduction

The Asian financial crisis of 1997, which was triggered by financial turmoil in Thailand in June 1997 and then spread to the rest of East Asia,[1] generated substantial interest in the nexus between financial globalization, financial liberalization, and corporate debt maturity. In particular, it has been argued that financial liberalization led to the shortening of debt maturity, since both firms and banks were given increased access and more choice over their portfolios without commensurate improvements in their long-term incentive structure and adequate prudential regulation. This in turn led to swift increases in macroeconomic fragility.

Researchers and policy-makers were thus led to reconsider the effects of financial liberalization, and eventually a new synthesis emerged, neatly captured by Kaminsky and Schmukler (2002), in which the effects of financial liberalization involve both short-term pain and long-term gain. The experience of South Korea became the archetype for this view, given both the relative importance of the South Korean economy in East Asia and the fact that the case strongly confirmed the new synthesis.[2]

In this paper, we examine the effects of financial liberalization on corporate debt maturity in Thailand, where the crisis began, and we consider whether the experience of South Korea generalizes to other countries. In particular, we consider whether Thai corporations increased their reliance on short-term debt in the run-up to the 1997 crisis, and whether this reliance resulted from financial liberalization or from other factors driving the maturity of corporate debt. We document the evolution of corporate debt maturity in Thailand during two different stages of international financial integration: early-stage financial globalization during 1993–94, and rapid financial globalization during 1995–97.

The remainder of this paper is organized as follows. Section two describes some specialized literature connected with this study and places this paper in context. Section three presents and discusses the main results of this investigation, including some robustness exercises. Section four concludes the paper.

## Debt maturity and Thailand's crisis

A number of studies have argued that debt maturity played a key role in the Asian financial crisis. Dadush *et al.* (2000) point out that half of all new loans from international banks in the period preceding the crisis had maturities of one year or less, and the volume of short-term debt grew fastest in East Asia. In Thailand short-term debt rose to around 120 per cent of reserves (a figure that pales compared to the Korean figure of 200 per cent), and since short-term borrowing was pro-cyclical with the macroeconomy, the reversal in the balance of payments that came with the crisis was thus dramatic.

Alba *et al.* (1999) argued that Thailand's financial crisis was fundamentally caused by private debt, and that financial liberalization was the main reason for this. Between 1990 and 1996, private external debt doubled as a share of Thailand's GDP, though the overall share of this debt that was short-term remained relatively stable, and the most dramatic expansion of international borrowing was by Thai banks and offshore institutions (i.e., the Bangkok International Banking Facility). Finance companies in particular began to borrow most of their funds with maturities of three months or less, and found their portfolio maturity increasingly mismatched. Financial liberalization, they argue, led to this borrowing because it increased competition and reduced profit margins, thereby increasing incentives to practice unsound banking behaviour in the absence of adequate prudential regulation. Financial liberalization was also accompanied by an increased international openness, so Thai firms had greater access to unhedged funds denominated in foreign currency, which made it susceptible to exchange rate risk.

What determines the maturity structure of corporate debt elsewhere? While much of the literature[3] on corporate debt maturity has concentrated on analyzing its effects on the value of the firm, there have been a number of studies on the external determinants of debt maturity and some of this literature has focused on international case studies and comparisons. Barclay and Smith (1995), for example, find evidence that larger firms in the US tend to have longer debt maturities, along with those firms under more regulation, while firms with more growth opportunities rely on shorter maturities, perhaps because of information asymmetries. These basic findings have been confirmed by several studies, including Stohs and Mauer (1996), Cunat (1999), Ozkan (2000; 2002) for a sample of British firms, Heyman *et al.* (2003) for a sample of small Belgian firms and Chen *et al.* (1999) for firms in Singapore.

Demirgüç-Kunt and Maksimovic (1999) examined the capital structure of firms in 30 developing and developed countries during the period 1980–1991 and found that the presence of well-developed stock markets was an important determinant of the positive relationship between firm size and debt maturity, since small firms in countries where bank lending was the dominant form of finance tended to use relatively less short-term debt. Niskanen and Niskanen (2001) found for a sample of Finnish firms that bank ownership of stock helped solve the contracting problem, so smaller firms with more bank ownership and growth opportunities were able to get longer maturities on their debts. Similarly, Datta *et al.* (2005) found that more managerial stock ownership led to shorter debt maturities.

Other studies have focused on the effects of specific policies or macroeconomic variables on the maturity of corporate debt, including, prominently, the impact of inflation on the shortening in the maturity structure of corporate debt (e.g. Klein 1975; Aarstol 2000; Guerrero 2004; 2007b). Miller (1997) found evidence that political instability and polarization have an important role in creating inflation uncertainty and thus shorter debt maturities.

Closer to this paper are studies by Schmukler and Vesperoni (2001; 2006) and Guerrero (2007a). Schmukler and Vesperoni (2001; 2006) conduct a cross-country study of the effects of globalization on firms' financing choices in an unbalanced panel of firms in eight Latin American and East Asian countries. Interestingly, Thailand is one of the countries in their study, though they did not derive country-specific conclusions and they were mainly interested in studying the effects of financial crisis on firms' financing choices. Guerrero (2007a) finds a reduction in corporate debt maturity prior to the Asian financial crisis for publicly-traded firms in South Korea, and traces back the origin of the phenomenon to the early stages of financial globalization. Finally, the debt maturity of Thai corporations in the run-up to the financial crisis has been studied by Wiwattanakantang *et al.* (2003), who found that firms with close relationships with banks were more likely to borrow with longer maturities.

## The effects of liberalization on corporate debt maturity in Thailand

Was the reduction in the maturity of international debt mirrored in the patterns of corporate debt in Thailand, and are the initial effects of financial liberalization generalizable beyond the banking and financial sector? Did Thai corporations also respond to financial liberalization by taking advantage of increased access to short-term lending markets? Did Thai banks try to match the maturity of their domestic lending to that of their own international borrowing?

In this paper, we examine the maturity structure of corporate debt in Thailand, and how it responded to globalization, as measured by proxies for financial liberalization, increased access to international bond and equity markets, and the increase in the development of the domestic equity and financial markets. This paper purposefully excludes the period after 1997, because the focus is on the effects of globalization on corporate debt maturity in the years that lead to the crisis. Our data is a subset of the dataset used in Schmukler and Vesperoni (2001; 2006), but given the differences in goals and scope between this paper and theirs, we use a balanced panel to be able track the evolution of the same firms during the run-up to the crisis.

### *Definition of variables*

The dependent variable in all our regressions is the ratio of long-term debt to total debt (LTD/TD). Following the recent empirical literature that studies firms' financing decisions (e.g. Demirgüç-Kunt and Maksimovic 1999; Booth *et al.* 2001; Schmukler and Vesperoni 2001; 2006) the vector of observable firm characteristics includes five variables. The first variable is a proxy for the size of the firm, the logarithm of a firm's net fixed assets (NFA). The second variable is an indicator of asset tangibility, the ratio of net fixed assets to total assets (NFA/TA). The third variable, an indicator of firms' revenues, is the ratio of net sales to net fixed assets (S/NFA). The fourth variable proxies the profitability of firms with the ratio of profits to total assets (PF/TA). Descriptive statistics for these five variables are shown in Table 14.1.

To capture the potential effects of expanded financing opportunities through increased access to international bond and equity markets on the maturity of corporate debt, two proxies for access to international debt and equity markets are included. The variable capturing access to international bond markets is a dummy variable (BONDS) that takes the value of one for periods in which a given firm issues bonds in international capital markets, and zero otherwise. The variable capturing access to international equity markets is defined as a dummy variable (EQUITY) that takes the value one from the moment when a firm starts trading (or raising capital) in international equity markets, and zero otherwise.

Two alternative measures to proxy for financial liberalization are used. First, we use the arithmetic average of four individual financial liberalization indices (AFLI) that capture the degrees of liberalization of interest rates caps, the degree of control

*Table 14.1* Summary statistics for microeconomic variables

| Variables | | Mean | Std. Dev. | Max. | Min. | # of observations |
|---|---|---|---|---|---|---|
| LTD/TD | overall[a] | 0.264 | 0.241 | 0.929 | −0.035 | $N^d = 883$ |
| | between[b] | | 0.209 | 0.788 | 0.000 | $n^e = 182$ |
| | within[c] | | 0.119 | 0.777 | −0.314 | T-bar[f] $= 4.851$ |
| NFA | overall | 8.943 | 0.673 | 11.153 | 6.923 | $N = 1107$ |
| | between | | 0.650 | 10.967 | 7.126 | $n = 230$ |
| | within | | 0.185 | 10.094 | 7.667 | T-bar $= 4.813$ |
| NFA/TA | overall | 0.358 | 0.257 | 0.967 | 0.001 | $N = 1107$ |
| | between | | 0.249 | 0.923 | 0.003 | $n = 230$ |
| | within | | 0.071 | 0.887 | −0.189 | T-bar $= 4.813$ |
| S/NFA | overall | 4.886 | 10.044 | 126.866 | −5.132 | $N = 1104$ |
| | between | | 9.317 | 84.042 | 0.079 | $n = 230$ |
| | within | | 4.582 | 47.711 | −74.707 | T-bar $= 4.8$ |
| PF/TA | overall | 0.029 | 0.089 | 0.364 | −1.108 | $N = 1106$ |
| | between | | 0.0633 | 0.295 | −0.310 | $n = 230$ |
| | within | | 0.0631 | 0.363 | −0.870 | T-bar $= 4.808$ |

Notes: [a] Overall means combined between and within variation. [b] Between means across firms. [c] Within means across years. [d] N = total number of observations. [e] n = number of firms. [f] T-bar = average number of years of data available for the firms included in the sample.

of private credit by the central bank, the level of marginal and average reserve requirements, and restrictions to both capital inflows and capital outflows. Each of the individual indices takes three possible values (1, 2, or 3), where 3 represents full financial liberalization, 2 partial financial repression, and 1 full financial repression. The information to construct these indices was taken from Kaminsky and Schmukler (2002). This multidimensional index of financial liberalization is reported in the tables below. We also considered a dummy variable that follows the stock market liberalization dates reported in Bekaert and Harvey (2000), but the results were unchanged.

To control for the effects of rapid development of the domestic equity and credit markets on the maturity of corporate debt, we follow Beck *et al.* (2000) and proxy for the degree of financial development (FD) with the sum of both stock market capitalization and the outstanding liabilities of the banking sector, expressed as a share of GDP.

The inflation rate, as measured by the rate of change of the Consumer Price Index, and the real GDP growth rate were both used to control for the effects of the macroeconomic environment on the maturity of corporate debt. Neither had a significant effect in our regressions, so we do not report these results in the tables below.

### Econometric estimations and baseline results

We estimate six different alternative specifications:

1  ordinary least squares;
2  firm-specific fixed effects;
3  random effects;
4  instrumental variables, with the right-hand-side regressors instrumented using first lags;
5  fixed effects and instrumental variables, using both the first and second lags as instruments; and
6  the Arellano-Bond (1993) specification, using a dynamic panel data Generalized Method of Moments procedure that controls both for the potential endogeneity of the microeconomic variables used as right-hand-side regressors, as well as for the potential time-series problems of the left-hand-side endogenous variable.

Results for these baseline regressions are shown in Table 14.2. All regressions include an unreported constant term.

The OLS estimate provides the basic multivariate correlation embedded in the data, and these results are shown in column 1 of Table 14.2. However, OLS estimates are usually criticized when used with individual or firm-level data because they do not control for unobservable characteristics that could be biasing the estimated coefficients or introducing a potential reverse causation problem. To control for some of these unobservable characteristics, the firm-specific

*Table 14.2* Baseline regressions

| | OLS (1) | Fixed effects (2) | Random effects (3) | IV(1) (4) | IV(2) + FE (5) | GMM (6) |
|---|---|---|---|---|---|---|
| *Dependent variable is (LTD/TD)* | | | | | | |
| NFA (size) | 0.217 | 0.194 | 0.210 | 0.215 | 0.286 | 0.236 |
| | (16.68)** | (5.31)** | (10.61)** | (14.15)** | (0.67) | (3.10)** |
| NFA/TA | −0.086 | −0.291 | −0.177 | −0.034 | −2.406 | −0.421 |
| (tangibility) | (−2.46)* | (−4.05)** | (−3.84)** | (−0.74) | (−2.04)* | (−2.96)** |
| S/NFA (sales) | −0.003 | −0.003 | −0.003 | −0.003 | 0.03 | 0.001 |
| | (−1.67) | (−1.60) | (−1.75) | (−0.86) | (0.30) | (0.42) |
| PF/TA (profits) | −0.053 | −0.181 | −0.129 | 0.047 | −1.052 | −0.123 |
| | (−0.71) | (−2.50)* | (−1.94) | (−0.35) | (−1.78) | (−1.11) |
| BONDS | 0.234 | 0.160 | 0.171 | 0.199 | 0.060 | 0.082 |
| (access) | (6.01)** | (5.12)** | (5.65)** | (4.44)** | (0.62) | (1.69) |
| AFLI (fin. | −0.294 | −0.356 | −0.381 | 0.533 | 0.176 | 1.323 |
| liberalization) | (−0.90) | (−1.45) | (−1.69) | (0.58) | (0.15) | (1.99)* |
| FD (fin. | 0.038 | 0.025 | 0.022 | 0.295 | 0.304 | 0.733 |
| development) | (0.66) | (0.61) | (0.57) | (0.97) | (0.45) | (2.69)** |
| Lagged | | | | | | 0.598 |
| (LTD/TD) | | | | | | (5.11)** |
| $R^2$ | 0.34 | 0.78 | | 0.32 | 0.65 | |
| F-Statistic | 63.38 | 12.87 | | 43.61 | 4.33 | |
| Chi-Squared Statistic | | | 205.7 | | | 47.38 |

Note: *t*-statistics in parentheses below coefficients. (**) significant at 1%; (*) significant at 5%. The variable EQUITY was dropped due to multicollinearity problems.

fixed effects estimation procedure is estimated, and the results are shown in column 2. Because the fixed-effects estimates disregard all the cross-sectional variation, we also include an alternative (static) panel data technique using random effects estimates, with a weighted average of the purely cross-sectional estimate and the fixed effects estimates. These estimates are shown in column 3.

The purely cross-sectional estimates are not included here for a couple of reasons. First, they are subject to similar criticisms as OLS estimates. There is also problem of the 'between groups', or purely cross-sectional estimate, in the present context is that by the very nature of our estimates completely disregards the time dimension of the data.

Given the potential endogeneity of most – if not all – of the observable firm characteristics (size, tangibility of assets and profitability, etc.), instrumental variable estimates that use the value of these variables lagged once are presented in column 4, while estimates that combine fixed effects with two lags as instruments are given in column 5.

Finally, column 6 contains the results produced by the Arellano-Bond (1993) estimation procedure, a more sophisticated instrumental-variables procedure that also takes care of potential problems of non-stationarity, by first differencing the data and including the lag of the dependent variable as a right-hand-side regressor.

As Table 14.2 shows, the most significant microeconomic determinants of corporate debt maturity are the firm's size (NFA) and the tangibility of its assets (NFA/TA). Consistent with the literature, we find that larger firms hold longer debts. The negative sign for the tangibility of assets implies that more tangible assets are associated with shorter maturity; this result is consistent across specifications and stands in opposition to what is usually observed in other case studies (in South Korea, for instance, as reported in Guerrero 2007a). No other microeconomic determinant of corporate debt is statistically significant for all or most econometric specifications, and this result is also different from results previously found for other emerging economies (e.g. Schmukler and Vesperoni, 2001, or Guerrero, 2004). The sales ratio is insignificant, and the effect of profitability is insignificant in all cases but the fixed effect model, where the effect on maturity is negative.

For the variables proxying the effects of financial globalization, we find that a firm's access to international bond markets (BONDS) is positive and statistically significant in the first four specifications, but not in the last two. This result is in line with the ones reported in Schmukler and Vesperoni (2001; 2006). We dropped the EQUITY variable due to multicollinearity problems in these initial estimations.

The next proxy for financial integration to the international markets is AFLI, the multidimensional index of financial liberalization. This variable is insignificant in all specifications but the last, where it is positive. In the GMM specification, the index for financial liberalization has a lengthening effect in corporate debt maturity, a finding that contradicts the ones in Schmukler and Vesperoni (2001; 2006) and Guerrero (2007a). This result suggests that it is not so clear that financial liberalization led to a shortening of debt maturity, at least for listed corporations in Thailand, and it may in fact have had the reverse effect.

Finally, the FD variable that proxies for the degree of financial development of the domestic financial sector displays a similar pattern to AFLI, in that that it is insignificant in all but the last and most relevant specification, the only one that explicitly controls for potential dynamic problems; the indicator for financial development displays a significant degree of inertia, as does the dependent variable, so a dynamic specification is probably the most appropriate. In the GMM specification, FD displays a strong and significant lengthening effect on the maturity of corporate debt. Therefore, the overall effect of increased financial integration during the early stages of globalization is probably to lengthen the maturity of corporate debt, a finding that is in contrast to those reported previously by Schmukler and Vesperoni (2001; 2006), for an unbalanced panel of East Asian firms during the period 1980–99, and Guerrero (2007a), for the case of South Korea at an early stage of financial globalization.

### *Robustness of the access measurements*

Given the collinearity problem affecting the dummy variables BONDS and EQUITY for access to international capital markets in the regressions reported above, we next consider an alternative proxy for the access variables. Specifically, we combine the two access variables into one, by measuring the number of times that firms had access to either the international bonds or equity markets. The results are not very different from the ones displayed in Table 14.2, and are not shown separately, but the combined access variable becomes statistically and economically insignificant in all specifications.

A legitimate concern with the baseline regressions shown in Table 14.2 and described above is related to the potential endogeneity bias introduced by the access variables. In particular, if the firms that had access to international capital markets are the same ones that also had access to long-term debt, the estimate of the effect of the access variable would be biased. To address those potential sources of trouble, two strategies were followed, along the lines of recent literature (Schmukler and Vesperoni 2006; Schmukler and Vesperoni 2001; Ozkan, 2000). First, we use first lags of the same proxies used in Table 14.2, under the assumption that these lags were predetermined variables. Second, we follow a twofold procedure in which we use lags of the same variable as instruments. For access to equity markets, following both Schmukler and Vesperoni (2006) and Ozkan (2000), we use two lags as instruments. For access to bonds markets, we construct an instrument that indicates whether capital markets were open. This instrument, first proposed by Schmukler and Vesperoni (2001), takes a value of one if two conditions are fulfilled: (i) At least one firm had access to international bonds markets during that period; and (ii) the firm was able to issue international bonds at least once during the sample period. Otherwise, the instrument takes a value of zero. The results provided by the two strategies are shown in Table 14.3.

Results are similar to the ones presented in Table 14.2 before. First, larger firms, and those with less tangible assets, have longer debt maturities. The sales variable remained insignificant in all cases and was dropped, while profit rates are now also insignificant in all cases. Access to the international bonds market continues to have had a positive effect on maturity in four of the specifications, though not the same four cases. Access to international equity markets has a mixed effect, positive in the OLS and IV specifications, negative in the dynamic GMM specification, and insignificant in the other three. Financial liberalization and the degree of financial development both continue to conform to the results in Table 14.2, with both having a significant and positive effect on maturity in only the GMM specification.

Indeed, if this last specification is the most appropriate, as we have argued, then financial globalization had a significant lengthening effect on corporate debt maturity through three different channels: financial liberalization, domestic capital markets development, and increased access to international bond markets. The only force that partially offsets these lengthening effects is given by the access to international equity markets.

*Table 14.3* Endogeneity of access variables

| | OLS | Fixed effects | Random effects | IV | IV w/FE | GMM |
|---|---|---|---|---|---|---|
| **Dependent variable is (LTD/TD)** | | | | | | |
| NFA (size) | 0.209 | 0.199 | 0.208 | 0.202 | 0.324 | 0.254 |
| | (15.93)** | (5.35)** | (10.30)** | (13.17)** | (−0.82) | (3.37)** |
| NFA/TA | −0.071 | −0.288 | −0.166 | −0.013 | −2.240 | −0.421 |
| (tangibility) | (−2.03)* | (−3.96)** | (−3.58)** | (−0.28) | (−2.21)* | (−2.99)** |
| PF/TA (profits) | −0.032 | −0.169 | −0.108 | 0.047 | −0.982 | −0.137 |
| | (−0.43) | (−2.30)* | (−1.61) | (0.36) | (−1.69) | (−1.23) |
| BONDS | 0.008 | 0.008 | 0.008 | 0.006 | 0.001 | 0.005 |
| (access) | (2.84)** | (3.94)** | (3.91)** | (1.89) | (0.11) | (2.03)* |
| EQUITY | 0.118 | 0.017 | 0.058 | 0.130 | −0.073 | −0.177 |
| (access) | (3.72)** | (0.40) | (1.67) | (3.97)** | (−0.40) | (−2.27)* |
| AFLI (fin. | −0.361 | −0.355 | −0.385 | 0.585 | 0.173 | 1.386 |
| liberalization) | (−1.11) | (−1.43) | (−1.69) | (−0.64) | (−0.15) | (2.09)* |
| FD (fin. | 0.024 | 0.019 | 0.015 | 0.331 | 0.332 | 0.775 |
| development) | (0.42) | (0.46) | (0.39) | (1.09) | (0.54) | (2.85)** |
| Lagged | | | | | | 0.586 |
| (LTD/TD) | | | | | | (5.14)** |
| R-Squared | 0.34 | 0.78 | | 0.33 | 0.7 | |
| F-Statistic | 52.07 | 10.34 | | 40.35 | 4.96 | |
| Chi-Squared statistic | | | 201.51 | | | 48.17 |

Note: *t*-statistics in parentheses below coefficients. (**) significant at 1%; (*) significant at 5%. The variable S/NFA was consistently insignificant and was therefore dropped.

## Conclusion

Using a balanced panel for publicly traded Thai firms, this paper documented the evolution of corporate debt maturity during the period prior to Thailand's financial crisis in 1997, and considered whether or not financial liberalization caused Thai corporations to increase their short-term debt, as the new synthesis has argued. While our results do confirm that larger firms used more long-term debt, we found the effects of financial liberalization to be not so clear. Using six different specifications, we found some evidence that access to the international bonds market actually increased debt maturity, and while the effects of financial liberalization and financial development were mostly insignificant, we found that the dynamic specification we thought most appropriate to the data yielded positive and significant effects for both of these variables. Our evidence here stands in stark contrast with previous findings for other East Asian economies, especially in South Korea, and thus our results call into question the generality of the new synthesis. Thailand's financial sector may have borrowed heavily using short-term debt instruments from international markets, but it is not so clear that Thailand's corporations did the same.

## References

Aarstol M. P. (2000) 'Inflation and debt maturity', *Quarterly Review of Economics and Finance*, 40 (1): 139–53.

Arellano M. and Bond S. (1993) 'Some tests of specification for panel data: Monte Carlo evidence and an application to employment equations', *The Econometrics of Panel Data*, 2: 176–96.

Alba P., Hernandez L. and Klingebiel D. (1999) 'Financial liberalization and the capital account: Thailand, 1988–97', World Bank Policy Research Working Paper, No. 2188.

Barclay M. and Smith C. W., Jr. (1995) 'The maturity structure of corporate debt', *Journal of Finance*, 50 (2): 609–31.

Beck T., Demirgüç-Kunt A. and Levine R. (2000) 'A new database on financial development', World Bank Policy Research Working Paper, No. 2146.

Bekaert G. and Harvey C. (2000) 'Foreign speculators and emerging equity markets', *Journal of Finance*, 55 (2): 562–613.

Booth J. (2001) 'South Korea braces for wave of maturing corporate debt', *Wall Street Journal*, June 1, 2001.

Booth L., Aivazian V., Demirgüç-Kunt A. and Maksimovic V. (2001) 'Capital structures in developing countries', *Journal of Finance*, 56 (1): 87–130.

Chen S.–S., Ho K. W. and Yeo G. H. H. (1999) 'The determinants of debt maturity: The case of bank financing in Singapore', *Review of Quantitative Finance and Accounting*, 12 (4): 341–50.

Corden W. M. (2002) *Too Sensational: On the Choice of Exchange Rate Regimes*, Cambridge, MA: MIT Press.

Cunat V. (1999) 'Determinantes del plazo de endeudamiento de las empresas espacolas. (Determinants of corporate debt maturity: Evidence for Spanish firms)', *Investigaciones Economicas*, 23 (3): 351–92.

Dadush U., Dasgupta D. and Ratha D. (2000) 'The role of short-term debt in recent crises', *Finance and Development*, 37 (4): 54–57.

Datta S., Iskandar-Datta M. and Raman K. (2005) 'Managerial stock ownership and the maturity structure of corporate debt', *Journal of Finance*, 60 (5): 2333–50.

Demirgüç-Kunt A. and Maksimovic V. (1999) 'Institutions, financial markets, and firm debt maturity', *Journal of Financial Economics*, 54 (3): 295–336.

Guerrero F. (2004) 'The reduction in the maturity structure of contracts during high inflation and its recovery after stabilization: The case of Argentine firms', *European Review of Economics and Finance*, 3 (1): 61–84.

—— (2007a) 'Early-stage globalization and corporate debt maturity: The case of South Korea, 1980–94', *Journal of Asian Economics*, 18 (5): 809–24.

—— (2007b) 'High inflation and corporate debt maturity: The case of Turkey, 1988–94', *ICFAI Journal of Monetary Economics*, 5 (2): 51–62.

Heyman D., Deloof M. and Ooghe H. (2003) 'The debt-maturity structure of small firms in a creditor-oriented environment', Working Paper D/2003/7012/35. Universiteit Gent, Faculteit Economie en Bedrijfskunde.

Isard P. (2005) *Globalization and the International Financial System. What's Wrong and What Can Be Done*, New York: Cambridge University Press.

Kaminsky G. and Schmukler S. (2002) 'Short-run pain, long-run gain: The effects of financial liberalization', World Bank Policy Research Working Paper, No. 2912.

Klein B. (1975) 'The impact of inflation on the term structure of corporate financial instruments: 1900–1972', in Silber W. L. (ed.), *Financial Innovation*. D.C. Heath and Company, Lexington, MA.

Ozkan A. (2000) 'An empirical analysis of corporate debt maturity structure', *European Financial Management*, 6 (2): 197–212.

—— (2002) 'The determinants of corporate debt maturity: evidence from UK firms', *Applied Financial Economics*, 12 (1): 19–24.

Miller V. (1997) 'Political instability and debt maturity', *Economic Inquiry*, 35 (1): 12–27.

Niskanen J. and Niskanen M. (2001) 'The effect of bank ownership on loan maturity', *Liiketaloudellinen Aikakauskirja*, 50 (1): 116–27.

Ravid S. A. (1996) 'Debt maturity-survey', *Financial Markets, Institutions and Instruments*, 5(3): 1–69.

Schmukler S. and Vesperoni E. (2001) 'Globalization and firms' financing choices: Evidence from emerging economies', IMF Working Paper WP/01/95.

—— (2006) 'Financial globalization and debt maturity in emerging economies', *Journal of Development Economics*, 79 (1): 183–207.

Stohs M. H. and Mauer D. C. (1996) 'The determinants of corporate debt maturity structure', *Journal of Business*, 69 (3): 279–312.

Wiwattanakantang Y., Kali R. and Charumilind C. (2003) 'Crony capital? Corporate debt maturity in Thailand before the financial crisis', Unpublished working paper. Institute of Southeast Asian Studies.

# 15 Foreign lending under limited enforcement

*Nedim M. Alemdar, Sibel Sirakaya and Stephen J. Turnovsky*

## Introduction

It is widely recognized that the well-established principle of sovereign immunity poses an additional risk for lenders of international capital. The lack of any notable collateral and the absence of a supranational institution with a recognized authority to enforce loan contracts limit lending to sovereign states. Assuming participants in international capital markets are rational, any sovereign loan contract must therefore be self-enforcing.

Several studies have indicated that credible sanctions against arbitrary defaults, implicit in the nature of the debtor/creditor relationship, can explain positive sovereign debt.[1] In an influential paper, Eaton and Gersovitz (1981) focus on the threat of exclusion of a defaulter from further borrowing. In their model, foreign borrowing cushions consumption from shocks to income so that a greater *variability* in export earnings increases the option value of access to credit markets thus diminishing the risk of a default. Bulow and Rogoff (1989) show, however, that if a defaulter can enter into outside financial agreements, the threat of exclusion from future borrowing alone will not support foreign lending. In a more recent study, Kletzer and Wright (2000) demonstrate that in a repeated borrowing/repayment game, if the defaulters of today can become defaultees of the future, then positive lending can be sustained without recourse to any exogenous punishments even with outside financial options. In general, incentive-constrained consumption loans are inefficient since they cannot provide for complete consumption smoothing.

For a developing economy, foreign borrowing is desirable not only because it enables consumption smoothing, but more significantly because it can free investment from constraints due to limited domestic sources of savings. For growth, the *level* of exports matters as well: exports facilitate imports of investment goods for which domestic substitutes usually do not exist. Hence, the prospect of losing valuable export markets may also work as a strong deterrent against an arbitrary default. Consequently, the extent of a debtor's dependence on creditor markets for exports becomes strategic. While building up an export presence in creditor markets is a signal of future willingness to repay debt, an expansion in the home goods market can be construed as a sign of potential recalcitrance. Thus, investment and lending decisions are strategically intertwined, distorting incentives for investment and creating opportunities for inefficiencies to arise.

For instance, in a two-period stochastic model, Aizenman (1991) assumes default sanctions in the form of a terms-of-trade deterioration and shows that in the presence of default risk and limited enforcement, investment subsidies to open sectors may be optimal. Nonetheless, investments in the open sectors are lower than full-commitment levels, resulting in an inefficiently small degree of openness.[2] But the two-period assumption is unnecessarily restrictive, since by assumption it excludes dynamic adjustment paths. A more serious drawback is that, without some stickiness in capital stocks, the assumed form of sanctions – a terms-of-trade deterioration – lacks credibility. A defaulter, anticipating an imminent worsening in the terms of trade, can rapidly divest the export capital and use the proceeds for consumption and investment in the import-competing sector, and thereby avoid any default costs. In models with limited enforcement, some *irreversibility* in capital stocks is essential for the credibility of sanctions. As such, we believe it may constitute one of the key identifying principles in foreign lending for export-oriented investment projects.

Admittedly, the full weight of the irreversibility assumption would be felt more acutely in a general stochastic environment where, given an adverse shock of sufficient magnitude, default would be optimal in equilibrium. In an uncertain world with irreversible investments, a debtor is best advised to keep his default option open. That is, in order to avoid inordinate potential default costs, less openness of the economy will be desirable. In a world of certainty such as we shall consider, irreversibility is still needed. Otherwise, the credibility of the lending equilibrium under the threat of trade sanctions is questionable.

The literature on sovereign debt has shown that, in the absence of an outside authority to enforce loan agreements, endogenous commitment mechanisms are likely to arise to mitigate, but not fully reverse, the welfare loss due to the lack of enforcement. This paper focuses on one such commitment mechanism, export-led growth, and also quantifies the welfare loss stemming from limited enforcement. We develop a model of a two-sector open economy that underscores the strategic nature of investment activities and foreign lending. In contrast to its predecessors, however, exports are not domestically consumed, and sector specific capital stocks are *locked-in* so that the threat of trade restrictions is credible. In the absence of full enforcement, the model emphasizes the commitment value of investment activities and shows how export-led growth can be supported as a second-best policy.

We study a self-enforcing lending scheme in which a debtor's repayment *resources* never fall below the default alternative at any point in time. We show that this strategy boils down to setting target debt/export ratios. Using these target debt/export ratios, we are able to derive analytical results that explicitly show the nature and the extent of the inefficiencies caused by limited enforcement. For instance, if a borrower's pure time preference exceeds the world interest rate, then the long-run productive capacities in the export and the home goods sectors depend also on the severity of creditor sanctions. More specifically, the marginal product of capital in the export sector is now bounded from above by the domestic pure time preference, as in autarky (no enforcement) and from below by the world interest rate, as in full integration (full enforcement). The size of the home goods, on the other hand, depends both on preferences and the available sanctions. If the home and the foreign goods are gross substitutes, then the home goods sector expands with limited sanctions.

When the pure time preference and the world interest rate are equal, so too is the marginal product of export capital in the long-run, regardless of how limited the sanctions are. The size of the home goods sector, however, is still inversely related to the potential sanctions. Ultimately, to the degree the home goods are poor substitutes for foreign goods, the future consumption is discounted heavily, and the potential sanctions are low, the welfare cost of limited enforcement will be substantial.

Finally, using a wide range of parameter values, we use genetic algorithms to optimize numerically the repayment program constrained by target debt/export ratios, thereby demonstrating the extent of inefficiencies due to limited enforcement.

The balance of the paper is organized as follows: Section 2 discusses the model, its justification, and the long-run analytical results. The simulation results are provided in Section 3, while conclusions are summarized in Section 4.

## The model

Consider a small open economy that produces an export, $Q^e = Q^e(K^e)$, and a home good, $Q^h = Q^h(K^h)$. The production technology in each sector is strictly concave. Home goods are only consumed so that $C^h = Q^h(K^h)$ in equilibrium where $C^h$ denotes the consumption of home goods. Sector-specific capital stocks, $K^e$ and $K^h$, grow over time according to:

$$\dot{K}^e = J^e, \text{ and } J^e \geq 0, \tag{15.1a}$$

$$\dot{K}^h = J^h, \text{ and } J^h \geq 0. \tag{15.1b}$$

where $J^e$ and $J^h$ are the amounts of imported goods invested in the respective sectors, which cannot be undone, i.e. are irreversible.[3]

The accumulation of capital stocks involves installation (or adjustment costs), so that the total resources involved in accumulating capital at the rates specified in equations (15.1a) and (15.1b) are[4]

$$C(J^e) \equiv J^e \left(1 + \frac{z}{2} J^e\right) \tag{15.2a}$$

$$C(J^h) \equiv J^h \left(1 + \frac{z}{2} J^h\right) \tag{15.2b}$$

where $z$ reflects the installation costs, assumed for simplicity to be common to both sectors. The absence of domestic production, irreversibility in capital accumulation and sectoral specificity of investment are adopted in order to highlight the value of investment as a commitment mechanism in the strategic interplay between debtors and creditors in an environment of limited enforcement.

As long as the outstanding debt is below the credit limit, the country has access to the world credit market and can finance its current account deficit by borrowing from abroad:

$$\dot{D} = rD + C^m + J^e + \frac{z}{2}(J^e)^2 + J^h + \frac{z}{2}(J^h)^2 - Q^e,$$

$$D \leq \tilde{D},$$

(15.3)

where $D$ is the outstanding debt, $\dot{D}$ is the rate of gross borrowing and $\tilde{D}$ indicates the credit limit yet to be determined by creditors. Note that the terms of trade is fixed at unity so that borrowing is in terms of foreign goods, with the import of consumption goods being $C^m$. The parameter $r$ denotes the fixed world interest rate at which the country can borrow as long as it is below its credit limit.[5]

At any point in time, $t$, given the initial stocks, $K^e(t)$, $K^h(t)$ and $D(t)$, if the debt is repaid, the debtor will then obtain a repayment utility:

$$V^P(K^e(t), K^h(t), D(t), t; \beta, r) = \max_{C^m, J^e, J^h} \int_t^\infty e^{-\beta(\tau - t)} U(C^m, Q^h) d\tau \quad (15.4)$$

where $U(C^m, Q^h)$ is a strictly concave instantaneous utility function and $\beta$ denotes the fixed pure time preference rate.

Alternatively, the debtor may opt for a default with the certain prospect of collective creditor sanctions of an indefinite duration. These include cutting off future lending and retaliatory measures that will disturb the debtor's normal flow of trade.[6] In this case, a defaulter has to conduct trade on a current basis, $\dot{D} = 0$, and will also come under direct trade sanctions. The external constraint, equation (15.3), then becomes,

$$C^m + J^e + \frac{z}{2}(J^e)^2 + J^h + \frac{z}{2}(J^h)^2 = (1 - \alpha)Q^e$$

(15.5)

This parameterization of sanctions is in keeping with the literature on sovereign debt.[7] The 'sanction' or 'enforcement coefficient', $0 \leq \alpha \leq 1$, can be motivated by arguments on various levels. For example, if a wilful default is countered by tariffs on the defaulter's exports in creditor countries, then $\alpha$ is the percentage deterioration in the defaulter's terms of trade so that $\alpha Q^e(K^e(t))$ is the direct default cost flow. Alternatively, if quantity restrictions are in force, then $\alpha$ is the fraction by which exports are reduced implying that the potential default cost flow is the same, namely, $\alpha Q^e(K^e(t))$. At a more general level, $\alpha$ measures the difficulty with which the debtor can shift its trade to alternative markets at favourable terms, and also the severity of trade restrictions it anticipates facing in creditor markets. As such, it parameterizes the dependency of the debtor on the creditor markets for exports and thus the ability of creditors to enforce sanctions.

If the debtor defaults, he will obtain a default utility:

$$V^R(K^e(t), K^h(t), t; \beta, \alpha) = \max_{C^m, \, J^e, \, J^h} \int_t^\infty e^{-\beta(\tau - t)} U(C^m, Q^h) d\tau \qquad (15.6)$$

with the same constraints, except now equation (15.5) replaces (15.3).

Having formulated the debtor's problem, we now turn to the determination of the credit ceiling, $\tilde{D}$, by the creditors.

### Lending

Lenders recognize the inherent time-inconsistency in extending loans to sovereign countries, but lack the capacity to compute the dynamically incentive compatible loan contracts. Neither they nor the debtor deem the pledges of future investment or loan plans as credible. Furthermore, the creditors are unable to compute the debtor's optimal default policies. Instead, loans are collectively made to ensure that the debtor's interest burden at any time not become too onerous, creating temptation for a default.

Creditors reason that by defaulting the debtor would save the face value of its outstanding debt, $D(t)$, and given its locked-in export capacity, it would at the minimum suffer a default penalty equivalent to the capitalized value of the current default cost, $\alpha Q^e(K^e(t))/r$. They reckon that if the outstanding debt is never allowed to exceed the minimum default penalty, $D(t) \leq \alpha Q^e(K^e(t))/r$, then a potential default can always be averted. Below, Proposition 1 establishes that this lending policy is self-enforcing.

**Proposition 1.** Assume $\beta \geq r$ and low initial indebtedness so that borrowing is desirable, $\dot{D}(t) \geq 0$. Then the lending policy that sets a target debt to export ratio, $\tilde{D}(t) = \alpha Q^e(K^e(t))/r$, is self-enforcing. Thus, creditors can prevent a default if they insist that the debt to export ratio at any given time $t$, $D(t)/Q^e(t)$, not exceed a 'vulnerability ratio', $\alpha/r$.

**Proof:** Note that the repayment and default programs are essentially the same except for the external constraints, (15.3) and (15.5). Indeed, if $\dot{D}(t) - rD(t) + \alpha Q^e(K^e(t)) = 0$, for all $t$, then $V^P(K^e(t), K^h(t), D(t), t; \beta, r) = V^R(K^e(t), K^h(t), t; \beta, \alpha)$ for all $t$ because both programs have identical utility functionals and equal resources. Suppose $rD(t) - \dot{D}(t) \leq \alpha Q^e(K^e(t))$ for all $t$. Then $V^P(K^e(t), K^h(t), D(t), t; \beta, r) \geq V^R(K^e(t), K^h(t), t; \beta, \alpha)$ for all $t$ as both programs start with the same initial capital stocks, $K^e(t)$ and $K^h(t)$, and have identical utility functionals. That is, so long as the net debt service is less than the default cost, the debtor has more resources under the repayment program, and therefore, is better off servicing the debt. Since $\dot{D}(t) \geq 0$, if $rD(t) \leq \alpha Q^e(K^e(t))$ for all $t$, then $V^P(K^e(t), K^h(t), D(t), t; \beta, r) \geq V^R(K^e(t), K^h(t), t; \beta, \alpha)$ for all $t$. Thus, Proposition 1 follows.

At first blush, this lending policy may appear overly restrictive since creditors have ignored new lending ($\dot{D}(t) \geq 0$) as a repayment resource in their default calculus. In fact, lending will not be unduly restricted. This is because, in a world of certainty, default can be optimal only after all available credits are exhausted. Thus, when weighing the costs and benefits of a default, it is reasonable to assume that credits have been used up.

### Long-run analytical results

Despite their widespread use by international credit institutions as measures of creditworthiness and their practical appeal, to our knowledge, an analysis as to the welfare costs of debt/export ratios on growth has not been addressed. The following analytical results should therefore be of interest both for their empirical relevance, and for the fact that debt/export ratios themselves have a rational foundation as we have demonstrated. We summarize our long-run results as propositions.

**Proposition 2.** Suppose that creditors adopt the lending policy $\tilde{D} = (\alpha/r) Q^e(K^e)$. Reconsider the repayment program described by equations (1) to (4), now constrained by $D(\tau) \leq (\alpha/r) Q^e(K^e(\tau))$ :
Given sufficiently low stocks of initial debt and export capital, if $\beta > r$ and $0 \leq \alpha \leq 1$, then the long-run credit constraint, $\tilde{D} = (\alpha/r) Q^e(K^e)$, is binding where export capital, $\hat{K}^e$, satisfies:

$$\frac{\partial Q^e}{\partial \hat{K}^e} = \frac{\beta r}{r(1-\alpha) + \alpha \beta}.$$

*If $\beta = r$ and $0 \leq \alpha \leq 1$, then in the long-run, the credit constraint does not bind, though in transition it may have, and the marginal productivity in the export sector is independent of sanctions; namely, $\partial Q^e / \partial \hat{K}^e = \beta = r$.*

Given a sufficiently small initial home goods sector and also a sanction rate, $\alpha$, if $\beta \geq r$, then the long-run capital stock in the home goods sector is determined by both sanctions and preferences:

$$\frac{\partial U}{\partial \hat{C}^m} \beta = \frac{\partial U}{\partial Q^h(\hat{K}^h)} \frac{\partial Q^h}{\partial \hat{K}^h}.$$

**Proof:** Note that the debtor faces an optimal growth problem with an additional target debt/export constraint. Kamien and Schwartz (1981) provide a set of necessary conditions for optimal control problems with bounded state variables. These involve a new definition of the Hamiltonian, now appended with the total differential of the state variable constraint and an accompanying multiplier which is non-increasing when the constraint is binding and a constant but not necessarily zero during a free interval. In our problem, H, the current valued Hamiltonian is:

$$H = U(C^m, Q^h) + \mu\left[rD + C^m + J^e + \frac{z}{2}(J^e)^2 + J^h + \frac{z}{2}(J^h)^2 - Q^e(K^e)\right]$$

$$+ \lambda^e J^e + \lambda^h J^h + \phi\left\{\alpha(\partial Q^e/\partial K^e)(J^e/r) - [rD + C^m + J^e + \frac{z}{2}(J^e)^2\right.$$

$$\left. + J^h + \frac{z}{2}(J^h)^2 - Q^e(K^e)]\right\}$$

For optimality, the following first order conditions are necessary:

$$\frac{\partial U}{\partial C^m} = \phi - \mu \tag{15.7}$$

$$J^e = \frac{1}{z}\left\{\frac{\lambda^e + W^1 + \dfrac{\phi\alpha}{r}\dfrac{\partial Q^e}{\partial K^e}}{\phi - \mu} - 1\right\} \tag{15.8}$$

$$J^h = \frac{1}{z}\left\{\frac{\lambda^h + W^2}{\phi - \mu} - 1\right\} \tag{15.9}$$

where $\lambda^e$, $\lambda^h$, and $\mu$ are the respective co-state variables for $\dot{K}^e$, $\dot{K}^h$, and $\dot{D}$. The variable, $\phi$ adjoins the time-differentiated credit constraint, $(\alpha/r)$ $(\partial Q^e/\partial K^e) \cdot \dot{K}^e - \dot{D}$. Optimal policies will satisfy (15.7)–(15.9) as well as the 'complementary slackness conditions' $W^1 \geq 0$, $J^e W^1 = 0$, and $W^2 \geq 0$, $J^h W^2 = 0$.

Equation (15.7) prescribes the optimal consumption of foreign goods while (15.8) and (15.9) indicate the rates of investment in each sector. Notice that the marginal utility of imported goods consumption is $\phi - \mu$ whereas in the absence of credit constraint it would have been only $\mu$. Hence the opportunity cost of borrowing is now higher, discouraging consumption. The term $(\phi\alpha/r)(\partial Q^e/\partial K^e)$ appearing in the numerator in equation (15.8) captures the beneficial effect of investment in the export sector on the credit constraint. Thus, the presence of the credit constraint tilts the optimal composition of investment in favour of the export sector relative to a decentralized borrowing or when the credit constraint is altogether absent.

The costate variables $\mu$, $\lambda^e$, and $\lambda^h$ evolve according to,

$$\dot{\mu} = \mu(\beta - r) + \phi r \tag{15.10}$$

$$\dot{\lambda}^e = \lambda^e \beta + (\mu - \phi)\frac{\partial Q^e}{\partial K^e} - \phi\alpha\frac{J^e}{r}\frac{\partial^2 Q^e}{\partial(K^e)^2} \tag{15.11}$$

$$\dot{\lambda}^h = \lambda^h \beta - \frac{\partial U}{\partial Q^h(K^h)} \frac{\partial Q^h}{\partial K^h} \tag{15.12}$$

$$\phi \geq 0, \ (\dot{\phi} - \beta\phi) \leq 0, \ (\dot{\phi} - \beta\phi)[(\alpha Q^e / r) - D] = 0, \tag{15.13}$$

with the transversality conditions

$$\lim_{\tau \to \infty} e^{-\beta(\tau - t)} \mu D(\tau) = \lim_{\tau \to \infty} e^{-\beta(\tau - t)} \lambda^e K^e(\tau) = \lim_{\tau \to \infty} e^{-\beta(\tau - t)} \lambda^h K^h(\tau) = 0 \tag{15.14}$$

From equation (15.10) notice that when $\beta = r$, for $\dot{\mu} = 0$, $\phi = 0$, that is the credit constraint is non-binding at that point, although it may have been previously. Consider first the export sector. Assume sufficiently low initial indebtedness and export capital so that an interior solution obtains in the steady state. Setting $J^e$ in equation (15.8) to zero implies

$$\lambda^e + \frac{\phi\alpha}{r} \frac{\partial Q^e}{\partial \hat{K}^e} = \phi - \mu. \tag{15.15}$$

Next, taking the time derivative of (15.15), substituting $\dot{\mu}$ and $\dot{\lambda}^e$ from (15.10) and (15.11), and then replacing $\beta\lambda^e$ in the resultant expression from (15.15) yields

$$\left(\frac{\alpha}{r} \frac{\partial Q^e}{\partial \hat{K}^e} - 1\right)(\dot{\phi} - \beta\phi) - (\phi - \mu)\left(\frac{\partial Q^e}{\partial \hat{K}^e} - r\right) = 0. \tag{15.16}$$

In steady state, $\dot{\phi} = \dot{\mu} = 0$, so that $\phi r = \mu(r - \beta)$. Substituting these relationships into (15.16) yields

$$\frac{\partial Q^e}{\partial \hat{K}^e}[\alpha\beta + r(1 - \alpha)] - \beta r = 0.$$

from which the first result in Proposition 2 immediately follows.

Next, turn to the home goods sector. Assume sufficiently small initial stocks and sanction rate so that the desired consumption profile of imported goods is not declining. Consequently, the irreversibility constraint does not bind, so that $W^2 = 0$. Setting $J^h$ to zero in (15.9) and combining with (15.7), implies $\lambda^h = \partial U / \partial \hat{C}^m$. Setting $\dot{\lambda}^h = 0$ in (12) and substituting $\lambda^h = \partial U / \partial \hat{C}^m$ yields the second result in Proposition 2.

Proposition 2 shows that the long-run marginal productivity in the export sector varies between the world interest and the domestic pure time preference rates, depending on the rate of enforcement. If no sanctions can be brought to bear upon a debtor, $\alpha = 0$, then the financial autarky results in, $\partial Q^e / \partial \hat{K}^e = \beta$. With full enforcement ($\alpha = 1$), on the other hand, perfect capital market integration leads to a convergence, $\partial Q^e / \partial \hat{K}^e = r$.

Note that in a more general stochastic environment a sufficiently large shock will trigger a default and thus sanctions in equilibrium. Consequently, the debtor's investment plans will have to cover this contingency as well. With default as a real possibility, the long-run sectoral mix as indicated by Proposition 2 would not be optimal. In order to plan for such an eventuality, and not to regret having invested so much in the export sector to bear such heavy default costs, the debtor will invest relatively less in the export sector than prescribed by Proposition 2. In other words, with irreversible investments in an uncertain environment the debtor will always keep its default option open.

Proposition 3, below, summarizes the sensitivity of the long-run equilibrium to the rate of enforcement as well as making more precise the role preferences play. Assuming an interior steady state and taking home and foreign goods to be gross substitutes, we may state

**Proposition 3.** If $\beta > r$, then in the long-run:

$$\frac{\partial \hat{K}^e}{\partial \alpha} \geq 0, \quad \frac{\partial \hat{D}}{\partial \alpha} > 0, \quad \frac{\partial \hat{C}^m}{\partial \alpha} < 0, \quad \frac{\partial \hat{K}^h}{\partial \alpha} < 0,$$

If $\beta = r$, the above qualitative results are still valid, with $\partial \hat{K}^e / \partial \alpha = 0$.

**Proof:** From Proposition 2, $\hat{K}^e$ solves,

$$\frac{\partial Q^e}{\partial \hat{K}^e} = \frac{\beta r}{r(1-\alpha)+\alpha\beta}. \tag{15.17}$$

Assuming that the debt/export and the vulnerability ratios are equal in the long-run, $\hat{D}$, satisfies,

$$r\hat{D} = \alpha Q^e(\hat{K}^e). \tag{15.18}$$

The long-run foreign goods consumption is given by,

$$\hat{C}^m = Q^e(\hat{K}^e) - r\hat{D}. \tag{15.19}$$

Finally, the home goods capital stock in the long-run is obtained from,

$$\frac{\partial U}{\partial \hat{C}^m}\beta = \frac{\partial U}{\partial Q^h(\hat{K}^h)}\frac{\partial Q^h}{\partial \hat{K}^h}. \tag{15.20}$$

Differentiating (15.16), (15.17), (15.18) and (15.19) and assuming home and foreign goods to be gross substitutes, we obtain the qualitative responses summarized in Proposition 3:

$$\frac{\partial \hat{K}^e}{\partial \alpha} = -\frac{\beta r(\beta - r)}{(r + \alpha(\beta - r))^2 \dfrac{\partial^2 Q^e}{\partial(\hat{K}^e)^2}} \geq 0,$$

$$\frac{\partial \hat{D}}{\partial \alpha} = \frac{1}{r}\left[Q^e + \alpha \frac{\partial Q^e}{\partial \hat{K}^e}\frac{\partial \hat{K}^e}{\partial \alpha}\right] > 0,$$

$$\frac{\partial \hat{C}^m}{\partial \alpha} = -Q^e + (1-\alpha)\frac{\partial Q^e}{\partial \hat{K}^e}\frac{\partial \hat{K}^e}{\partial \alpha} < 0,$$

$$\frac{\partial \hat{K}^h}{\partial \alpha} = \frac{\dfrac{\partial \hat{C}^m}{\partial \alpha}\left[\dfrac{\partial Q^h}{\partial \hat{K}^h}\dfrac{\partial^2 U}{\partial \hat{C}^m \partial \hat{C}^h} - \beta \dfrac{\partial^2 U}{\partial(\hat{C}^m)^2}\right]}{\beta \dfrac{\partial^2 U}{\partial \hat{C}^m \partial \hat{C}^h}\left(\dfrac{\partial Q^h}{\partial \hat{K}^h} - \dfrac{\partial^2 U}{\partial(\hat{C}^h)^2}\left(\left(\dfrac{\partial Q^h}{\partial \hat{K}^h}\right)^2 - \dfrac{\partial^2 Q^h}{\partial(\hat{K}^h)^2}\dfrac{\partial U}{\partial \hat{C}^h}\right)\right)} < 0.$$

Proposition 3 establishes that a stronger enforcement will support a larger debt and openness in equilibrium. Since increased inflows also finance foreign consumption and investment in the home goods sector, indebtedness will grow more than exports so that foreign consumption falls in the long-run. Furthermore, as shown in the proof of Proposition 3, if foreign and home goods are gross substitutes, the home goods consumption drops as well. Dynamic inefficiency in the home goods sector occurs in the opposite direction. Namely, lower sanctions lead to an inefficiently large home goods sector. The upshot of the comparative static exercise is that limited enforcement also limits openness. These results are intuitive and also verified by our numerical experiments.

Finally, to conclude our analytical inquiry, and also to better appreciate how the locked-in export capital serves as a commitment mechanism, compare the long-run export capacity had investments been irreversible with the capacity when they could be undone. Had the debtor been able to disinvest after a default, the long-run capital stock in the export sector would have satisfied, $\partial Q^e/\partial \hat{K}^e = \beta/(1-\alpha)$. Clearly, a defaulter would have preferred to have a much smaller export capacity than the one it got locked into. Thus, the capacity created in the export sector under the lending regime, $D(t)/Q^e(K^e(t)) \leq \alpha/r$, is "too high" should the debtor default. As such, this "excess capacity" provides the guarantee to the creditors that their loans will be repaid.

## Simulations of transition paths

Since the purpose of our numerical experimentation is to discover how limited enforcement impacts equilibrium paths, we approximate the repayment and default programs with a low, $\alpha = 0.1$, and a high enforcement, $\alpha = 0.8$, rates. The equilibrium paths are also affected by the relative magnitudes of the pure time preference and the interest rates so that the experiments are run with $\beta = r$ and $\beta > r$. Altogether, four cases are considered.[8]

In order to control for the effects of technology and tastes on the experiments, we assume symmetry in production technologies and preferences over domestic and foreign goods. The economy is assumed initially to be almost closed with no outstanding foreign liabilities and a relatively small export sector. Parameter values and functional forms are discussed in the Appendix. Figures 15.1 and 15.2, and Table 15.1 summarize our numerical findings.

Notice that in a loose enforcement regime where the borrower is allowed to hold a debt stock about 1.25 times its exports, $\alpha = 0.1$, the credit limit binds around the tenth quarter (after the first time period) and remains so thereafter. Once the credits tighten, the creditors allow gross lending to grow at the same rate as exports and also start extracting a fixed fraction, $\alpha = 0.1$, of the debtor's exports as interest payments.

As shown in Figures 15.1 and 15.2, the debtor starts with no foreign debt and a relatively low export capacity, and quickly accumulates both. The home goods

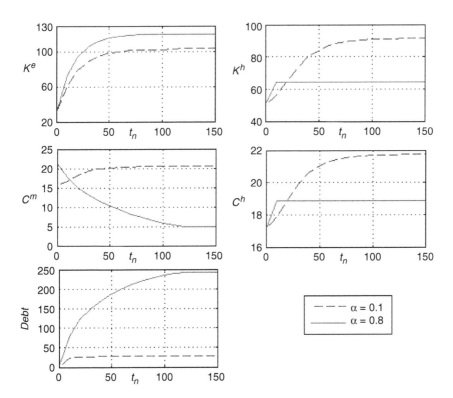

*Figure 15.1* Capital, consumption and debt paths ($\beta > r$).

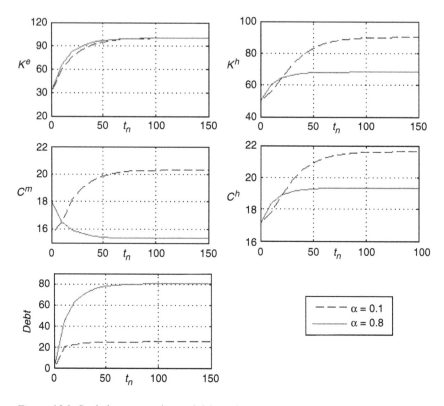

*Figure 15.2* Capital, consumption and debt paths ($\beta = r$).

sector expands as well, albeit, at a slower pace. If $\beta > r$ and $\alpha < 1$, credit constraints eventually bind and remain tight thereafter. That is, for some $t$, $D(s) = \tilde{D}(s)$ for all $s \geq t$.

Increased enforcement speeds up the adjustment process and allows debtor to shift consumption to earlier periods. Since, the home goods are only consumed, the rapid initial growth in the home goods sector indicates the borrower's impatience to attain the long-run consumption level. Furthermore, since the home goods sector shrinks with a stronger enforcement in the long-run, adjustments run their due course faster.

In a tight enforcement regime, larger initial inflows also finance higher consumption of foreign goods while exports are still low. When the debtor's desire to consume in the present is strong, $\beta > r$, and severe sanctions are in force against a default, $\alpha = 0.8$, the time profile of foreign goods consumption starts to decline. If $\beta = r$, as in Figure 15.2, consumption shifting is less desired so that time profiles become more balanced and increase monotonically. In this instance, earlier capital inflows largely finance investment in both sectors.

When $\beta = r$, the long-run productive capacity in the export sector is *independent* of the severity of sanctions as also witnessed in the simulations of the next section.

*Table 15.1* Comparison of lending strategies

| $\alpha$ | $N$ | $t_n$ | $K^e_{t_n}$ | $K^h_{t_n}$ | $D_{t_n}$ | $C^m_{t_n}$ | $C^h_{t_n}$ | $K^e_{t_n}$ | $K^h_{t_n}$ | $D_{t_n}$ | $C^m_{t_n}$ | $C^h_{t_n}$ |
|---|---|---|---|---|---|---|---|---|---|---|---|---|
| | | | $\beta = 0.09, r = 0.08$ | | | | | $\beta = r = 0.09$ | | | | |
| | 0 | 0 | 30.00 | 50.00 | 0.00 | 15.86 | 17.08 | 30.00 | 50.00 | 0.00 | 15.61 | 17.08 |
| | 1 | 10 | 60.88 | 55.96 | 23.10 | 16.62 | 17.87 | 60.09 | 55.52 | 20.42 | 16.50 | 17.81 |
| | 2 | 20 | 78.74 | 64.08 | 25.60 | 18.37 | 18.86 | 76.22 | 63.98 | 22.46 | 18.12 | 18.85 |
| | 3 | 30 | 89.39 | 73.16 | 26.93 | 19.33 | 19.89 | 86.07 | 72.60 | 23.58 | 19.04 | 19.82 |
| | 4 | 40 | 94.85 | 79.94 | 27.58 | 19.82 | 20.60 | 91.93 | 78.92 | 24.21 | 19.57 | 20.50 |
| | 5 | 50 | 99.59 | 84.03 | 28.12 | 20.22 | 21.02 | 95.15 | 83.18 | 24.55 | 19.86 | 20.93 |
| | 6 | 60 | 100.48 | 87.28 | 28.22 | 20.31 | 21.34 | 97.11 | 85.83 | 24.75 | 20.03 | 21.20 |
| 0.1 | 7 | 70 | 101.87 | 88.79 | 28.38 | 20.42 | 21.49 | 98.76 | 87.43 | 24.91 | 20.17 | 21.36 |
| | 8 | 80 | 102.32 | 89.86 | 28.43 | 20.46 | 21.59 | 99.37 | 88.62 | 24.98 | 20.22 | 21.47 |
| | 9 | 90 | 102.54 | 90.45 | 28.45 | 20.48 | 21.65 | 99.73 | 89.29 | 25.01 | 20.26 | 21.54 |
| | 10 | 100 | 102.57 | 90.76 | 28.46 | 20.49 | 21.68 | 99.94 | 89.68 | 25.03 | 20.27 | 21.57 |
| | 11 | 110 | 103.29 | 90.81 | 28.53 | 20.54 | 21.68 | 100.07 | 89.91 | 25.05 | 20.29 | 21.60 |
| | 12 | 120 | 103.86 | 91.01 | 28.60 | 20.59 | 21.70 | 100.15 | 90.04 | 25.05 | 20.29 | 21.61 |
| | 13 | 130 | 103.88 | 91.29 | 28.60 | 20.59 | 21.73 | 100.19 | 90.12 | 25.06 | 20.30 | 21.62 |
| | 14 | 140 | 103.88 | 91.42 | 28.60 | 20.59 | 21.74 | 100.22 | 90.17 | 25.06 | 20.30 | 21.62 |
| | 15 | 150 | 103.88 | 91.49 | 28.60 | 20.59 | 21.75 | 100.23 | 90.20 | 25.06 | 20.30 | 21.62 |
| | | | Welfare: 338.177 | | | | | Welfare: 336.576 | | | | |
| | 0 | 0 | 30.00 | 50.00 | 0.00 | 21.33 | 17.08 | 30.00 | 50.00 | 0.00 | 18.00 | 17.08 |
| | 1 | 10 | 73.40 | 64.17 | 79.85 | 17.50 | 18.87 | 65.82 | 59.90 | 45.37 | 16.50 | 18.36 |
| | 2 | 20 | 94.44 | 64.17 | 121.73 | 14.99 | 18.87 | 82.19 | 64.29 | 62.62 | 15.92 | 18.88 |
| | 3 | 30 | 105.91 | 64.17 | 149.88 | 13.10 | 18.87 | 90.51 | 66.32 | 70.91 | 15.65 | 19.12 |
| | 4 | 40 | 112.44 | 64.17 | 170.82 | 11.57 | 18.87 | 94.93 | 67.26 | 75.21 | 15.50 | 19.23 |
| | 5 | 50 | 116.24 | 64.17 | 187.36 | 10.28 | 18.87 | 97.32 | 67.71 | 77.53 | 15.42 | 19.28 |
| | 6 | 60 | 118.46 | 64.17 | 200.91 | 9.16 | 18.87 | 98.63 | 67.92 | 78.80 | 15.38 | 19.30 |
| 0.8 | 7 | 70 | 119.66 | 64.17 | 212.17 | 8.17 | 18.87 | 99.36 | 68.01 | 79.50 | 15.36 | 19.31 |
| | 8 | 80 | 120.12 | 64.17 | 221.50 | 7.30 | 18.87 | 99.76 | 68.06 | 79.89 | 15.34 | 19.32 |
| | 9 | 90 | 120.12 | 64.17 | 229.24 | 6.54 | 18.87 | 99.98 | 68.08 | 80.11 | 15.33 | 19.32 |
| | 10 | 100 | 120.12 | 64.17 | 235.57 | 5.86 | 18.87 | 100.10 | 68.09 | 80.23 | 15.33 | 19.32 |
| | 11 | 110 | 120.12 | 64.17 | 240.15 | 5.27 | 18.87 | 100.17 | 68.10 | 80.29 | 15.33 | 19.32 |
| | 12 | 120 | 120.12 | 64.17 | 242.43 | 4.85 | 18.87 | 100.21 | 68.10 | 80.33 | 15.33 | 19.32 |
| | 13 | 130 | 120.12 | 64.17 | 242.43 | 4.85 | 18.87 | 100.23 | 68.10 | 80.35 | 15.32 | 19.32 |
| | 14 | 140 | 120.12 | 64.17 | 242.43 | 4.85 | 18.87 | 100.24 | 68.10 | 80.36 | 15.32 | 19.32 |
| | 15 | 150 | 120.12 | 64.17 | 242.43 | 4.85 | 18.87 | 100.25 | 68.10 | 80.37 | 15.32 | 19.32 |
| | | | Welfare: 342.946 | | | | | Welfare: 337.303 | | | | |

Depending on the initial size of the export sector and $\alpha$, the credit limit may or may not bind. If the initial export capital and the rate of enforcement are sufficiently large, as per our numerical exercises with $\alpha = 0.8$, the credit limit will not bind at all so that no loss of efficiency ensues. Otherwise, (e.g., $\alpha = 0.1$) the credit constraint will eventually bind and remain tight thereafter. Since, in the long-run, all marginal investment opportunities will have been completely exhausted, the value of extra credit will be nil. In this instance, limited enforcement will be costly because, restricted foreign lending will slow down adjustments and will also lead to an inefficiently large home goods sector. As different from the export sector, the size of the home goods sector in the long-run is also affected by the preferences over the two goods.

Ultimately, a tighter enforcement, as captured by a higher $\alpha$, reduces the effective opportunity cost of foreign borrowing. The borrower not only invests and consumes more in the present, but also invests relatively more in the export sector and consumes more of the imported goods. To the extent home goods can substitute for foreign goods with ease, as assumed in our exercises, the loss of welfare due to the lack of enforcement is limited. Otherwise, with a wide margin between the domestic time preference and the world interest rate, the welfare cost can be substantial.

Finally, we note that a target debt/export ratio is a credible lending policy as it aligns the debtor's ex ante and ex post incentives. *Ex ante*, it imparts to a potential borrower the *ability* to borrow contingent on its investment and trade policies; *ex post*, it measures the creditworthiness as the *willingness*, due in part to the borrower's past investment decisions, to service a given level of debt.

## Concluding remarks

In the absence of conventional legal and institutional structures, participants in international loan markets have incentives to develop alternative relational mechanisms to provide support for the contingency needs of loan transactions. Specifically, in an environment of limited enforcement, investment decisions and long-term debtor/creditor relationships become strategically interlocked.

Creditors may set a target debt/export ratio to keep a debtor's interest burden below a certain fraction of its exports so that servicing debt does not become too onerous triggering a default. Within the repudiation/retaliation framework, this fraction can be construed as a measure of the severity of creditor sanctions that may come about in various guises. Thus, the upper bound on the debt service gains a special meaning as the potential default cost. We show that, under the assumptions of our model, target debt/export ratios generate self-enforcing trajectories of debt should a default ever be entertained as an option.

Borrowers, on the other hand, may deliberately alter their investment patterns to increase their vulnerability to potential creditor sanctions to attract increased foreign capital. To the extent investments are irreversible, when present governments commit to export-led growth, they also limit the possibilities for future governments to re-optimize. A large export sector which has been financed by foreign debt is then a 'firm pledge' not to default, for the costs of a default have increased as well.

The inefficiencies arising from the lack of enforcement, however, cannot completely be done away with. Lending under limited enforcement is too restricted to support an efficient foreign and home goods mix. By and large, the trade sector is relatively too small. To the degree the home goods are poor substitutes for foreign goods, the future is discounted more heavily domestically than by the rest of the world, and the potential sanctions are low, the welfare cost of limited enforcement can be substantial.

## Appendix: Genetic simulations with target debt/export ratios

Throughout our exercises, we assume identical sectoral production functions, $Q^i(K^i) = a(K^i)^b$, $i = e, h$. Consumption preferences are represented by $U(C^m, C^h) = (C^m C^h)^\gamma$, which is symmetric in the two goods. Two enforcement regimes exist: a low $\alpha = 0.1$ and a high $\alpha = 0.8$. Other parameter values are:[9] $a = 3.57146$, $b = 0.4$, $\gamma = 0.5$, $z = 0.05$, $r = 0.08$, $\beta = 0.09$, $K^e(0) = 30$, $K^h(0) = 50$, and $D(0) = 0$. When $\beta = r$, the same parameter values are used with the exception, $\beta = r = 0.09$.

Assuming both programs become stationary at some arbitrary date $T$, we discretize the repayment and default programs using the time aggregation method proposed by Mercenier and Michel (1994) to ensure that the discrete models have the same steady-states as their continuous analogs. In time aggregation, we assume 15 periods with a dense equally spaced gridding of the time horizon $T = 150$, which is sufficient to capture convergence.

In all of our numerical experiments, we use the genetic operators in the public domain *GENESIS* package by Grefenstette (1990) on a *SUN SPARC-1000* running

```
procedure Debt/Export GA;
begin
  i = 0;  /* Generation counter */
  initialize Kᵉ(i), Kʰ(i), D(i);  /* Initial population of Kᵉ, Kʰ and
                                        D paths */
    n = 0;  tₙ = 0;
    evaluate Kᵉₜₙ, Kʰₜₙ, Dₜₙ;
    n = n + 1;  tₙ = tₙ₋₁ + 10;
      evaluate Kᵉₜₙ, Kʰₜₙ, Dₜₙ;
      check Dₜₙ/Qᵉₜₙ ≤ α/r
      repeat until (tₙ = T)
  i = i + 1;
      select new population Kᵉ(i), Kʰ(i), D(i);
      crossover and mutate Kᵉ(i), Kʰ(i), D(i);
      n = 0;  tₙ = 0;
      evaluate Kᵉₜₙ, Kʰₜₙ, Dₜₙ;
      n = n + 1;  tₙ = tₙ₋₁ + 10;
        evaluate Kᵉₜₙ, Kʰₜₙ, Dₜₙ;
        check Dₜₙ/Qᵉₜₙ ≤ α/r
        repeat until (tₙ = T)
  repeat
  until(terminal condition);
  end;
```

*Solaris 2.5*. In a typical run, we use a *population size* of 50 a *crossover* rate of 0.60, a *mutation* rate of 0.03, and a generation number of 200,000.

Using these parameter configurations, we approximate the repayment program by genetic algorithms. Genetic algorithms are powerful general purpose optimization tools in irregular and complex search spaces. A drawback, however, is the lack of any obvious and generally accepted method of dealing with constraint violations. Given that repayment program is heavily constrained by target debt/export ratio, irreversible investments as well as non-negativity restrictions this difficulty may seem especially troubling. Nonetheless, we successfully incorporate constraint violations into fitness evaluations by way of severe penalties. The following is a sketch of the algorithm.

## Acknowledgement

N. M. Alemdar thanks Lance Girton for fruitful discussions and many helpful suggestions.

## References

Aizenman J. (1991) 'Trade Dependency, Bargaining and External Debt', *Journal of International Economics*, 31(1–2): 101–20.

Auerbach A. J. and L. Kotlikoff (1987) *Dynamic Fiscal Policy*, Cambridge; New York: Cambridge University Press.

Bardhan P. K. (1967) 'Optimum Foreign Borrowing', in: K. Shell (ed.), *Essays on the Theory of Optimal Economic Growth*, Cambridge, MA: MIT Press, pp. 117–128.

Bulow J. and K. Rogoff (1989) 'A Constant Recontracting Model of Sovereign Debt', *Journal of Political Economy*, 97(1): 155–78.

Cohen D. and J. Sachs (1986) 'Growth and External Debt under Risk of Debt Repudiation', *European Economic Review*, 30(3): 529–560.

Cohen D. (1994) 'Growth and External Debt', in: R. van der Ploeg (ed.), *Handbook of International Macroeconomics*, London: Basil Blackwell, pp. 480–505.

Corden M. (1989) 'Debt Relief and Adjustment Incentives', in: J. Frenkel, M. Dooley and P. Wickham, (eds), *Analytical Issues in Debt*, International Monetary Fund, Washington, DC, pp. 242–257.

Diwan I. (1990) 'Linking Trade and External Debt Strategies', *Journal of International Economics*, 29(3–4): 293–310.

Eaton J. and R. Fernandez (1995) 'Sovereign Debt', in: G. M. Grossman and K. Rogoff, (eds), *Handbook of International Economics 3*, Amsterdam: North-Holland. pp. 2031–77.

Eaton J. and M. Gersovitz (1981) 'Debt and Potential Repudiation: Theoretical and Empirical Analysis', *Review of Economic Studies*, 48(2): 289–309.

Eaton J., M. Gersovitz and J. E. Stiglitz (1986) 'The Pure Theory of Country Risk', *European Economic Review*, 30(3): 481–513.

Grefenstette J. J (1990) *A User's Guide to GENESIS Version 5.0*. Manuscript.

Helpman E. (1989) 'Voluntary Debt Reduction: Incentives and Welfare', in J. Frenkel, M. Dooley and P. Wickham, (eds), *Analytical Issues in Debt*, International Monetary Fund, Washington, DC, pp. 279–310.

Kamien M. I. and N. L. Schwartz (1981) *Dynamic Optimization: the Calculus of Variations and Optimal Control in Economics and Management*, North Holland, New York.

Kletzer K. M. and B. D. Wright (2000) 'Sovereign Debt as Intertemporal Barter', *American Economic Review*, 90(3): 621–639.

Lipton D. and J. Sachs (1983) 'Accumulation and Growth in a Two-Country Model: A Simulation Approach', *Journal of International Economics*, 15(1–2): 135–59.

Mercenier J. and P. Michel (1994) 'Discrete-time Finite Horizon Approximation of Infinite Horizon Optimization Problems with Steady-State Invariance', *Econometrica*, 62(3): 635–56.

Sachs J. (1984) 'Theoretical Issues in International Borrowing', Princeton Series in International Finance, No. 54, Princeton NJ: Princeton University Press.

—— (1985) 'External Debt and Macroeconomic Performance in Latin America and East Asia', *Brookings Papers on Economic Activity*, 2: 523–564.

Turnovsky S. J. (1997) *International Macroeconomic Dynamics*, Cambridge, MA: MIT Press.

# Notes

### Introduction

1 Earlier versions of some of the papers included in this book were presented in the second annual conference of the Asia Pacific Economic Association held at the University of Washington in July 2006.

### 1 Flying geese or sitting ducks: China's impact on the trading fortunes of other Asian economies

1 See also Carolan, Singh and Talati (1998), Diwan and Hoekman (1999), Kojima (2000) and Loungani (2000).
2 This paper updates our previous work, Ahearne *et al.* (2003), by extending the data to 2005 and – in section 3 of the paper – including three economies in South Asia (Bangladesh, India and Pakistan) among the group of emerging Asian economies.
3 Fernald *et al.* (1999) argue that it makes economic sense to combine data for China and Hong Kong even in the period preceding formal unification, since many goods use Chinese labour and Hong Kong management and distribution skills. It makes statistical sense to use trading-partner statistics, to avoid double-counting Chinese and Hong Kong exports.
4 'Rest of Asia' consists of Korea, Singapore, Taiwan, Indonesia, Malaysia, Philippines, Thailand, Bangladesh, India, and Pakistan.
5 Chinese export growth has also been helped by structural reforms of the exchange and trade system, as detailed in Cerra and Dayal-Gulati (1999). Examples include allowing local governments and exporting enterprises to retain a proportion of foreign exchange receipts, eliminating mandatory export and import planning, and opening up the economy to foreign direct investment. Despite occasional reversals, the overall trend has been to reduce the role of central planning in China's foreign trade.
6 In fact, there are 48 industries in the aggregate, but there is not trade between the United States and Asia in electric energy, industry 104.
7 For more on the impact of China on ASEAN-4 see Gochoco-Bautista and Socorro (1995), Voon (1998) and Tambunan (2006).
8 The data is augmented with data from the CEIC database as needed. In particular, data for Taiwan are not up to date in the DOTS database.
9 So, for example, exports from the ASEAN-4 to the ASEAN-4 represent total exports from each of the ASEAN-4 economies to the other three economies in the ASEAN-4 – in essence, an intra-subregional trade measure. Similarly, exports from China to China capture mainland China's exports to Hong Kong and Hong Kong's exports to the mainland.
10 Prasad and Rumbaugh (2004) present complementary evidence by looking at how important China has become to various economies as a destination for their exports.

In the case of some of the Asian NIEs the increase in the importance of China as an export destination has been quite dramatic. For example, China has gone from accounting from under 0.1 per cent of Korea's exports in 1990 to over 10 per cent in 2000 and nearly 15 per cent in 2002. See also Abeysinghe and Lu (2003).

11 For a detailed discussion of the rise in intraregional trade in Asia, see Zebregs (2003). He concludes that 'the rise in intraregional trade is largely driven by rapidly growing intra-industry trade, which is a reflection of greater vertical specialization and the dispersion of production processes across borders. This has led to a sharp rise in trade in intermediate goods ... but the EU, Japan and the United States remain the main export markets for final goods'.

## 2 A decade of flow of funds in China (1995–2006)

1 In this paper we use the terms individual, household and private interchangeably. By definition, any investment or savings not undertaken by the production or government sectors is defined as the individual sector.

2 In fact, we should also subtract out portfolio inflows into China to get the broadest measure of gross capital outflows. Doing so, however, would break the equality between national investment and national savings; maintaining the usefulness of the definition of national investment as non-FDI investment seemed more important than altering this definition.

3 Data on investment can be found in Chapter 6 of the *China Statistical Yearbook*. Data on profitability can be found in Chapter 14 for recent years and Chapter 13 for earlier years. Data on private savings and consumption can be found in Chapter 10.

4 In this paper, estimates for 2005 are based on either preliminary data or are simply extrapolated by the authors in the absence of a preliminary estimate.

5 When we later work with domestic savings and domestic investment, we will no longer be working with net lending abroad but an approximate gross lending measure. Specifically, the concept of net lending nets out FDI inflows against China's, increase in foreign exchange reserve holdings, for example.

6 This is not completely true since domestic savings also includes savings of productive entities in China which are jointly or wholly owned by foreigners. But we assume that even these decisions are in practice locally determined.

7 Recent EIU estimates are US$ 875.1 billion.

8 In that discussion we will attempt to follow along the lines of World Bank (1995) where we make the distinction between goods produced *for use* by the public sector as opposed to goods *supplied* by the public sector (by SOEs).

9 Basing shares of government investment on GDP is preferable to basing shares on total investment since the latter is confounded by the presence of FDI. Though it is an intermediate scenario in the World Bank paper, the fact that the estimate is for 1992 makes it a 'High Investment Scenario'.

10 We note that in the G-7 economies in 2004, corporate savings represented about 11 per cent of GDP and household savings about 4 per cent, so the finding of a higher production sector savings rate in China is not unique. Historically, however, household savings have exceeded corporate savings in the industrialized economies.

11 We are assuming that net profits are a sufficient measure of savings. Given the limited level of dividend distribution in China, we believe this assumption is reasonable.

12 Beginning in 1998 coverage was changed from type of ownership to the size of the enterprise. All enterprises with sales over 5 million Yuan (about US$ 750,000) were covered in the CSY data for Chapter 14. Earlier years selected entities based on whether or not they had an 'independent accounting system'.

13 Using the profit distribution method, the SOE flow balance becomes positive at 1 per cent in 2004.
14 From the perspective of household and productive entities, we treat the activities of insurance companies as similar to that of banking institutions. They accept premiums and channel those premiums into productive investments after deducting costs.
15 This result is even more dramatic since one would assume that bank deposits represent a multiplier effect above and beyond actual savings. It is in this sense that our estimate for informal intermediation is conservative.
16 We make this assumption regarding holding of foreign instruments since it is assumed that the decision to hold these instruments is made by the PBOC after having issued some type of local currency counterpart financial instrument to the general public. Those instruments would already be accounted for in Figure 2.12.
17 No doubt this in part reflects the secular decline in United States savings relative to the long history of financial innovation and intermediation in the United States.

## 3 China's approach to capital flows since 1978: A brief overview

1 For example, see Whalley and Xin (2006), and Wei (1992).
2 For example, McKinnon (2007) argues that, given that China's financial market is not ready to support 'normal' operations of monetary policies to allow the central bank to control inflation and that the Fed has proved to be credible in keeping US inflation under control, China's policy of pegging its currency to the dollar fixed exchange rate allows it to eliminate inflation expectation, thereby keeping price stability and fostering an environment conducive to investment and growth.
3 To relieve the rising pressure on the yuan to appreciate, the People's Bank of China announced a change in the exchange rate regime on July 21, 2005, replacing the yuan's *de facto* peg to the US dollar peg by a crawling-peg regime which uses a basket of currencies as a 'reference' for the central parity that will be announced at the end of each previous trading day. The yuan was allowed to appreciate or depreciate a maximum of 0.3 per cent each day from that parity. On May 21, 2007, that band was further widened to 0.5 per cent. In practice, the movement of the yuan has been within a narrower band than officially allowed, even though the yuan's appreciation against the dollar has quickened in pace since early 2007. (The yuan appreciated 7.5 per cent against the dollar over the 12 months since to January 2007, more than double the 3.6 per cent rise over the 12 months since January 2006.)
4 See Exhibit 1 in Hung (2008).
5 It should be noted that a portion of FDI inflows from Hong Kong are likely to be due to round tripping (i.e. capital originating from China that returns in disguise as FDI to take advantage of tax, tariff and other benefits) and inflows that actually originated from other countries. Estimates of total round-tripping ranged from 7 per cent of inflows in 1996 to almost 25 per cent in 1992.
6 According to Whalley and Xin (2006), FIEs controlled by US investors sold more than 80 per cent of their products locally in 2002. In comparison, FDI inflows from Japan have been more balanced between vertical and horizontal investment, with about 45 per cent of production for China's domestic market.
7 As pointed out by Prasad (2007), because of the high content of imported material in Chinese exports, net exports' direct contribution to China's nominal GDP growth (from the perspective of growth accounting) was not significant until after 2004 when China's trade surplus surged. But the overall effect of net exports on growth, including investment growth which is stimulated in part by exports but counted as a component of domestic demand growth, should be much bigger.
8 Because of capital controls, the vast majority of foreign investment is FDI.
9 Data on the share of industrial FIEs in total FIEs are not available before 1996. That share was 58 per cent in 1996.

10 Labour movements have continued to be restricted by the household registration (hukou) system, even though some reforms to that system have been initiated since the mid-1990s. Migrant workers who could not obtain household registration are considered illegal immigrants, deprived of social benefits – such as police protection and public education for their children. Consequently, China's employment growth mainly occurred in cities, with little growth in rural areas. Even though firms in the booming cities are facing a labour shortage, they cannot easily tap the surplus labour from rural areas or other cities. See Whalley and Zhang (2004).

11 See the article, 'Trojan Dragons', in *The Economist*, November 1st, 2007.

12 For example, Zhao (2006) notes that, 'In mid-1978 the China Communist Party ... established a philosophy that "*Practice is the sole criterion to test truth*". ... Following this philosophy, (China's) external liberalization has been experimental and gradual, making it evolutionary rather than revolutionary'.

13 For example, since 2004 the government has allowed multinational corporations operating in China more freedom to move funds in and out of the country, insurance companies to invest in foreign-currency-denominated assets overseas, social insurance funds to invest in overseas securities markets, qualified foreign institutions to issue yuan-denominated bonds in China, and emigrants as well as overseas citizens receiving inheritances to transfer their properties abroad. In 2005, the first foreign company was listed on the Shanghai Stock Exchange. Corporations were allowed to keep all of their foreign exchange earnings in their own accounts, up from 80 per cent previously. Since early 2006, Qualified Domestic Institutional Investors (QDII) – basically local fund managers and banks – have been permitted to invest money offshore. Most recently (December 17, 2007), the China Banking Regulatory Commission also announced that Chinese citizens would soon be able to buy shares and mutual funds in London and New York through their local banks.

14 Those economists include McKinnon (2007) and Eichengreen (2006). Even analysts in the Peterson Institute for International Economics, who are among the most critical of China's slowness in allowing its currency to appreciate, do not believe China is ready to exit to a free float yet. Goldstein and Lardy (2003) and more recently Goldstein (2004, 2007), maintain that 'full capital account liberalization in China has to wait for a strengthening of China's banking and financial system – not that exchange rate appreciation has to wait for financial-sector reform'. Since a free-floating exchange rate is not advisable without full capital account liberalization, they have advocated that China should first revalue its currency in one big step (20 to 25 per cent from its level before July 2005) and widen the currency band substantially (to between 5 per cent and 7 per cent). After that first-stage reform and after China has strengthened its domestic financial system enough to permit a significant liberalization of capital outflows, then China should then adopt a managed float.

15 In countries where FX trading is not inhibited and is well functioning, large banks normally have direct access to this international market and are the dealers that match buy and sell orders for the domestic currency. In the absence of government intervention (including playing the role of a market maker), these dealers must continually take open positions – for or against the domestic currency – in order to 'make' the foreign exchange market. In doing so, they provide depth and liquidity to the market, helping to stabilize the currency (at least in a well-behaved market). Thus, a sufficient number of market makers is an important factor for a reasonably smooth market-based float.

## 4 The estimation of domestic value-added and employment induced by exports: An application to Chinese exports to the United States

1 See Fung and Lau (1998, 2001) and Fung *et al.* (2006).

2 Of course, there are other economic benefits, such as increased competition, lower prices, and increased efficiency. We only consider value-added and employment in this study.

3 There is another difficulty of using net exports of the unit of exogenous change. In order to produce an additional US$ 1 of gross output for export, it will usually be necessary to import intermediate inputs, so that in general it is difficult to assure that there is exactly US$ 1 of additional net exports.

4 A new input-output table for China, based on data for 1997, was published at the end of 1999, after substantial effort was made to construct database and input-output table for the production of processing exports. The latest benchmark input-output table is for the year 2002.

5 Adjustment is necessary because a large portion of Chinese exports are first exported to Hong Kong. Hong Kong middlemen add a mark-up to these goods and then re-export them to their final destinations. In the process of exporting and re-exporting, transport and insurance costs have to be incurred. To arrive at the correct shares of Chinese exports by sector, we need to adjust the trade data by re-exports, re-export mark-ups and transport and insurance costs. The methodology of these adjustments follows closely that adopted in Fung and Lau (2001) and details can be obtained from the authors by request.

## 5 External shocks, transmission mechanisms and inflation in Asia

1 The eight countries are Mainland China, Hong Kong SAR, Korea, Malaysia, Philippines, Singapore, Taiwan and Thailand. Apart from not including Japan and Indonesia these countries are also those studied in Disyatat (2003) and Gerlach *et al.* (2003). I have excluded Japan and Indonesia from the analysis since I am focusing on the reaction of the smaller economics in the region. Indonesia is excluded since it is somewhat of an outlier in the 1997–8 period with a peak year-on-year inflation rate of 59.2 per cent (in 1998:4) whereas the next largest was 9.9 per cent in the Philippines in 1998.

2 The spike in the average in 1994 owes much to the high inflation rate in mainland China during this year. Considering only the seven other countries does not change the essence of the overall picture however. For this group the averages were 5.5 per cent in 1991–5, 2.8 per cent in 1996–2000, and 0.9 per cent in 2001–03.

3 The terms 'crisis' and 'no crisis' to identify countries should not be taken to mean that only the former suffered in a real sense from the crisis. Judged by the slow-down in real economic activity all countries in the group, with the possible exception of mainland China, experienced significant difficulties.

4 The US is of course not the only relevant external source of macroeconomic shocks for the countries in question. The US inflation rate should therefore be thought of as a proxy for more general external factors.

5 The group of countries is the same as those described briefly in the previous section plus Indonesia and Japan.

6 The clearest example of this is Hong Kong where interest rates are very highly correlated with corresponding rates in the United States because of the currency board arrangement.

7 The study covers the period 1995 to 2002.

8 This channel is emphasized in the study by Genberg and Pauwels (2004) on Hong Kong.

9 In a more complete structure one should also give a special role to Japan in the context of the countries under study. Here Japan is implicitly included in 'world market influences'.

10 A number of authors have recursive structures of this type to identify partially estimated VAR systems for small open economies. A partial list includes Genberg *et al.* (1987), Cushman and Zha (1997), Hoffmeister and Roldos (1997) and Genberg (2003).

11 Checks for robustness of the results were carried out with two alternative model specifications: one in which $y_t^i$, $y_t^C$ and $y_t^U$ each contained two variables, the rate of

CPI inflation and the growth rate of real GDP, and another in which mainland China was eliminated and where $y_t^i$ and $y_t^U$ each contained the rate of CPI inflation, the growth rate of real GDP, and a short-term interest rate.

12 Even though there is only one Chinese shock in the model, I will not be able to identify it as a structural shock because it presumably represents a linear combination of supply and demand shocks in China.

13 The arguments in this and the following two paragraphs are adapted from Genberg (2003).

14 The results in Table 5.4 refer to VAR systems with four lags of each variable in each equation. Very similar results are obtained with systems estimated with three lags. For example, the correlation coefficient between the 16 quarter horizon FEVs for the 3 lag systems and those for the 4-lag systems are 0.95 for inflation and 0.85 for real growth.

15 Our results for Hong Kong and Taiwan are consistent with those reported in Kumar *et al.* (2004) who found, that prices in these two economies were strongly influenced by price developments in mainland China. Contrary to our findings, their results also showed significant influences of the mainland on Singapore and no effect on Malaysia. A possible reason for the discrepancy is that their results were based on bi-variate VARs including only prices, whereas ours also control for the influence of US variables.

16 When VAR systems were estimated in which a domestic short-term interest was included instead of the inflation rate in Mainland China (i.e. where both $y_t^i$ and $y_t^U$ contained the rate of CPI inflation, the growth rate of real GDP and a short-term interest rate, and $y_t^C$ was eliminated), there was a tendency for the external component of the FEVs for the domestic inflation rate and the interest rate to be correlated across countries i.e. in countries were domestic shocks accounted for a relatively larger portion of interest rate movements, the inflation rate was also less dependent on external shocks.

## 6 External balances in five Asian countries

1 See Lee and Chinn (2006) for more details on econometric issues.

2 The real exchange rates for Korea, India, and Indonesia were obtained from the internal database, which calculated the real exchange rates by the same methodology as the other currencies. See Bayoumi *et al.* (2006) for details on the effective exchange rate calculation.

## 7 What drives business cycle correlation in the Pacific Rim?

1 For instance, Cheung and Yuen (2005) argue in favour of a greater China currency union.

2 Recently, Mink *et al.* (2007) have suggested an alternative way to assess similarities of business cycles.

3 We calculated the transformed correlation coefficient as $\rho' = \frac{1}{2} \ln \frac{1+\rho}{1-\rho}$, where $\rho$ denotes the original correlation coefficient.

4 The remainder of this section draws heavily on Sturm and De Haan (2005).

5 Here we deviate from Baxter and Kouparitsas (2005) who either have no variables in the $M$ vector, or only gravity variables. Since gravity variables do not have a direct impact on business cycle alignment we do not include them in the EBA analysis. See Inklaar *et al.* (2008) for a further discussion.

6 Sala-i-Martin *et al.* (2004) propose a so-called Bayesian Averaging of Classical Estimates (BACE) approach to check the robustness of different explanatory variables in growth regressions. This approach builds upon the approach as suggested by Sala-i-Martin (1997) in the sense that different specifications are estimated (by OLS)

to check the sensitivity of the coefficient estimate of the variable of interest. The major innovation of BACE as compared to the Sala-i-Martin's approach is that there is no set of fixed variables included and the number of explanatory variables in the specifications is flexible. The biggest disadvantages of the BACE approach are the need of having a balanced data set, i.e. an equal number of observations for all regressions (due to the chosen weighting scheme), the restriction of limiting the list of potential variables to be less than the number of observations and the computational burden.

7  This part heavily draws on Sturm and De Haan (2005).

8  Note, however, that if $x_i$ is near the centre of the set of explanatory observations, as is the case in Figure 7.3(a), it will mainly affect the constant and hardly alter the slope.

9  We would have preferred to include the share of a particular product sector in a country's GDP as specialization measure in our model as well, but detailed data on the composition of national GDP was not available for many countries considered in this research.

10  Gruben *et al.* (2002) suggest multiplying this measure with total bilateral trade between countries in order to decompose the trade in an inter- and intra-industry component. Since both components are highly correlated, however, their separate impacts cannot be distinguished in a regression analysis. We therefore simply include the intra-industry trade measure as a third specialization variable in our regressions.

11  We would have preferred to include the share of a particular product sector in a country's GDP as specialization measure in our model as well, but detailed data on the composition of national GDP was not available for many countries considered in this research.

## 8  Have exchange rate regimes in Asia become more flexible post crisis? Re-visiting the evidence

1  Of course, apart from differences in methodologies and estimating techniques, divergences in results could be because of different time periods and frequency of data used (daily, monthly or quarterly).

2  The monthly data are from the IMF-IFS CD and from the ADB-ARIC database from January 1990 to June 2004. Exchange rates per US dollar are taken from line *RF* of IFS, exchange rates per yen are calculated from the US/yen rate, and real effective exchange rate (REERs) are from the ADB-ARIC database. Reserves data are taken from lines 11, 14 and 16*c* of IFS, and interest rates are taken from line 60*B* of IFS.

3  The standard deviations for 2004 are for the first half of the year (January to June).

4  Of course the *ceteris paribus* condition is critical as the implicit assumption is that there is no substantive change in the external environment. In order for a full analysis to be undertaken we would need to estimate a monetary model or a related model that is able to capture the external factors that might have an impact on the exchange rate. The problems with fundamentals-based models of exchange rates are well known and do not need to be repeated here. Also see Willett (2004) for a useful discussion of the issue of trends versus volatilities when attempting to decipher exchange rate behaviour.

5  We are abstracting here from issues relating to sterilization of reserve intervention. See Ouyang *et al.* (2007).

6  Money market rates (IFS line 60*B*) are used as they appear to adequately represent the policy rate and offer sufficient volatility for the purposes of analysis.

7  Thus, we define the crisis period as being between 1997:4 and 1999:5. There is, admittedly, a degree of ad-hocism in the choice of these periods. For instance, Hernández and Montiel (2001) and Taguchi (2004) take the post-crisis period to be 1999:1. Our choice of 1999:5 as being the end of the crisis is derived from simple robustness tests – we found that, by and large, the post crisis results were reasonably robust as we kept working backwards from the end of the sample and expanding the sample size until 1999:6, beyond which the results began to change (quite significantly in some cases).

8 Of course, it could also be that the market risk element of interest rates (i.e. risk premium) has become more volatile as well.
9 New Zealand is an interesting case in that it has not chosen to hold its own reserves, the bulk of its reserves having been borrowed. However, the Reserve Bank of New Zealand (RBNZ) has recently taken steps to bolster its capacity to intervene in the foreign exchange market to influence the level of the New Zealand dollar in certain circumstances.
10 Of course, it could also be that the floaters are faced with a different set of shocks to the Asian countries.
11 The indices presented in this paper are essentially second order constructions of the simple EMP measures derived from a simple monetary model. For examples of models of this type, see Girton and Roper (1977), Pentecost *et al.* (2001) and Tanner (2001).
12 Willett (2004) uses a measure referred to as the 'intervention index', which is merely $1 - Index\ 1$, i.e. $\sigma_{NFA}/(\sigma_{ER} + \sigma_{NFA})$.
13 Cleansing the data to focus only on reserves change due to policy intervention rather than valuation changes is not possible as most countries do not provide data on the currency composition of reserves.
14 The calculation of weights in indices of this type is a critical feature of the literature on EMP. In some cases theory is used as the basis for determining the weights (for instance, see Girton and Roper 1977), while in other cases, empirical methods are employed to select the weights (for instance, Pentecost *et al.* 2001 make use of principal components analysis).
15 Oh (2004) also finds that the Korean won has displayed increasing co-movements with the yen post-crisis.
16 A common choice in studies of this type (see Baig, 2001).
17 When interpreting the significance levels of the coefficient estimates, it is important to be aware of the possible existence of multicollinearity in models of this type.
18 The update estimates of the state and covariance are given as follows:

$$\beta_{t|t} = \beta_{t-1|t-1} + S_{t-1}X_t(X_t'S_{t-1}X_t + R_t)^{-1}(ER_t - \alpha - X_t'\beta_{t-1|t-1})$$

$$P_{t|t} = S_{t-1} + S_{t-1}X_t(X_t'S_{t-1}X_t + R_t)^{-1}X_tS_{t-1}$$

where: $S_{t-1} = P_{t-1|t-1} + Q_t$
$\mu \sim N(0, Q_t)$
$\varepsilon \sim N(0, R_t)$

19 The $\beta$s are assumed to follow a random walk and the covariance matrix of the measurement and the transition equation is diagonal. This is the usual practise (see Cuthbertson *et al.* 1992 for a discussion). The robustness of the Kalman Filter tests can be checked against recursive OLS estimations of 8.3. This exercise has been performed and results are quite robust. They are available from authors.
20 Eichengreen (2004) and Willett (2004) explore Korean exchange rate and monetary policies in some detail. However, neither specifically addresses or entangles the issue of the won-yen nexus. Also see Oh (2004).

## 9 The evolution of the East Asian currency baskets – still undisclosed and changing

1 If hedging instruments are available, the cost of hedging dollar liabilities, i.e. the premium on buying dollars forward with the domestic currency, is high.
2 Schnabl (2006) shows how the Central Bank of Russia has promoted the role of the euro as anchor, intervention and reserve currency since early 2005.

3  For small countries that have one major trading partner, it makes more sense to peg to only one currency instead of a basket.
4  In July 2005 China announced a currency basket which claimed to contain dollar, yen and euros as well as a substantial number of smaller currencies such as the Korean won, the Thai baht, the Malaysian ringgit, the Russian rouble, the Canadian dollar, amongst others.
5  If large countries such as China and Japan would start converting dollars into euros this could have a strong destabilizing effect on the dollar. To avoid such an effect both countries may tend to maintain their dollar stocks but to built up new reserve position in euros.
6  In former estimations we used the Swiss franc as a numéraire.
7  Before January 1999 the euro is represented by the German mark as the anchor currency of the European Monetary System. Before 1999 the German mark was also used as an international currency rather than the synthetic euro which is used in other studies.
8  There is no evidence for any co-integrating vector between the four exchange rate levels.
9  Note the different scale compared to Figure 9.5.
10  The spike in mid 2005 captures the one time appreciation against the dollar, rather than a change a higher weight of the yen in the currency basket.
11  Kawai (2006) shows the prospects of East Asian monetary integration.

## 10  Implications of refined renminbi effective exchange rates with Asian entrepôt and intra-regional trade

1  For applications in policy and market analysis, see Leahy 1998; Buldorini *et al.* 2002; Hargreaves and Carlton 2003; Suttle and Fernandez 2005.
2  Different treatment of China-US trade through Hong Kong has given rise to a much remarked-on and considerably analysed discrepancy between the US and Chinese measures of their bilateral trade balance (Feenstra *et al.* 1999; Fung and Lau 1998; Lardy 1996; US Department of Commerce 1995).
3  Given the paths of other bilateral dollar exchange rates, the effective volatility as calculated depends on the weights assigned to different currencies in the basket. At the limit, a 100 per cent weight on the dollar bloc means that the bilateral dollar exchange rate and effective exchange rate would be essentially the same. In other words, under a tight dollar link and a (mis-assigned) 100 per cent weight on the dollar bloc, the RMB volatility would be zero in both effective and bilateral terms.
4  Cooper (1971) ascribed the tendency of finance ministers that devalued their currencies to lose their jobs to, among other causes, such valuation gains on liabilities. See also Calvo and Reinhart 2002; Goldstein and Turner 2005.
5  Ho and McCauley (2003) show that large effective exchange rate changes are associated with missed inflation targets for a sample of emerging market countries.
6  Recall our assumption that the other currencies in the RMB EER basket would follow their observed paths against the dollar, not responding to the hypothetical shifts in the RMB/USD rate. However, as argued by Ogawa and Ito (2002), regional currencies may respond to each other. In general, China's trading partners would be expected to react to a hypothetical shift of the RMB from bilateral dollar stability to an orientation to effective stability with a reduced weight on the dollar. Thus, to maintain effective stability, China would need to allow for even greater offsetting bilateral moves vis-à-vis the dollar than in Figure 10.1. Hence, the implied movements in the bilateral RMB/USD rate in Figure 10.1 should be interpreted as the minimum movements needed to keep the effective RMB stable. That is, to maintain the effective stability of the RMB, the required variability in the RMB/USD rate would probably have been even larger, once the possible reaction functions of China's trading partners are factored in, a topic to be discussed in Section 5.

7 Latter (2004) finds that Hong Kong adopts the same currency system as China when that is possible.

## 11 Foreign bank lending and bond underwriting in Japan during the lost decade

1 Another potential implication of foreign bank entry is on the competitiveness of the domestic banking sector; see Claessens and Glaessner (1998) for example.
2 See Gorton and Winton (2003) for an overview of bank-like financial intermediation.
3 Due to data limitations, Greece and Ireland are also excluded.
4 The *International Financing Review* is a weekly publication covering the international bond markets.
5 For 91% of Eurobonds, the issue is coordinated by one bookrunner.
6 US studies have used two primary approaches to proxy underwriter reputation: a ranking based on the underwriter's hierarchical bracket position in new issue tombstone announcements (e.g. Carter and Manaster 1990); and the market share of the underwriter in dollar terms over a prior period (e.g. Megginson and Weiss 1991). Since Kollo (2005) finds a high positive correlation between the rankings and tombstone rankings are not available for the Eurobond market, we use the market share approach.
7 For example, as reported in the IFR in December 1993, the Japanese Ministry of Finance lifted the requirement of a 90-day lock-up period for Euro-yen issuance by sovereigns, which will lead to more issuance in Eurobonds because these underwriting fees are lower than in Samurai issues.
8 For a discussion of the Japan premium, see Peek and Rosengren (2001).

## 12 The core-AMU denominated Asian bonds for local investors in East Asia

1 In ABF 2, there was another USD 1 billion invested in the Pan Asia Index Fund (PAIF), which is a US dollar denominated passive fund tracking the total returns of the iBoxx Pan Asian Index.
2 We calculate the AMU Deviation Indicators for each East Asian currency, which shows the degree of deviation from the hypothetical benchmark rate for each of the East Asian currencies in terms of the AMU. At a glance of the graph of them, we can easily find the current situation of misalignments among the East Asian currencies. We suggest that such a deviation measurement is useful indicator for monitoring misalignments of intra-regional exchange rates in the surveillance process.
3 Iwata (2005) explained that the reason for this prospects were from the lack of convergence of interest rate and inflation rate within Asian and some restrictions of capital movements in some Asian countries. He indicated that these circumstances are similar to that of early development of private ECU from 1979 to 1987.
4 It was treated as a 'foreign currency' by the monetary authorities of the communities. Consequently, European countries could use the ECU for their international commercial and financial dealings, such as ECU denominated syndicated loans, ECU denominated Eurobond, ECU in the international bank credit and deposit market, and ECU in invoicing and payments currencies between community countries.
5 We download these data from the website of AsianBondsOnline by the ADB (http://asianbondsonline.adb.org/regional/regional.php).
6 PAIF also introduce 'market openness' as one of the currency weight factors. According to this, Japan and Singapore are 'highly open', Indonesia, Korea, Malaysia, Philippines and Thailand are 'generally open', and China and others are 'relatively less open'.
7 Forward swap bid-ask spreads of each currency are calculated by bid and ask quotations on Bloomberg screens of both spot and forward rates against the US dollar in May 2006.

8  We use the data of GDP measured at PPP from World Development Report of World Bank. When we compare other sources, such as IMF and CIA, which offer the GDP measured at PPP we confirmed that there are not so large differences among them.
9  For the data of trade volume from Direction of Trade Statistics (IMF), we use averages of recent three years from 2001 to 2003.
10  We use the yield data of Japanese government bonds 10 years, exchange fund notes 5 years for Hong Kong, treasury bonds 10 years for Singapore, Loan bonds 10 years for Thailand and treasury bonds 5 years for South Korea. All data except for Indonesia come from Datastream. Due to data constraints, we use 3 month deposit rate for Indonesia from the website of Bank Indonesia.
11  We suppose the case in which investors do not use forward swap transactions for covering foreign exchange risk.
12  We suppose that each local bond is a zero coupon bond. In addition, the yield data are annual basis, we convert them to a monthly basis.
13  A similar calculation is conducted for investors who invest in the US dollar denominated bond and the euro denominated bond to calculate a correlation matrices in the next section.
14  The interest returns for each of the bonds are calculated from yield data of local bonds. Foreign exchange returns are calculated from actual ex-post returns which are rate of change changes in spot exchange rate from the beginning of the month to the end of the month.

## 13  A new framework for analyzing adequate and excessive reserve levels under high capital mobility

1  See, for example, Willett *et al.* (2005) and the references cited there.
2  For surveys, see Claassen (1976) and Willett (1980)
3  See, Aizenman (1998); Aizenman and Marion (2003); Aizenman *et al.* (2004) and Bird and Rajan (2003).
4  See Edison (2003); Jeanne and Rauciere (2005) and Kim *et al.* (2004).
5  In a recent paper similar in spirit to ours, Bar-Ilan *et al.* (2004) have shown that a country might wish to accumulate reserves over a long period of time if the cost of adjusting reserve levels is high in relation to the cost of holding reserves. Generalizing from the conventional buffer stock models, Bar-Ilan *et al.* developed a model of optimal reserve holdings where the reserve authority controls the upward and downward drifts of international reserves and chooses the trigger points that induce changes in drifts. In their model, a country entails a fixed cost while adjusting the drift of reserves. If this fixed cost is high enough, the country prefers to tolerate the cost of high reserve holdings.
6  See Sula (2006) for more details.
7  See Sula and Willett 2006 for more details.
8  The published statistics likely overstate the safety of FDI flows, however, since outflows generated by foreign direct investors would frequently show up under other categories in the balance of payments statistics.
9  Scale ups of reversals are not calculated since Korea was the only country in our sample that had resumed net financial inflows by 2003.
10  There is still an ongoing debate about whether East Asian countries' reserve holdings are excessive. Cheung and Ito (2007) argue that China's reserve level is not terribly high, partially based on the fact that China has the largest population in the world. Others question whether population size is a relevant factor.
11  This framework is similar to Garcia and Soto (2004) and Li and Rajan (2006).
12  See, for example, Sachs *et al.* (1996); Bussiere and Mulder (1999); Li (2006) and Willett *et al.* (2005).

13 The choices of the fundamentals as the determinants of a currency crisis vary across different studies. Among those which are relatively more agreed among different papers are real effective exchange rates, fiscal deficits, credit booms and sometimes current account deficits. On the correlates of the Asian crises, see the analysis and references in Willett *et al.* (2005).

14 This form of using reserves is far from universal but even when not adopted it reflects an important opportunity cost of reserve holdings. There are several experiments going on in some high-reserve countries. More than $45 billion of reserves has been injected into three big state-owned commercial banks in China to boost the capital base of the fragile financial system. India is conducting domestic infrastructure construction using some of its reserve holding as well. Singapore has been investing some of its reserves overseas in higher yielding investments for a long time.

15 For recent literature on the scope for sterilizing capital inflows into emerging markets, see the analysis and reference in Edison *et al.* (2007) and Ouyang *et al.* (2007).

16 Such negative cost could occur if a country is in some type of liquidity traps and finds it difficult to undertake domestic monetary expansion. Some have argued that this was the case in Japan for several years in the early 2000s.

17 Notice that we need to throw in one more assumption here: the cost of crisis is zero without a crisis. Thus, we can get the expected total cost of a crisis as the product of the fixed cost of a crisis and the probability of it.

18 Alternatively we could state the analysis in terms of the benefits of avoiding a crisis and then describe the optimum condition as the familiar marginal costs equal marginal benefits.

19 An analytical solution can be found in Li and Rajan (2006) with an explicit assumption of the probability function.

20 These adjustment costs can be interpreted as either sterilization cost or cost of adjusting exchange rates.

## 14 Financial liberalization and corporate debt maturity in Thailand, 1993–97

1 See Corden (2002: 209–12) and Isard (2005: 142–4) for fascinating accounts of this crisis.

2 See Booth (2001), for the relevance of the issue for the South Korean macroeconomy, and Guerrero (2007a), for a systematic documentation of the link between increased financial globalization and the shortening in corporate debt maturity in South Korea.

3 The literature on corporate debt maturity is much more extensive than what we review here and a good summary can be found in Ravid (1996).

## 15 Foreign lending under limited enforcement

1 The literature on sovereign debt is vast. See among others, Sachs (1984); Cohen and Sachs (1986); Eaton *et al.* (1986); Cohen (1994). Eaton and Fernandez (1995) survey the issues involved in sovereign debt.

2 Diwan (1990) on the other hand, stipulating a complete isolation of a defaulter from international trade, finds that a protracted debt renegotiation and a large inherited debt will tilt the *ex-post* investment incentives towards the import-competing sector. Sachs (1985); Corden (1989) and Helpman (1989) also focus on the adverse effect of heavily discounted inherited debt on the debtor's incentive to pursue aggressive growth strategies. However, possible adverse incentive effects of a reduction in the debt overhang on creditor countries to keep their markets open to debtor country exports are underplayed.

3 Time is continuous, and unless otherwise stated, all variables are functions of time. A dot over a variable denotes its time-derivative. For simplicity, capital does not depreciate.

4 Convex adjustment costs play a critical role in macrodynamic models of small open economies, facing perfect world capital markets; see Turnovsky (1997). These are adequately captured by the quadratic specification, which has the added advantage of analytical tractability.

5 We may contrast our approach with the alternative where the country's risk is internalized in the form of increased borrowing costs, which are tied to its national debt position; see Turnovsky (1997) for a detailed discussion of this specification which has been widely employed in a variety of contexts, originating with Bardhan (1967).

6 In a more general stochastic environment, the distinction between a default due to circumstances outside the control of the debtor and an outright repudiation would become important in the design of loan contracts. In our deterministic setup, we focus on the effects of limited enforcement on growth.

7 For similar specifications see for instance, Sachs (1985) and Cohen and Sachs (1986). Also, in contrast with Diwan (1990), the trade loss is partial here.

8 Since we are limited by computational costs, we cannot experiment with other parameters of the model.

9 Similar values are used by Lipton and Sachs (1983) in a similar context and by Auerbach and Kotlikoff (1987) in a different context.

# Index

page references followed by f indicate an illustrative figure; t indicate a table

# Journal of Chinese Economic and Business Studies

**The international scholarly journal of the Chinese Economic Association UK (CEA-UK)**

**Increase in frequency for 2008**

**MANAGING EDITOR:**

Xiaming Liu, *Birkbeck College, London, UK*

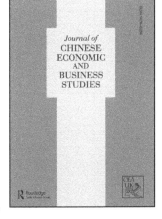

*Journal of Chinese Economic and Business Studies* is a peer-reviewed journal aiming to publish current and relevant findings from cutting edge research in Chinese economic, business and related issues. More specifically, it aims:

- to provide a forum for exchange of information and ideas among people in academic, business and government professions who are interested in the Chinese economy.
- to foster and enhance research activities that advance knowledge in transition economies.
- to discuss the relevance of Chinese economic and business studies to our society.

The journal specialises in both theoretical and empirical research on the Chinese economy, business and related issues including economic theories and policies for transition economies, economic reforms in the agricultural sector, state-owned enterprises, financial and fiscal systems and management styles, R&D and technology, marketing, human resources, business strategy, business culture and ethics, foreign trade and direct investment, similar issues for Hong Kong and Taiwan, and their relevance to other parts of the world.

**SUBSCRIPTION RATES**
Volume 6, 2008, 4 issues per year
Print ISSN 1476-5284
Online ISSN 1476-5292
Institutional rate (print and online): US$515; £311; €412
Institutional rate (online access only): US$489; £295; €391
Personal rate (print only): US$157; £95; €126